THE BATTLE FOR THE ARAB SPRING

REVOLUTION, COUNTER-REVOLUTION AND THE MAKING OF A NEW ERA

Lin Noueihed and **Alex Warren**

YALE UNIVERSITY PRESS
NEW HAVEN AND LONDON

For information about this and other Yale University Press publications, please contact:
U.S. Office: sales.press@yale.edu   yalebooks.com
Europe Office: sales@yaleup.co.uk   www.yalebooks.co.uk

Set in Janson MT by IDSUK (DataConnection) Ltd
Printed in Great Britain by TJ International Ltd, Padstow, Cornwall

Library of Congress Cataloging-in-Publication Data
Noueihed, Lin.
   The battle for the Arab Spring : revolution, counter-revolution and the making of a new era / Lin Noueihed and Alex Warren.
      p. cm.
   ISBN 978–0–300–18086–2 (cl : alk. paper)
1. Arab Spring, 2011. 2. Arab countries—Politics and government—21st century. 3. Revolutions—Arab countries—History—21st century. 4. Protest movements—Arab countries—History—21st century. 5. Democracy—Arab countries. I. Warren, Alex. II. Title.
   JQ1850.A91N68 2012
   909'.097492708312–dc23

                                                                      2012003580

A catalogue record for this book is available from the British Library.

ISBN 978–0–300–19415–9 (pbk)

10 9 8 7 6 5 4 3 2 1
2017 2016 2015 2014 2013

THE BATTLE FOR THE ARAB SPRING

A dual Lebanese/British national, **Lin Noueihed** has spent ten years as a Reuters correspondent in the Middle East, covering politics, economy and conflict.

Alex Warren is a director of Frontier, a Middle East and North Africa consultancy. He has lived and worked around the region, and since 2009 has specialised in Libya.

Contents

List of Illustrations

Acknowledgements

This book would not have been possible without so many people and organizations. We are indebted to our publisher, Yale, and to Phoebe Clapham for her meticulous editing of our many drafts and her suggestions on structure and tone. Her encouragement was indispensable as we raced to complete the manuscript to a tight deadline while events on the ground continued to move at a breakneck pace. We are also grateful to our agent, Andrew Lownie, for his faith in this project, his hospitality and his support. This book would have been impoverished were it not for the dozens if not hundreds of people we interviewed both on and off the record, across many countries, and who generously committed their time, shared their experiences and offered their insight. This goes not only for our research in 2011 and 2012, but in the many years preceding it too, and their names are too numerous to list here.

For regular access to his encyclopedic knowledge of the region, we thank Walid Noueihed. For generously sharing their photographs, we thank Lana Asfour, Camilo Gomez-Rivaz and Mohamed Abbas. For his valuable comments on the final draft, we thank Dr Warwick Knowles. Both authors would like, of course, to extend their gratitude to their families, for their love and their home cooking as we worked non-stop to finish on time. This book is dedicated to them. We thank Beth Hepworth for her support and for sharing her photographs of Libya, while emphasizing that this book does not reflect her views nor those of Frontier. Finally, we extend our deepest appreciation to Reuters for giving Lin the opportunity and the time to write this book. While this book was written during Lin's employment as a Reuters journalist, Reuters has not been involved with the content or tone of this book, which are the authors' responsibility alone.

When writing about such a complex region in so few words, and in such a short space of time, omissions are necessary and inevitable. The bulk of this book was written in a period of four months and, while we have visited and worked in many Arab countries, it would not have been possible without the scholars, journalists and colleagues whose preceding work and years of advice and insight enriched our understanding of the region long before the Arab Spring. As always, while we thank all those who assisted in this project, any shortcomings are our responsibility alone.

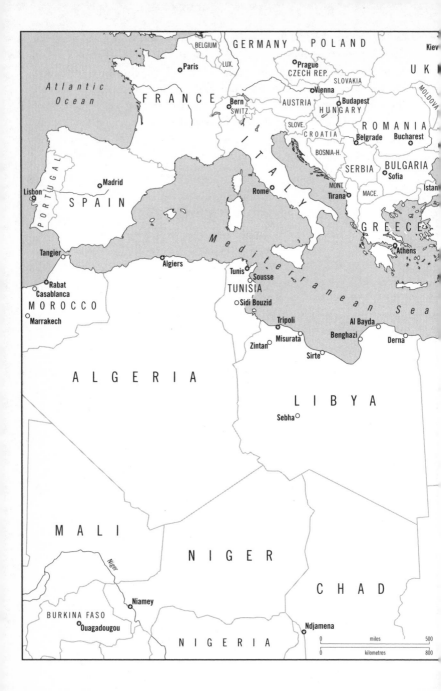

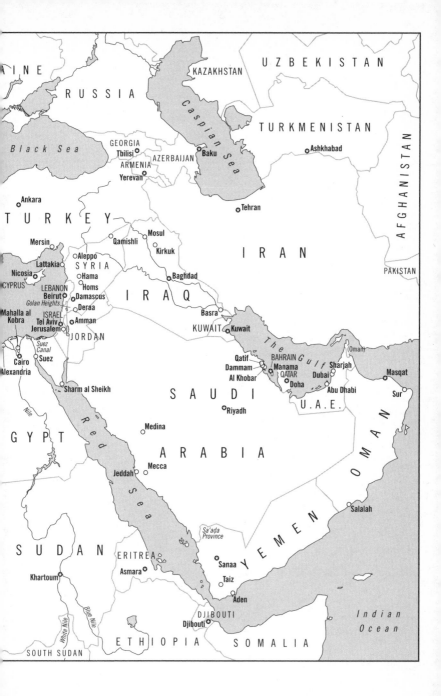

Introduction

On 1 September 2010, Tripoli residents awoke to the public holiday marking the anniversary of Muammar Gaddafi's 1969 revolution. The celebrations were not as lavish as the previous year, when Gaddafi triumphantly commemorated 40 years in power by inviting thousands of musicians, dancers and politicians from around the world, but they offered a rare insight into the preoccupations of one of the world's longest-serving leaders.

Strings of coloured lights were draped from buildings, and shiny new billboards designed by foreign PR agencies loomed over Tripoli's main streets. Some recreated scenes of the Libyan 'guide' in a desert tent, dreaming up his *Green Book* in the 1970s. Others showed him addressing the United Nations in 2009 on his first-ever trip to the United States. A towering poster of Gaddafi and Italian Prime Minister Silvio Berlusconi, standing side-by-side, hung from a building close to his Bab al-Aziziyah compound, marking the colonel's return to the international fold.

All seemed well for Gaddafi, and hundreds of dignitaries would gather that night to celebrate the flamboyant leader's longevity in the rapidly-shrinking international club of dictators. Gaddafi did not bother with elections, palming off his diffuse *jamahiriya* system of popular councils as the rule of the masses. Faced with US pressure or popular demand, however, most other Arab rulers obligingly dressed their authoritarian regimes in the ceremonial robes of democracy.

Almost three months after Gaddafi's celebrations, Hosni Mubarak's National Democratic Party (NDP) would take 83 per cent of seats in an Egyptian parliamentary election marred by violence, arrests and allegations of fraud.[1] In October, elections in the Gulf monarchy of Bahrain would see the opposition Al Wefaq group win nearly half the seats in the lower house, despite accusations of gerrymandering, the detention of civil society activists, and the closure of publications and websites in the months leading up to the poll.[2]

A year earlier, Tunisia's Zine al-Abidine Ben Ali had secured a fifth term with 89 per cent of the vote.[3] Over a thousand well-known figures, including singers, film-makers, doctors and businessmen, had already put their names to a petition exhorting the ageing president to run in 2014, despite a law stipulating that Tunisia's head of state must not be aged above seventy-five.[4] In Yemen, parliamentary elections initially scheduled for 2009 had been postponed for two years because of disagreements over electoral reforms intended to level the playing field. And in Syria, Bashar al-Assad was only three years into his second seven-year term as president. The constitution had been amended when his father died in 2000 to allow the then thirty-four-year-old ophthalmologist to inherit the country's highest office, despite his youth.

It had been a turbulent decade in the Arab world, home to some of the world's richest countries, like Qatar, and some of its poorest, like Yemen. In late 2010, food prices were scaling the heights they had reached in 2008. Runaway costs were as much a headache for populous countries as for desert emirates with tiny populations but little agriculture of their own, squeezing household budgets and raising demands for state subsidies. Fuel prices were stubbornly high – a relief for the crude exporters but a serious problem for oil-poor Arab countries like Tunisia and Morocco. In a region where 61 per cent of the population was under 30, widespread youth unemployment was a fact of life.[5]

So was a lack of change at the top. While satellite television and the internet had created a new public space in the Arab world, eroding the personality cults that surrounded stalwart rulers, freer expression did not translate into political change. A dangerous disconnect was developing between ageing leaders, security-obsessed and seemingly stuck in a Cold War paradigm, and the restless youths they ruled. Lacking the resources to marry and still living with their parents, members of what has come to be called the 'generation-in-waiting' could not express their dissatisfaction at the ballot box.[6] While few rulers went so far as to hold no elections at all, polls that ranged from the fraudulent to the meaningless only fed a belief that leaders and the cliques that surrounded them were not serious about ceding any real political power.

Mubarak had been in power since 1981, longer than the majority of Egyptians had been alive. Only two men had occupied the post of president since Tunisia won independence from France in 1956. When Gaddafi seized power in 1969, Richard Nixon was president of the United States and Barack Obama had just celebrated his eighth birthday. The United States has seen eight presidents occupy the White House since the colonel, then a youthful twenty-seven-year-old, deposed King Idris.

Arab intellectuals and journalists railed against what they saw as their atrophied political and cultural life, and bemoaned their diminished place in the world. When the first Arab Human Development Report was published in cooperation with the United Nations in 2002, it stirred heated debate. While praising countries for combating poverty and raising life expectancy, it outlined three so-called deficits that were holding the region back – the freedom deficit, the women's empowerment deficit and the knowledge deficit.[7] The report revealed that the Arab world had lower literacy levels than the developing countries' average, and invested less in research than most regions of the world.[8] Then came the humbling observation that almost as many books were translated in Spain each year as had been translated into Arabic since the ninth-century reign of Islam's Caliph Ma'amoun.[9]

The report was not authored by a team of Western policy wonks but by a group of Arab scholars respected in their own countries and research fields. It echoed a deepening sense of despondency in a civilization that, during the golden age of Islam, had been at the forefront of world science, medicine and philosophy, preserving and expanding on the works of Greek philosophers that Europe, then mired in the Dark Ages, had forgotten. It was a loss of confidence that had been exacerbated by the 11 September 2001 attacks, ushering in a new era in which Muslims at airports and on university campuses were now viewed as potential practitioners or sponsors of terrorism. The US invasion of Iraq, pursued despite broad Arab misgivings and worldwide protests, unleashed years of sectarian civil war that inflamed tensions between Sunni and Shi'ite Muslims to levels not seen in decades.

'It's not pleasant being Arab these days. Feelings of persecution for some, self-hatred for others: a deep disquiet pervades the Arab world,' Samir Kassir, a critic of Syria's domination over Lebanon, wrote in *Being Arab*.[10] 'Even those groups that for a long time have considered themselves invulnerable, the Saudi ruling class and the Kuwaiti rich, have ceased to be immune to the enveloping sense of malaise since a certain September 11.' Published a year before he was assassinated in 2005, Kassir's soul-searching book on the 'Arab malaise' was an appeal to rediscover the cultural renaissance that Arabs had enjoyed a century earlier as the Ottoman Empire crumbled. More and more Arabs, it seemed, were disappointed with their lot and their place in the world. And as Ted Gurr argued in his seminal book, *Why Men Rebel*, the gap between what people have and what they believe they are entitled to lies at the heart of revolution.[11]

One day before Ben Ali fled Tunisia, US Secretary of State Hillary Clinton warned America's Arab allies that they could not delay reforms forever. 'In too many places in too many ways the region's foundations are sinking into the sand,' Clinton told a regional conference in Doha. 'Those who cling to the status quo may be able to hold back the full impact of their countries' problems for a little while, but not forever.'[12]

The fact that change was so much talked about inside and outside the Arab world suggests that many had wanted and expected it to happen. Far from being a sudden awakening, the Arab Spring capped a decade of protest, political activism and media criticism that had laid the ground for more open political systems. Movements against rising prices and unemployment, against corruption and political stagnation, had gained traction in Tunisia and Egypt in the five years before the uprisings. Strikes posed serious challenges to governments struggling to maintain the economic growth that was so vital to creating jobs and mollifying the angry and unemployed youth. In Syria, big business was booming but years of drought had wrought havoc in the rural hinterlands. A web of struggles for power had already destabilized Yemen and a decade of political reform in Bahrain had ended in disappointment and pushed protesters back out onto the streets.

Arab populations were indeed young, but that was because the previous generation had produced so many children. In the decade since the publication of the first Arab Human Development Report, fertility rates had fallen in most Arab countries. In North Africa, women had an average of 2.2 children in 2010, lower than the world average. The rate was 2.7 in the Gulf countries and 3 in the Levant, though it has remained higher in Yemen. This was a significant decline from an average of more than 6 children in the previous generation.[13] People were getting married at an older age, and more and more were choosing their own life partners, breaking the traditional hold of fathers over their lives.

Enjoying more time, fewer responsibilities, more personal freedom and better education, this younger generation had enjoyed something of a cultural and communications boom in recent years. To many, change was not inevitable, change was already happening. It was an ongoing, invigorating process.

Yet as Gaddafi celebrated his forty-one years in power and Mubarak's NDP stole another election in the last few months of 2010, few, inside or outside the Arab world, would have predicted that three of the region's veteran rulers would be gone before the next year was out.

These states looked stable from the outside, their leaders seeming invincible to those who had known no other. A succession of pan-Arabists, national socialists and liberal nationalists had smashed or co-opted opposition forces, first the left and then the Islamists. Their leaders were exiled or imprisoned. A lack of political participation forced many to retreat to the narrow and cosseted protection of religion, sect or tribe.

Allowed to rise to the surface, all of these bottled-up tensions and conflicts could, as authoritarian rulers liked to remind the world, end in chaos or civil war. From Lebanon to Iraq to Algeria, Arab experiments with democracy had descended into violence that claimed lives by the hundreds of thousands. Yet change was something that millions of people around the region would be prepared to risk their lives for in 2011.

Before January was out, Tunisia's leader had been despatched into exile by peaceful protests that gravitated towards the capital through the country's forgotten hinterlands. The following month, demonstrations that had broken out around Egypt and drawn hundreds of thousands into Cairo's Tahrir Square had removed a president who would next appear six months later in a courtroom cage. By the end of a long hot summer, Libyan fighters backed by NATO air strikes had captured Tripoli and would soon hunt down their eccentric former leader, sodomize him with a stick, and send him to his maker. After fending off ten months of domestic and international pressure, Yemen's leader would finally sign a power transfer deal in November that offered him a face-saving exit.

And when the United States killed Osama bin Laden after a decade of 'war on terror' that had infuriated Muslims around the world, and withdrew the last of its combat troops from Iraq, it tied up more loose ends in an old Arab world order that was unravelling at a furious pace. The paradigm that had divided Arab states into the 'moderate' pro-Western camp, involving countries like Jordan, Egypt and Saudi Arabia, and the resistance axis of Syria and Iran and their allies in Hezbollah and Hamas, was melting away. A new order was emerging in which old certainties were uncertain and the unlikely suddenly seemed possible.

In the heat of revolutionary turmoil in January and February 2011, with seething crowds on the streets of Cairo, Tunis, Benghazi, Casablanca and Amman, it appeared as if every Arab regime was under threat. The protesters were successful by dint of what they did not have – a clear programme, a hierarchical organization with figureheads and followers – and by what they did not want – a specific ruler, his party, his family, his policies that had enriched his elite and impoverished the people.

They were young. They spoke English or French. Their voices dominated Twitter and Facebook. They looked and sounded like people might on the streets of London or New York. They were not chanting religious slogans. They did not carry weapons. They drew satirical cartoons and penned sardonic raps about their leaders. The Western media adored them. They all voiced similar aspirations for freedom of expression, for decent jobs and pay, for better opportunities, for the right to choose their governments. With both the plodding Islamist parties and the state spies and torturers taken by surprise, it appeared that a youthful, dynamic, secular and liberal Middle East might now be in the making.

It was never going to be that simple. The flash of that first revolutionary moment blinded both observers and the protesters themselves to the more ruthless battles that would now burst into the open. To see the Arab Spring as a series of popular uprisings against unelected governments would be to oversimplify the struggles that are under way, and to underestimate what is at stake. The Arab Spring also pitted people against people and states against states, complicating the transition to new systems of government. Some battles will be fought and won at the ballot box. Others will be fought and won and retained by the gun. Three of the region's leaders may have gone by the end of 2011, but the majority who remained would struggle ever-harder to cling on to power.

We completed the first edition of *The Battle for the Arab Spring* in early 2012, just as Egyptians had voted the Muslim Brotherhood into parliament, Libyans were celebrating the first anniversary of their revolution, Yemenis waved goodbye to Ali Abdullah Saleh and the Syrian opposition was trying to unite around a single leadership. Looking in turn at Tunisia, Egypt, Bahrain, Libya, Yemen and Syria, we analysed the turbulent events of 2011, asking if the hopes of youthful protesters had been fulfilled, how much these countries had really changed and what minefields lay ahead. This paperback edition continues the story, analysing events up to early 2013, most of which have borne out our original arguments. The Arab monarchies have all survived the Arab Spring but none is unchanged. Islamist political parties in Egypt and Tunisia have already been compromised by their first taste of power and, as we wrote in the first edition, their electoral success may well have already peaked. Bahrain remains trapped in a cycle of protest and repression. Yemen faces the same daunting economic and social challenges as it did when Saleh was still in power. In Syria, a complex web of conflicts is ripping the country apart. And our central argument, reflected in the title of the book, has – often tragically – come to pass.

The battle for the Arab Spring is a battle for the identity of a region buffeted through the past century by the rise and fall of European empires, by Cold War rivalry and by the encroachment of a triumphant US superpower that aggressively pressed its interests. It is a battle for satisfying jobs, decent housing and the right of young people to grow up and build families and futures of their own. Most of all, it is a battle for dignity and justice after years of repression. But other conflicts, simmering below the surface for decades before 2011, have also been unleashed.

Policies that favoured cities over provinces, one region over another, wealthy business elites over ambitious graduates, are coming home to roost. Struggles for control of councils and committees have reawakened old feuds between rival families, villages and clans, not over religion but money, land, resources and power.

And policymakers are at odds over how best to tackle economic problems, which worsened in 2012 and if left unaddressed will only trigger future upheaval. Can new governments provide the jobs that young people so desperately need? Will they bow to popular opinion and increase state salaries, offer better benefits, raise subsidies and drop taxes? Or will they push ahead with measures that are painful in the short-term but would make their economies competitive in the long-term? Which approach emerges victorious will be crucial to the shape and direction of the region.

New Arab governments do not face this dilemma alone. The Arab Spring was part of a season of upheaval that has made Western governments tremble before the markets, seen protesters occupy Wall Street in the name of the 99 per cent who fear big business has usurped their democratic rights, and prompted Indians to protests against runaway corruption in the world's largest democracy.

At stake is not just the future of individual countries. The Arab world is perched on the axis of the world's busiest trade routes that link Europe, Asia and Africa, and at the centre of the biggest energy-exporting region, and what happens here has the potential to shake the entire globe.

This book draws on our first-hand experiences and interviews from the front lines of the Arab Spring and from a decade of reporting, analysis and research that has provided a ringside seat at some of the Middle East's most dramatic moments. Between us, we were on the first flight to Tunisia after

Ben Ali's departure in January 2011 and among the first to visit post-uprising Sidi Bouzid, where it all began. We were in Bahrain in March when Saudi troops rumbled over the bridge and we were in the Rixos Hotel in Tripoli as Gaddafi held out in the summer of 2011. We watched in Cairo as the standoff between Egypt's army and its protesters turned violent in October, as Egyptians cast their ballots in their first post-Mubarak elections in the ensuing months and as Islamists took control of the new parliament in January 2012.

Over the past decade, we have attended Hafez al-Assad's funeral in 2000, witnessed Lebanon's 2005 Cedar Revolution, and watched the bombs crash down in Israel's 2006 war with Hezbollah. We were in Najaf in 2005 as Iraqis cast their ballots in the first elections after Saddam Hussein's defeat and watched that country descend into civil strife. We spent time all over Libya in the final years of Gaddafi's rule. From Dubai, we watched the oil boom fuel a property bubble that reached its height in 2008, and we were there to see it burst. Between us, we have also reported from and worked in Oman, Yemen, Jordan, Morocco and beyond. Speaking Arabic and French, and having lived in countries across the region, we have attempted to bring some of this context to events that surprised the world in 2011.

Two years on, there is much to suggest that the Arab Spring should have been predictable. A media revolution had prepared the ground. Elite corruption was insulting to ordinary people who struggled with soaring food costs, rising rents and miserable job opportunities. Strikes were breaking out. Protests were increasingly common. Yet in 2010, right on the eve of change, plenty of evidence suggested that regimes in Egypt, Tunisia, Libya and elsewhere were impregnable, that popular protest could never achieve anything, and that talk of an 'Arab exception' was perhaps true. Few realized that a new chapter in Arab history was about to open.

PART 1

THE ROOTS OF RAGE

CHAPTER 1

An Arab Malaise

Good rulership is equivalent to mildness. If the ruler uses force and is ready to mete out punishment and eager to expose the faults of people and to count their sins, (his subjects) become fearful and depressed and seek to protect themselves against him through lies, ruses and deceit ... They often abandon (the ruler) on the battlefield and fail to support his defensive enterprises ... The subjects often conspire to kill the ruler. Thus the dynasty decays, and the fence (that protects it) lies in ruins.
– 14th-century Tunisian philosopher Ibn Khaldun, *Al-Muqaddimah*

Not a single Arab country made it onto the 2011 list of top global risks issued by Eurasia Group, a multinational consulting firm that helps clients identify looming instability. Some perennials, such as the Iranian nuclear standoff, were mentioned, but domestic change in the Middle East was simply not on its radar – even though protests had been spreading since late 2010.[1] After all, despite their dysfunctional economies and ossified political systems, Arab rulers had proved remarkably resilient to both domestic pressures and external shocks. They had survived the end of the Cold War and the so-called 'third wave of democratization' that swept away dictators from Portugal to Indonesia, from the 1970s onwards.[2]

Arab regimes, if not individual leaders, had made it through a series of wars and three unpopular peace deals with Israel. They had largely crushed violent Islamists. They had adjusted, as mostly Sunni Muslim rulers, to the Shi'ite resurgence ushered in by Iran's 1979 revolution, and they had survived the sectarian and political tensions wrought by two US-led wars against Saddam Hussein's Iraq.

Syria, Morocco, Jordan, Saudi Arabia, Bahrain, Kuwait and the United Arab Emirates had all survived the deaths of veteran leaders and managed relatively smooth successions. Syria, the only republic on this list of monarchies and dynasties and the one most vulnerable to a succession crisis, had set a precedent with Bashar al-Assad's carefully-choreographed takeover in 2000 from his father Hafez, who had ruled for the previous three decades. Mubarak, who had led Egypt for thirty years without naming a vice president, took note as he groomed his son Gamal for the presidency.

Democrats around the Arab world lamented the birth of the first Arab '*jumlukiya*'. Literally translated as 'republarchy', the word fused together *jumhuriya*, Arabic for 'republic', and *malakiya*, Arabic for 'monarchy'.[3] With the creation of this monstrous hybrid dropped the last fig leaf of legitimacy. There could be no more pretence that national interests came before the interests of the ruling family, and the sect or tribe to which it belonged. In Tunisia, another Arab republic, it was widely suspected that Ben Ali, whose only son was a toddler, was grooming his son-in-law for the top job. There were fears that the first lady, Leila Trabelsi, derided by Tunisians as a latter-day Marie Antoinette, had her own eye on high office.

Rather than invest in the future of their countries, these leaders dedicated much of the wealth and power of the state to ensuring their own survival. Coercion, or the threat of it, was widely used in a region whose governments spend a higher proportion of their state budgets on defence and security than any other. In 2009, an average 4.6 per cent of Arab GDP went on military spending, compared to a global average of less than 2 per cent.[4]

Much Gulf Arab military spending is intended as a deterrent against Iran, a non-Arab Shi'ite power in a region dominated by Sunni rulers, but the aura of an impregnable state, possessed both of the latest weaponry and of support from Western countries, also put off potential opponents from mounting any serious challenge for power. It was not just the amount spent on the armed forces, but also their composition, that discouraged revolt. Some rulers and their families fortified their power bases by filling the military and interior security forces with members of their own tribe or sect, creating a patronage network and ensuring that those who bore arms owed their allegiance to the leadership rather than the state itself. The Saudi Arabian National Guard, for instance, is a separate force that bypasses the defence ministry and draws its soldiers from tribal elements historically loyal to the royal family and dedicated to protecting the king from a family rebellion or a challenge from the regular army.[5] Bahrain, meanwhile, has resorted to recruiting foreigners, who were less likely to balk at shooting or beating protesters and had no stake in local politics.

Tellingly, the army in Tunisia was considerably more professional than most in the region and considered itself to be an institution of the state rather than the private security wing of the ruling family or party. In Tunisia and Egypt, furthermore, tribal ties are weak and both countries are home to majority Sunni populations ruled over by Sunni rulers, who focused on crushing opposition parties or rival elite figures rather than shielding themselves from competing sects or clans.

An underlying sense of fear was also perpetuated by intelligence agencies, or *mukhabarat*, that employed spies at every level of society. This was manifested in different ways in different countries. Egypt or Bahrain did not feel oppressive day-to-day, but Syria was another story. Men in lurid shirts and leather jackets loitered in hotel lobbies, hiding behind newspapers and listening to the conversations that went on. It was casually assumed that phones were tapped and on no account was any political conversation to be undertaken in taxis, whose drivers were widely believed to be informants. One in Damascus openly admitted that he worked for Syrian intelligence, describing how he had been based in Beirut before the 2005 withdrawal of Syrian forces but by 2010 was forced to supplement his paltry civil servant's salary with taxi fares.[6]

Intelligence agencies operated in a legal grey area, carrying out arrests and operating secret jails where political prisoners, numbering thousands, were abused or tortured. Many of these prisoners were Islamists, but any journalist or academic worth his salt could expect to be in and out of jail on trumped-up charges, or no charges at all.

The Syrian regime had maintained emergency law since the Ba'ath Party coup of 1963, Egypt had done so since 1981 and for long stretches before that, while in Algeria emergency law had been in place since 1992. This effectively suspended constitutional protections and gave rulers much wider scope for arbitrary arrests. It meant that a journalist who stepped over the line could suddenly find him- or herself in a military or security court on charges of undermining national security that would normally be reserved for cases of terrorism or espionage. The absence of the rule of law meant that no one knew exactly what was permitted and what was not, forcing critics to play a dangerous game of self-censorship as they tried to make their point without tripping up on one of the many red lines that criss-crossed the public sphere.

But it was not all repression. Authoritarian rulers also built alliances among prominent tribes, families and business elites to bolster their rule. Libya's Gaddafi rewarded the clans who helped him to recruit fighters in the war against Chad with plum government jobs, or put the scions of loyal families in charge of public sector companies. In Syria, the ruler was Alawite but the established Sunni business families were among the main beneficiaries of Assad's economic liberalization policies of the 2000s. In Saudi Arabia and among some Sunni monarchies, political bonds were strengthened through marriage, much as they had been among European aristocracies in centuries past.

The economic reforms introduced in Syria, in Tunisia, in Libya and beyond had lifted the pall of oppression that hung over these countries in the 1980s and 1990s. New cafés, restaurants and shops opened up. Foreign high-street brands arrived in upmarket districts. The lot of most Syrians and Libyans had improved a great deal since the 1980s, when imports were effectively banned but local industries could not produce enough goods of sufficient quality to meet demand. Yet such reforms were intended to protect the incumbent rulers by relieving economic discontent and staving off calls for deeper change.

Facing US pressure or domestic demand, some Arab dictatorships and dynasties even introduced more meaningful elections, but they worked to curtail any concrete changes the ballot box might bring. When one party can change the laws to its benefit, can wield the security forces to intimidate its opponents, the judiciary to jail its critics and the state-run media to campaign on its behalf, there is no real choice. Either electorates were not allowed to vote freely or the body that they were voting for lacked any meaningful powers. This system proved effective on at least two fronts. Firstly, it applied a veneer of plurality to systems that were in reality based on a single party that saw itself as the state. Secondly, it divided the opposition. After years underground, some activists felt that, since they could not beat the system, they should try to change it from the inside.

Together with this ran the promotion of a cult of personality. Rulers projected the image that they would be there for eternity and that, if they were not, their son or other relative was waiting in the wings. A giant poster showing Bahrain's King Hamad bin Isa Al Khalifa, his son, the crown prince, and his uncle, the prime minister, hung from the side of a building just a few metres from the Pearl roundabout where protests would be concentrated in early 2011. In Libya, billboards were filled not with ads but with pictures of Gaddafi showing the number of years he had been in power. Faded posters showing the Colonel next to a large number 39 were juxtaposed with newer ones of Gaddafi 40 or 41. Visitors could buy Gaddafi watches, baseball caps and T-shirts from shops in central Tripoli.

Alongside this crude propaganda that appeared to belong to another era, Arab rulers demonstrated a knack for 'upgrading authoritarianism' to survive the challenges posed not only by globalization but also by new media and the growing international emphasis on human rights.[7] One of several tactics they employed was to curtail, co-opt, compete with and thereby undermine efforts to build a strong civil society through the creation of non-governmental organizations (NGOs).

Arab NGOs first started to proliferate in the 1980s, largely in response to openings from above. Authoritarian rulers apparently thought that tolerating small and powerless groups would burnish their democratic credentials abroad while incurring little cost at home. But local NGOs that focused on issues from human rights to corruption eventually became a thorn in their sides. Rather than attract bad press by banning all groups, they harassed and repeatedly detained offending members. They introduced laws that required NGOs to register, which then allowed the state to legally reject troublesome critics, limit their sources of funding, or restrict the scope of their activities. While weakening independent groups, Arab governments also set about sponsoring semi-official NGOs that received privileged access to donors, conferences and officials. These could not act independently and were muted in their criticism while competing for funds and publicity with the weaker and smaller independent groups.

Many of these government NGOs, or GONGOs, were led by the glamorous wives of Arab kings and presidents, and were dismissed by grassroots activists as 'First Ladies' Clubs'. Asma al-Assad, the wife of the Syrian president, was the sponsor of seven NGOs focused on issues such as youth, women's rights and rural development. All operated under the umbrella of the Syria Trust for Development, which she also chaired, and which advertised itself as a non-profit and non-government organization through which the state would partner with local NGOs to foster development. Yet it was notoriously difficult for any rights-based NGOs to operate legally in Syria, which is home to 1,500 civil society groups compared to 5,000 in its much smaller but much freer neighbour Lebanon.[8]

Gushing Western media coverage also made it easier to present a sanitized view of developments in the Arab world. Asma al-Assad was glamorous, charming, British-born, and the subject of a fawning *Vogue* story which described the democratic principles governing her family's life, and was published the same month that Mubarak was overthrown. Jordan's Queen Rania, another beautiful first lady, boasted a string of accolades from *Glamour* magazine's Woman of the Year to a place on *Forbes'* Most

Powerful Women list, thanks to her work for charity and for NGOs that sought to empower women.[9] These first ladies were popular abroad, but their unveiled, slick and empowered images bore little resemblance to the lives of ordinary women and made no mention of the undemocratic ways of their husbands.[10]

If one generalization could be made about countries as different as Yemen and Tunisia, it is that their rulers were survivors, adept at repressing or co-opting their enemies and adapting to changes, from the end of the Cold War to the rise of social media. They had simply been around so long that they exuded an air of stability that masked the growing discontent among their people.

The Arab Exception

The club of Arab dictators had proven so resilient that a whole body of academic literature and journalistic commentary had developed to explain why emerging countries were industrializing, growing, creating jobs and shifting towards more representative government, while the Middle East fell ever further behind. Pundits spoke of the 'Arab exception', unfavourably comparing Arab countries first to Asia's 'tiger economies', then to the BRICs, the rising powers of Brazil, Russia, India and China.

There were several permutations to the 'Arab exception' argument, ranging from the suggestion that these societies were simply not 'ready' for democracy because their patriarchal nature predisposed them to authoritarian rule, to the opinion that Islam, as a religion, was intrinsically incompatible with democracy. Another explanation was that the United States had propped up authoritarian rulers in countries including Egypt, Jordan, Saudi Arabia, Yemen, Bahrain and Tunisia because a confluence of geopolitical interests in the region – its desire to defend Israel, to ensure a steady supply of affordable oil, to hold back Iranian influence following the 1979 revolution, and to curtail any Islamist threat – trumped any ideological desire to spread democracy.

The US commitment to protecting Israel's security has, indeed, led it to work closely with leaders in Egypt, Jordan and the Palestinian territories, all of whom signed peace deals with the Jewish state, and to apply pressure to those who had not. When Egyptian leader Anwar Sadat broke ranks and signed a unilateral peace treaty with Israel in 1979, the deal was sealed with the promise of $1.3 billion a year in US aid and unwavering support from Washington. The Camp David peace accord won back Egypt's Sinai Peninsula, which had been captured by the Jewish state in the 1967 Arab-Israeli war, but cost Sadat his life in 1981, when he was assassinated by an Islamist militant.

So unpopular was the agreement both at home and among other Arab states, that Sadat's funeral was attended by three former US presidents, as well as Israeli Prime Minister Menachem Begin, but only one Arab leader.[11] Once host to the Arab League, Egypt had been thrown out and its leader was as unpopular among his own people as he was in the region. Sadat's economic liberalization, or *infitah*, policies also cemented Egypt's shift from the Soviet into the Western sphere and, though they provoked bread riots in 1977, the reforms were lauded by the United States.

US financial, military and political support continued under Sadat's successor. Mubarak worked with the United States and Israel to enforce a blockade of Gaza that began in 2007, with the aim of isolating Hamas, despite television images of widespread civilian suffering and protests on the streets of Cairo. Even as thousands of Egyptian protesters braved tear gas and rubber bullets to demand Mubarak's resignation in 2011, US officials appeared reluctant to admit that his record on human rights and democracy was, to put it mildly, an embarrassment.

'Mubarak has been an ally of ours in a number of things and he's been very responsible ... relative to geopolitical interests in the region; Middle East peace efforts, the actions Egypt has taken relative to normalizing the relationship with Israel,' US vice president Joe Biden said two days after the start of protests in Egypt on 25 January 2011. 'I would not refer to him as a dictator.'[12]

There was a sense in the region that the United States not only propped up its allies, but also turned a blind eye to its enemies as long as they served its interests. While Syria has sheltered and supported armed anti-Israeli groups such as Hamas and Lebanon's Hezbollah, for instance, both Assads have stuck to a 1974 ceasefire on the Golan Heights, allowing Syria to maintain its anti-Israeli stance while avoiding direct conflict. Whatever misgivings the United States and Israel may have had about the Syrian regime, they appeared more willing to live with the Assads than venture into the unknown.

Many Arabs clearly saw US support for, or tolerance of, authoritarian leaders in Egypt, Jordan, Syria and the Palestinian territories, as serving the Jewish state. Beyond the borders of Israel, however, oil had been a chief strategic consideration for Washington.

The United States, still the world's biggest energy consumer, has sought to ensure the steady supply of crude to world markets even if that means supporting illiberal and undemocratic rulers who it trusts to keep the taps on. And the Middle East and North Africa is the world's largest energy-exporting region, producing crude oil equivalent to about two-fifths of total global consumption in 2010.[13] It includes the world's biggest oil exporter, Saudi Arabia, plus another six of its top 20 producers – the UAE, Kuwait, Iraq, Algeria, Qatar and, before 2011, Libya.[14] Saudi Arabia single-handedly produces about 12 per cent of the world's oil consumption, and in 2010 had become yet more important to global energy markets when it completed a $100 billion, six-year expansion programme that upped its total crude production capacity to 12.5m barrels per day (b/d) and provided a generous cushion of unused capacity.[15]

While the United States pumps a significant amount of oil itself and sources most of its crude imports from countries outside of the Middle East, any serious disruption to Saudi production, whether through domestic unrest or problems in its export routes, would send shockwaves through the famously jittery global oil market.[16] In the wake of the global financial crisis, ensuring a steady supply of cheap crude took on added importance. Any repeat of the 2008 spike, which saw prices reach almost $150 a barrel, could seriously undermine any recovery in the United States and, by extension, the global economy. Saudi Arabia, in banking crisis parlance, was too big to fail.

While the Israel and oil arguments apply to some, but not all, of the Arab countries, all rulers worried to differing extents about what they saw as the Islamist threat. This concern was conveniently shared with the United States and its allies in Western Europe. Whereas, with the end of the Cold War in 1989, the United States no longer needed to prop up friendly dictators from Latin America to Asia to guard against democratic movements that threatened to bring in socialist or populist leaders, in Arab countries the threat of communism was immediately succeeded by the threat of Islamists who had once been exploited as a bulwark against the left.

For decades before the 2001 attacks and the ensuing war on terror, Arab rulers from Tunisia's Ben Ali to Egypt's Mubarak had veered between repressing Islamists and co-opting them for their own ends. It is us or the Islamists, they said, and any free and fair elections that had been held in the Arab world, like those in Algeria, Iraq and the Palestinian territories, appeared to prove them right.

When Hafez al-Assad crushed an armed Islamist insurgency that began in the late 1970s and culminated in a bloodbath at Hama in 1982, the United States brought the fighting to the world's attention but took no action.[17] Journalists, initially banned from the central Syrian city, had to rely on Western diplomats estimating the death toll at 5,000 people.[18] However, in a detailed report published in 2006, the Syrian Human Rights Committee said at least 25,000 people had died.[19]

Western governments threw money at Yemeni president Ali Abdullah Saleh, despite endemic corruption in the public sector, to help him crush an Al-Qaeda franchise active in the lawless south and east of the country. In 2010, the United States more than doubled its official military aid to Yemen after an Al-Qaeda-linked militant trained in the country tried to blow up a passenger plane by hiding explosives in his underwear.[20]

It was a similar story elsewhere. As long as the alternative was the Islamists, the United States appeared to turn a blind eye to all but the worst repression by Arab rulers. And while it publicly criticized the arrest of activists, it continued to offer some of these rulers financial or military aid that they could direct against their opponents.

The United States had also helped to create a monster. In what proved to be the last decade of the Cold War, it had helped to fund the Afghan *jihad* against the Soviet Union. Thousands of Arab Muslim men, who became known as the 'Afghan Arabs', arrived to help expel the 'Godless' Soviets from Afghanistan. Many of them were backed by Saudi money, and Pakistani intelligence. Among them was Saudi-born Osama bin Laden. When the Soviet Union withdrew from Afghanistan in 1989, many of these men, trained militarily and indoctrinated to fight for Islam, went on to fight in other troubled regions such as Chechnya,[21] or returned home and turned their guns against their own governments.

Al-Qaeda turned the war against the United States, the Arab rulers Washington supported, and even those rulers whom it did not support. It is worth noting that Libya, not the United States, was the first country to issue an international arrest warrant for Osama bin Laden, via Interpol in 1998, for the murder of a German intelligence officer and his wife four years earlier.[22] And when nineteen Arab and Muslim hijackers from Al-Qaeda flew passenger planes into the World Trade Center, the Pentagon and Pennsylvania on 11 September 2001, it was not just US-allied rulers such as Egypt's Mubarak who proved indispensable to the ensuing US 'war on terror', but also ostensible enemies such as Assad and Gaddafi.

Some Al-Qaeda suspects were subjected to what is euphemistically known as 'extraordinary rendition', meaning they were abducted and trans-ferred to secret CIA detention centres or to their home countries, where they faced potential mistreatment. One widely reported case was that of

Maher Arar, a Canadian citizen who was arrested in 2002 while passing through New York and transferred to his country of origin, Syria, where he was imprisoned for a year and says he was tortured.[23] Abdel Hakim Belhaj, the Islamist and rebel placed in charge of securing Tripoli following the taking of the capital in August 2011, has publicly said he was detained at Kuala Lumpur airport in 2004, questioned by the CIA, and then repatriated to Libya, where he spent the next six years in jail.[24]

Arab rulers also used the 'war on terror' as a handy excuse to round up domestic opponents on the flimsiest evidence. Now, even the most moderate of Islamists could be jailed on charges of supporting terrorism, adding to increasing domestic repression.

As we will discuss in more detail later, Islamists range in their outlooks from religious democrats campaigning peacefully within their own countries to *jihadis* fighting a global war to establish direct Islamic rule across vast swathes of majority-Muslim land. But in the Western media, the words Islam and *jihad* were heard together all too often. As US-led forces fought the Taliban in Afghanistan, ordinary people across the world watched news features on women forced to wear the *burqa* or banned from going to school. A slew of books hit the shelves warning of the dangers of the global *jihad*, a war against the United States, the West and anyone who did not believe in the narrowest interpretation of Islam.

Samuel Huntington's 1993 prediction of a coming 'clash of civilizations' was the subject of renewed debate, while pundits explained how Islam's emphasis on community good clashed with the Western emphasis on individual rights, and why Islam could not provide for the separation between mosque and state required for a liberal democracy.

These arguments are likely to have come as a surprise to Turks and Indonesians, whose majority-Muslim countries were already functioning, if flawed, democracies. They also appear to ignore the historical tradition of *shura*, or consultation, that the early Islamic community engaged in and that many Muslim scholars consider to embody the democratic values of Islam. Amid the fears that swirled in the aftermath of 9/11, the enormous variety of views held by Muslims, on everything from democracy, to sex, to banking, were glossed over. When George W. Bush declared that you were either 'with us or against us', virtually all Arab dictators screamed that they were 'with'. Without us, they warned, the Islamists will come to power, the borders of Israel will no longer be secure and the supply of oil may be disrupted, and it was hard for the United States, as it hunted down Al-Qaeda supporters and invaded two Muslim countries, not to listen.

Yet the 2003 invasion of Iraq, opposed by many of Washington's Arab allies, inflamed anger across the Arab world and raised a new generation of *jihadis*. Men too young to have fought in Afghanistan in the 1970s and 1980s now went to Iraq to fight the US invasion. From the perspective of Washington's long-time allies – particularly the Sunni rulers of Saudi Arabia and the other oil-exporting Gulf states – the biggest winner from the invasion of Iraq was their common enemy, the Shi'ite Muslim theocracy Iran. Tensions flared between Sunni and Shi'ite Muslims from Pakistan, to Bahrain and Saudi Arabia in the Gulf, to Lebanon on the Mediterranean coast. Jordan's King Abdullah spoke with concern in 2004 about the rise of a Shi'ite crescent from Lebanon, through Iraq, to Iran.[25] That, along with the widely-held belief that Iran was pursuing a nuclear weapons programme, provided another reason for the United States to maintain its support both for Sunni Arab rulers and for Israel.

The Democracy Dilemma

All this did not deter Bush from officially launching his so-called 'freedom agenda' in 2005. In it, Bush recognized that US support for authoritarianism in other countries might breed anger against the United States, but apparently failed to grasp that sermons on freedom would ring hollow while hundreds were held without trial in Guantanamo Bay, and that democracy enforced by the barrel of a gun might not be welcomed by all those struggling against unelected rulers. 'We are led, by events and common sense, to one conclusion: The survival of liberty in our land increasingly depends on the success of liberty in other lands. The best hope for peace in our world is the expansion of freedom in all the world. America's vital interests and our deepest beliefs are now one,' Bush said in his second inaugural address.[26]

The Bush administration's public enthusiasm for accelerated Arab democracy appeared to be waning by 2006. The 2005 Egyptian parliamentary election lauded by Bush had again shown the Muslim Brotherhood to be the strongest opposition force there. Washington's carefully groomed secular exiles had failed to win votes in Iraq, trounced in 2005 elections by Shi'ite Islamist groups who now dominated the government. The 2006 Palestinian elections had brought a clear win for Hamas, who had rejected the Oslo accords with Israel. By 2007, the noisy US demands for Arab rulers to accelerate democratic reforms and hold elections had shifted focus.

More emphasis was placed on empowering civil society, activists and NGOs. Arab bloggers were invited to the United States, while activists were given training and in some cases funding. Signed into law on 3 August 2007, the ADVANCE Democracy Act enshrined Washington's declared commitment to promote democracy abroad into law. Similar measures were passed through National Security Presidential Directive 58, which was signed by Bush in July 2008. Rather than pushing for change from the top, the United States appeared to settle for a longer-term strategy of empowering young, secular activists to establish the bedrock on which more stable and organic democracies could later be built. To many activists, such efforts were little more than window-dressing, hopelessly overshadowed by continued US support for unelected rulers.

Warmly welcomed when he first became president in 2008, Barack Obama changed the tone of engagement with Arab leaders and people, but his handling of the Arab Spring would suggest that the US dilemma remained essentially unchanged. How does it balance its oft-stated desire to promote democracy and free markets in the Middle East and North Africa with its often conflicting political, economic and security interests in the region? On the eve of the Arab Spring, only 20 per cent of Arabs saw Obama in a positive light compared to 45 per cent the previous year. Some 63 per cent were discouraged by his Middle East policy, compared to 15 per cent a year earlier.[27]

In the decade before Mohammed Bouazizi's desperate suicide sparked the 2011 uprisings, people in the Arab world had witnessed Israel's crushing of the second Palestinian *intifada*, marked by a spree of Palestinian suicide bombings that had shocked world opinion. They had watched Islamic extremists fly passenger jets into buildings on 9/11. They had suffered the darkest side of the US 'war on terror'. They had witnessed the US-led invasion of Iraq in 2003, and Israel's war against Hezbollah in 2006 and then against Hamas in the Gaza Strip in 2009.

Writing after the invasion of Iraq but before Israel's war with Hezbollah, Samir Kassir encapsulated the feelings of helplessness that pervaded the region at the time. 'The Arab people are haunted by a sense of powerlessness; permanently enflamed, it is the badge of their malaise,' he wrote in *Being Arab*.

> Powerlessness to be what you think you should be. Powerlessness to act to affirm your existence, even theoretically, in the face of the Other who denies your right to exist, despises you and has once again asserted his

domination over you. Powerlessness to suppress the feeling that you are no more than a lowly pawn on the global chessboard even as the game is being played in your backyard. This feeling, it has to be said, has been hard to dispel since the Iraq war, when Arab land once again came under foreign occupation and the era of independence was relegated to a parenthesis.[28]

With the odds so stacked against them, it seemed no wonder, as the first decade of the twenty-first century came to a close, that many people in the region lived in one of two equally-depressing situations: under the thumb of authoritarian rulers, be they monarchs or presidents-for-life, or in the midst of chaos, sectarian strife and foreign meddling. It seemed to reinforce these leaders' oft-repeated warning that their heavy-handed rule was the only thing preventing anarchy, and it seemed to underscore the helplessness felt by millions who could see little hope of change.

Arab rulers had crushed opposition parties, preventing any meaningful consolidation among their ranks and dispersing their members between jail, exile and hiding. Their repression had left opponents nowhere to gather but the mosque, breathing life and legitimacy into religious movements that would defeat weakened secularists in the aftermath of the Arab Spring. They had undermined civil society, ensuring that NGOs were under-resourced and under pressure, and limiting the role they could play after the uprisings. And they had strengthened the networks of patronage and nepotism that weakened state institutions and forced people to look to sects or tribes for protection and favours, complicating the transition to new systems of government.

This legacy of repressive policies and foreign meddling would define some of the battles that would unfold in the post–2011 era, but, as the next chapter explains, deep economic divides and inequalities were stoking just as much anger.

CHAPTER 2

Bread, Oil and Jobs

The most dangerous moment for a bad government is usually when it begins to reform itself.

– Alexis de Tocqueville[1]

In the spring of 2008, popular discontent flared up around the Arab world. In Morocco, protests left 300 people injured and persuaded the government to cancel a planned 30 per cent cut in the bread subsidy. In Egypt, textile workers in the Nile Delta town of Al-Mahalla Al-Kobra took to the streets to complain about high prices and low wages, burning banners of the ruling National Democratic Party (NDP) and stamping on a poster of President Hosni Mubarak. Eleven people were killed in clashes and hundreds more arrested as a wave of strikes and demonstrations around the country descended into the worst unrest Egypt had seen since the late 1970s.

A similar movement had swept through deprived parts of central Tunisia since January, a direct precursor to the 2011 protests that would snowball into outright revolt. Smaller-scale demonstrations had also taken place in Algeria, Lebanon, Jordan, Yemen and dozens of other countries around the world as the cost of basic foodstuffs skyrocketed thanks to a combination of high oil prices, poor harvests, rising speculative investment in commodities, and biofuel subsidies that discouraged farmers from growing food.

As Egyptians fought each other in bread queues and soldiers were drafted in to bake loaves, energy-rich Gulf states like the UAE and Saudi Arabia were seeking to buy up millions of hectares of farmland in Africa and south-east Asia. This was not just a strategic move to secure future food supplies, but part of a wider reinvestment of revenues from oil, which by the spring of 2008 was approaching the peak of an extraordinary price spike that showered the major exporters with a wealth that was unprecedented, even by their standards.

While that wealth allowed Arab oil-exporters to provide for their citizens on a scale that was beyond the reach of governments in Tunis or Rabat, the very same boom was eroding the living standards of families in oil-poor countries around the region. The burden of food, fuel and housing costs piled pressure on household budgets that were already squeezed by unemployment and low incomes, breeding dissatisfaction that would so readily find an outlet in 2011. The 2008 protests in North Africa and elsewhere may have been subdued by a familiar combination of arrests and concessions, but their underlying causes remained unresolved.

Every revolution has its economic roots, though they are often inseparable from the politics. They formed two of three promises made to the Russian people in Lenin's 'Peace, Bread, Land!' slogan in the summer of 1917. Uncontrolled inflation stoked unhappiness with the Shah's regime in late 1970s Iran. Marie Antoinette's apocryphal suggestion that her people eat cake had its origins in the bread shortages which afflicted 1780s Paris. Economic stagnation in the 1980s meant that Eastern Europe lagged behind its Western counterparts to the extent that even those who believed in socialism had lost faith in their governments.

And it was no coincidence that demonstrators on the streets of Tunis, Amman or Cairo would brandish baguettes or flatbreads as a symbol of their rage in 2011. The cost of living had spiralled in the years before the uprisings, with the poorest hit harder than most. Impressive GDP growth had failed to create anywhere near enough jobs to satisfy the legions of university graduates who entered the job market each year with expectations that could only be dashed on the rocks of unemployment or the unskilled, low-wage jobs that awaited them.

Nor was it a coincidence that most oil-rich countries in the Arab world experienced neither bread protests in 2008 nor inflation-inspired uprisings in 2011. True, none were immune from rampant inflation during the oil boom, but they had long utilized their financial resources to offset price rises and neutralize the threat of serious economic discontent among their citizens – even though other manifestations of malaise would trigger revolts in Bahrain or Libya.

The financial clout that the Gulf monarchies – especially the region's economic, political and religious giant Saudi Arabia – derive from their energy resources would carry powerful political weight in 2011. It could be seen in the six-member Gulf Cooperation Council's (GCC) decision to intervene in Bahrain, in the reaction by Washington to signs of unrest in the Gulf, or in Qatar's role in funding and assisting Libya's National Transitional Council (NTC). Long a central factor in the political economy of the region, hydrocarbons were cast by the boom into an even more prominent role.

But while the economic picture was far from rosy in many Arab countries on the eve of 2011, problems like youth unemployment and income inequality were no worse than they were in parts of Europe. There was no sudden market crash or severe budget cuts in 2010, and economic discontent alone cannot explain why the uprisings spread so quickly through the region. Unlike people in Spain or Italy, most Arabs were helpless to change their condition. They could not realistically vote out their governments or their ageing presidents, could not criticize their policies in the media and, in many cases, could do little more than try to emigrate to the Gulf or to the West, where they at least had the assurance of a job or a vote, if not always both.

The majority, with nowhere else to go, watched with growing frustration as the gap between rich and poor widened and as government privatizations appeared to benefit the ruling elites at the expense of ordinary people who were locked out of job markets and sometimes unable even to pay for a wedding.

Preferred Partners

On the eve of the Arab Spring, there was a growing sense that those ordinary people were being excluded from the benefits of economic growth, especially the sort being fuelled by big-ticket foreign investments and economic liberalization policies. The petrodollars pouring into the banks of Abu Dhabi, Doha or Kuwait in the late 2000s needed an outlet, and the foreign companies riding the global economic boom and enjoying access to easy pre-2008 credit were on the prowl for investments. With Arab investors keen to focus on their home turf in the post-9/11 world, many looked to the Levant and North Africa for new opportunities.

Between 2003 and 2008, the countries of the six-member GCC invested an estimated $120 billion in the Middle East and North Africa out of their $900 billion in total spending.[2] Most of that investment came from the smaller Gulf states. At the peak of the oil price spike in 2008, outbound foreign direct investment (FDI) was $1.5 billion from Gulf leviathan Saudi Arabia, compared to $6 billion from tiny Qatar, $8.9 billion from Kuwait and $15.8 billion from the UAE.[3] But, ironically, it was an oil-poor entity, the emirate of Dubai, which became the poster child for this model of large-scale investment.

Dubai's oil production might be meagre, but its ruling family had long been reaping the financial benefits of operating an investment-friendly, international city at the epicentre of the world's most energy-rich region.[4] The ruling Al Maktoum dynasty wove a web of funds and vehicles to invest at home and overseas, joining other Gulf states, as well as Libya, whose relatively conservative sovereign wealth funds (SWF) now became more acquisitive. While this new wave of multi-billion-dollar spending certainly massaged foreign investment statistics in Tunis or Cairo, it did little to improve life for the average person on the street, and contributed in several ways to popular discontent in the countries that were on the receiving end.

Privatization programmes being pursued by governments around the region were one magnet for oil money. In 2006, UAE-owned Etisalat paid $3.1 billion for Egypt's third mobile phone licence, while the National Bank of Kuwait purchased Egypt's Al Watany Bank for $1 billion in 2008. The opening-up of Syria's banking and insurance sector from 2005 onwards attracted a series of Gulf banks, while privatization in Morocco's power generation sector brought investment from Abu Dhabi and elsewhere.

Shiny billboards sprouted up everywhere from Rabat to Muscat as Gulf property developers like Emaar, MAF, Damac, Qatari Diar and Sama Dubai announced grandiose new projects. Real estate was the single biggest target for Gulf investors. Between 2004 and 2010, property developments accounted for an estimated $132 billion out of a total $171 billion in FDI that poured into North Africa from West Asia (the Levant and the Gulf, plus Turkey), and for 59 per cent of all greenfield FDI projects.[5]

On the surface, this was a boon for countries like Tunisia and Egypt, which both received more foreign investment in the three years between 2006 and 2009 than in the 15 years between 1990 and 2005.[6] But any positive effects were diluted by crony capitalist systems that ensured the benefits of foreign investment went to a small clique of businesses owned or controlled by key regime figures, people like Rami Makhlouf in Syria and Sakher al-Materi in Tunisia, who were related by blood or marriage to the ruling families. These men and their networks were ideal conduits for rulers reluctant to share profits, now super-sized by the oil boom, and looking for ways to siphon off generous commissions. A handful of businessmen attained a new level of wealth with these big contracts. They increasingly owed their fortune to the status quo and they defended the regimes more fiercely than ever, despite growing public frustrations.

Either facing international pressure to liberalize their economies, or responding to a domestic need to find new sources of income and jobs, many Arab regimes embarked on privatization and deregulation policies that were packaged as reform but were, in reality, carefully managed to ensure that the benefits and the power remained in the hands of the regime or the elite that surrounded it.

Opening up the economy to overseas trade and investment often involved offering local distribution licences, joint ventures or franchise agreements to foreign companies. It was not difficult for governments to channel these opportunities towards a favoured clique. Larger foreign firms seeking to enter new markets naturally look for powerful local partners with the financial clout and political connections to drive sales and cut through red tape. What resulted was an oligarchy of quasi-private sector companies controlled by figures related to the ruling elite.

A couple of examples from Tunisia illustrate the point. In 2009, two front-runners had emerged in the auction for the country's third mobile phone licence. The first, and the eventual victor, was a consortium of France Telecom and a Tunisian telecoms company owned by prominent local businessman Marouane Mabrouk, the husband of Cyrine Ben Ali, the president's daughter from his first marriage. The second was a joint bid by Turkcell in partnership with Sakher al-Materi, the husband of another Ben Ali daughter. Materi was the scion of an established Tunisian business family and his union with the Ben Alis had propelled him to such rapid wealth and status that some speculated he was being groomed as a potential successor to the ageing president.

Meanwhile, the local dealerships of Fiat, Ford, Jaguar, Volkswagen, Audi, Seat, Land Rover, Hummer, Porsche and Mercedes were all controlled by Materi, Mabrouk or Belhassen Trabelsi, the brother-in-law of Ben Ali.[7] Big companies that did not play by the rules found it tough to make inroads. McDonalds' refusal to grant an exclusive licence to a regime-connected partner, for instance, torpedoed its planned entry into Tunisia.[8]

High-level corruption was no secret. It was fodder for juicy gossip on the street and details of corrupt dealings occasionally found their way into the press, particularly when they involved a regime insider who had fallen out of favour. In the spring of 2010, state-controlled newspapers in Libya carried stories of a major corruption scandal at the Economic and Social Development Fund (ESDF), a sprawling state-owned entity where senior managers had allegedly been siphoning off millions in illegal commissions. Dubai's ruler, Sheikh Mohammed bin Rashed Al Maktoum, led something of a witch-hunt against corruption in government-owned developers and financial firms in the wake of the property market collapse in 2009.[9] High profile Emiratis, not just foreign executives, were sacked and arrested as inefficiency and graft left these firms unable to withstand a downturn while the government was scrambling to pay or write off their debts.

When WikiLeaks released 90,000 US embassy cables in December 2010, it simply confirmed what people had been gossiping about for years. Some of the more potent material was penned by Robert Godec, the US ambassador in Tunis between 2006 and 2009, whose dispatches often carried sarcastic headings such as 'Yacht Wanted', referring to the alleged theft of a French businessman's yacht by a close relative of Leila Trabelsi, or 'Mob rule', which described the mafia-like behaviour of the Tunisian regime. A July 2009 cable included the following passage:

> And corruption in the inner circle is growing. Even average Tunisians are keenly aware of it, and the chorus of complaints is rising. Tunisians intensely dislike, even hate, first lady Leila Trabelsi and her family. In private, regime opponents mock her; even those close to the government express dismay at her reported behaviour. Meanwhile, anger is growing at Tunisia's high unemployment and regional inequities. As a consequence, the risks to the regime's long-term stability are increasing.[10]

Another leaked cable, written in December 2009, reported other goings-on in Morocco. The source quoted in the report accused the palace of using state institutions to 'coerce and solicit bribes' and asserted that 'contrary to popular belief, corruption in the real-estate sector during the reign of King Mohamed VI is becoming more, not less, pervasive.' This trend, the cable's author said, 'seriously undermined the good governance that the Moroccan government is working hard to promote'.[11]

Of course, some benefits from foreign investment and economic liberalization did cascade down to the broader population. Retail franchises, car dealerships and mobile phone companies all create jobs and spin-off businesses, while privatization generates proceeds that contribute towards government spending. But their main beneficiary was nonetheless an increasingly ostentatious clique that was able to accumulate ever-greater wealth and power, to the growing frustration of the masses.

At the other end of the corruption spectrum, but just as corrosive to the building of trust in the institutions of state, was petty graft. Swedish social scientist and Nobel prize-winning economist Gunnar Myrdal, whose description of corruption in south-east Asia in the 1960s could easily apply to many Arab countries in the early twenty-first century, describes this in terms of 'soft states'. Such countries are 'dominated by powerful interests that exploit the power of the state or government to serve their own interests rather than the interests of their citizens'. It is a system, Myrdal wrote, that 'easily leads people to think that anybody in a position of power is likely to exploit this in the interest of himself, his family, or other social groups to which he feels loyal. If corruption becomes taken for granted, resentment amounts essentially to envy of those who have opportunities for private gain by dishonest dealings.'[12]

Galal Amin, professor of economics at the American University in Cairo (AUC), argues that 'the soft state came to Egypt about thirty-five years ago' and had appeared 'both totalitarian and soft' since the 1980s, restricting individual freedoms on the one hand but constructing bureaucratic frameworks that by their very nature encourage law-breaking on the other.[13]

Under this sort of system, rules exist in theory but are not imposed in practice; they appear to exist with the widespread knowledge that they will be bent or ignored. The payment of invoices can be accelerated by greasing the palms of an underpaid clerk in the accounts office. Tax bills can be reduced by paying a willing official to 'handle your account' and rubber-stamp a falsified return. A traffic policeman threatening to impose a speeding fine can be dissuaded by the surreptitious palming of a note through the car window. Construction permits can be purchased from those with the right *wasta*, a word which has no direct equivalent in English but suggests the use of one's connections to curry favour or get out of a sticky situation, something akin to 'pulling strings'.

Such transactions permeate down to the most mundane aspects of life. In Damascus, landlords who rented out property were obliged to register the details of their tenants with the local authorities and theoretically also had to pay tax on any income they made. To give one real-life example, a two-bedroom apartment in the upmarket Abu Romaneh district of the Syrian capital was worth an annual rent of about $20,000 in early 2011. But the annual rent that the landlord lists in the contract might be little more than $1,000, a ludicrously low amount which in turn reduces the tax bill. The official registering the contract realizes that the listed value is highly unrealistic, but either does not question it, given that he or she stands to make no personal gain or loss if the real market value is listed, or uses the situation as leverage to extract a small bribe in exchange for turning a blind eye.

This is a classic example of an opaque and inefficient system in which more or less everyone is forced to commit a crime because the laws are 'there to be broken'. If you aren't breaking them, so the reasoning goes, then someone else is, even their supposed enforcers. But the very process of breaking them gives birth to a niggling fear that somebody, somewhere, in the security services or the bureaucracy, has a record of your crime. You are therefore part of the system and have no interest in exposing other abusers.

It all creates a vicious circle in which the government fails to collect sufficient taxes to make improvements that could remedy the situation, such as raising public-sector wages to a level where taking bribes would no longer be necessary to supplement incomes. The size of the informal cash economy keeps growing, and those making the rules have no incentive to change them.

One important implication is that loyalty to the organized state is necessarily weak. People learn not to rely on talent or meritocracy to further their careers or business interests, but turn instead to connections within their own communities, whether defined by religion, family or geography, for the provision of jobs, favours and opportunities.

This lack of loyalty to the state, we will show, is at the heart of the dangers that Arab countries face in making their transition from dictatorship to more participatory and transparent political systems. The more entrenched the networks of patronage and corruption, the harder the country will have to work to avoid sinking into civil war or falling victim to a new dictatorship.

Both petty graft and elite corruption helped plant the seeds of discontent in the Arab world. In Tunisia, Syria and Egypt corruption created figures of hate against which popular anger could be targeted. Ben Ali's wife, Leila Trabelsi, was reviled by Tunisians for what they saw as her desire not only to keep major international investments in the family, but to demand a stake in any profitable private enterprise. The Trabelsi family's predatory behaviour had reached such an extent on the eve of revolution that Tunisians cited it as a reason why they were not interested in growing their own companies. Tellingly, an early concession promised by Bashar al-Assad in an effort to extinguish protests in June 2011 was to announce that Rami Makhlouf, the president's cousin and one of the country's wealthiest men, would 'retire' from business.

By that time, it was too late. Assad and other Arab leaders were seeing a popular rejection of the uneasy marriage of inefficient Soviet-style bureaucracy with crony capitalism that had bred corruption, encouraged nepotism, and left the growing mass of young people unable to access anaemic job markets and faced with a punishing rise in the cost of living.

Inflation, Uninterrupted

Despite the grand plans and the computer-generated images of pristine new skyscrapers, many Gulf-funded real-estate projects in oil-poor Arab countries never broke ground. Some were scuppered by incompetent management and disputes with local partners, others by stultifying levels of corruption or labyrinthine local bureaucracy. Many Gulf investors attempted to copy and paste a Dubai-style business model that involved making bumper profits very quickly by selling luxury properties off-plan to speculators who would resell them within days at inflated prices. But a more complicated web of regulations and taxation in poorer Arab countries made this model problematic to export, as did the fact that a much higher proportion of potential buyers were actually people who would live in the apartments or villas when they were finished. Unlike the speculators, they preferred to wait and see the finished product before opening their wallets.

And the finished product in many of these swanky new developments was often far beyond the reach of the average person. Marketing campaigns in Tunis, Casablanca or Cairo showed futuristic towers, luxurious apartments with gyms and swimming pools, or images of smiling families buying Western designer brands in air-conditioned shopping malls.

True, there was an elite who could afford this lifestyle. But for the bulk of the population, battling with high unemployment, low incomes and rising prices, these images were not just an inaccessible dream but painful evidence of a growing rich-poor divide. They bolstered a sense that foreign investment, often from the Gulf, was only benefiting the upper crust of society, whether through corrupt deal-making and the sale of state assets, or by building new districts for the rich. Meanwhile, the poor languished in crumbling accommodation squeezed into overcrowded districts that lacked basic services or decent roads.

Foreign investment in real estate was also one driving force behind a property price spike that spread across the region in the years leading up to the Arab Spring. Others included a common preference for investing in bricks and mortar rather than riskier stocks and bonds, natural population growth, rapid urbanization and easier access to credit. Social trends were also changing, with more and more young couples wanting to move immediately into their own home rather than taking the traditional route of living with the groom's parents.

More importantly, overseas remittances had been pouring into property. The boom in oil-rich countries had created hundreds of thousands of jobs for Egyptians, Syrians, Moroccans, Lebanese or Jordanians, work that Emiratis, Saudis or Qataris were either unwilling, unqualified or insufficiently numerous to do. Saudi Arabia is the second-biggest remittance-sending country in the world after the United States.[14] Remittances wired home by expatriates in the Gulf, including some 10 million Arab nationals, totalled $40 billion in 2008, up almost a third on the previous year. Remittances from Gulf countries to Egypt alone stood at more than $4 billion in 2008–9,[15] while Jordanians working overseas sent back some $3.2 billion in 2008,[16] 45 per cent more than in 2005 and equivalent to about a fifth of the country's GDP. Much of this was reinvested in property because the aim of most single men who went off to work in the Gulf was to save enough money to buy a house in their own countries, giving a major boost to their desirability in an increasingly competitive marriage market.

The end result was a region-wide property boom in the second half of the 2000s, pushing house prices and rents to levels that were out of proportion with incomes. A 20-something university graduate working in a respectable private company in Damascus might take home a monthly salary of about $750, but to rent a one-bedroom apartment in a mid-range district would easily cost more than $500 a month. A 2008 survey found that property prices in many parts of Tripoli had risen by an average of 70 to 80 per cent in the previous year alone. In Tunisia, only 41 per cent of respondents to a 2010 poll said they were satisfied with the availability of affordable housing, compared to 74 per cent in 2009.[17]

Wages rose, and access to credit did get easier, but not enough to close another gaping divide between expectation and reality. Life was made more difficult because landlords would frequently ask for large upfront payments on rent, often for six months or even a year, to give them security. And if you worked in the informal sector, as many people did, or in any job that was not full-time and could not be proven with a formal letter from your employer, then no bank would even think of offering you a loan.

Researchers at Tunisia's statistics authority went on strike during the summer of 2011 to protest about years, sometimes decades, of working on a continuous succession of short-term contracts that made them ineligible for either mortgages or pensions.[18]

The cost of housing was just one element among widespread price rises that stoked popular discontent. In the region's largest non-oil economy, Egypt, the cost of food and drink rose much faster than the overall consumer price index between 2005 and 2009.[19] It was the same story in Syria, where food and fuel prices rose more rapidly than any other items over the same period, partly because the government had cut diesel and heating oil subsidies.[20] In Morocco, grain prices jumped between 2006 and 2008 while the government's subsidy bill in the first four months of 2011 was more than three-quarters higher than in 2010.[21] In Tunisia, where many suspected that the government massaged its economic figures, food, drinks and transport costs rose more quickly than those of any other product in the years before the revolution.[22] Even bribes got more expensive. 'A traffic stop used to cost you 20 dinars and now it's up to 40 or 50!' complained a source in a US embassy cable from Tunis released by WikiLeaks.[23]

Inflation was cushioned to some extent by state subsidies, and Arab regimes were all too aware of the potentially explosive effect of removing them. When late Egyptian President Anwar Sadat reduced bread subsidies as part of Western-inspired liberalization policies in 1977, riots in Cairo left some 80 people dead. In 1984, when ageing Tunisian leader Habib Bourguiba announced that the price of bread would double, dozens died in a wave of clashes across the country. In both cases the subsidies were soon reinstated. In 2008, the Moroccan government happily accepted a Saudi grant of $500m to help pay subsidy bills after the cost of its crude oil imports rose by 69 per cent in the first quarter of the year.

But price rises were also being fuelled by a burgeoning consumer culture and easier access to debt. More and more households took out loans or overdrafts to fund the purchases of TVs, cars, houses or even medical treatment. In Tunisia, for example, the value of bank loans to individuals rose almost fourfold in the eight years between 2002 and 2008, and the value to professionals almost doubled.[24] The value of short-term loans only increased by 5.5 per cent between 2001 and 2005, but then soared by 67 per cent between 2005 and 2010. Bank claims on private companies and households in Morocco rose by an average of 14 per cent per year between 2005 and 2010.[25]

Other issues contributed. The Tunisian dinar depreciated by 12 per cent against the euro between 2006 to 2011, making imports from the Eurozone – the country's largest trading partner – more expensive. The global food price spike that afflicted North Africa more than many other regions was exacerbated by a heavy reliance on imports and rising consumption. Egypt, for example, is the world's largest per capita consumer of bread and its largest importer of wheat.[26] Per capita wheat consumption in North Africa rose by about a fifth in the first decade of the 2000s, and in 2010 the region imported a quantity of wheat surpassed only in 2008.[27] In January 2011, the UN's food price index set a new record high, surpassing the previous peak of 2008 when protests had erupted across North Africa and beyond.[28]

High energy prices also took a particularly high toll on many Arab economies because of their reliance on oil and gas for power generation. Of Egypt's total primary energy consumption in 2008, 94 per cent came from crude oil and natural gas, whereas the equivalent in the United States was 69 per cent and in France 53 per cent.[29] The remainder there was provided by burning coal or came from renewable and nuclear sources, but Arab economies had fallen sharply behind the rest of the world in diversifying their power sources. This meant that rising local energy consumption ate up greater proportions of domestic oil and gas production, leaving less available for export and bringing fewer dollars into state coffers. This lack of diversification presents long-term problems for Arab economies, even for the major oil producers like Saudi Arabia.

Rising prices did not exclusively affect those countries that saw upheaval in 2011. Prices had skyrocketed in supercharged economies growing from a small base, like the UAE or Qatar, and also in Saudi Arabia, where high inflation was a relatively new phenomenon. The kingdom's cost of living, which had actually fallen below 1999 levels in the first five years of the 2000s, rose rapidly after 2005, and inflation touched almost 10 per cent in 2008.[30] But as discussed at the start of this chapter, most oil-rich countries had the financial resources to ensure that living standards were not dangerously eroded, even if the social contract only papered over the same structural cracks as in other Arab countries – a youth bulge, a lack of 'real' jobs as opposed to manufactured public-sector positions, and a reliance on food imports.

The argument that consumers were protected from inflation by government subsidies is true to some extent, but fails to take into account the abuse of the system by wholesalers. The widening gap between subsidized local prices and rising global prices only encouraged unscrupulous merchants to sell basic foodstuffs on the black market at inflated prices or to smuggle fuel across borders to countries where it would fetch more money. More importantly, every extra dollar spent by the state on keeping petrol or food prices artificially low was a dollar not spent on improving education or healthcare standards. State budgets, at least in oil-poor countries like Syria or Tunisia, were not bottomless.

Rising prices might not have fomented such frustration had incomes and employment matched their growth. But in deprived areas of many Arab countries, the worst-off were being pushed below the poverty line, with serious implications for stability. Anger was not only inflamed by rising prices, but by the growing sense of injustice at the ruling elite who were lining their pockets with the proceeds of economic liberalization while many wallowed in unemployment or underemployment.

Jobless Growth

The word *hittiste* has its origins in 1980s Algeria. It refers to a young, male urban dweller who spends much of his time leaning against a wall, or *hit* in Arabic, because he has no work and nothing else to do. It is a phenomenon visible not only in Algeria but in most towns and cities across the Arab world, even though the *hit* might now have been replaced by an internet café or a shopping mall, depending on the country.

Youth unemployment was without doubt one of the main roots of discontent in many parts of the Arab world. The overall jobless rate varies from around 10 per cent to 20 per cent across the region, depending on whose figures you believe, but for those between 15 and 30 years of age, it is far higher – just as it is in the Western world. In virtually every country in the region, 15- to 30-year-olds made up more than half of the unemployed population and represented a dangerous hotbed of resent- ment. By 2010, only 29 per cent of Egyptians thought their government maximized the potential of youth, compared to 41 per cent a year earlier.[31]

Job creation did take place, but generally favoured older people or even expatriates. In Jordan, for example, foreign workers took some 63 per cent of the 55,000 jobs created every year between 2001 and 2007.[32] An increasingly bloated public sector still dominated the labour markets and was apparently preferred by most jobseekers for its better average pay, laxer work ethic and greater security than 'real' jobs in the profit-driven private sector. There were exceptions. 'For every twenty people in government, eighteen sit around doing nothing,' said one Kuwaiti entrepreneur whose explanation of why she didn't want a public sector job summed up the issues of underemployment and invisible unemployment that masked the true scale of joblessness.[33] Anyone who has wandered through the labyrinthine corridors of public-sector companies and ministries anywhere in the Arab world would probably agree with her. One efficient, well-paid person could do the same job as three inefficient, low-paid people, but governments did not want another two unemployed people on the streets.

Unemployment also varied sharply within each country, reflecting geographical divides in several states that saw revolts in 2011. In Tunisia, towns and cities on the eastern seaboard enjoyed higher incomes, lower unemployment and better infrastructure than the deprived central, southern and western areas that were such fertile ground for protests in both 2008 and 2011. Nationally, average unemployment was 14.8 per cent in 2010 but in southern towns like Redeyef, Metlaoui and Moulares it was often above 25 per cent, even by official figures, which means the real total was likely to be higher still. Some have put it above 50 per cent in the most deprived areas.[34]

Jobless figures in the smaller Gulf monarchies are heavily skewed by the fact that there is theoretically zero unemployment among expatriates, who are not officially allowed to live in the country without full-time employment contracts, nor remain beyond retirement age unless they own property. Among Gulf nationals, however, unemployment is still a reality. The official unemployment rate in 2009 was 13 per cent among Emiratis[35] and 4 per cent among Qataris,[36] but this does not take into account the relatively high number of people who choose not to work and are therefore not counted as unemployed. A reliance on the public sector is even more marked here than anywhere else in the Arab world. In 2010, 46 per cent of UAE nationals were employed by federal government institutions, 39 per cent in local government, and 6 per cent in institutions that spanned the two. Only 7 per cent of the country's private-sector workers were UAE nationals.[37]

The problem is even graver in Saudi Arabia. Although around 716,000 new jobs were created in 2009, unemployment among Saudi nationals rose from 9.8 per cent to 10.5 per cent, and some 39 per cent of 20–24-year-olds were without work. Some 92 per cent of the Saudi workforce was employed in the public sector, despite the government's efforts to cajole private-sector companies into hiring Saudis.[38]

Unemployment was also exacerbated by intense demographic pressures from the so-called 'youth bulge' – a swelling cohort of 20- and 30-somethings with little prospect of finding a job. In proportionate terms this demographic problem is most extreme in Yemen, which had a mean average age of 21 in 2010, making it the youngest Arab country. Yemen's population explosion has exacerbated various other political, social and economic calamities that are described later in this book. The single biggest growth in youth numbers was in Egypt, whose overall population increased by 23 per cent in the first decade of the 2000s to reach 78 million in 2010, by far the largest in the Arab world. Just under a third of those are aged between 15 and 30, and their numbers grew by 1.8 million in the second half of the 2000s.[39]

Near the other end of the demographic spectrum is Tunisia. Within a few years of gaining independence from France in 1956, late President Habib Bourguiba had banned polygamy, promoted contraceptives and legalized abortion. Tunisia's average annual population growth was less than 1 per cent in the 2000s, compared to 2 per cent in Egypt or 2.3 per cent in Saudi Arabia. But Tunisia's problem is one that afflicts so many others in the region, namely a surplus of university graduates with skills mismatched to the job market and with unrealistically high career expectations. Sharp growth in higher education in the late 1990s and early 2000s was partly a result of higher education being prioritized by government. Parents believe that respectable jobs require university degrees, and therefore push their children to enter university, funding their higher education at the expense of other spending. But the outcome is often a surplus of graduates with worthless degrees from poor-quality universities and skills that are not suited to real-world, private-sector jobs. An emphasis on learning by rote has also tended to discourage independent inquiry and initiative.

Of the 2.4 million unemployed people in Egypt in 2009, over a third had university level education or better, and in the capital, Cairo, the figure was 54 per cent.[40] An additional 7.2 million people are forecast to enter the job market between 2008 and 2020, and to create jobs for them would require annual GDP growth of at least 7 per cent a year, even before taking into account all the existing jobseekers on the market.[41] Every year, the Tunisian economy creates around half as many jobs as there are new graduates entering the labour market. The result is that Tunisian chambermaids and restaurant waiters are often graduates with fluency in two or three languages, frustrated with the lot that life has offered them.

Crisis? What Crisis?

There is little to distinguish the origins of the 2008 protests from those of the 2011 revolutions. Both began for essentially the same reasons in the same region of Tunisia, a deprived and little-known area but in many ways a microcosm of the economic malaise that affected so much of the Arab world. Where those protests faded away in 2008, they snowballed in 2011.

Was it the global financial crisis and the recession in Europe – the main trading partner for all North African countries – that made the difference? The answer is yes and no. There was no dramatic stock-market crash or sovereign debt crisis on the eve of 2011, but nor were most countries immune from the crippling economic problems that were striking fear into the hearts of governments and consumers on the northern side of the Mediterranean.

Several Arab bourses had crashed in 2008, notably Saudi Arabia's Tadawul, by far the region's largest stock market by capitalization, whose main index shed more than half of its value that year, as did the Cairo stock exchange. It was a similar story in Dubai, Abu Dhabi and Doha, as big institutional investors who had adventurously entered these high-risk, high-profit markets during the boom times quickly sold off their holdings.

Individual local investors were the biggest losers. On Riyadh's bourse, retail investors accounted for the vast majority of share trades. In Egypt, where middle-class interest in the stock market had perked up in recent years, a fifty-six-year-old man was found hanging at his home in October 2008 after losing most of his savings in the crash.[42]

Yet many Arab stock exchanges were too small, illiquid or disconnected from global financial markets to be seriously affected by the credit crunch or to make any widespread impact on a meaningful proportion of the population. After years of planning, the Syrian government had finally re-established the Damascus Securities Exchange (DSE) in early 2009. It rode out the global downturn and subsequently became one of the best-performing stock markets in the world, its overall index rising by more than 70 per cent in 2010, testament to its latent wealth and the lack of other investment outlets in the country.[43]

Tunisia's tiny stock exchange, with just 55 listed companies, saw strong gains in 2009 and 2010, while a renewed upswing in sentiment in the Gulf meant Riyadh's main index rose by 27 per cent in 2009 and 8 per cent in 2010.[44] And the country that arguably emerged strongest from the credit crisis and global downturn was Libya, whose uprising was bloodier than any. This was as much by accident as by design – the country had no housing credit bubbles and no financial system sophisticated or interconnected enough to be directly affected by international markets.

Nonetheless, the 2008 slowdown in the Gulf certainly sent ripples throughout the Arab world. Job losses began to gather pace, especially after the property and construction crash in Dubai and decelerating growth elsewhere. Many companies imposed hiring freezes at best, and at worst went bust as the juggernaut of real estate speculation shuddered to a halt. The outcome was fewer job opportunities for workers from oil-poor countries, and less money sent back home to support families. Remittances to Egypt dropped by a fifth in the first half of 2009 and by 6 per cent in the second half.[45]

Many projects set to be funded by Gulf investors were cancelled or shelved. SAMA Dubai, which had promised to create 350,000 jobs for its Mediterranean Gate project in Tunis, essentially ceased to exist after a corruption probe in Dubai saw some of its management arrested. The land it was meant to build on around the Lac du Sud, close to central Tunis, still sat empty in late 2011. Overall foreign direct investment (FDI) into Tunisia in 2010 was 45 per cent lower than in 2008, in Egypt it was 33 per cent lower, and in Morocco it was 48 per cent down. But there was an even bigger collapse in the Gulf states themselves, where FDI into the UAE was more than three times lower than in 2008. In Bahrain, it was ten times lower.[46]

The tourist industry stopped growing in the region's most popular destinations, but did not collapse. Tunisia and Egypt benefited from their status as low-cost package destinations that appealed to cash-strapped European holidaymakers.[47] And tourism in Syria – a growing source of jobs and foreign currency earnings – was booming. Arrivals rose by 46 per cent year-on-year in the first eight months of 2010 and the economy as a whole grew at 5 per cent in the year before the revolt against Assad, with inward FDI remaining steady.[48]

Housing markets collapsed in overheated cities like Dubai, Abu Dhabi and Doha, where years of speculation and lax regulation finally came home to roost, but there was no real property crash in most other Arab cities, which were facing a genuine shortage in low and mid-range housing. Nor was there any other economic emergency, like a sudden currency depreciation or sovereign debt crisis of the type that prompted riots on the streets of Athens several times in 2011.

The global financial crisis and the ensuing downturn was not the direct trigger for the 2011 revolts, and indeed barely affected countries like Syria and Libya: the most vulnerable countries, in general, were those with close financial and business ties to the global economy but whose governments were not able to cushion the shock using energy revenues. And what evidence we do have about changes in sentiment between 2008 and 2010 suggest that living standards were being eroded. A rare poll in Tunisia, for example, found that while 56 per cent of respondents felt the overall economy was improving in 2009 and 2010, public satisfaction with schools, roads, transport and housing was decidedly lower than it had been in 2008.[49]

More broadly, the events of 2011 took place against a backdrop of deep global economic uncertainty that has historically tended to be fertile ground for political change. Extreme spikes and troughs in the price of oil, which plays such a central role in the region, carried crucial implications for rulers and ruled in both resource-rich and resource-poor countries. This is not to say that all citizens of oil-rich countries were kept happy by the benefits that their rulers provided, while those in oil-poor countries had their patience drained by stagnant or deteriorating qualities of life. The reality is clearly more complex, and a better way to characterize the economic roots of the 2011 uprisings might be to see them as a series of divides.

Most evidence, both empirical and anecdotal, suggests that the rich-poor divide was widening in most Arab countries. Those closest to the poverty line were the worst-hit by rising food and fuel prices that meant basic essentials still ate up most of their incomes. At the other end of the spectrum, financial and political elites in places like Syria, Tunisia, Libya and Egypt were gathering ever-larger concentrations of wealth and power in their hands as the chief beneficiaries of privatization and economic liberalization programmes.

An extreme rich-poor divide is also obvious in the tiny Gulf monarchies like Qatar and the UAE, neither of which saw any real instability in 2011. But the beneficiaries in that divide were nationals of those countries, enjoying advantages and privileges denied to the foreign workers who made up the bulk of the overall population. As the final section of this book outlines in more detail, nationals in these countries are essentially an elite stratum in a many-layered system that has, in general, helped to neutralize the threat of revolt and enhanced a sense of national cohesion and identity.

Geographical divides were equally striking. Stark variations in incomes and unemployment rates between coastal and central Tunisia help explain why the protest movement began in deprived areas before anywhere else. The perception in north-eastern Libya that Tripoli had neglected them for decades was a serious cause of discontent. It was no coincidence that this region fell first from Gaddafi's grip. In Syria, impoverished families in rural eastern and southern areas lived a very different life from the urban elite in Damascus who spent their weekends partying or shopping in Lebanon.

There was also a crucial gap between expectations and reality, one closely linked with a sense of injustice. In Bahrain, where the ruling family is Sunni, the majority Shi'ite population felt economically as well as politically disenfranchised, believing that access to government jobs or housing was deliberately more restricted for them than for their Sunni compatriots. Tens of thousands of new graduates in Tunisia and Egypt expected to find jobs commensurate with their skills. They were disappointed to find no employment, or that their qualifications were ill-suited to whatever work was available.

But none of these divides are unique to the Middle East and North Africa. In fact they are often more pronounced in the developed world. Income distribution in the United States, for instance, is far more unequal than in most Arab states, and regional variations in unemployment and income are just as bleak in many Western European countries as they are on the other side of the Mediterranean. Youth unemployment in Spain was 40 per cent in 2010, higher than Tunisia, Syria or Egypt, and new graduates were faced with very similar mismatches between expectations and reality.

Nor were state finances on the verge of crisis. Net government debt was 17 per cent of GDP in Syria or 40 per cent in Tunisia in 2010, compared to 142 per cent in Greece or 101 per cent in Italy.[50] Stock market crashes in developed economies were far deeper and more damaging than they were in the Arab world. Bank bail-outs in Britain or the United States could be seen as a sophisticated technique of crony capitalism little different in essence from what authoritarian rulers had applied in Syria or Tunisia.

Perhaps the key difference in the Arab world was the combination of economic hopelessness with political powerlessness. Angry, poor and disenfranchised people in Greece, Spain or Britain had outlets to express their displeasure with policy-makers. They could read and write criticism of their governments, they could watch TV shows and enjoy cartoons that openly mocked their political leaders, they could stage peaceful protests without being shot, and they could ultimately voice their disapproval at the ballot box. They had a belief, whether real or imaginary, that they could influence the course of events.

The absence of this belief in most of the Arab world fuelled a frustration that, as the next chapter explains, was being shared and spread through new forms of media and communication that had already undergone their own revolution in the preceding decade.

CHAPTER 3

The Media Revolution

If you want to free a society just give them internet access because ... the young crowds are all going to go out and hear and see the unbiased media, see the truth about other nations and their own nations and they're going to be able to communicate and collaborate together ... Definitely, this is the internet revolution. I'll call it Revolution 2.0.

— Egyptian activist Wael Ghonim, February 2011[1]

In a Damascus courthouse in May 2002, Riad al-Turk, then 71, was on trial after taking part in the political salons that had sprung up after Bashar al-Assad inherited Syria from his father.[2] Assad had promised reforms when he took office in 2000. Hopes were high for the new president, a seemingly affable eye doctor who had only been fast-tracked for leadership after his older brother, the heir apparent, was killed in a car crash. Assad had freed political prisoners, encouraged free speech and condemned corruption.

Intellectuals, many of them graduates of the Syrian prison system, began to cautiously criticize the lack of political freedom while Turk, head of a banned faction of the Communist Party, condemned the hereditary turn the Syrian republic had taken. A respected cartoonist, Ali Ferzat, who would have his hands crushed by regime thugs in 2011, opened a daring new magazine called *al-Domari*, or the lamplighter, which flew off the shelves in its first week. Soviet-style housing blocks still loomed over the grey streets of Damascus and an army of spies still occupied street corners, taxis and hotel lobbies, but the erstwhile capital of Islam's Ummayad Empire was buzzing. And this new vigour had a name: the Damascus Spring.

It was not to last. While an economic reform programme picked up speed over the ensuing decade, Assad shut down the political salons, tried their hosts in security courts and sent them to jail, or in some cases back to jail. The experiment with political liberalization was over.

Barred from entering the courthouse on that spring morning in 2002, a crowd of several dozen had gathered outside. Most were friends and fellow dissidents, lawyers and human rights activists. Among them were some Western diplomats and a few reporters.

One man walked past a journalist, whipped a pamphlet from its hiding place inside his jacket, stuffed it in the journalist's hand, and kept walking.[3] The leaflet would have got the man arrested not just for its content, but also for distributing publications without a licence in a country where the state controlled the media. Only a few pamphlets could be printed at any one time and they could only be distributed to Syrians who were brave enough to show up in person at the courthouse, watched by the secret and not-so-secret police. Internet and mobile phone services had only arrived in Syria in 2000, and glacially slow dial-up connections initially had to go through the Syrian Computer Society, headed by Assad himself before he became president. Hotmail and Yahoo! were banned. Widespread restrictions meant few people used e-mail, so Syrian authorities could monitor users easily. Some critics had been arrested for forwarding jokes about the president, reinforcing suspicions that the internet, like the phones, were under surveillance.

Ten years and a technological revolution later, Syrian activists harnessed Facebook and Twitter to criticize the regime and rally protesters. Though Syria still has one of the most regulated internet and telecoms sectors in the Middle East,[4] demonstrators could take shaky footage on camera phones, once an expensive gimmick but now cheap and ubiquitous, and upload it for free onto video-sharing sites. The arrival of third-generation telecoms services in Syria in 2009 also meant images could be instantly shared with the world, albeit at an exorbitant price.[5]

Activists smuggled in satellite phones, considered espionage equipment by the Syrian government, to get around state closures of mobile phone networks or the internet. Net-savvy internet users turned to proxies and mirror sites and worked with fellow activists abroad to bypass state censorship. Activist groups such as Shaam News Network,[6] which claims to have no party affiliation or foreign backing, were dedicated entirely to collecting evidence of protests and alleged state brutality and disseminating it to the world in both English and Arabic. The message could be spread instantly and anonymously to reach a far larger audience than dissidents could have hoped for with their printed leaflets, their faxes, or even their e-mails, just a decade earlier.

The Arab Spring may have taken the world by surprise in 2011, but another upheaval had long been underway. It was a media revolution that, through satellite television and the internet, had connected people from the Atlantic to the Gulf like never before, had eroded the cults of personality nurtured by authoritarian rulers, and had helped to empower civil society which is the bedrock of democracy.

Breaking Taboos

The spread of satellite television in the Arabic language took the region by storm in the 1990s, boosting access to information, breaking taboos, bringing the Arab world closer together and powering a whole new industry of writers, actors, directors and producers of dramas, comedies, game shows, music videos and newscasts. Combined with rising literacy, falling birth rates and a young generation raised on the internet and coming of age, satellite television was part of a cultural revolution that had taken place across the Arabic-speaking world in the decade leading up to 2011.

Since the 1950s, controlling the media in Arab countries had been closely associated with controlling the reins of power. One of the first acts of Gamal Abdel Nasser's 'free officers' after their 1952 coup in Egypt was to take control of state radio and deliver Communiqué Number 1, announcing the change of the country's leadership. The same routine was repeated by Nasser's imitators in Iraq, Libya and Yemen. Controlling a mouthpiece was essential to feeding the propaganda machine that turned these military coups into 'revolutions' that could not be criticized.

Millions of people around the region tuned into Nasser's Voice of the Arabs radio station, which started broadcasting in 1953 and delivered a mix of the Egyptian leader's rousing pan-Arab and anti-imperialist rhetoric alongside music from legendary Arab singers like Egyptian diva Umm Kalthoum. Voice of the Arabs galvanized opposition to British-installed monarchs and Western policy. But its allure faded after the 1967 war when, as swathes of Arab territory was lost to Israel, its chief presenter, Ahmed Said, lied across the airwaves about an impending Arab victory.[7] The disappointment, when the truth began to seep through other channels in the following days, was made worse by the enormity of the untruth.

The station lost its credibility, and throughout the 1970s and 1980s Arabs viewed state television, radio and newspapers with a mixture of boredom and contempt. Syrians knew something interesting was going on when a

Lebanese or French magazine would be turned back at the border, or when certain pages were torn out. In Arab countries where independent newspapers were allowed, journalists and editors had to perform linguistic acrobatics to get a controversial point across without breaching one of the many red lines that criss-crossed public life.

Regardless of what had happened in the region on a given day, state news bulletins would typically begin with a report on the president or monarch receiving a delegation of well-wishers or cutting a ribbon. The anniversaries of each country's 'revolution' would be marked by endless military parades and hours of empty speeches that were televised live. Across the Arab world, state television fed the public on a stale diet of propaganda that appeared to belong to another era and was increasingly out of step, not just with modern technology, but with reality. Media output would be controlled by a ministry of information or its equivalent, often housed in an imposing Soviet-style block where censors combed through the newspapers and from where press accreditation and visas for foreign journalists could be both issued and withdrawn.

With the arrival of satellite television in the 1990s, people suddenly had a choice. Based in London, the Middle East Broadcasting Center (MBC) became the Arab world's first private free-to-air satellite channel when it launched in 1991.[8] Offering a mix of popular Arabic entertainment shows with programmes that were already successful in the West, it was an instant hit among the millions of Arabic-speakers who lived in Europe. Overseas dissidents also began to set up their own television broadcasts from Europe. Rifaat al-Assad, the exiled brother of Syria's late president, ran the Arab News Network from London, which became a favoured base for Arab exiles and their broadcasts.[9]

Yet until the launch of Al-Jazeera in 1996, those who wanted to watch professional news broadcasts rather than entertainment and competing propaganda bulletins were still forced to turn to English- or French-language television. During the 1990–1 Gulf War, Arabic-speakers, like the rest of the world, watched events unfold on the US network CNN, and many felt the coverage to be one-sided.[10] Those with a particular interest in current affairs tuned in to the BBC World Service or Radio Monte Carlo, which both ran Arabic radio broadcasts. Yet none of those services could hope for mass appeal.

Hailed as an Arabic CNN, Al-Jazeera was not only the first dedicated news channel in the Arabic language but also an antidote to the stale newscasts of old. Owned by the Qatari government and considered by friend and foe to be a tool of the tiny emirate's increasingly muscular foreign policy, Al-Jazeera nevertheless transformed the media landscape.

The channel's approach to news, encapsulated by the tagline '*Al-Rai* … *Wal Rai al-Akhar*', or 'The Opinion … and the Other Opinion', helped to create what Marc Lynch has called a 'new Arab public'.[11] For the first time, Arabs were able to watch commentators, activists and politicians offering conflicting points of view on the news rather than guests carefully selected to cheerlead for the government or, on opposition stations, parrot an incendiary opposition line. A more professional and nuanced approach to news was not all that Al-Jazeera, whose original staff were mainly graduates of a failed Arabic-language joint venture between Saudi-owned Orbit and the BBC, brought to Arab airwaves. Through its controversial political talk shows, the station had, over the years, played a significant role in eroding the cult of personality that Arab dictators had so carefully tried to construct.

Similar to CNN's *Crossfire*, *Al Itijah al-Mu'akis*, or 'The Opposite Direction', was one programme that was accused of polarizing public opinion. Its host, Faisal al-Qasim, a Syrian Druze, chose a deliberately divisive theme each week and invited two people he knew would disagree strongly to debate it. The show often brought together pro- and anti-regime commentators speaking from European exile or in Al-Jazeera studios in Doha. Egged on by the provocative questions of the bespectacled Qasim, the show often collapsed into a shouting match and guests had been known to walk off.[12]

In January 2011, with Tunisia's Ben Ali still in his presidential palace and protests yet to take off in Egypt, Qasim invited two journalists onto his show to discuss whether citizens should have the right to criticize their rulers. In an Al-Jazeera online poll, 86 per cent had answered yes. In his typically provocative introduction, Qasim asked: 'Has it not become much easier to insult a prophet or even God himself than it is to insult an Arab ruler? Why do Arab rulers consider themselves holier than all that is holy? Why do criminals, thieves … and thugs get imprisoned for a few months in our countries before they are released, while anyone who insults an Arab ruler disappears behind the sun?'

He then compared the Arab world to the West: 'Don't people pelt rulers in the West with tomatoes, rotten eggs and even shoes, without any punishment? Why does a ruler in the West accept all insults from his people, bearing in mind that he is democratically elected, whereas the Arab ruler does not accept any criticism, bearing in mind that he enjoys no legitimacy?'[13]

Such a televised discussion would have been unthinkable in the Arab world in the 1970s or 1980s. A testimony to the taboos Al-Jazeera broke was the fact that it irritated just about everyone from Israel, to the United States, to other Arab rulers, who had at various times closed it down, banned its reporters, or even withdrawn their ambassadors from Qatar over the channel's coverage.[14]

When US-led forces invaded Afghanistan in 2001, Al-Jazeera was the only foreign television station with a correspondent based in the country. It beamed footage of the airstrikes and video messages from Osama bin Laden, enraging the US government of George W. Bush. Some US commentators labelled it 'Jihad TV' and campaigned to prevent cable networks from carrying Al-Jazeera English when that channel was launched in 2006. Coverage from Arabic-speaking reporters in Iraq and around the Arab world, rather than journalists embedded with US-led forces during the 2003 invasion, produced a far more negative perspective on the build-up to and the aftermath of the war.[15]

Al-Jazeera also became the first Arab channel to seriously compete with the Israeli media's version of events. It had made its name in the region with wall-to-wall coverage of the second Palestinian *intifada*. But at the same time, Al-Jazeera shocked viewers when it became the first Arab TV channel to begin hosting Israeli officials and spokespeople.

It was not only the variety of perspectives represented on Al-Jazeera that changed the media landscape in the Arab world, but also the fact that it engaged its viewers. Al-Jazeera organized shows where viewers could call in and air their political views live and uncensored, and many did. It became not just a station that informed its audience about the different points of view that were out there, but a station that engaged with them in a continuous, cross-border conversation. Whatever the Qatari emir's objectives in financing the project, and dozens of theories abound, there was something essentially democratizing about a channel that allowed people to have their say.

As we will discuss later, Al-Jazeera and other satellite channels would come in for severe criticism over their partisan coverage of the upheaval that would spread through the region in 2011. They would end the year more compromised and less popular than they began it. Be that as it may, the Arab Spring took place in a media landscape that was much more inter-active and democratic than had been the Voice of the Arabs at the height of pan-Arab nationalism. Listeners across the region had indeed tuned in to Nasser's rousing speeches, but that was a one-way conversation. It offered one voice and one ideology. It spoke for the Arab people, who were not invited to speak back. Now, with a plethora of Arabic-language channels to represent a multitude of views, they could.

While some Arab governments place theoretical restrictions on the ownership of satellite dishes, it is not a rule that any have seriously tried to enforce. A look at the Damascus skyline from the Qasyoun ridge reveals a sea of dishes across the city. Satellite dishes lurched, rusting and dusty, from every balcony of even the shabbiest apartment blocks and sat atop the breeze-block dwellings of the bleakest villages, built along motorways surrounded by sand. A 2010 opinion poll found that 85 per cent of Arabs relied on the television for their news, and 78 per cent listed Al-Jazeera as either their first or second choice for international news.[16]

Shrinking the Arab World

Satellite TV and the internet played another role that would prove vital once the protests in Tunisia had begun. Over the previous two decades they had made the Arab world smaller, consolidating the sense of community among a group of people who shared the same language, and many of the same concerns, but lived in a vast area that stretched from the Atlantic Ocean off Morocco to the Indian Ocean off Oman.

Well into the 1990s, populations had been limited largely to the newspapers and channels available in their own country, subject to varying levels of censorship, self-censorship and legal restrictions. But pan-Arab news stations meant that a person sitting in Damascus could closely follow developments in Tunisia and Bahrain and gauge different perspectives on different channels. From 2003, it was not just Al-Jazeera that facilitated this consolidation. The Saudi-owned Al-Arabiya, launched just before the Iraq war as a counterweight to its Qatari rival, quickly took off. Its coverage was more conservative, but just as slick, and it offered some of the strongest coverage of business and stock markets in the Arab world, another sea change from the days when the state controlled the economy too.

Beyond the news bulletins, young people from all over the region watched and participated in shows such as Lebanon's *Star Academy*, a copy of a French concept that mixes elements of the British reality TV show *Big Brother* and the talent contest *The X-Factor*. The series was a sensation. Dozens of entertainment channels played endless selections of the latest Arabic music videos, which ranged from Lebanese sex symbol Haifa Wehbe frolicking in a wet dress, to Egyptian pop star Amr Diab in his jeans and styled black hair, to Kuwaiti crooners in traditional white robes singing in the desert. Lebanese multi-platinum star Nancy Ajram became the Arab face of Coca-Cola and Arab pop stars appeared in advertising campaigns around the region.

Alongside these symbols of popular culture, satellite television also played host to preachers from Sheikh Yousef al-Qaradawy, who appeared on Al-Jazeera's *Al-Sharia wal-Hayat*, or 'Religion and Life', to Amr Khaled, an Egyptian accountant turned superstar televangelist. With his dapper suits and neat moustache, Khaled proved popular among the young middle classes who may have been turned off by the dour sermons of the traditional bearded clerics. Khaled's television show attracted more viewers than Oprah Winfrey before the uprising, and he has two million fans on Facebook.[17] During the month of Ramadan, when Muslims fast from dawn to dusk, television viewing shoots up in the prime-time evening slot that follows the *iftar*, or breaking of the fast. Egyptian- and Syrian-made soaps and dramas exploring themes from the complications of polygamy to forbidden love have enthralled sated viewers across the Middle East and North Africa. The Syrian-made soap opera *Bab al-Hara*, or 'The Neighbourhood Gate', a historical drama set in a quarter of the old city of Damascus in the interwar period, returned season after season.

This plethora of regional news, regional music, regional soap operas and regional game shows, however trivial some of them might have been, helped to bolster the feeling of 'Arabness' and the sense that what happened in the Palestinian territories or Iraq or Morocco mattered to all. In the decade before the Arab Spring, satellite television had made it easier than ever before for Arabs to coalesce around a cause of importance to the whole community. Al-Jazeera's coverage of the second Palestinian *intifada* electrified audiences and helped spur protests that erupted in Beirut, Cairo and Tunis. Those protests not only expressed sympathy for the Palestinians but expressed anger at rulers from Mubarak in Egypt to King Abdullah in Saudi Arabia for their reluctance to help or to complain to their US allies.[18] The anger was palpable on the streets. In Cairo, protesters congregated around the Israeli embassy, in Syria they attacked the US embassy and, in the Palestinian refugees camps of Lebanon, demonstrators burned effigies of Ariel Sharon and torched Israeli flags.[19]

It was a reaction that would be repeated with the invasion of Iraq in 2003, the war between Israel and Hezbollah in Lebanon in 2006 and the Gaza War of 2008–9. Expatriates around the world could communicate through television, share experiences and spread a sense of community that at once unified them and reflected the diversity of their opinions. Available internationally, satellite television also helped to connect the huge Arab diaspora with their compatriots back home.

By the time the uprisings of 2011 came around, the wooden sounds of state TV had long been exposed for what they were. Criticism of leaders was already on people's minds, and from there it quickly tumbled onto their lips. Many were already thinking beyond borders. Al-Jazeera's initial coverage of the protests in Tunisia, when Western media had hardly registered that something deeply troubling was taking place, was unparalleled, and appreciated by Tunisians.

Al-Jazeera's partisan coverage of the Arab Spring, like its previous programming, would attract much criticism. In Tunisia, Egypt and Libya, the channel's wall-to-wall coverage was instrumental in boosting protests and was widely seen as reflecting its Qatari owner's backing for the rebels. In the aftermath of the revolts many secularists would accuse it of giving more airtime and therefore more credence to their Islamist rivals and Al-Jazeera was increasingly derided for apparently promoting Qatar's regional allies. As the biggest advertising market in the Middle East and North Africa and home of both Al-Jazeera and Al-Arabiya, the Gulf would later emerge as a red line for the majority of Arab satellite channels, even those that might otherwise be committed to independent news coverage. Al-Jazeera and Al-Arabiya's coverage of the Bahraini uprising was subdued and unrest in Kuwait and the UAE passed almost unnoticed in any media well into 2012. Al-Jazeera barely covered Qatar at all. Critics have widely accused Al-Jazeera of promoting the Muslim Brotherhood and related Islamist groups in the region. In 2010, a number of well-known anchorwomen quit the channel, saying they had come under pressure to dress more conservatively. By the time Wadah Khanfar, a Palestinian who had led Al-Jazeera for eight years, left in September 2011, the channel was widely seen as no more than an arm of Qatari foreign policy.

But it was not just television that had revolutionized communications in the lead-up to the Arab Spring. The mobile phone had become ubiquitous, and the internet had arrived – in Arabic.

The Connected Generation

In 2008, a Facebook page set up by Esraa Abdel Fattah, a young Egyptian woman with little experience of political activism, helped transform a months-long strike for better pay and conditions at the industrial town of Al-Mahalla Al-Kobra into a political crisis. Within two weeks of the online call for a general strike in support of the textile workers, 70,000 supporters had signed up. Political bloggers promoted the strike and most of the opposition political parties swung behind it. On the day, 6 April, thousands of workers and students around Egypt stayed at home, though the sit-in at Al-Mahalla Al-Kobra itself was broken up by police and sparked three days of clashes.

While the strike was only a partial success, it convinced young Egyptian activists of the powerful role that new media technologies could play, not just in disseminating their message, but in organizing action and forming instant networks that rallied thousands of people around a single cause. Internet use had exploded in the Arab world in the decade leading up to the uprising, eroding the state's monopoly on information as a new breed of internet-savvy young people found ways around government controls. Blog sites had mushroomed, breaking the hold of traditional newspapers with their censors and self-censors on information. A new generation of so-called 'hacktivists' brought traditional activism to the new battleground of cyberspace. The spread of social media such as Facebook and Twitter allowed millions of people who had never met to form instant communities of common interest that would play a major role when the time came. The change had been rapid and revolutionary.

The first Arab Human Development Report of 2002 had found fewer internet users in the Arab world than in sub-Saharan Africa, but that digital divide had narrowed sharply in the decade before the uprising, connecting people in new and unpredictable ways.[20] By 2005, internet users in Arab states numbered just 25 million. By 2011, their numbers had more than quadrupled.[21] Young people were using the internet not just to mobilize politically or to follow the news but also to chat online to members of the opposite sex, challenging powerful social traditions, particularly in the conservative Gulf region.[22]

The spread of the internet also coincided with an explosion in the use and capabilities of mobile phones. The number of mobile subscriptions in the region quadrupled between 2005 and 2011, and soared far more quickly in certain countries. In Syria, it grew a spectacular 393-fold in the decade before the uprising, and had still only reached slightly more than half the population. In Yemen, it grew by 346 times, and still less than half the population owned a phone by 2010 – in contrast to Tunisia, where there was an average of more than one phone per person. In wealthy oil-exporting countries such as Saudi Arabia and Libya, there were almost two mobile phones per person on the eve of the Arab Spring.[23]

By now, mobile phones had spread to distant villages where inhabitants had never even had a landline. And where once the mobile phone had allowed users to conduct a conversation from anywhere with people they already knew, by 2010 the smartphone had revolutionized communications. Now users could access the internet from anywhere. They could capture photographs and footage on their phones and instantly upload the images to the world.

Facebook penetration rates remained low on the eve of the Arab Spring, averaging 6.7 per cent in December 2010, compared to 46 per cent in the United Kingdom, but social media was spreading at a phenomenal rate.[24] In December 2010, the total number of Facebook users in the Arab world stood at 21 million, up 78 per cent from January of the same year.

It would be wrong to overemphasize the role of social media once the uprisings began. The five Arab countries with the highest level of Facebook penetration in December 2010 were the UAE, Bahrain, Qatar, Lebanon and Kuwait. Of all those countries, only Bahrain, and to a far lesser extent Kuwait, saw significant unrest in 2011.[25] In Yemen, where protests would break out in January, only 0.7 per cent of the population used Facebook and only 12 per cent were internet users at all. In Egypt, once at the forefront of Arab culture and politics, only 5.5 per cent of the population used Facebook on the eve of the revolt, and just a quarter used the internet. In Libya, 3.7 per cent were Facebook users and 14 per cent used the internet. Even in Tunisia, which would become the birthplace of the Arab Spring, 17.6 per cent were Facebook users in 2010, and overall internet penetration was still only slightly more than a third.[26]

Yet to assess whether the internet and social media were used successfully or unsuccessfully to organize specific protests and disseminate specific information in the Arab Spring is to miss the point. Whatever its role in the mechanics of the revolts, the rapid rise in internet use, blogs and social media over the preceding five years had already had a democratizing effect on Arab society that authoritarian governments could not roll back. From the invention of the wheel to the printing press to the internet, technology has consistently revolutionized the world, connecting people in new ways, shrinking the globe, and breaking down established power structures. This type of change is far more fundamental and has had more lasting effects on states and societies than a single change of government or the reform of a political system in an individual country.

As the printing press did 600 years ago, the internet eroded old elites, forcing the traditional media to re-evaluate its role and weakening the power of national governments and hierarchical organizations. New communication technologies and new media have historically played a key role in movements of political and social upheaval. In Iran, activists smuggled in casette tapes, then a modern technology, of exiled Ayatollah Ruhollah Khomeini's speeches in the lead-up to the 1979 revolution. New media allows activists to spread their message faster and to more people than was possible before, which is crucial in breaking down the barrier of fear that would normally prevent the mass of ordinary people from joining the hardcore of committed activists and turning a humdrum sit-in into an engine for major political upheaval.

Under authoritarian regimes that try to instil a cult of personality, and where the costs of dissent can be as high as arrest, torture or even death, a large number of people tend to oppose the government but few will take the risk of making that opposition public, so the extent of opposition remains hidden. The state appears strong, but is in fact only fierce, as Nazih Ayubi described it in *Overstating the Arab State*. This becomes evident the day that a mass of people realize that dissent is widespread. With that knowledge, a growing number join the protests and the regime crumbles much faster than anyone had expected.[27] These factors would be seen at play once the Arab Spring broke out, as social media, combined with satellite television, would play a crucial role in creating a sense of communal fearlessness.

Thus, through a single Facebook page, an individual could rally thousands of supporters around a cause, thousands of supporters who had never met, who may live in different countries around the world and who, at any other time in history, would not have been able to connect.

But the internet can be misleading. A blog pertaining to be written by a Syrian lesbian gained widespread coverage in the Western media in 2011, before it was revealed that the author was a man living in Scotland. The incident highlighted the difficulty involved in verifying information posted online and the ease with which journalists, denied access to Syria and desperate for sources, could be misled.

Journalists following events through Twitter have also tended to portray the opinions expressed online as broadly reflecting public opinion. Some were surprised when the secular-dominated voices of the young and urban Arab 'twitterati' were revealed by post-revolutionary elections to represent a far smaller proportion of the wider population.

Critics have also warned that so-called 'slacktivism' could undermine revolutionary movements as time spent on virtual activism is time not spent on real activism that carries very real risks.[28] They argue that it can be useful for those who want to lazily burnish their activist credentials by clicking a button to support a cause online, similar to those who may have bought a bumper sticker twenty years ago, but that it cannot change the world in the way protest can. Evgeny Morozov, author of *The Net Delusion*, correctly argues that governments had been quick to exploit social media for their own ends, using it to monitor dissent and spread propaganda. Indeed, Bahrain's government posted pictures of protesters on Facebook and asked its supporters to identify them for arrest, while Syria's government set up an 'Electronic Army' to fight its war online.[29]

Online activists themselves acknowledge that uprisings require a combination of old methods such as pamphleteering and new methods such as Twitter, and would amount to nothing unless large numbers of people were ultimately willing to brave the rubber bullets, tear gas and, in some countries, tanks and snipers. But the internet, social media and even WikiLeaks undoubtedly played a role.

When in December 2010, days before protests broke out, WikiLeaks published a batch of US diplomatic cables that detailed the corruption and mafia-like practices of Ben Ali and his wife, some commentators immediately began to write of the first 'WikiLeaks Revolution',[30] describing a narrative of 'hacktivists' changing the world, or at least individual countries, by leaking government documents through the democratizing medium of the internet. This is overstated. Few within Tunisia would trace their anger back to WikiLeaks, but what the leak did was to confirm what Tunisians had known all along and to reveal that the United States was no big fan of Ben Ali, information that simultaneously galvanized opposition and weakened the president in the eyes of the people.

A Decade of Activism

On the eve of the Arab Spring, then, a new generation was coming of age. It was a generation that had grown up watching satellite television in Arabic, with a deluge of political opinions and news spin, with television dramas and Arabic music videos, with televangelists and call-in chat shows. It was a generation that was connected by mobile phone, by BlackBerry and by iPad. It was a generation that was internet-savvy; that harnessed e-mail and Twitter and Facebook to build networks with like-minded young people in other Arabic-speaking countries and beyond.

It was the 61 per cent of Arabs who were under 30. Unlike their parents, swathes of whom were illiterate, most of this generation could read and write. Some could read and write in English or French as well as Arabic. It was a generation with high expectations of life, a generation that had delayed marriage in favour of university, and had delayed child-bearing in favour of a career. Enjoying more time, fewer responsibilities, more personal freedom and a better education than their parents, these younger Arabs had also benefited from a cultural and communications boom in recent years.

Television programmes such as *Prince of Poets* had reinvigorated enthusiasm for the best-loved of Arab literary forms. In 2007, the Emirates Foundation had launched the International Prize for Arab Fiction, which aims to become a sort of 'Arab Booker', and had helped to bring a wider variety of Arab voices to the West. A renewed effort to ensure that the best of Arabic literature found its way into English translation had flowered into a new cultural conversation. Arab film festivals were annual events in Beirut, Dubai, Abu Dhabi, Doha, Marakech, Cairo and beyond.

Indeed, Emmanuel Todd and Youssef Courbage have argued that civilizations are not heading for the inevitable clash that was predicted by Samuel Huntington, a theory that gained so much currency during the 'war against terror'. Rather, civilizations are converging. Changing marriage patterns and rising literacy were already revolutionizing Arab countries much as they had revolutionized Europe, shifting the emphasis when it came to political, social and economic choices from the traditional patriarchal family to the individual.[31]

It had also been a decade of activism. Fed up with the lack of change at the top, impatient with the cautious and long-term strategies of the mainstream Islamist parties, appalled at the violent antics of the *jihadis*, disgusted with the corruption that had eaten away at state institutions, angry at the abuse carried out by spies and police with seeming impunity, a handful of young people were taking action. In the midst of the apathy and the hopelessness, youth activists from Egypt, from Syria, from Lebanon and elsewhere were turning to the ideas of an American academic.

Gene Sharp's 1993 work *From Dictatorship to Democracy* had become a handbook for non-violent revolutionaries around the world, inspiring the young Serbian activists who overthrew Slobodan Milosevic in 2000 and setting off a chain of revolutionary change around Eastern Europe in the 2000s. Otpor, the Serbian group that orchestrated the non-violent opposition to Milosevic, trained and aided other East European revolutionaries as well as young activists battling authoritarian regimes from Burma to Egypt to Lebanon.

In many ways, the Arab world's wave of popular action did not begin in 2011, but in 2005, when Lebanese activists used non-violent resistance tactics not to overthrow a dictator but to push the Syrian army out after twenty-nine years. Like the removal of Ben Ali or Mubarak, it was a huge achievement for unarmed activists facing military might. Lebanon and Syria signed an accord establishing diplomatic relations and opening an embassy, the first time Syria had officially treated Lebanon as a sovereign and independent neighbour rather than an outlying province. Lebanon's revolt, known in Arabic as *Intifadat al-Istiqlal*, or the Independence Uprising, but to the foreign media as the Cedar Revolution, was heavily branded. Its proponents wore the red-and-white sashes that were the same colour as the Lebanese flag. Banners and symbols representing different political parties or religious factions were nowhere to be seen. The protesters all united behind Brand Lebanon, beginning their demonstrations with candle-lighting vigils and growing into a mass sit-in in Martyrs' Square where a hardcore of activists camped out until the Syrian army was gone.

Yet as soon as that main goal had been achieved, the country collapsed into the worst bout of infighting since the end of its 1975–90 civil war, the ranks of the anti-Syrian independence movement decimated by a series of assassinations that were claimed by no one but served Syria and its allies. Blinded by the red-and-white flags, the Western media had taken the cosmopolitan and liberal young demonstrators in Martyrs' Square to be representative of Lebanon, but Hezbollah, the main Shi'ite Islamist group backed by Syria and Iran, had been lying low. The Shi'ites were believed to be the single largest sect in Lebanon, a country comprised entirely of minorities, and most of them had been absent from the protests in central Beirut.

When Hezbollah called its supporters out on 8 March 2005 in a display of appreciation for Syria, legions of bearded men and women wrapped in black *chador* cloaks filled downtown Beirut. Within two years, Syria had managed to re-establish its political influence over Lebanese politics, even though its soldiers were gone. In the third year, Hezbollah turned its guns on its anti-Syrian rivals inside Lebanon, further asserting its military and political domination with the blessing of its friends in Damascus and Tehran. The demonstration effect of the Lebanese protests was powerful, and the tactics of its young activists would be mimicked in Egypt and elsewhere in the years leading up to the 2011 uprising, but the battle that emerged for the future of Lebanon was more instructive of the challenges that protesters would face in the aftermath of the Arab Spring.

By the time Mohammed Bouazizi set himself alight in a desolate town in central Tunisia, the region was a tinderbox waiting for a spark. Protests that had broken out a decade earlier in support of the Palestinians, then against the US invasion of Iraq in 2003, then again against Israel's war with Hezbollah in 2006 and then against its war on Gaza in 2009, had turned repeatedly against the Arab rulers who sat idly by, unwilling to stand against their allies in Washington. On television, taboos had been broken and the cults of personality had been eroded. Waves of strikes had convulsed factories, mines and offices in Tunisia, Egypt and elsewhere. Once easily isolated and crushed, labour movements increasingly teamed up with the new generation of dissident bloggers who harnessed the internet and social media to raise awareness of strikes and generate wider public support. Once the protests began, despite government efforts to close down the internet, ban specific sites or cut off mobile phones, they would not be able to halt the momentum.

Lacking the hierarchical structures of traditional organizations, the loose and leaderless networks flummoxed police, who could not identify ring-leaders and did not see the young internet-savvy activists as a serious threat. Focusing on a single demand with general appeal, protesters would build coalitions that brought together the Islamist and the secular, the trade unionist and the businessman, the young and the old. Those coalitions would be broad, but they would necessarily be loose and easily divided. The online networks that were formed were able to grow very large, very quickly, but they lacked the cohesion of smaller, tight-knit networks based on face-to-face interactions over a long period, and they could vanish as quickly as they had appeared.

When it came to persuading the average person on the street that they could govern, the weaknesses of youth movements would be exposed and the older, more established groups would outmanoeuvre them. So it was in Tunisia, where by mid-January 2011 a cross-border protest movement that had already started to ripple through Morocco, Algeria, Jordan and elsewhere, was on the verge of claiming its first scalp.

PART 2

THE BATTLEGROUNDS

CHAPTER 4

Tunisia's Jasmine Revolution

If, one day, a people desires to live, then fate will answer their call, And their night will then begin to fade, and their chains break and fall
                                                    – Tunisian poet Abu Qasim al-Chebbi[1]

On the evening of 14 January 2011, Tunisian President Zine al-Abidine Ben Ali, his wife, their five-year-old son, one of his daughters and her fiancé sped to the airport.[2] Around them, the normally sleepy capital was in tumult. A general strike had paralysed the economy. Thousands were on the streets demanding that the president step down. It was less than twenty-four hours since Ben Ali, in a televised address, had promised not to run for re-election. The following day, he sacked his government, called early elections and declared a state of emergency. Tour operators had evacuated tourists from the Mediterranean hot spot. A curfew was imposed. Yet the army had refused to use force to quell demonstrations after four weeks of police crackdowns that had only swelled the ranks of protesters now braving bullets in towns from the deepest south to the furthest north of the country.

At 6.40 pm, Al-Jazeera and other television stations began to report that Ben Ali had left the country. At 6.44 pm, Prime Minister Mohammed Ghannouchi appeared on television to tell Tunisians that the president was temporarily incapacitated and that he would take over in the interim. Conflicting news began to emerge. First it appeared Ben Ali was heading to Malta, then Qatar, then France. Hours after Ghannouchi had made his staggering announcement, Paris, realizing the tide of history had turned, said Ben Ali would not be welcome on French soil.[3]

It had taken some time for France, the former colonial power, to abandon its long-standing ally. Soon after the vegetable seller Mohammed Bouazizi set himself alight in the central town of Sidi Bouzid on 17 December 2010, the new French foreign minister, Michèle Alliote-Marie, her partner, also a minister, and her elderly parents had arrived to spend their Christmas break in Tunisia, a favoured winter destination. As protests spread from town to town, Alliote-Marie took complimentary flights on the private jet of businessman Aziz Mled, an associate of Ben Ali's family.[4] On the same trip, her parents signed a property deal with Mled. Then, days before the president's departure on 14 January and with dozens dead in the Tunisian riots, Alliote-Marie appeared to suggest that Paris could offer Tunis its crowd-control know-how.[5] Shipments of tear gas and anti-riot gear to Tunisia had been approved during the uprising, though they were never sent.[6] In the early hours of Saturday morning and with virtually nowhere else to turn, Ben Ali and his family touched down in Jeddah, a port city of Saudi Arabia, where his family would embark on a religious pilgrimage, or *'umra*, until the situation in Tunisia had calmed down.[7]

The mechanics of Ben Ali's departure had caused uproar, not because he was gone but because the door was left open for his return. Legal and constitutional experts filled the airwaves to argue that, contrary to Ghannouchi's announcement, Ben Ali was not temporarily but rather permanently incapacitated, meaning that power should pass to the speaker of the parliament, in this case Fouad Mobazza', pending new elections. With thousands on the street, Ghannouchi and other officials perhaps saw their opportunity to rid the country of what had come to be known as 'The Family', and transfer power with the minimum possible disruption to the system or threat to their own positions.

Tales of the corruption that had tainted Ben Ali's rule had become the stuff of lore. His second wife, a social-climbing former hairdresser, was a figure of hate. Since marrying the president in 1992, Tunisians say Leila Trabelsi had cultivated a penchant for seizing successful private businesses or attractive properties at will. Rumours abounded of the regime's excesses, some confirmed in US diplomatic cables published by WikiLeaks, which described a pet tiger, Pasha, that was kept by Ben Ali's daughter Nisrene and her husband Sakher al-Materi, and consumed four chickens a day. Invited to dinner at their house, the US ambassador Robert Godec wrote in 2009 of the frozen yoghurt he had been served for dessert, flown in from St Tropez on a private jet.

With disgust at his family's greed and decadence reaching the top circles of government, Tunisia's highest court declared that Mobazza' was indeed president. Ben Ali was gone for good and the Arab world would never be quite the same again. What had begun as localized protests in a struggling town had ended as the Jasmine Revolution, named in the Western press after the fragrant national flower that is hawked on the country's sandy beaches and in its street-side cafés.

From Riyadh to Tripoli, authoritarian rulers watched events unfold with growing unease. Tunisia had demonstrated how brittle these Arab dictatorships were, how quickly they could be swept away. By overcoming the barrier of fear, Tunisians had shown that peaceful protest could succeed, and at a heady pace. They had removed their ruler in less than a month of popular action in an unarmed uprising. They were as shocked by their own success as the world was. And success sells.

Overnight, the United States, France and Britain found that their long-standing foreign policies required a hasty rewrite. They appeared to dither and agonize, seemingly caught between their populist instinct to support protesters and their interests in propping up the dictators on whom their foreign policies had for so long relied. With little oil and less clout, this North African country of 10 million had been all but ignored by journalists busy prophesying what might become of the regional colossus, Egypt, as Hosni Mubarak sank deeper into his dotage. In Saudi Arabia, diplomats tracked the fluctuating fortunes of the myriad geriatric pretenders to the throne. Rulers in Syria, Yemen, even Bahrain, had occasionally found themselves blinking in the unforgiving glare of international attention while Tunisia's uprising brewed quietly, almost unnoticed.

Yet of all the countries that saw mass uprisings in 2011, Tunisia possessed more of the ingredients for a home-grown, successful revolution than any other. Its long history of political activism, which Ben Ali and his predecessor curbed but did not kill, its resilient civil society, its educated and unarmed people, its relatively neutral army, its relative religious homogeneity and its pragmatic Islamist movement, also meant it had more of the ingredients necessary for success.

Tunisia faces a historic opportunity in the wake of a revolution that has threatened the old political order from Cairo to Damascus to Manama. It also faces significant challenges. This was not an Islamic uprising, but it would unleash a battle over the role of religion in a country with perhaps the strongest secular legacy in the region. It would dramatically revive a banned Islamist party and bring back its long-exiled leader, it would see hardline Salafist Islamists attack television stations, cinemas, art exhibitions and alcohol vendors and it would stoke a heated debate over the nature of the country's new constitution. Yet whatever role Islam plays in the new Tunisia, it cannot offer a solution to the economic problems that lay at the heart of this remarkable uprising and which will take years to resolve.

The Kings of Carthage

In September 2010, less than three months before Bouazizi's fateful suicide, the IMF issued a glowing report on Tunisia. The government had weathered the global financial crisis well. Growth had reached 4.5 per cent in the first quarter, a notable achievement in the midst of a crisis that had hit demand in the country's biggest export market and mired its European trading partners in debt. At 43 per cent, Tunisia's debt-to-GDP ratio was almost half that of France. Tunisia would need more dynamic sources of growth to ease joblessness, the report said, but the official unemployment rate of 13.3 per cent was not incomparable to that of southern Europe.[8] In a region beset by poverty and instability, Tunisia was seen as an economic success story. Its workforce was educated. It attracted foreign investment, mainly from Europe. The World Economic Forum judged it the 32nd most competitive country in the world in its 2010–11 Global Competitiveness Report, above Italy and Spain, and international organizations never tired of praising its 'economic miracle'.[9]

Yet it did not feel like a miracle to many Tunisians. While per capita GDP was growing, only 14 per cent of Tunisians classified themselves as 'thriving' in 2010, down from 24 per cent just two years earlier. Tunisians were increasingly unhappy with the state of housing, healthcare and roads, and they complained about bureaucracy.[10] A newborn's birth certificate might be endlessly delayed if the tip was found ungenerous, while a trail of backhanders accompanied any official document requiring the stamps and signatures of underpaid civil servants and go-betweens.[11]

Dig deeper beneath the headline economic indicators, or drive an hour outside of the capital, and you would find another Tunisia, one where young people with university degrees and no jobs loitered in cafés and on street corners with nothing to do. Tunisia's economy had grown by an average of 5 per cent each year over the previous two decades, according to the IMF. By the World Bank's definition, just 7 per cent of Tunisians lived in poverty on the eve of the uprising, one of the lowest rates in the region. And yet the number of unemployed graduates had doubled over the past decade. Astonishingly, perhaps, the better educated the individual, the more likely he or she was to be jobless. Half of graduates with a masters degree were unemployed in 2010.

Unemployment was also far higher among younger people than it was on average, and much worse in the interior and southern regions, where the uprising began, than it was on the coast. By the accounts of Tunisians themselves, perceptions of corruption, inequalities and a lack of opportunity had dramatically worsened in the last two or three years before the uprising.

Yet economic malaise does not a revolution make, at least not on its own. Economic frustration was compounded by political repression. Those who were considered the biggest threat, and who suffered the severest crackdowns from the 1980s, were the Islamists. Hundreds of them, mostly members of the group now called Ennahda, or Renaissance, were thrown in jail by Habib Bourguiba, who had led Tunisia from independence in 1956, his New Destour Party consistently dominating politics through sham elections. Ben Ali's so-called 'medical coup' in 1987 initially came as a relief for Tunisians. Ben Ali freed political prisoners and promised free and fair parliamentary elections two years later. Despite complaints of irregularities, the Islamists officially won 17 per cent of the national vote and some 30 per cent in certain areas.[12] Though the electoral system was organized in a way that meant parliament was dominated by the ruling party, with the new and less catchy name of Rassemblement Constitutionnel Démocratique (RCD), Ben Ali was alarmed.[13]

By 1992 some 8,000 suspected Ennahda supporters had been arrested, 279 of whom were charged with plotting to assassinate the president and take over the state.[14] So severe was the crackdown on Islamists that Tunisian men were rounded up for growing beards or attending dawn prayers, while mosques were closely watched by secret police. Ennahda members arrested in this early crackdown had mostly been released by the end of the 1990s, but they did not go back to lead normal lives. They were watched and harassed, could not get the security clearance needed for formal jobs, and were sometimes banned from travelling abroad or required to check in at the local police station every month, every week or, in some cases, several times a day.[15]

'In Tunisia, if you wanted to get a permanent job, you had to go through a security check on your political views, whether you are leftist, Islamist, nationalist,' Rida Harrathi, a self-proclaimed Islamist, said as he prepared to enter a Tunis mosque for the first Friday prayers after Ben Ali's departure. 'I was expelled from work and when I asked why, they said, "Your problem is with the interior ministry" ... If you are honest about yourself, and especially if you are an Islamist, you would lose your job or you would not be confirmed in it.'[16]

By the time the revolution began, the Islamists were unable to meet or organize, but they were present in other civil society organizations like the unions, professional syndicates and human rights and advocacy groups, which managed to survive if not to flourish. Islamists were not just Islamists, after all. They were also doctors, teachers, journalists or lawyers. They worked alongside the nationalist and the secular, the apolitical and the socialist in every walk of life.

Despite the best efforts of Ben Ali and his predecessor, Tunisia had a long history of political and civil activism. Working around police and legal restrictions in the years before the uprising, human rights and union activists had built cross-regional and cross-class networks. Set up in the 1970s, the Tunisian League for Human Rights (LTDH) is one of the oldest such groups in the Arabic-speaking world.

Ben Ali was wary of civil society groups but, loath to attract the kind of international criticism invited by an outright ban, he sought to undermine them in more subtle ways. In 1992, Tunisia passed an associations law that forced all non-governmental organizations to admit anyone who wanted to join, allowing the regime to stuff the ranks of NGOs and undermine their activities.[17] The law also required all NGOs to obtain approval from the interior ministry, which could deny or permanently delay their licence, leaving the groups to act in a legal grey area.[18] External funding for NGOs had to pass through the state, where it would often be deliberately held up by paperwork. Ben Ali's government had refused to licence new human rights groups for the last decade of his rule and activists were sometimes intimidated, dismissed from work, monitored or arbitrarily prevented from travelling.[19] But while hampered at every turn, civil society survived, establishing a precious bedrock for participatory politics.

Activists could also draw on the long heritage of Tunisia's union movement, which traces its origins back to the colonial era of the 1920s, played a key role in the fight for independence alongside Bourguiba, and later fought against the government to remain autonomous.[20] While the RCD claimed to have two million members, a fifth of the whole population and a figure widely disputed by opposition activists, the Tunisian General

Union of Labour (UGTT) claimed to represent almost 500,000 workers in various sectors across the country, making it Tunisia's second-largest organization and a force to be reckoned with.[21]

In the fifteen years before the 2011 uprising, Ben Ali had succeeded in co-opting the UGTT to the extent that it was often dismissed as little more than a semi-independent contractor for the state, sapping the power of the unions as a potential counterweight to the ruling RCD.[22] By the time Bouazizi set himself alight, the UGTT leadership's reluctance to stand up to the state had already undermined its authority with the rank and file, and disputes between the leaders in Tunis and the regional and local representatives were reaching crisis point.[23]

The Arab Spring had a dry run in the first half of 2008, when Tunisia's mining basin of Gafsa was paralysed by a series of strikes and demonstrations. Amid rising food inflation, the unrest spread through the south-west, escalating into riots and prompting a violent police crackdown. The protest was led by local unionists and activists from a handful of opposition parties. Journalists were banned from reporting on the demonstrations, preventing the miners from garnering sympathy and support in other parts of the country. The UGTT leadership, moreover, was widely seen to have abandoned the miners and colluded to isolate them, damaging its credibility in the eyes of its members. Two years later, in July and August of 2010, riots broke out in the southern province of Ben Guerdane. Grievances were again socio-economic and, again, dithering by the UGTT and its efforts to mediate in the crisis rather than lead the workers damaged its standing.

Similar tensions were developing inside some of the legal political parties. Tunisia's bicameral parliament held elections every five years for the Chamber of Deputies in which a handful of licenced political parties competed. Most outspoken among them were Nejib Chebbi's Progressive Democratic Party (PDP) and Mustafa Ben Jaafar's Democratic Forum for Freedom and Labour (FTDL), or Ettakatol, which was born out of a conference of democratic activists in 1993. Among the others were Ahmed Ibrahim's secular left Ettajdid, or Renewal, and the Social Democratic Movement, established in the 1980s by Bourguiba ally-turned-opponent Ahmed Mestiri.

Some 20 per cent of the 241 seats in parliament were reserved for this legal 'opposition', keeping up the facade of pluralism over a system that ensured the house was overwhelmingly dominated by the RCD. Even if they did win seats, the smaller parties could not seriously propose or block legislation and some offered no real opposition at all, serving only to maintain the pretence of democracy that Ben Ali wanted to project to his Western allies.

Presidential elections had been held every five years, but Ben Ali did not allow rival candidates until 1999 – when official figures show he won 99 per cent of the vote. The legal opposition parties found that their presidential candidates might be disqualified because they did not have enough seats in parliament or, in the case of Chebbi, because he was no longer the head of a party. Ahmed Ibrahim was the only serious rival for the presidency in the 2009 election, though he acknowledged that he was not allowed to mount an effective campaign. Ben Ali romped home again with over 89 per cent of the vote. Official turnout would regularly be reported at over 80 or 90 per cent, though it was not hard to find Tunisians who had never voted.

The system created a dilemma for parties that had often fought hard to obtain a licence. Keen to protect the gains they had already made, even the more outspoken leaders were often unwilling to confront Ben Ali head-on. In many cases they opted for accommodation, a situation that suited the Tunisian government well but did not always please the party rank and file.[24]

Not only were Ben Ali's efforts to crush, co-opt or undermine potential challengers beginning to crack, but the septuagenarian leader appeared increasingly disconnected from his youthful population. Communication was breaking down with the urban, educated and broad middle classes that had been the engine of Tunisia's economic growth and the gatekeepers of its stability since independence. Connected to the world, a new generation of multilingual Tunisians was increasingly frustrated with the lack of free speech. Tunisian newspapers were so repressed as to be utterly unreadable. When an unfavourable book about Leila Trabelsi was released by a French publisher in 2009, the authorities not only outlawed it in Tunisia but also tried – and eventually failed – to ban it in France. The restrictions seemed increasingly anachronistic in the world of 24-hour satellite news channels and fast internet, and Ben Ali's government was among the most draconian in the Arabic-speaking world when it came to online censorship.

Yet on the eve of the uprising, almost two million Tunisians – or 17.6 per cent of the population – were Facebook users, the second-highest level for an Arab country outside of the wealthy and technologically advanced Gulf. E-mails were filtered and hacked, and cybercafés watched by secret police; so pervasive were the restrictions that the Tunisian dissident and technology entrepreneur, Slim Amamou, set @Slim404 as his Twitter name in reference to the '404 not found' message that would appear when internet users tried to access one of the many banned sites.

Despite these restrictions, vocal Tunisia-based bloggers were breaking new barriers in terms of what could be reported, what questions could be asked, and what footage and pictures posted. Sites began to collate blogs, news and interviews under one umbrella, establishing themselves as rare one-stop sources for those seeking to find out what was really going on in the country.

In December 2010, a site called Nawaat began to publish WikiLeaks documents related to Tunisia in its 'Tunileaks' campaign, enraging the government and prompting it to block sites carrying US cables that described 'The Family's' plummeting popularity. While media coverage of the Gafsa mining strike was banned, bloggers found ways to visit the area and report on the violent police crackdown. This constant battle with the authorities gave birth to a generation of Tunisian bloggers with a wealth of experience in circumventing state controls, who had built ties and swapped advice with a network of online activists in other Arab countries and beyond. That experience would stand them in good stead once the uprising was under way in December 2010.

By that time, it was not just the rights activists, the Islamists, the unionists and the youth that Ben Ali had alienated. Perhaps his biggest mistake was to erode the foundations upon which his rule was built. During his twenty-three years in power, former RCD officials later complained, Ben Ali had hollowed out the ruling party to monopolize power within his own family and that of his wife. Former ministers bemoaned how their access to the president was limited by Trabelsi, that they no longer had his ear, that his decisions were driven by his desire to keep his wife and her family happy.[25] As described in the first section of this book, major privatizations or sales of state assets such as mobile phone licences went to the first couple's extended clan, causing widespread disgust and anger.

'After 2002–3 there was a sense that these guys were bandits profiting from the reputation and riches of the country. They were not like a monarchy whose fate was tied to the country,' said Zyed Krichen, editorial director of *Le Maghreb* newspaper, which was shut down by Ben Ali in the 1990s and restarted in the wake of the uprising. 'So businessmen and intellectuals gradually became liberated from this wall of fear because of the gossip and rumour around the corruption. There was also a sense that Ben

Ali wasn't in control any more, couldn't exert power over the clan, and the cult of personality was weakening.'[26]

Businessmen large and small complained that members of the elite clan would seek to take a cut in any company that was doing well and making profit. If the demand was refused, a rival firm would be set up, while its adversary would suddenly find itself under investigation for tax or other irregularities. This is what happened to Mohammed Bouebdelli, a businessman who ran a chain of private schools and a private university, and fell foul of the president.

Bouebdelli describes his 2002 conversation with Ben Ali: 'I told him that I have a lot of demand to set up a pharmacology college and he said, in that case, 50–50. He said it in English not in French. I was sorry inside that a president puts his hand out like that … I am an educator. I am not a businessman with billions of dollars. I said to myself, a person like this could sell the country …'[27]

Two years later, Bouebdelli clashed with Ben Ali once more when he refused to let a failing pupil from 'The Family' graduate from her class. Bouebdelli came under pressure from the education minister to change his mind. Soon after, his school was seized by the authorities. An investigation was launched into his social security and tax payments. Then, in 2007, Leila Trabelsi decided to open a rival private secondary school in Carthage, purchasing cheap state land for the purpose, and Bouebdelli was forced to close the existing Louis Pasteur school he ran. By 2009, the situation had deteriorated so much that he wrote a book entitled *The Day I Realised Tunisia is Not a Free Country*. Soon after, he was removed from the private university he had set up. He left the country, visiting the US State Department, White House and Congress, as well as the European Parliament, to discuss Tunisia's human rights situation. When he returned in April 2010, he was questioned by the police, and on 4 December 2010, thirteen days before the uprising, police demolished a house he had built outside Tunis, saying he did not have a permit.[28]

Ben Ali and his wife hailed from neither Tunisia's old moneyed classes nor its educated middle classes. The president himself had risen through the ranks of the security services and interior ministry, helped by his first marriage to Naima al-Kefy, the daughter of a general. Ben Ali had subsequently attempted to cement alliances with business elites, strategically marrying his daughters, three of them from his first marriage, to the scions of wealthy families. But by keeping the riches in this narrow circle, the first couple undermined their support among business elites.

Ben Ali's mismanagement of the security forces would prove to be the final straw. Tunisia's army, which numbers about 35,000 active members, had always been small and largely separate from politics. Both Bourguiba and Ben Ali had enforced their rule through the interior security forces that were estimated to number some 150,000 on the eve of revolution.[29] Yet, as a police protest held soon after Ben Ali fled would show, many of these employees were poorly paid and in some cases open to legendary levels of corruption: traffic police, for instance, would regularly stop motorists for no other reason than to elicit a small bribe. Among these interior security forces, the Presidential Guard was the elite, a highly trained, well-paid, competitively selected group of about 5,000 that was trusted by the president. It was called in to restore order around the country once the uprising was under way, causing tension with local police, while its high-handed behaviour was also resented by the military and other security units who could find fewer and fewer reasons to protect Ben Ali in the face of unarmed popular protest.[30]

Once the uprising reached a critical momentum, Ben Ali would have few loyalists left to turn to. He had undermined his own ruling party's political power, made life harder for big business, and alienated both the army and a large section of the police. As cracks in his regime began to show, civil society had rushed in to fill the space. Human rights activists, the courageous lawyers of the Bar Association, the active teachers' syndicate, trade unionists, political party members and dissident bloggers had become increasingly active and increasingly resilient. They were mostly leaderless, a network working around and in spite of the docile union and political chiefs. And when the time came, they were able to rally together and focus on the big prize – the fall of the regime.

The Slap That Was Heard Around the World

Residents of Sidi Bouzid, a town where weeds grow in the dust that covers the streets, said anger had been building for years before Mohammed Bouazizi set fire to himself. Frustration at widespread joblessness and anger at local officials had reached tipping point. The crumbling infrastructure and stretched health facilities, a world apart from the upmarket coastal suburbs that are home to Tunisia's elite, fed resentment.

Local authorities had confiscated Bouazizi's unlicenced cart several times before, but the turning point for the twenty-six-year-old, and for his country and ultimately the entire region, came on 17 December 2010. The breadwinner in a family of eight, Bouazizi had argued with a policewoman who took away his goods and scales. Though a court later found her innocent of the assault, Bouazizi's family say the policewoman slapped him and insulted his dead father.[31] Bouazizi bought a can of petrol and set himself on fire outside the provincial headquarters. 'What kind of repression do you imagine it takes for a young man to do this? A man who has to feed his family by buying goods on credit when they fine him ... and take his goods,' his sister Leila said. 'In Sidi Bouzid, those with no connections and no money for bribes are humiliated and insulted and not allowed to live.'[32]

In the absence of clear leaders in Tunisia's uprising, Bouazizi came to symbolize the hopelessness and frustration of a generation of Arabs. His death captured the imagination of millions and inspired copycat burnings in Egypt, Algeria, Mauritania and even Saudi Arabia.[33] But it was Bouazizi's friends and family, and the union leaders and political activists in his home town, who mobilized his anger into a national revolution. Locals had already begun to protest in solidarity with the Palestinian uprising a decade earlier, and had demonstrated against the Iraq war. They had learned from the Gafsa mining strike that solidarity protests could quickly be mobilized in neighbouring towns. 'The fear had begun to melt away and we were a volcano that was going to explode. And when Bouazizi burnt himself, we were ready,' said Attia Athmouni, a union leader and official of the PDP in Sidi Bouzid. 'Protesters demanded payback for the blood of Bouazizi and this developed into economic, social and political demands. We started calling for an end to corruption.'[34]

Among the first to join were members of the Bar Association, which boasted a history of activism against extrajudicial detentions and the mistreatment of prisoners of conscience. 'The unions got involved, teachers, lawyers, doctors, all sections of civil society, and set up a Popular Resistance Committee to back the people of Sidi Bouzid and back the uprising. The efforts meant the uprising continued for 10 days in Sidi Bouzid with no support,' said Lazhar Gharbi, a head teacher and union member. 'As the protests spread, the headlines changed from bread to call for the removal of the head of state.'[35] Demonstrations spread across the province of Sidi Bouzid as groups of youths clashed with police who fired tear gas at the crowds. Protests were turning into riots.

The community of cyber-activists formed over the preceding decade also rolled into action. A Facebook group called 'The Tunisian People Are Burning Themselves, Mr President' began to publish pictures and footage from Sidi Bouzid, and raise awareness of events there. Within ten days, online activists had begun to tweet news on the Tunisian protests under the hashtag #sidibouzid. Across Facebook, activists and sympathizers replaced their profile photograph with the red and white Tunisian flag.

Protests and riots began to spread from town to town, engulfing the centre of Tunisia. Before the end of December, they had reached the capital. Mid-level and rank-and-file trade unionists held small protests. Using Facebook, blogger and journalist Sofiane Chourabi called for one of the first independent, citizen-led political protests in Tunis on 28 December. It was the same day Ben Ali delivered his first speech, saying the protests were 'unacceptable'. More and more activists began to independently organize protests online, spreading the message using mobile phones and fliers.

'When I saw some young people I would never have imagined would stand against Ben Ali, young people who have nothing to do with politics, shouting slogans against the regime and facing the police and overcoming their fears, even then I was not thinking we would get rid of Ben Ali. But perhaps I was convinced that we had broken the barrier of fear,' said Chourabi.[36]

It was no longer a call for jobs and freedom, nor for an end to corruption and police brutality. '*Dégage!*', or 'Get out!', had become the rallying cry of the Tunisian revolution, while *The Will to Live*, a rousing liberation poem written by Tunisia's Abu Qasim al-Chebbi when the country was still a French colony, became the anthem of a revolution, sung by hundreds during peaceful protests. And when Bouazizi finally succumbed to his burns on 4 January 2011, crowds of people turned out for his funeral.

Alarmed by the powerful role of the internet, police arrested Slim Amamou and Aziz Amami two days later. The arrests backfired. Both, it turned out, were well known, and an internet campaign was launched for their release, which came days after. Ben Ali made another mistake by arresting the twenty-two-year-old rapper Hamada Ben Amor, whose song 'Mr President, Your People are Dying' was widely circulated online. The move made the song even more popular and provoked disgust that Tunisians could be arrested for singing. Ben Amor, better known as 'El Generale', was released three days later.[37]

By 10 January, at least twenty-three protesters were dead, most of them killed by police and interior security forces in a single weekend of rioting in the central provinces. Images of those killed in Kasserine, Tala and Rgeb spread on the internet.[38] The police response galvanized Tunisians in the coastal areas and in the capital, and drew sympathy from people who were not normally politically active. Ben Ali appeared on television to give his second speech, promising to create 300,000 jobs over two years but still denouncing the riots as 'terrorist acts'. After the death toll of the previous weekend, the speech fell flat.

Meanwhile Ali Seriati, the head of the elite Presidential Guard, had called in the army chiefs, as well as top commanders of the interior security forces, to coordinate a response. Army Chief of Staff Rachid Ammar refused to take orders to use the army in the crackdown. It was a pivotal moment; Ben Ali had now lost the army as well as the people.[39]

On 12 January, Ben Ali fired the interior minister over his handling of the protests, freed jailed protesters, and called a night-time curfew in the capital as riots spread. Protesters burned tyres and threw stones at police. Five more had been killed.[40] 'I understand you, I understand you,' Ben Ali pleaded in his final speech on state television, just a day before he fled, breaking for the first time from formal Arabic into the colloquial language of the people. They were the same fateful words Charles de Gaulle had uttered on his visit to Algeria in 1958, not long before France was forced to grant it independence.

Yet even after demonstrations had engulfed the capital, Ben Ali could not muster a single pro-regime demonstration. The greed of 'The Family', its reluctance to share the spoils of power even among trusted party loyalists, its battles not just with the Islamist but also the nationalist and leftist opposition, not only with human rights activists but also with the business elite, had cost it dearly.

A call went out for a general strike and mass protests across the country on 13 January 2011. It was successful. Finally, as it risked losing both its relevance in the struggle and its rank and file, the UGTT leadership made its own call for a nationwide general strike on 14 January. Thousands filled Bourguiba Avenue, a tree-lined boulevard of street cafés and hotels that leads to the old *medina* in the heart of Tunis.

Unknown to Tunisians, Trabelsi was already making plans to escape. That same night, thirty-three members of 'The Family' were arrested at the airport waiting to board a flight out. Later, it emerged that Samir Tarhouni, head of Tunisia's anti-terrorism unit, had decided that the game was up and had instructed his wife, who worked at airport control, not to allow them to fly.[41] Seriati, who is rumoured to have encouraged Ben Ali to leave in a possible ploy to take over, was also detained.

By the time Ben Ali landed in Saudi Arabia on 14 January, at least 147 people had been killed in the revolt.[42] But no sooner had their president beaten a hasty retreat than Tunisians began to worry that their revolution would be lost to the remnants of his ruling party. Some immediately feared that loyalists would continue to hold positions of power and were working behind the scenes to curtail dramatic change in the economic, social and bureaucratic structure.

It may have appeared like a tiny detail in the avalanche of revolutionary change, but the decision for the speaker rather than the prime minister to take over was crucial. Ben Ali had not officially resigned and it later transpired that he had been planning a comeback. Ghannouchi had announced a new government that kept the interior, defence and foreign ministers unchanged and added three UGTT representatives plus the three legal opposition party leaders – Chebbi, Ibrahim and Ben Jaafar – to the line-up.

Demonstrators could still have gone home at this point, but their demand was never the fall of the president. Indeed, it was Tunisian protesters who coined the chant 'The people want the fall of the regime,' which would soon echo from the squares of Cairo to the streets of Sana'a. From the very first day after they had unseated Ben Ali, protesters spoke soberly of the fear that they had decapitated the regime but left its structure in place, ready for a new dictator. Realizing their credibility was again at risk, the UGTT members quit the cabinet along with Ben Jaafar. The new government freed political prisoners, lifted a ban on parties, and closed down the media censor. The RCD ministers all resigned from their party, but this too was rejected by the demonstrators. The executive committee of the RCD was dissolved, but again, this was not enough to persuade protesters off the streets.

Finally, Ghannouchi reshuffled the cabinet once again to bring in ministers untainted by RCD membership. The move satisfied the UGTT and some opposition parties, but not for long. Less than three weeks after Ben Ali had fled, the RCD's activities were suspended. Senior police officials and provincial governors accused of corruption, brutality or close links to the old regime were replaced. On 27 February, with protests still ongoing, Ghannouchi stepped down and a new interim government was appointed, containing no former regime members. The first phase of the Tunisian revolution was complete.

By the time of the constituent assembly elections in October 2011, Tunisians had cleared every hurdle that had come their way, but the challenges that lie ahead are no less significant than those they leave behind them.

In the aftermath of Ben Ali's removal, a new battle front has emerged, one that does not pit people against their system but pits Tunisia's Islamists, who faced the most brutal repression under the old regime but have emerged as the biggest winners in the country's first elections, against its powerful secularists. It is a struggle that has deep roots in Tunisia's history, and it is a struggle for the very identity of the new country Tunisians seek to build.

The Islamist Renaissance

Few of the Tunisians who went to greet Rachid Ghannouchi, when he returned to his homeland after twenty-one years in exile, managed to catch a glimpse of the diminutive Islamist leader. Then nearly seventy, Ghannouchi was swamped by the crowds that awaited him at Carthage International Airport on 30 January 2011. Thousands of men, neatly dressed in jeans and shirts, and women in muted head scarves and matching overcoats, thronged the car park and the arrivals lobby, threatening to spill across a bulging cordon into the baggage hall beyond. In the relative peace near the whirring luggage belts, small groups of relatives tearfully and privately embraced the returning exiles before they exited to the adulation of the waiting public. Some had found prime spots where they held bunches of flowers to hand to emerging returnees, only to be thrown into disarray as the crowd surged spontaneously forward with the arrival of Ghannouchi, the leader of Tunisia's once-banned Ennahda party and no relation to the eponymous former prime minister.

Further back, a handful of secularist and feminist activists, conspicuous by their tight clothes and glossy hair, held a small protest that warned against what they feared would be the inevitable outcome of Ghannouchi's return: the Islamization of Tunisian politics and society. Standing at the edge of the scrum, their chants drowned out by the buzz of conversation and occasional cries of 'Allah Akbar', or 'God is Greatest', that rippled through the crowd, one of the activists held up a sign that encapsulated an attitude widely held in this most secular of North African countries: 'No Islamism, no theocracy, no *sharia* and no stupidity'. Another secularist stuck in the traffic that gridlocked the streets outside later muttered that Ghannouchi thought himself Tunisia's answer to Iran's Ayatollah Ruhollah Khomeini, who returned from exile in

1979 to throngs of people and what history has called Iran's Islamic Revolution.

The handful of secularists at the airport were vastly outnumbered by Ennahda supporters, but sensing the fear and potential hostility among their less religious brethren, and perhaps confident in the strength of their numbers, the Islamists held aloft their own, more conciliatory, banners. 'No to extremism, yes to moderate Islam' and 'Do not fear Islam', they implored in slogans that spoke directly to US and European as well as domestic concerns.[43]

With airport security hardly anywhere to be seen, volunteers, all of them young men sporting white T-shirts and baseball caps so that they could recognize one another, tried to marshal the throngs. Yet when he finally spoke in the car park, Ghannouchi's words were barely audible to the crowds that seemed to fill every corner of the tarmac, even through a loudspeaker. Some supporters had scaled pylons and street lights to catch a glimpse of the old man with the salt-and-pepper hair. Others looked down from a nearby bridge and, as the crowds dispersed, a cluster of men could be seen kneeling in prayer on a grassy verge, an unimaginable sight only weeks before. Struggling to keep Ghannouchi from being crushed, the volunteers clearly knew each other, they were organized, they were polite and softly spoken, and they had a plan – no mean feat for an organization whose members had been jailed, exiled or driven underground for most of the three decades since it was formed in 1981.

Ennahda played no organized role in the Tunisian revolt, but like Sunni Islamist groups in nearby Egypt, it was by far the biggest winner from the first phase of uprisings. It emerged as the single most popular and organized political force in the North African country, winning 41.7 per cent of the seats in Tunisia's constituent assembly which was tasked with rewriting the constitution, much to the alarm of secularist Tunisians who feared it would use its newfound political influence to gradually push for the Islamization of Tunisian laws.

Tunisians are overwhelmingly Sunni Muslims and tribal loyalties are weak, potentially avoiding the bloody tussles that convulse more religiously or ethnically diverse democracies like Iraq or Lebanon, but a struggle over the appropriate role of religion in politics has coloured much of Tunisia's post-independence history and polarizes public opinion like no other issue. Mistrust runs deep between the two camps and has been the source of deepening tensions as the country picks its way along the treacherous road from dictatorship to multi-party democracy. The stakes are high not only for Tunisia but for other Arab countries which have sought to emulate its uprising and which face similar challenges in the post-election phase. Unlike in other Arab states, Tunisia's secular tradition is strong and while secular parties are splintered with no single dominant player, together they won about half of seats in the constituent assembly. Any change in the secular approach to politics in Tunisia would be difficult to achieve and would mark a break with the national identity nurtured since independence and with the idea of *laïcité*, or secularism, imported by the former colonial power.

Independence leader Habib Bourguiba had championed the fight against the French but, once they were gone, he had accelerated their drive to banish the trappings of religion from public life and appropriated the functions of existing Islamic institutions for the newly sovereign state. In 1956 he abolished the *sharia* courts, which had been run in accordance with Islamic laws, and nationalized the *habous*, religious trusts that owned 150,000 hectares and funded mosques and religious institutions as the church once did in Europe.[44] In 1958, Bourguiba began a programme to abolish the religious curriculum in favour of French-style education that had been fast gaining popularity, and by 1961 Tunisia's ancient Islamic college of al-Zaitouna was given over to the new and secular University of Tunis.[45]

Bourguiba also introduced the Personal Status Code. Jealously defended by Tunisian feminists to this day, the code abolished polygamy and gave women greater rights in marriage and divorce, introducing a minimum age for marriage and demanding that it be mutually consensual. The Personal Status Code afforded women more freedoms in the 1950s than constitutions in most Arab countries half a century later. It was a daring move. Even today, many Arab governments impose civil law on all areas of life except the family, which remains under the control of the religious courts. In a society that frowned upon those who broke the fast – publicly, at least – during the holy month of Ramadan, Bourguiba launched a campaign in 1960 to denounce fasting as an impediment to the economy. He was even shown on television drinking a glass of orange juice during Ramadan.[46]

Bourguiba, who later declared himself president-for-life, was not merely concerned with crushing old elites who might threaten his power. In the mould of Turkey's Kemal Ataturk, the bespectacled autocrat saw himself as a modernizer, seeking to move Tunisia away from what he saw as outdated religious customs and towards a new secular nationalist identity. In that vein, Bourguiba discouraged women working in the public sector from wearing the *hijab*, the traditional Muslim headscarf, going so far as to call it a rag. In a 1957 speech, Bourguiba argued: 'If we understand that middle-aged women are reticent about abandoning an old habit, we can only deplore the stubbornness of those who continue to oblige their children to wear a veil in school. We even see civil servants going to work in that odious rag...'[47]

He also granted Tunisian women the right to an abortion, regardless of their marital status, and in 1957 allowed women to vote for the first time in municipal elections. Even by European standards, the reforms were progressive. In France, women were only granted the vote in 1944, and in Switzerland in 1971. Abortion remains a highly divisive issue in the United States today and is banned in many Christian-majority countries around the world. By the standards of North Africa and the Middle East, Bourguiba's policies were revolutionary and they made him deeply unpopular among some Tunisians, who felt their identity as Muslims was under assault.

Bourguiba's Tunisia was not secular in the strict sense of the word – the constitution clearly identified Islam as the religion of the state – but his reforms shaped Tunisia into the country it is today and defined the cleavages that still divide it long after his death. Significant swathes of Tunisia's elite, even if they profess personal faith, are secularists in the Bourguiba tradition and are deeply suspicious of efforts to return Islam to political life. 'Tunisia will not change to adapt itself to the Islamists and their ideas. The Islamists must adapt to modern Tunisia,' Neji Bghouri, then head of the journalists' union, said soon after the revolution. 'This is an issue of great sensitivity among Tunisia's political elite.'[48]

Other Tunisians, however, have yearned to return to the Islam that they equate with an identity that was ripped painfully away from them first by the French and then by the independent state. It was a yearning that Ghannouchi both felt and sought to respond to with the establishment of Ennahda. Asked at Ghannouchi's triumphant return how a group banned for so long had managed to organize itself so quickly, one of the young volunteers touched his chest and answered softly that the faith had remained in his heart: 'Our activities were stopped, but you cannot disperse an ideology.'[49]

Understanding that it would be a kiss of death for the nascent Tunisian revolution, Ennahda was careful not to issue any statements during the uprising, and no Islamists among the crowds raised religious slogans. Ghannouchi waited two weeks to return to the country, partly to avoid any accusations that he was returning Khomeini-style to claim victory. In an atmosphere of post-revolutionary suspicion, Ghannouchi took pains to strike a conciliatory tone, saying he took Turkey's ruling Islamist AK Party as his inspiration for Tunisia. Despite winning such a large chunk of the vote, Ennahda did not field a candidate in the first presidential nominations, trying to reassure sceptics that it did not aspire to seize the highest office and declare an Islamic state.

After the elections, it backed the nomination of Tunisia's first post-revolutionary president Moncef Marzouki, a former human rights activist and leader of a non-religious party banned under Ben Ali. Even before the election, Ennahda had agreed not to challenge the Personal Status Code, a major concession for an Islamist party, though it clashed with outspoken Tunisian feminists who pushed to have these rights guaranteed in the new constitution.

In fact, Ennahda's position on the Personal Status Code was not new. In November 1988, as a prelude to Ben Ali's fateful 1989 election, Ennahda, along with all other groups, signed up to a National Pact that involved the acceptance of the code, a position it reiterated in 2005 when it signed up to a charter with liberal, leftist and nationalist opposition groups including Chebbi's PDP and Marzouki's Congress for the Republic.

More generally, by the end of 2011, there was no real dispute among the main parties on the form of future government. All the largest parties, including Ennahda, agreed on the principles of democracy, political pluralism and rotation of power. There was already a general consensus on the principle of a separation of powers among the executive, the legislative and the judicial branches of government. Though they differed on whether to introduce a fully parliamentary or a semi-presidential system, learning from their lengthy experience with authoritarian rule, most favoured limiting the power of the president and vesting more authority in the government. Even in the elections for the constituent assembly, Ennahda accepted the system of proportional representation, though this is often less advantageous to larger parties, tends to give smaller parties a role in parliament, and encourages coalition-building. The election rules also required half of the candidates fielded on a list to be women, another progressive principle that Ennahda accepted, going as far as to run at least one unveiled woman. Of the 49 women who won a place in the 217-seat constituent assembly, 42 were Ennahda candidates.[50] The sight of so many veiled women in parliament may be a shock for secularists, but boasting a similar ratio of female MPs as parliaments in Europe, the assembly refuted any suggestion that women's rights had been set back.

Among the men sporting jeans and T-shirts and waiting at the airport to greet Ghannouchi, one man stood out. He had a long, orange-tinted beard, wore an Islamic skull cap and a traditional white *jalabiya* robe cut above the ankles in the style of conservative Salafist Islamists, and he was holding aloft a Koran. Approached by a young woman journalist, he declined to answer her questions, refused to look her in the eye and, sensing her confusion, eventually traced his hands around the edge of his face, as if to signal that she should be veiled. Seeing this, a group of female Ennahda supporters fell upon the man, thumping his arms. 'Ennahda would never tell you to wear the *hijab*. It is your choice. We are against these extremists who misrepresent us,' said Samda Jbeili, one of the main detractors, dressed herself in a muted pastel-colour headscarf.[51]

Those are sentiments echoed by Ghannouchi himself, who was careful to distance himself both from Iran's Shi'ite theocratic model, where a cleric is the head of state and is considered the representative of the infallible imam on earth, and from the Taliban's narrow and inflexible interpretation of Sunni Islam in Afghanistan. 'There are countries that, in the name of Islam, force women to wear particular attire, and there are countries that, in the name of modernity like Tunisia, ban women from wearing particular attire,' he said. 'We are against either. We consider one a theocracy and the other a secular theocracy. We are with a woman's freedom to decide her clothes, to decide her life partner and not be forced into anything.'[52]

The day after winning Tunisia's first free multi-party elections, Ennahda officials visited the bourse to reassure the business community that it would not impinge on business or ban the paying and earning of interest (considered usury in Islam), reversing an initial drop in share prices on news of the Islamist victory. Ennahda has not banned alcohol, which would enrage secularists and hurt the tourism sector that provides 400,000 jobs. It has not imposed modest clothing and would, in fact, do nothing to damage a sector so vital to the country's oil-poor economy.[53]

Ghannouchi has been careful to say that the creation of a pluralistic, democratic and civil state running according to the rule of law is Ennahda's priority and, since it emerged as the biggest single winner in the first elections, there is little reason to imagine that it would oppose a system from which it has the most to gain. Winning less than half the seats in parliament, however, Ennahda could not and did not attempt to govern alone. In late 2011 it entered a coalition with the parties of Mustafa Ben Jaafar and

Moncef Marzouki, both non-religious groups that performed strongly in the polls and could force it to compromise. Significant tensions have since developed within the ruling troika, as they are wont to do in any coalition, but despite Tunisians' discomfort with the tense political atmosphere post-revolution, differences have tended to be resolved politically.

Indeed, if Ennahda can live up to its democratic and inclusive rhetoric, Tunisia could become the first Sunni-majority Arab republic in which Islamist, secular and other minority groups compete in a multi-party democracy to govern a civil state in tune with local specificities. In much the same way as it became a model for peaceful revolution against a rotten regime, it could set the standard for post-revolutionary rule in other Arab countries that are still struggling to throw off the yoke of dictatorship. Yet mistrust between secularists and Islamists remains deep, and many secularists fear that Ennahda is striking a conciliatory tone to defuse opposition in the short term, and will set about slowly but surely Islamizing society and building grass-roots support for increasingly religious and conservative laws with a view to eventually declaring an Islamic state.

Secular Tunisians already accuse Ennahda of using a 'double discourse', saying one thing in public and another to their own followers. Secularists were alarmed when a video surfaced on the internet showing Hamadi Jbeli, a senior Ennahda official who was soon to take up the newly empowered post of prime minister, triumphantly declaring to supporters that 'we are in the sixth caliphate', referring to the Islamic empires that dominated the region until early last century. Ennahda said his comments were taken out of context but they caused an outcry among secularists, who saw them as proof of a secret agenda. A similar furore was caused when a video was leaked showing Ghannouchi meeting with Salafists and advising them to be patient and think long term, working through outreach not confrontation. Ennahda has said Ghannouchi was trying to defuse Salafist anger over its refusal to impose *sharia* law. Secularists saw it as evidence that Ennahda was in cahoots with hardliners.

Most Tunisians are too young to remember the Ennahda of the 1980s, but older generations recall a spate of violence that was linked to Islamist militants and raised fears that their country would go the same way as neighbouring Algeria, which descended into years of civil war from the early 1990s. Secularist critics point to violent demonstrations held by Islamists in the 1980s, to the 1991 arson attack on the offices of the ruling RCD, and to a spate of acid attacks.[54] This was evidence, they said, that

Islamists would accept democracy so long as they won elections but would turn violent if they did not. Rumours spread like wildfire in the brittle atmosphere of suspicion that surrounds the issue of religion in Tunisia. Secularists denounce Ghannouchi as an extremist posing as a moderate, pointing to fiery speeches he made in the early 1980s.

In reality, Ghannouchi's views have evolved over the decades from a more conservative focus on prayer and morality to an explicit embrace of democratic principles that have manifested themselves in the internal functioning of Ennahda from the outset, and through a number of writings that have influenced Turkey's AKP.

In contrast to French-educated Bourguiba, who came from the affluent coastal town of Monastir, Ghannouchi was born and raised in Hamma in the south-east of Tunisia. His father was a farmer and a Koran teacher who at one point was married to four women, and Ghannouchi was educated partly at a French-system school and partly at a local Islamic school before completing his degree at al-Zaitouna's Islamic university just before it was closed.[55]

Ghannouchi left Tunisia in the 1960s to complete his studies in Egypt and Syria, finding then losing hope in Arab nationalism, recovering his waning faith and taking a growing interest in political Islam, which he pursued while undertaking postgraduate studies in Paris in 1968.[56] Back in Tunisia in 1970, Ghannouchi became the head of a secret organization named al-Jamaa al-Islamiyah, or Islamic Group.[57] In a classic case of divide and rule, he and his friends played into the hands of Bourguiba, who turned a blind eye while the group attacked his communist enemies rather than the state itself.[58] Due to their extensive contacts with the liberal democratic and leftist opposition, however, Ghannouchi and his group slowly moved away from their uncompromising Salafist approach and turned to the reformist school of Islam that in the late-nineteenth and early-twentieth century had sought to reconcile Western democratic principles with the Islamic concept of *shura*, or consultation, and *ijmaa*, or consensus, through which the early Islamic community had been ruled.

The first incarnation of Ennahda, co-founded in 1979 by Ghannouchi, was far more austere and radical than the party of 2011. Busy attacking Bourguiba's ban on polygamy, the party initially saw no role for women in politics. By his own admission, Ghannouchi's ideas were turned on their head during a visit he paid to Sudan in 1979 to find out about the Sudanese Islamic Movement led by Hassan Turabi, where he saw how women were fully included in political life. On his return in 1980, Ghannouchi criticized his earlier position, called for equality between the sexes, and argued that innocent mixing of men and women was not banned.[59]

By the time the group went public in 1981, announcing the formation of what was originally called the Islamic Tendency Movement (MTI), its democratic credentials had already been established through internal elections for the president, the executive committee and the *shura* council.[60] Its founding manifesto expressed its commitment to democracy, making it the first Islamist movement to do so, and was criticized by other Islamists, and by some in Iran.[61]

But Bourguiba was not especially interested in democracy. In the same year it was created, MTI's leaders and 500 of its members were arrested. Ghannouchi spent the years 1981 to 1984 in jail.[62] He was rearrested within two years of his release, along with eighty-nine other leading MTI members, and released after Ben Ali's coup. As a prelude to applying for a licence, which demanded that no party be based on religion, MTI changed its name to the appropriately vague Ennahda.

Its members were allowed to run as independents in the ill-fated April 1989 elections, which along with events in Algeria had convinced Ben Ali that the Islamists were a serious threat. Sensing an impending crackdown, Ghannouchi went into exile in September of that year.[63] Being marooned in London, where he was able to observe the workings of an old democracy at close quarters, also convinced Ghannouchi of the important role of civil society. Contrary to what his critics suggest, his espousal of democracy is more than lip service. Ghannouchi is more than just an Islamist political leader: he is a theoretician who has formulated in Arabic an influential defence of the compatibility of Islam and democracy, and Islam and freedom. Indeed, Ennahda under Ghannouchi is so liberal that more conservative Islamists denounce its members as not being Islamists at all.

But while Ghannouchi himself may be an Islamic democrat, he is not Ennahda. As in any party, the movement includes more progressive and more conservative wings jostling for influence. Its leader is now in his seventies, and bursting to the surface is a new generation of activists who are not all as mellow or compromising. There are differences among those who lived harassed, underground or jailed in Tunisia and those, like Ghannouchi, who spent more than two decades abroad and have been influenced by their experience of life in Western democracies. Some secularists fear some elements may take the group down a more hard-line road, influenced by the spread of more conservative Salafist Islam in North Africa. Ennahda's dilemma over the role of Islamic law, or *sharia*, in the new constitution was a case in point. Ghannouchi had promised before the elections that his party would not seek to mention *sharia* in the constitution as long as the existing clause identifying Tunisia as a country whose religion is Islam remained.

This was the position outlined in the party's election manifesto. But a call by MPs from a rival party for the inclusion of *sharia* in the constitution and a series of subsequent rallies by Salafists and other hardliners forced a heated debate on the issue inside the party.

An internal vote ultimately saw Ennahda, being pulled in different directions by its own more conservative constituents and by secular political rivals, keep its original pledge. However, internal tensions over the issue highlighted the challenges the group faces not just from secularists, whose trust it has predictably struggled to win, but from more fundamentalist groups that have come out of the woodwork since the revolution.

In practice, the biggest political challenge may not come from Ennahda or other Islamist groups that have sought party licences since the revolution, but from hardline groups who reject democracy altogether and who have exploited the uncertainties of the transitional period to press their more divisive demands, sometimes through violence. Chief among them are the Salafists, a term that spans a spectrum of views but which generally refers to those who believe Muslims went awry when they stopped following the examples set by the Prophet Mohamed and his Companions in the earliest Islamic community. They tend to call for Islamic rule, though they differ on whether this should be achieved peacefully or by violent means.

Whereas under Ben Ali and Bourguiba it was virtually unheard of to see a woman in a *niqab*, or full-face veil, or a man in a long beard and short *jalabiya* robe, they are no longer an uncommon sight. Believed by analysts to be insignificant in number but claiming for themselves up to 100,000 sympathisers in 2012, the Salafists have asserted themselves through attention-grabbing and sometimes violent antics. They were accused in July 2011 of attacking a cinema showing the film *Ni Dieu, Ni Maitre* or *No God, No Master*, by director Nadia El-Fani, an atheist and outspoken critic of political Islam. In October, a gang of Salafists tried to attack the offices of a television station that had aired *Persepolis*, an animated film made from a moving graphic novel by Marjane Satrapi that follows the experience of a young woman in Iran's Islamic Revolution. In it, the protagonist loses her faith and finds it again, and the film includes a graphic depiction of God that has enraged Islamists who believe such images to be sacrilegious.

In June 2012, Islamist outrage over an art show they deemed insulting to Islam spilled over into days of rioting not seen since the revolution. Art works were destroyed and the names of artists listed online. The Ennahda-led government cracked down hard on the rioters but at the same time criticized the artists, raising fears that there would be limits to free expression in the new Tunisia.

Those fears have been exacerbated by a handful of court cases against journalists or activists accused of blasphemy or upsetting public morals by publishing revealing photographs or mocking religion. And in September, at least two people were killed as government forces tried to quell protesters who ransacked the US embassy over a low-budget Californian-made movie that denigrated the Prophet Mohammed. Again, Ennahda had condemned the film and called for peaceful protests but had been apparently unable to control more extreme elements who ran amok, terrifying secularists.

Salafism remains a relatively small movement in Tunisia compared to Egypt or Algeria, for instance, but fear of a lurch towards violent extremism fuels a rumour mill that is constantly spinning with alleged evidence of the Salafists' latest efforts to disperse beach goers or attack prostitutes in the country's red light districts. Certainly, religious extremists have clashed with alcohol vendors and even attacked a hotel serving liquor in Sidi Bouzid, the birthplace of the revolt. Local and official resistance to their efforts to impose their morals has seen Salafists armed with petrol bombs, knives and clubs attack police stations and the offices of secular parties. Their actions have alarmed secular Tunisians and left many yearning for the security – if not the repression – they felt under the *ancien régime*. They have also placed Ennahda in a difficult position: the group has distanced itself from violent attacks but has proven reluctant in government to suppress fellow Islamists as it was once itself suppressed. It has sought instead to engage Salafists and encourage them to join the political process, a policy secularists suggest is at best naive and at worst tantamount to collusion with an ideology that threatens the state.

Some also worry that Al-Qaeda, whose North African franchise is active in Algeria, might take advantage of the erosion of Tunisia's police state and the power void in Libya to recruit and to mount attacks. Indeed, Ben Ali had cracked down hard on suspected terrorists or militant Islamists in the last five years of his presidency, with at least 1,500 political prisoners languishing in jail when he fled, according to human rights activists. There is some basis for concern. In 2002, Islamic extremists bombed a synagogue on the island of Djerba killing twenty-one people, including fourteen German tourists. In December 2006 and January 2007 a group calling itself Soldiers of Ibn Furat, after a ninth-century Tunisian jurist, clashed with security forces in an area called Suleiman. The government said the fighters were killed but security forces later rounded up about thirty men it accused of having links to the group in Sidi Bouzid, where the 2011 uprising began.

In the murky world of post-revolutionary politics it is difficult to predict how much appeal extremist elements have in Tunisia. But groups that sympathise with Al-Qaeda have come out into the open since the revolution, particularly as many of their members have been released from jail as part of an amnesty for political prisoners. Chief among them is Ansar al-Sharia, or Partisans of Islamic Law, which counts among its members graduates of Guantanamo Bay detention camp and young men who have fought US forces in Afghanistan and Iraq and are now joining jihadist groups fighting in Syria. Ansar al-Sharia's first national conference in May 2012 drew thousands of Salafists, some of them waving the black flags of Al-Qaeda's affiliates in Iraq. Its members say they will not attack an Islamist government, even though they are disappointed by its policies. But what, secularists ask, would these hardliners do if Ennahda lost the next election? Throughout 2011 calls for moderation have abounded on all sides and it is only extremists, of both Islamist and secular varieties and the high level of mutual distrust, that have threatened to derail Tunisia's transition.

'The danger for us is the hard-line extremist Muslims who do not believe in democracy and believe in violence,' Moncef Marzouki, a veteran dissident who would later become Tunisia's new president, said two months before the elections. 'But when you look at the spectrum, you will find that the extremist secularists are as dangerous as the extremist Islamists and the only solution is for the moderate secularists and the moderate Islamists to build a consensual democracy that excludes no one and guarantees the rights of the majority of people.'[64]

Yet in the grimy streets of rundown towns in the centre of Tunisia, democracy has yet to bring what the disenfranchised youths want the most – jobs.

The Other Tunisia

Blue ropes were left hanging from makeshift gallows outside the education board in the central town of Kasserine, where five unemployed graduates had tried to commit mass suicide eight months after the departure of Ben Ali.[65] Even two years on riots, sit-ins and hunger strikes were a feature of life in these central Tunisian provinces, where cactus lines the shabby roads and almost half the inhabitants are jobless. There was no emergency law in

Tunisia before the uprising began, but swathes of the interior were intermittently cast under military rule in 2011 as the young and the desperate demanded the spoils of a revolution they had ignited.

This dusty hinterland, a world away from the well-heeled seaside towns in the north and east, was where it all began. It is also where Tunisia's most serious challenges lie in wait. Whoever wins the battle over the role of religion in the new Tunisia will face huge expectations to remedy income and regional inequalities that have only worsened since the revolt. Unlike the tussle over the role of Islam in politics, demands for jobs, equality and dignity cannot be satisfied by politicians negotiating in smoky rooms. They could take years, if not decades, to meet.

As elsewhere in the region, Tunisia's regional imbalances are significant. For decades, both government investment and foreign investors had been focused on the coast, which is greener, better connected by road and rail, and from where Bourguiba and Ben Ali both hailed. A few numbers tell the story. About 973 foreign firms employed nearly 94,000 people in the eastern coastal provinces of Monastir, Sfax, Mahdia and Ben Ali's home town of Sousse in December 2010. Greater Tunis boasted 990 foreign firms employing 91,489 people. That compared with just 59 foreign firms employing 7,720 people in the interior provinces of Sidi Bouzid, Kairouan and Kasserine. The south-west provinces of Gafsa, Kebili and Tozeur fared worse, with 32 foreign employers providing 3,500 jobs.[66] Poverty levels ranged from 0.5 per cent in Monastir, home town of Bourguiba, to 15.1 per cent in the central shrine town of Kairouan. Unemployment among graduates was 47.3 per cent in the central mining region of Gafsa compared to 10.9 per cent in coastal Ariana.[67]

Realizing the dangers that economic discontent could pose to the transition, both successive interim governments and opposition parties have been at pains to show their commitment to redressing the imbalances. The Ennahda-led government, whose payroll was already bloated, promised to create 25,000 public sector jobs in 2012 and to employ the many hundreds wounded in the revolt and one relative of each of more than 300 people killed. It also announced plans to develop impoverished areas, improve housing quality and build roads to more remote regions, which it hopes will dampen anger in the country's long-marginalised interior.

But it struggled to do more without pushing the budget deficit in this oil-poor economy above the official 2012 target of 6.6 percent of GDP.

In many ways, Tunisia's economy had already come a long way before the 2011 uprising. Despite stark regional divisions, rural poverty pales in comparison to that found in Egypt, where millions live on less than $2 a day. Though it lacks the colossal hydrocarbon wealth of neighbouring Libya or Algeria, Tunisia has long been better developed, and its economy is more diversified. Any Libyan with cash to spare would travel to Tunisia for healthcare, for instance, and many Tunisian clinics made the bulk of their money from medical tourism. While most Libyans struggle to speak any language other than Arabic and have suffered from a notoriously outdated and inadequate education system, many Tunisians speak Arabic and French, with English gaining traction.

To some extent, Tunisia is a victim of its own success. Its large middle class aspires to the higher incomes and benefits enjoyed by Europeans just across the Mediterranean, rather than comparing itself to fellow North Africans. Unfortunately for many who want to taste the fruit of their revolution now, however, the challenges their economy faces are to a large extent structural and will take years to unscramble. Not least among those issues is unemployment. Tunisian economist Murad Ben Turkiye said Tunisia's GDP must expand by about 7 per cent a year to create enough jobs to satisfy the 60,000 educated young people entering the job market each year. The economy had been growing at about 5 per cent a year before the revolution, enough to create at least 25,000 to 30,000 jobs, but the uprising initially hit Tunisia hard, with the economy shrinking some 1.8 percent in 2011. Even with the benefit of robust and sustained growth, a lot must be done to ensure the economy creates the right kinds of jobs.

About a third of Tunisians enter tertiary education compared to less than 13 per cent of people in Morocco which, like Egypt, still suffers from widespread illiteracy. Yet Tunisia's economic policies have tended to create low-wage jobs in tourism, industry and the public sector. To eliminate the mismatch, Tunisia must implement wide-ranging reforms in education to develop the sort of vocational skills that employers require, while rethinking the incentives structure to attract foreign and private investments that will create high-value rather than just factory jobs. These are long-term policies that will take years to bear fruit, as will efforts to root out corruption, which require a deep and painful overhaul of the civil service to bring in higher state salaries and discourage bribe-taking. A culture of accountability and transparency in government and the wider public sector will not appear overnight and may only take root under sustained public pressure.

In the months following the uprising, illegal buildings sprouted up around the country as police, no longer receiving their kickbacks, have mellowed. The tendency has been to drop some of the rules and relax the bureaucracy. The challenge for Tunisia is to reform the sprawling public sector so that the rules do apply, but apply equally to all.

Sitting in his office in a dilapidated French-era building off Bourguiba Avenue in August 2011, Abdel Jelil Bedoui, an economist and long-time UGTT official, who was briefly a minister in the first interim government after Ben Ali's departure, was realistic about what could be achieved.

'No government has a magic wand. There are no magic wands when it comes to the economy,' said Bedoui, who was getting ready to vacate the UGTT office, piled with studies he had overseen over the years, to devote himself to the new Tunisian Labour Party he had set up. 'It takes time to solve problems, particularly problems that have been building over many years.'[68]

Yet dissatisfaction with the pace of economic progress has already plunged Tunisia into a vicious cycle, prompting protests and strikes that in turn only undermine government efforts to revive growth. Shortly after being sworn in as president, Marzouki implored the protesters to give the government a six-month respite to try and improve the economy, promising to resign if it failed.[69] From teachers to airport workers to police, state employees had been striking to demand better pay and conditions, which they see as the rightful rewards of the revolution. Sustained labour upheaval could frighten off the foreign investors Tunisia needs so much to retain and attract. In the weeks after Ben Ali's departure, workers at a major hotel went on a brief strike aimed at removing their apparently unpopular manager. Even at banks and big businesses, employees complain that senior managers have remained in place, though they worked closely with the former regime. If we do not secure deeper changes in the midst of revolution, Tunisians ask, when will we secure them? Many saw this period of upheaval as a once-in-a-lifetime window to push through the gains they would have little hope of securing once the dust had settled.

'It is as if a big cake has come along and everyone wants to try their luck with the cake, because if he does not get a slice now, tomorrow it may not be there,' Bedoui said. 'There are a lot of movements, social and protest movements, and these do not always represent legitimate demands. Some of these movements have been provoked and are being pushed by people who want to abort the revolution.'[70]

And whereas the Tunisian economy needs to boost incentives for private-sector investment to create jobs, the revolution may actually usher in an era of increased protectionism. While Ennahda has emphasized that its policies will be pro-business, there is immense public pressure for social justice after the predatory economic approach of Ben Ali and his wife. Tunisia's experience under 'The Family' has given privatization a particularly bad name.

At the same time, the European Union, Tunisia's biggest trading partner, is battling a sovereign debt crisis and struggling to revive growth at home. Developed countries can ill afford to spend the money required to support Tunisia's transition or give it the full technical and political support it needs to democratize and liberalize the economy. Tunisia has secured US guarantees that will help it borrow more cheaply. The European Bank for Reconstruction and Development has expanded its mandate to support the private sector in post-Arab Spring countries, with $1.3 billion to spend. But pledges of support made by the Deauville Partnership of Western and Middle Eastern countries are longer term and partly technical. In the immediate aftermath of the uprising, the cheap bilateral loans came not from the West but from Qatar, Turkey and Libya, which have different agendas.[71]

'If the Arab Spring is going to work anywhere, it is Tunisia. So it is strategically important that Europe supports Tunisia in achieving that. But Europe has its own problems,' said one Western diplomat. 'The sort of money we put into Eastern Europe just isn't there. They can get money from the Gulf, but the Gulf's interest is in stability, not in the transition to democracy.'[72]

The New Tunisia

For all the dangers it faces, Tunisia has made more progress towards democracy than any other Arab country that saw unrest in 2011, and has a greater chance than any other of making a relatively peaceful transition. Despite secular fears over the Islamization of state and society, Ennahda is the single most progressive Islamist movement in the Arab world working in the most overtly secular society in the Arab world. If the party lives up to its self-proclaimed moderation, democratic values and pragmatism, then including the Islamist movement in political life could turn out to be a stabilizing factor that imbues the new system with legitimacy from the widest possible spectrum of Tunisians. Ennahda has struggled to reconcile its religious ideals with the day-to-day compromises of government, upsetting both secularists and hardline Islamists along the way. But that, say many observers, is politics.

Many Tunisians said they voted for the party not because it was Islamic but because it was untainted by the corruption that has sullied politics for so long. But power itself corrupts. Governments and deputies make mistakes for which, in the new democratic system to which Tunisians aspire, they must be held accountable. And if their economic policies are unable to create the jobs that young Tunisians want, they will be punished. There is nothing as effective as life in government and the accountability of genuine democracy for tempering extremism and encouraging accommodation. The main challenge for Tunisia's transition comes not from Ennahda and other Islamists who have chosen to join the democratic process, but from harder line elements that may ultimately resort to violence to impose their own vision.

In the months that followed the overthrow of Ben Ali, more than one hundred political parties registered for the elections. Most of the new parties won no seats in the assembly and were quietly wound down after the elections. Those that performed well were opposition parties that had existed, legally or illegally, before the uprising. Youth activists who played a role in disseminating information or organizing protests online have since fallen out and non-religious parties have splintered in the face of the organized and cohesive Ennahda, which immediately began canvassing door-to-door, undertaking charitable works and organizing mass weddings for couples with limited means – behaviour opponents said was tantamount to vote-buying. Yet 2011 was only the first phase in a prolonged period of change ushered in by the uprising. In the new Tunisia, new groups will have time to build experience and to present themselves and their vision in the future elections.

Two weeks after Ben Ali left Tunisia, secularist blogger and journalist Sofiane Chourabi set up a group that raises political awareness among younger people with the aim of building a new generation of active citizens and political leaders of the future. 'The years that Tunisians lived in a political and cultural desert did not allow the birth of a new youth generation able to lead a political life in a mature and responsible way. The challenge is to create a mechanism to encourage the political culture,' he said. It is a long-term project that will take years to bear fruit, but the next generation of Tunisians is already in the making.

So can we call the Tunisian uprising a revolution? Debate still rages among Tunisians themselves. Many of those who remain unemployed, or who found that policies have not gone their way, or that their strike failed to secure their demands, say nothing has changed. Yet no one who had visited Tunisia before January 2011 could deny that the country has indeed been transformed. By late 2011, political parties were freely competing for popularity in a country that had essentially been a one-party state since independence. Anyone could organize and hold a peaceful protest or strike, and they did so every day. The media has some way to go in overcoming its bad old habits, but journalists are mostly free to write what they want and criticize who they like. Tunisians can express their political views without fear of the secret police, now disbanded, though some worry that political red lines have been replaced by religious red lines that could see them arrested for offending social conservatives or insulting religion.

The reality is that Tunisia is midway through a political revolution that has a relatively high chance of success. It has an educated population and an active civil society, an effective education system and good healthcare. The overwhelming majority of its people are Sunni Muslims and tribal loyalties are weak, minimizing the risks of sectarian or clan violence. Its main Islamist movement is pragmatic. And Tunisia has a long history as a state. It is not a country that was created by imperial powers, like Iraq or Libya, which are riddled with ethnic, religious or regional divisions. It has the basic institutions of a democratic state, a bicameral parliament, and a separate judiciary. Tunisians say the parliament needs to have its powers expanded, the presidency must be curbed and the justice system needs to be truly free of political interference. There is much to build upon, but it takes decades to construct a culture of democracy.

And of all the uprisings in 2011, Tunisia's was the most organic. It did not require a spark from elsewhere to make it happen, nor did it require a foreign military intervention to achieve its aims. One of the biggest factors in Tunisia's favour is that it is simply not important enough to be interfered with by external actors. The country is physically isolated from the geopolitical quagmire of Iran in the Gulf and the Israeli-Palestinian conflict in the Levant. It lacks the energy resources that so complicate politics in Saudi Arabia or Bahrain. Foreign powers do not have a vested interest in ensuring that a costly and risk-laden intervention will be considered a success, as they do in Libya.

Unlike elsewhere in the region, the battle for Tunisia will largely be fought by internal parties rather than external players. Only time will tell, but should Tunisia succeed in making its transition to democracy, it could become a model for other Sunni Arab countries making a transition from dictatorship, much as it became a model of peaceful protest that within a month of Ben Ali's departure had brought down the pharaoh next door.

CHAPTER 5

Egypt: The Pharaoh Falls

You know when you have a scruffy old shirt that's in an awful state and stinks, and it's been too small for you for ages? And you've got into fights in it as well and it's spattered with blood and you'd bought it secondhand in the first place and the guy who had it before you was a criminal who's hiding out in Sharm el-Sheikh . . . That's what's happening now with the political system after Mubarak scrammed and went off to Sharm el-Sheikh.

— Khaled al-Khamissi's new foreword for the novel *Taxi*[1]

On 10 February 2011, Cairo's Tahrir Square was abuzz with rumour. The Supreme Council of the Armed Forces had met earlier that day and issued a coup-like Communiqué No. 1, vowing to protect the legitimate demands of the people.[2] The communiqué caused a stir, not just because of this vague pledge but because it divulged an extraordinary fact. The meeting had been chaired by the veteran defence minister, Hussein Tantawi. President Hosni Mubarak and his newly-appointed deputy Omar Suleiman were both absent.[3] Was Mubarak gone? Had the army taken over? Was this the revolution that so many had taken to the streets for?

Not long afterwards, Prime Minister Ahmed Shafiq told the BBC that Mubarak would make a speech and that his resignation was indeed on the cards. CIA chief Leon Panetta informed the US Congress that there was a 'strong likelihood' that Mubarak would step down that night, suggesting that consultations on his departure had been taking place with the United States, a staunch ally for more than three decades.[4] Rumours began to circulate that Mubarak had already left for Sharm al-Sheikh, the Red Sea resort he favoured. The head of Mubarak's ruling National Democratic Party (NDP) then offered the staggering opinion that it would be best for the man who had ruled Egypt since 1981, longer than the majority of Egyptians had been alive, to step aside.[5] It seemed the game was finally up.

Soon, however, doubts began to surface. US officials said the situation was fluid. The information minister said the octogenarian leader was not going anywhere.[6] Yet when Mubarak appeared on a big screen in Tahrir, or Liberation, Square the same evening, expectations among the cheerful protesters, their faces painted in the black, white and red of the Egyptian flag, were high. Here, finally, was the moment they had been waiting for. A carnival atmosphere had prevailed through the afternoon. There was music, fanfare, excitement and finally, as Mubarak began his speech, silence.[7] As part of an orderly transfer of power, the president promised to amend several offending articles of the constitution. He reeled off the numbers: articles 76, 77, 88, 93, 189 and 179.[8] None of them dealt with the state of emergency Egyptians had lived under throughout his rule, which allowed police to arrest opponents without charge and which protesters were demanding should end.[9] As the speech went on, the disappointment was palpable. The president appeared completely out of touch. Even as he lamented the loss of life among demonstrators, his tone was paternalistic rather than apologetic.

He repeated a previous promise, rejected by protesters as too little too late, not to run in a presidential election due after seven months. By the time he gave a vaguely worded vow to hand undefined powers to Suleiman, Egypt's long-time intelligence chief and new vice president, people were too disappointed to notice. Shouts of 'Down, down with Hosni Mubarak' filled the square and demonstrators waved their shoes in a mark of contempt. Suleiman, then seventy-five, promised an orderly transition, but his words fell on deaf ears. US President Barack Obama had unusually strong criticism for one of Washington's main Arab allies. 'The Egyptian government must put forward a credible, concrete and unequivocal path toward genuine democracy and they have not seized that opportunity,' he said following Mubarak's speech. After Washington's early dithering, those words could not have been clearer. Mubarak had lost US support. The next day, protests that the speech was intended to quell had swelled instead. Demonstrators expressed disgust at the lack of respect for popular opinion and a determination to keep up protests until Mubarak was gone.[10] Finally, with pressure mounting from the streets and the White House, Suleiman issued another statement, this time saying that Mubarak had stepped down and handed power to the military. The Supreme Council for the Armed

Forces, referred to as the SCAF, promised to lead the country to elections and hand over power to a civilian government within six months.

Celebrations broke out all over Egypt as people tumbled out into the streets waving the Egyptian flag. Cars sped around cities honking their horns, ecstatic passengers hanging dangerously out of the windows. Scenes of jubilation were beamed to television screens across the world. This was big news. Tunisia was a small country and a regional backwater, its revolution a possible anomaly, but Egypt was by far and away the most populous country in the Arab region. It was the Arab world's colossus and its ideological centre of gravity, the one-time cradle of both pan-Arab nationalism and political Islam. It had produced some of the most influential Arab ideologues, novelists and journalists and some of the greatest Arabic films and music. Egypt's status had no doubt declined, but its location at the very heart of the region, with one foot in North Africa and another in the Levant, meant that ripples of political upheaval in Cairo would be felt on the streets of Damascus, Benghazi or Sana'a. If Egypt had changed, the whole Arab world had changed. In Bahrain, Libya and Yemen, opposition activists took heart and began to plan their own revolutions.

Egyptians seemed in February to have matched the achievement of diminutive Tunisia but it soon became clear that their revolution was far from over. The army had not handed over power as promised. Reforms were halting and limited. Protesters who once hurled rocks and petrol bombs at the police were now clashing with the army they had welcomed into power as a guardian of the nation. Thousands of activists were languishing in jail. In late November, when Egyptians should have been focused on planning for their first free and fair parliamentary elections, a new protest movement demanding that the army hand over power to civilians was in full swing. Confusing and chaotic, the elections nonetheless marked a watershed for Egyptians who queued, in some cases for hours, to test their newly won democratic rights. And they voted overwhelmingly for Islamist groups. The 2012 presidential election saw Muslim Brotherhood candidate Mohammed Morsi win by the narrowest majorities against Mubarak-era prime minister Shafiq, who appealed to Egyptians either worried about Islamist domination or convinced that only an army man could restore stability after months of protest and economic crisis.

Efforts by the military to keep power by controlling the constitution-writing process failed. Before 2012 was out, Morsi had retired the ruling generals and rushed through a new constitution for a new Egypt. It had been a turbulent two years. Lives had been lost and Egyptians had, at times, appeared to be hurtling towards civil strife, but by early 2013, the first phase of Egypt's transition was almost complete.

Yet much more was at stake in Egypt than in out-of-the-way Tunisia. From the United States and Israel, keen to protect the first Arab-Israeli peace treaty, to Saudi Arabia or neighbouring Libya, everyone had something to lose if change in Egypt did not go their way. Unfortunately for ordinary Egyptians, the interests of foreign states rarely matched their own. Unlike Tunisia, with its large and educated middle classes, Egypt suffered from chronic poverty and had struggled to provide services to keep up with its burgeoning population. Egypt's Muslim Brotherhood was far more conservative than Tunisia's Ennahda. Egyptian society had become more insular. Narrow interpretations of Islam were spreading. And unlike Tunisia, where all but a tiny minority of Jews shared the same Sunni Muslim faith, at least 10 per cent of Egypt's population were Christians, who complained of increasing discrimination. Trust in the judiciary was low.

Even more importantly, perhaps, the police, the secret police and the interior ministry had been the backbone of the Ben Ali regime. They had cracked in the face of four weeks of nationwide protests, leaving the army as a guardian of the transition to democracy. In Egypt, while the interior ministry forces and the NDP had played an important role in maintaining Mubarak in power, the army had been the real backbone of the regime for sixty years and the new constitution, pushed through in a hurried and controversial referendum in December 2012, protected the military budget from parliamentary scrutiny and permitted the military trial of civilians in certain circumstances.

The gains made during two years of upheaval were fragile, divisions over the role of Islam and the rights of women and minorities festered, and economic problems were huge and worsening. A disconnect had developed between the young and often middle-class protesters in Tahrir Square, and the bulk of Egyptians who were not politically active and were struggling to feed their families. After decades of authoritarianism, Egyptians knew their political and economic system needed to change, but many were afraid that change would usher in a long period of instability, or even chaos, and push them further into poverty.

Kefaya!

Egypt's economy was motoring ahead in the five years leading up to the uprising. Helped by an emerging markets boom, foreign direct investment multiplied from some $400 million in 2003/4 to about $13 billion by

2008/9, peaking in 2007 before the global financial crisis hit.[11] The Egyptian government's economic reforms sought to privatize state-owned factories and companies, bringing much-needed cash into state coffers, bolstering the private sector, and drawing praise from the IMF.[12] Egypt could boast galloping GDP growth, which reached 7.2 per cent in 2008 before the global crisis pulled it back to a still respectable 4.7 per cent in 2009.[13] The pace of growth had resumed its upward trajectory in 2010 and investors had begun to return. It seemed like Egypt was doing everything right. Yet the impressive growth rates masked widening income inequalities and fell short of the aspirations of the young and educated generation who would take to the streets in 2011.

Despite living in one of the largest and most diversified economies in Africa, many Egyptians were on low incomes, with over 21 per cent below the poverty line in 2008 compared to 16 per cent at the start of the decade.[14] In 2008/9, more than 2.5 million people lived on less than $1.25 a day, designated as extreme poverty by the UN.[15] That figure had more than halved in the previous two decades, but on the eve of revolt millions[16,17] of Egyptians were still just one illness or pay cheque away from hunger. There were huge regional disparities too, with poverty in some rural areas, especially Upper Egypt, running at more than twice the national average. Rather than decreasing, urban poverty was on the rise, with almost half the population now resident in the largest cities and exerting enormous pressure on infrastructure and services. Cairo was home to almost nine million people in 2011 and stretched on through miles of urban sprawl, its skies filled with desert dust and smog.[18] For every gleaming new suburban development that attracted wealthy Cairenes desperate to flee the overcrowding and the pollution, there were informal neighbourhoods built or expanded using shoddy materials and lacking proper sewage works or paved roads.

Rapid economic growth was also failing to create enough jobs for the rising number of young people entering the labour market each year, and was not creating enough of the skilled jobs that educated young Egyptians sought. Of the 2.4 million unemployed people in Egypt in 2009, some 35 per cent had university-level education or better, and in the capital, Cairo, the figure was 54 per cent.[19] And many of those unable to find government jobs were forced to work in the vast informal economy, meaning they were unable to obtain mortgages or car loans and lacked proper health coverage, while an increasing proportion of family income went on private lessons to compensate for the poor state of public schools. With incomes low and youth unemployment stubbornly high, the rising cost of living hit Egyptians particularly hard. Inflation was running at 16.2 per cent in 2009, falling to a still eye-watering 11.7 per cent on the eve of the uprising,[20] with the cost of foodstuffs rising particularly sharply as a global spike in grain, sugar and fuel prices hit home. While basics such as bread and fuel were state-subsidized, loaves had shrunk and scuffles broke out in bread queues at the height of the commodities boom in 2008.

Even more striking was the statistic that more than 34 per cent of Egyptians were illiterate in 2006.[21] Literacy rates had improved over the previous three decades, with less than a fifth of 15–24-year-olds unable to read or write in the years leading up to the 2011 revolt, but a gulf remained between the middle-class or wealthy young Egyptians, who campaigned for political freedoms on Twitter and Facebook, and the women of Upper Egypt, illiterate and economically at the bottom of the pile. It had been a steady decline for Egypt, considered in the 1950s to be one of the world's fast-industrializing economies and emerging powers, but long since left behind by what were once its Asian and Latin American peers.

The privatization policies that were so lauded by the IMF were perceived by Egyptians as no more than a ploy by Mubarak and his cronies to line their pockets at the expense of the people. Big state industries were sold off to businessmen close to the regime for what many Egyptians believed to be knock-down prices, exposing what had been safe state jobs to new bosses motivated by profit. Despair at the economic situation was exacerbated not just by the disturbingly regular high-level scandals that found their way into the press, but also by the corruption that was eating away at the entire system. When a ferry sank in 2006, killing about 1,000 people, a parliamentary investigation found that the operator had forged safety certificates and conspired with the authorities to overlook its lack of lifeboats and firefighting equipment. Yet the owner, a wealthy businessman close to senior officials, was able to flee the country, and his eventual seven-year sentence was a Pyrrhic victory for families of the victims.[22, 23]

Egyptians were not just appalled at these economic challenges but at the political stagnation that seemed to have frozen their country in time, making it unable to adapt to new challenges and aspirations. Forty-seven per cent of Egyptians expressed satisfaction with their freedom in life on the eve of the uprising, down from 77 per cent in 2005. A devastating 28 per cent said in 2010 that they had confidence in the honesty of elections. Some 88 per cent believed democracy would help their country to progress, the highest level of democratic enthusiasm in a pool of twenty-three majority-Muslim countries polled.[24] Of the 1,000 Egyptian adults polled, 97 per cent said any new constitution should allow freedom of speech and three-quarters said it should allow freedom of religion, suggesting both were sorely missed in Egypt, a cradle of ancient civilizations whose proud moniker 'Umm al-Dunia' or 'Mother of the World' sat ever more uneasily with the country it had become.

The half-hearted pretence at multi-party democracy was wearing dangerously thin. Under US pressure, Mubarak had allowed multi-candidate presidential elections for the first time in 2005, a change from the old polls in which he was the only candidate. Despite this ostensible step towards democracy, Egyptian authorities had arrested opposition leader Ayman Nour, who was seen as a potential rival. Nour declared his candidacy from jail and was released following international pressure, going on to win 7 per cent of the vote before being rearrested over allegations that he falsified documents in his application to set up the Ghad, or Tomorrow, party.[25] He spent four years in prison, a clear signal to any other politician who thought of challenging Mubarak.[26] Over the next two years, the Egyptian leader oversaw a series of constitutional amendments that ostensibly legislated for multi-candidate presidential elections, but set so many conditions it seemed to some activists that only his younger son Gamal could realistically qualify, run and win.

A former investment banker, Gamal returned to Egypt in the mid–1990s, quickly rising through the ranks of the ruling NDP to become head of the powerful new Policies Committee, focused on economic reforms.[27] Surrounding himself by a coterie of influential businessmen who formed the NDP's 'new guard', Gamal became a driving force behind free-market reforms. Several names had been mooted as potential successors to Mubarak in the decade that preceded the uprising. Omar Suleiman, the intelligence chief so trusted by the United States, had long been considered a potential candidate, but the longer Mubarak refrained from naming him deputy, the more his star faded. Received Cairene wisdom also saw former Arab League chief Amr Moussa as a potential civilian candidate. By 2010, however, it was clear to Egyptians that Gamal was being groomed for the top job and that the ground was being smoothed for his rise at the ballot box. Indeed, to some activists, it appeared Mubarak had only opened up the presidential race so he could rig it with his son in mind.[28] For many who had lived for three decades under Mubarak senior, the thought of being led by Mubarak junior was galling.

And it was not just the presidential race that appeared to be rigged. The NDP was not the only party in Egypt. The Wafd, Egypt's oldest political group, was among some ten licenced parties that ran in elections but could be relied upon not to put up too much of a fight in parliament. The rules made it incredibly difficult for a new political party to register in the first place and even if it did manage to clinch a licence, elections were consistently marred by allegations of vote-buying, intimidation and other irregularities. Votes were considered so meaningless that most Egyptians were no longer bothering to cast a ballot. While tolerated as a religious charitable organisation, the Muslim Brotherhood, considered the single largest and most organized opposition group in Egypt, was officially banned. Its members were forced to run as independents and operated in a grey area that left them open to sudden imprisonment if they crossed a line. The Muslim Brotherhood had suffered repeated crackdowns since its inception in 1928, with thousands of members imprisoned and tortured, and some even executed, under Gamal Abdel Nasser's military regime.

Indeed, the Mubarak regime was the direct descendent of the 1952 coup mounted by the Free Officers under Nasser. The colonel swiftly turned his coup into a revolution, throwing out the aristocratic political class that had ruled Egypt under the deposed King Farouk's constitutional monarchy and replacing them with a new political class led by military officers. Nasser instituted land reforms, nationalized private companies and embarked on an industrialization drive that expanded the middle classes, but drove much of the old business elite, a cosmopolitan mix of Christians, Jews and Muslims, as well as Greeks, Italians, Levantines and Armenians, to friendlier shores. Nasser became an Arab hero, exporting his pan-Arab nationalism around the region and cementing Egypt's position as an emerging regional power, but his repeated crackdowns against all political opponents, from Islamists to communists, saw him transform Egypt not just from a largely feudal monarchy into a socialist republic, but into the security state that it still was when the uprising of 2011 broke out.

The prestige of the armed forces and of Nasser suffered a heavy blow in the 1967 Middle East war, when Israel captured Arab territory from Egypt's Sinai Peninsula, through the West Bank to Syria's Golan Heights. Yet when he died in 1970, Nasser was succeeded by his vice president Anwar Sadat, another man who had risen through military ranks. Sadat launched the more successful 1973 war and signed a peace deal with Israel in 1979 that won back the Sinai Peninsula and earned Egypt $1.3 billion a year in US military aid. He also rolled back his predecessor's socialist policies as part of his move into Washington's sphere of influence, introducing economic *infitah*, or openness, that was aimed at reviving the private sector. Sadat's regime used the reforms to build its power base, handing out contracts, concessions, agencies and investment opportunities to cronies, many of whom, unsurprisingly, were former military and intelligence officers. Conflicts of interest abounded, while income inequalities widened and failed to improve the living standards of the new middle classes that relied on ever-diminishing state salaries and pensions.[29] When Sadat was assassinated in 1981, he was succeeded by yet another military man, none other than Mubarak. The armed forces had now supplied all of Egypt's presidents since Nasser's coup, with the people locked out of genuine decision-making.

In addition to Egypt's powerful army, Mubarak had also bolstered the interior ministry forces over the years. On the eve of 2011, it was the internal security apparatus that carried out the regime's dirty work, clamping down on activists who complained of beatings and torture. Their ranks had doubled since Sadat's day to reach an estimated 1.4 million by 2007, and Egyptians routinely expected violence if they fell foul of security officers or police for the most trivial of offences.[30]

For many, the surprise was not that a mass uprising had happened in Egypt, but that it had taken so long. For years, books had predicted that the country was on the brink of momentous change. From Washington to Tel Aviv, scenarios had been plotted for what would happen when Mubarak eventually died.

National pride was ebbing to a new low. Egypt, which half a century earlier was the undisputed political leader of the Arab world, sending teachers and civil servants to the nascent Gulf monarchies, now exported its labourers to Libya, Saudi Arabia and the United Arab Emirates. In a book published in 2000 and bluntly entitled *Whatever Happened to the Egyptians?*, economist Galal Amin charted his country's social and intellectual decline.[31] In his 2002 novel *The Yacoubian Building*, Egyptian dentist-turned-writer Alaa al-Aswany traced the decline of Cairo from the cultural and political jewel of the Arab world into an overcrowded Third World city through the changing fortunes of a once-elegant apartment block.[32] The bestselling book, which was made into a film, cut to the heart of so much that was afflicting the country, from unemployment and overcrowding to the squeezed middle class, to the widespread corruption, to the lure of Islamic fundamentalism for disillusioned and hopeless young men. For these Egyptian intellectuals, a *fin de régime* stench had been lingering in Cairo's polluted air for years.

Protest had been a feature of life in Egypt for the best part of a decade. The so-called Kefaya movement, literally meaning 'Enough', had grown out of demonstrations in support of the Palestinian *intifada* of 2000 and against the US invasion of Iraq in 2003. It brought together opponents of many stripes – Nasserist, communist, liberal and Islamist – and focused on the one outcome that many Egyptians did not want: a Mubarak dynasty. Even though it never mustered more than a few hundred or thousand protesters, and had fizzled out long before the 2011 uprising, Kefaya had broken a taboo.

Wildcat strikes by workers demanding better wages and complaining about the privatization of state factories had also become widespread. Union leaders say that more than 3,000 strikes took place between 2006 and 2011, with persistent labour action and international pressure succeeding in establishing four unions that were independent of the state-controlled Egyptian Trade Union Federation.[33] The momentum had been accelerating since a December 2006 strike at Al-Mahalla Al-Kobra, Egypt's largest textiles factory, when 28,000 workers succeeded in winning unpaid two-month bonuses. Mimicking their counterparts in Mahalla, real estate tax collectors came away from their own protracted strike in 2007 with a five-fold pay increase.[34] 'It exploded in 2006 with the workers of Mahalla,' said Adel Zakaria, a spokesman for the Centre for Trade Union and Workers' Services, an NGO that had essentially been running a parallel independent labour federation for over twenty-one years.[35] 'The workers saw this beautiful thing called the spread of protests. One workplace protests and achieves successes so the one next to it protests to get the same gains. It causes an infection. The idea of success sells.'

NGOs were becoming so outspoken that Egypt revised its association law in 2002, banning them from receiving foreign funding and requiring all 16,000 to register with the Ministry of Social Affairs, which rejected the applications of some already well-established rights groups.[36] Powerful dissident blogs boomed, written in English or Arabic and reflecting a spectrum of political leanings. Egyptians were active on the micro-blogging site Twitter and on Facebook, providing a refreshing break from the self-censored pages of the leading newspapers. While the regime focused on crushing the Muslim Brotherhood, it was slow to recognize the danger that the new tech-savvy youths were beginning to pose.

The 6 April Youth Movement, which has emerged as one of the leading activist groups in Egypt, grew out of another Mahalla strike in 2008, which was backed and promoted by a Facebook group set up by the activists. In

June 2010, when a twenty-eight-year-old graduate and activist called Khaled Said was beaten to death by police in Alexandria, he became an online martyr thanks to a Facebook page set up in his honour.[37] Called 'We are all Khaled Said', the page became a lightning rod for public disgust with police brutality and corruption that appeared to have become routine.

When Muslim Brotherhood candidates won some 20 per cent of seats in parliament in 2005, they were reluctant to endanger their electoral gains and did not join the ongoing street protests. The opposition was fragmented, the NDP still dominated a parliament whose powers were, in any case, restricted, while legislative rules were skewed in favour of the regime, but Mubarak was alarmed by the Islamists' performance.

By the time the November-December 2010 elections rolled around, new constitutional amendments had made it harder for Muslim Brotherhood candidates to compete.[38] Claims of electoral fraud, arrests and intimidation were widespread. An NDP landslide was such a foregone conclusion that few bothered to vote – the turnout was officially 35 per cent but activists believed it to be lower and the Muslim Brotherhood candidates pulled out at the second round after failing to secure any seats.[39]

The net result was that in late 2010, on the eve of the uprising, the spectrum of Egypt's opposition movement had been thrown out of political institutions and onto the street.

Eighteen Days That Changed Egypt

When Facebook groups had first called for protests on 25 January, a public holiday honouring the police, the response was muted. The 25th had become an annual occasion for anti-Mubarak protests that rarely attracted more than a few hundred protesters, most of them dedicated political activists, who would be ludicrously outnumbered by walls of riot police. They would call on ordinary people – the silent majority referred to in Egypt as the 'party of the couch' – to join them, but few did. Their cause was perceived to be hopeless, even by many of the activists themselves. Even those Egyptians who privately complained about Mubarak, about the state of the economy and about the decline of their country, stayed off the streets. What was the point, after all, of being tear gassed and beaten when it would make no difference?

The departure of Tunisia's Zine al-Abidine Ben Ali in mid-January 2011 changed all that. Here was elusive proof, not that protests were possible, but that they could succeed. Arab satellite channels played over and over again the electrifying footage of a Tunisian lawyer, standing alone at night on Bourguiba Avenue shouting 'glory to Tunisians, Ben Ali has fled'. Interviews with elated Tunisians told the story of defenceless civilians who had rolled the dice in a dangerous gamble for freedom, dignity and jobs, and had won. The Tunisian people numbered only 10 million compared to Egypt's mighty 80 million, Egyptians reasoned. If the Tunisians could do it, then the Egyptians no longer had a choice. Amr al-Ansari, who in 2011 became an activist and an aide to Egypt's first female presidential candidate, had never joined a protest before. 'The Tunisian revolution happened and in the 10 days from when Ben Ali left to when 25 January came, people were boiling, saying they are fewer than us and they were able to do this,' said the twenty-seven-year-old. 'We had seen the model.'[40]

For the first time, residents came down from their homes to join the swelling demonstrations. In the weeks leading up to 25 January, youth activists from several opposition groups had been secretly meeting to devise tactics that would outfox the police and give the demonstrations a stronger momentum. Instead of setting off from one point they named twenty meeting points, announcing them on Facebook and Twitter and stretching the police's capacity to respond. They also used traditional means of communication, distributing leaflets to the residents of Cairo's Bulaq al-Dakrour slum encouraging them to join another protest that would begin outside a bakery in that area. Most of the marches were successfully dispersed by the police but others, including the Bulaq al-Dakrour demonstration, made it through to the centre of town, swelling on the way.[41] The success of the protests galvanized activists who lit up social media sites the same night with calls for another demonstration on the following Friday, the main weekend day in Egypt. The so-called 'Friday of Rage' was set for 28 January and the aim was to occupy Tahrir Square.

The day before the protest, the internet suddenly went down. It was to stay down for almost a week, but rather than take Egypt off the front pages, it drew attention from the international media which predicted that the Egyptian regime was turning the lights out pending a massive crackdown. On the day, the internet shutdown did little to deter protests. People were already congregating at the city's mosques for Friday prayers and from there they marched towards Tahrir. Thousands of protesters confronted police on the bridges leading into central Cairo. The Muslim Brotherhood had swung behind the protests, instantly multiplying the numbers. The promised crackdown was as vicious as many had feared, with tear gas and rubber bullets fired into the crowds. Protests broke out in Ismailia, Alexandria and other cities.

Around Tahrir Square, youths, many of them supporters of Egypt's Ahly football club, were at the forefront of pitched battles with the police. Drawing on their extensive experience in confronting the police at football matches, these so-called Ultras were old hands at making Molotov cocktails to hurl at riot squads. By some accounts, they were instrumental in tiring out and confusing the police. Activists had also been in touch with their counterparts in Tunisia and picked up tips. They brought onions and vinegar with them to counteract the effect of the tear gas. Many brought first aid kits. Those who were involved speak of an uplifting sense of camaraderie among the protesters who picked up the wounded and brought them to nearby mosques and offices for medical aid.

After a day of battles, the police melted away. The protesters had occupied the square. When Mubarak ordered tanks and troops in to restore order, the protesters cheered the soldiers, welcoming them as guardians of the people. Protesters gave the soldiers flowers and clambered on their tanks to have their photos taken. To some degree, this was a tactic used by non-violent demonstrators the world over, aimed at bringing soldiers onside and dividing their loyalties. For many demonstrators, though, there was a genuine affection for the army. By not involving itself in domestic repression over the years, the military had been able to distance itself from some of the more unpopular policies of successive presidents, and maintain its reputation as the honest and trusted guardian of the state. In times of crisis, the army had often emerged as one of the few competent organizations in a decaying and bloated public sector. Conscription for all men, with up to three years' service for those with only a basic education, also reinforced a widespread identification with the military. Cries of 'The people and the army are one hand' spread through the crowds, and most demonstrators were willing to trust the Supreme Council for the Armed Forces (SCAF), a body of which few Egyptians had previously heard, to manage the transition from Mubarak's presidency to a multi-party democracy.

Through the ensuing two weeks, protesters camped out on the traffic island that is Tahrir Square, overlooked by the *mogamma*, a Soviet-funded edifice associated with labyrinthine bureaucracy and grasping corruption; by the red-hued Egyptian Museum, by the imposing headquarters of the ruling NDP and by the head office of the Arab League. Protesters, men and women, Muslim and Christian, secular and Islamist, young and old, waved the Egyptian flag and painted their faces in its red, white and black colours.

But with the police gone and the army unprepared for routine policing duties, chaos and fear soon spread. Looters, who protesters believe were paid by Mubarak to instil fear, rampaged through the streets. Armed with sticks and rolling pins, Egyptians set up vigilante groups to protect their building, street or neighbourhood from attack. *Baltagiya*, paid thugs, infiltrated Tahrir Square and began to attack and intimidate protesters. A campaign by state media first sought to ignore the demonstrators, then to label them traitors involved in outlandish US-Israeli-Iranian-Qatari conspiracies involving – depending on the account – Hamas, Hezbollah and some US-funded NGOs. The chaos culminated in the so-called Camel Battle on 2 February, when touts who normally sell camel rides to tourists at the pyramids were brought in to attack the protesters.[42] Images of camels careening through the crowds stunned viewers of satellite television and made the rounds online. The move backfired as those who had initially feared the chaos saw a clear attack on the people. Yet as time passed and Mubarak clung on, the protests began to lose momentum and to anger many Egyptians yearning for a return to normality. Penned inside Tahrir, the demonstrators risked becoming a sideshow, their numbers only swelling at weekends, while nearby shops complained of lost business.

The momentum shifted again when Wael Ghonim, a youthful Google executive and Facebook activist, was released on 7 February 2011 after eleven days in jail. His appearance on the private Dream TV channel, in which he told the presenter through his tears that the protesters were not traitors and the hundreds of deaths were the fault of those who refused to relinquish power, drew widespread sympathy and galvanized support.[43] The crowds swelled the next day.[44] At the same time, labour unrest accelerated across the country. The main labour union, controlled by the government, had stood against the protesters, so unionists were not represented as a coherent group. But with hundreds of thousands in the streets, the four independent unions and the CTWS began to organize. An independent labour confederation was established in Tahrir Square, in the midst of the protests. By 10 February, a general strike was more or less in effect, paralyzing both public and private sector companies and factories.[45]

When Mubarak finally stepped back on 11 February, many of those who had stayed and returned to Tahrir Square for those eighteen days and nights welcomed the army's new role at the pinnacle of political power.

Many Egyptians said they trusted the military to defend what became known as the '25 January Revolution', and to lead the transition to democracy. That trust was not to last.

Devouring its Children

The Egyptian military's gleaming hardware was on display on 6 October 2011. Every year, the parade marking the 1973 war with Israel displayed the prowess of the armed forces, but the show had taken on a special meaning with the country under the naked rule of the generals. Fighter jets sliced through the air during the week of the public holiday, a visual reminder of who was in charge and how powerful they really were. Yet the very same day, as state TV broadcast the parade, the newly-empowered unions were holding their own rally. Buses were at a standstill all week and strikes at Egypt's universities were slowly but surely easing out Mubarak-era appointees. The following afternoon, protests in Tahrir Square were held under the banner of 'Thank you, now please return to your barracks'.

Eight months on from February, military rule was beginning to chafe. The army's initial six-month timeline for the transfer of power had come and gone with a return to civilian rule not on the horizon for many more months. Activists and politicians who had welcomed the army began to ask if it would ever relinquish power, and allow the Egyptian people's success in removing Mubarak to be completed with a transition to rule by elected civilians.

While Tunisians were preparing for their first free elections, Egyptian activists found themselves facing not only the coercive might of the army, but its perceived high moral standing and the respect it enjoyed among large parts of the population. For Egypt's revolutionaries the struggle for freedom, dignity and the rule of law was far from over, but it would be a lopsided fight against a military establishment that had not only provided all the presidents since the overthrow of the monarchy sixty years earlier, but controlled a network of business interests too.

The land holdings of the army, as well as its exact size, manpower and budget, have long been considered state secrets. The defence publisher, Jane's, estimated that Egypt's military expenditure in 2010 was $4.6 billion, excluding US aid. The army was broadly reckoned to employ more than 450,000 active personnel, including over 250,000 conscripts, making it the largest in both Africa and the Middle East. In 2010, about a third of Egypt's provincial governors had military backgrounds, about a third had police backgrounds, and a third were civilians.

Over the decades, the armed forces had also developed vested economic interests they were loath to leave open to the vagaries of a democracy, with its emphasis on accountability and parliamentary oversight. The military began its proper foray into civilian industry in the late 1970s, when the prospect of peace with Israel left it with spare industrial capacity and lots of young men with no wars to fight. When the 1979 peace deal prompted Saudi Arabia, Qatar and the UAE to withdraw from the Arab Organization for Industrialization, which had been set up a few years earlier to develop a regional military-industrial complex, that spare capacity was put to use. Employing 16,000 people, by 2011 the AOI was one of the largest industrial organizations in Egypt and produced everything from televisions to DVDs, wooden furniture, hospital beds, incubators, ambulances, garbage trucks, train carriages, farm equipment and the ubiquitous blue butane gas canisters Egyptians use to fuel their cookers.[46] A similar role was played by the National Service Products Organization, which was established in 1978 and controls a range of subsidiaries specializing in everything from construction to the manufacture of the Safi brand of bottled water.[47]

The military does not pay taxes and has access to abundant cheap labour in the form of conscripts, giving it an edge over profit-making private-sector industries and generating a revenue stream that was independent of the budget it received from Egypt's treasury. Its industrial complex was large enough to have its own Ministry of Military Production, which in 2010 employed 40,000 civilians.[48] The armed forces controlled anything between 5 and 40 per cent of the economy, depending on who you asked and what they counted as being under military control. The army's opacity makes it impossible to know for certain. What is clear, however, is that the Egyptian economy had shifted from being 67 per cent public-sector in the 1990s to 62 per cent private-sector in 2008/9.[49] Even assuming the military's economic activities had continued apace, its share of a growing overall economy would likely have fallen. While Egypt's estimated annual military spending has not fallen, at least two studies estimate that its share of a growing GDP has been in steady decline, falling from 14 per cent in 1984 to 2.1 per cent in 2008.[50]

Whatever the military's actual economic weight, it was certainly seen by most Egyptians on the eve of the uprising as a major, if diminished, force in politics, having a decisive say and perhaps even a veto over the choice of president. By grooming his son Gamal to take over, then, Mubarak threatened to dilute the army's influence on the top office. In this sense, the 2011 uprising resolved a problem that had been hanging over the military for more than a decade, allowing it to remove Gamal with popular blessing and restore its flagging political influence.

By overwhelming the interior security forces on 28 January, burning down the NDP headquarters and ultimately forcing the military, with US encouragement, to remove Mubarak, the protesters had gone some way to undermining the two main counterbalances to the military's power. That power had hitherto been diminishing in terms of its political influence, economic clout and control of the coercive forces of the state. The revolt had removed Mubarak, a momentous achievement when many Egyptians had known no other leader. It had also ensured that there would be no Mubarak dynasty, another major triumph. But by entrusting the transition to the military, an integral part of the old order with a stake in so many economic and political interests, the protesters had increased the risk that Egypt's revolution would only be half-completed.

Chaired by the defence minister, Hussein Tantawi, the ruling military council, SCAF, promptly dissolved parliament and set up a committee to draft an interim constitution that was ratified in March in a largely free and fair referendum. And after a summer and autumn of arrests, military trials and intimidation, it also held parliamentary elections that saw unprecedented numbers of Egyptians cast their ballots in a largely free vote.

Throughout the year, however, youth activists, opposition politicians, bloggers and newspaper columnists became increasingly concerned that the military was stretching out the transition and exploiting the associated uncertainty to foment divisions within the opposition camp and limit the scope and depth of change. Not only did the military fail to lift the emergency law throughout 2011 – a move demanded by opposition activists of all stripes – but it seemed to take over the disgraced police force's campaign of repression.

An assault on freedom of speech appeared to gather pace as 2011 dragged on, though it failed to suppress the new trend for outspoken criticism which had taken hold. At a reading of his novel *Taxi* in London in October 2011, Egyptian intellectual Khaled al-Khamissi said that none of his columns had been rejected or censored in the previous ten years, but three of his articles had been turned down in the six months after the uprising. Some 12,000 people were arrested and tried in military courts between February and October, more than the number tried in such courts in Mubarak's entire thirty-year tenure and more than the estimated 5,000 prisoners held without charge under the emergency law that had suspended constitutional protections throughout Mubarak's term.[51]

The leading lights of Egypt's uprising appeared before military courts. They ran into trouble for no more than holding protests against military rule, writing articles, blogs or even tweets criticizing the army, and in some cases for distributing critical fliers or hanging up posters.

By the end of 2011, the Egyptian government was threatening to prosecute NGOs that had received foreign funding for 'treason', using essentially the same tactics that Mubarak had once employed to discredit vocal critics of his human rights record and to starve them of funds.[52] Human rights groups, pro-democracy groups and women's organizations found their bank records scrutinized for foreign cash and some had accounts shut down.[53]

An initial revolution in state media coverage appeared by the end of 2011 to have been cosmetic. Accustomed for decades to self-censorship and to burnishing the image of those in power, they had simply switched from being a mouthpiece for Mubarak to being a mouthpiece for the generals. Controlling dozens of terrestrial and satellite television stations, radio stations, newspapers and magazines, the sheer size of state media had long given it enormous influence over public opinion.[54]

The way in which the elections were organized also smacked to some activists of a deliberate attempt to undermine the whole process. After protracted to-ing and fro-ing, the military council settled on a complicated electoral system where two-thirds of the seats would be decided on a list basis by proportional representation, and the other third would go to candidates running as individuals. Allowing individuals to stand should have bolstered former NDP candidates who had dominated certain districts for years, but in the event the *felool*, or remnants, were roundly punished by the electorate. To complicate matters further, the list constituencies were different from the individual constituencies, confusing voters. Preparations for the elections began in September, allowing only two months of campaigning for those parties that had managed to form and register since the new parties law was introduced in March.

The time to build alliances, haggle over lists, sign up for the polls and campaign was too short for many Egyptians to even understand the rules, let alone get to know the hundreds of new names that had emerged.[55] Many of the youth activists were not party members, had little funding or political experience, and ended up running as individuals against better-known and better-financed Islamists or Mubarak-era deputies. Others did set up parties and ran in a coalition called The Revolution Continues, but lacked the resources or the experience to scoop a large share of the vote. In contrast, the Muslim Brotherhood, an eighty-three-year-old organization with established networks of hospitals and charitable groups, had a clear head start. More conservative Salafist Islamists, who seek to emulate the sayings and doings of the earliest Muslims, also had an immediate advantage, using their presence in some of Egypt's 40,000 independent mosques to campaign for Islamic rule.[56]

The elections would also take place over several rounds, plus runoffs and reruns, sapping momentum as the results of one round affected the results of the next in a voting season that stretched out over some eight months from the first poll for the lower house to the end of the presidential election. Overall, elections were organized in much the same haphazard way as they had always been, with no new and independent electoral commission, and there were accusations of irregularities, though Egyptians were able to cast their ballots without being harassed by *baltagiya* and there appeared to be little sign of the ballot-stuffing and violence that activists say had marred previous polls. In a clear endorsement of the process, some 62 per cent of eligible Egyptians voted in the third round of post-Mubarak elections in January 2012, a major improvement on the 2010 poll, when some activists put turnout as low as 10 per cent.[57]

Throughout 2011, the motives of the military junta were difficult to discern. It was not clear how the SCAF took its decisions. It seemed unwilling to make any major changes by drafting laws or amending controversial policies unless faced with significant pressure. It also appeared to respond more seriously to demands from the Muslim Brotherhood than other groups. In response, the Muslim Brotherhood was more muted in its criticism of the military council and largely stayed off the streets, preferring to focus on the elections it knew would bring it into power. Secular and Islamist groups had already fallen out over the pace of transition, with the Muslim Brotherhood seeking to consolidate its advantage by backing the military's plan for earlier elections while nascent youth and non-Islamist groups called for more time to organize.

Despite the military's historic suspicion of the Islamists, the SCAF seemed to find itself better able to deal with the Muslim Brotherhood, a traditional hierarchical organization whose senior leaders were from the same generation as the generals, than with the fragmented secular opposition and the essentially leaderless youth activists. Yet at the same time, the military-backed government sought to impose a set of 'supra-constitutional principles' to guide the process of writing a new constitution, widely seen as an attempt to limit the influence of the Islamists, or whoever won most seats in parliament, and to keep itself and its budget independent of government oversight.[58] The principles divided some liberals, who were keen to see limits imposed on the Islamists but also worried about undermining elected bodies and giving the army too much leeway to meddle in government. The principles outraged the Muslim Brotherhood, which organized a huge protest in November, and they reignited a bout of protest by youth activists who clashed with the internal security forces and the army in and around Tahrir Square in the run-up to the elections, leaving forty people dead. Protests resurfaced again in December, with the military's violent response drawing rare criticism from the United States. For youth activists, removing the military from politics had become a priority, but the generals were refusing to budge.

All in all, an atmosphere of mutual mistrust pervaded Egypt for much of 2011. For the youth activists and opposition groups, the revolution was not over, yet that old disconnect between the politically active few and the silent majority had re-emerged. The day after the 6 October military parade was a Friday, and protests were scheduled in Tahrir Square to demand that the generals return to their barracks. Instead of presenting a united front that might have forced a concession, only a few hundred turned up in the square and the Muslim Brotherhood was not officially taking part. The protest demonstrated the divisions that plagued the opposition and failed to galvanize the support of the ordinary person on the street. On one side of Tahrir Square, from a double-height stage behind a wall of amplifiers, Salafists drowned out the speeches from a handful of other platforms and stalls set up by embryonic political parties. Nearer the Egyptian Museum, the 6 April Youth Movement was handing out red cards, apparently telling the military to get off the pitch. Carrying their trade-mark black flags with a symbol of the clenched fist used by non-violent revolutionaries the world over, they marched out of the square.

Taxi drivers cursed the traffic jams caused by the regular protests, while those who could not afford to take taxis cursed the striking bus drivers. Since police no longer dared to ask for 'tips', they no longer bothered themselves with minor offences, so the practice of double parking had spread. Street-sellers had flourished. Many Egyptians, who were used to stability and stagnation under Mubarak, feared that the longer the transition dragged on, the more likely it was to bring chaos and economic gloom. These were fears that the military stoked in its apparent effort to sap the momentum of the labour and protest movements. A poll found that the proportion of Egyptians who did not feel safe shot up from 18 per cent on the eve of the uprising to a peak of 51 per cent five months later, before declining to 38 per cent in August. At the same time, the number who had reported being assaulted or having money or property stolen had actually fallen.[59] The revolts had not brought chaos, but perceptions of danger had dampened the enthusiasm of those Egyptians who were not normally politically active, but had joined the protests in January and February. A poll conducted between March and October found that 90 per cent of Egyptians had confidence in the military and 85 per cent thought that continuing protests were a bad thing.[60]

These tensions came to a head with the presidential elections that took place in May and June 2012, some sixteen months after Mubarak's departure. Since taking power, the generals had essentially made up the rules as they went along. The new constitution had yet to be written, creating uncertainty for candidates who were running for a post without knowing what powers it would hold. The Muslim Brotherhood had initially promised not to field a presidential candidate – but now, fearful that the army would engineer a new system that minimized the movement's political powers, it reconsidered. At the same time, the Islamist victory in the parliamentary elections had alarmed secular and leftist Egyptians, who were now desperate to stop the religious right from taking control of both legislative and executive branches of government.

With mutual suspicions deepening, the constitution-writing process fell ever deeper into disarray. Determined to use their electoral victory to influence the constitution, the Muslim Brotherhood and Salafist Islamist groups pushed to dominate the constituent assembly that would write it, ignoring calls by secularists and Christians for a more inclusive membership. Secularists, Christians and others sought, in turn, to paralyze the entire process with repeated walkouts and boycotts. The divisions polarized the debate and played into the hands of the military, which now saw an opportunity to influence the whole process and claw back the democratic gains made since the uprising had begun.

Knowing it could not impose its choice of military president, the ruling junta instead used its powers to influence the outcome of the vote. In April 2012, the body organizing the presidential elections disqualified ten candidates from the race – including Hazim Salah Abou Ismail, a populist preacher who had managed to amass a significant following and was the only Salafist with a reasonable chance of victory. The Muslim Brotherhood's first-choice candidate, businessman Khairat al-Shater, was also banned, forcing the organization to select one of its former MPs. Omar Suleiman, the ex-intelligence chief long tipped as Mubarak's successor, was excluded and later died. Ahmed Shafiq, a military man and Mubarak-era prime minister, was also banned, but successfully appealed to have his candidacy reinstated, thus becoming a serious contender in the race.

The results of the first round in May were a shock for many observers. Amr Moussa, the former foreign minister tipped as a front runner, performed poorly, defeated even by Abdel Monem Aboul Futouh, a lesser-known defector from the Muslim Brotherhood. Hamdeen Sabahi, a Nasserite popular with the left and the unions, performed particularly strongly, almost securing a place in the second round. But the run-off came down to the two men who embodied the country's divisions: Shafiq and the Muslim Brotherhood's Mohammed Morsi. For many Egyptians, Shafiq represented a return to stability after months of turbulence that had hurt the economy. But the Muslim Brotherhood's electoral behemoth had also swung into action, bringing out the vote among its disciplined members and benefitting from the support of Salafist voters who had backed Aboul Futouh in the first round.

The military junta now sought to insure against the very real possibility of a Brotherhood president. Days before the vote, the constitutional court announced that the first set of elections were invalid and that Egypt's newly-elected parliament would have to be dissolved. This audacious move robbed the Islamists of their parliamentary majority. After the polls closed on 17 June, SCAF issued a decree that granted the generals legislative powers until new parliamentary polls could be held and gave them veto power over the new constitution, which it now announced must be finalised before a new ballot was held. As news began to emerge of a Muslim Brotherhood win at the polls, it seemed that Morsi would have to choose between accepting his powerless position and preparing for a showdown with the army.

The final numbers showed that Morsi had pipped Shafiq to the post, winning just under 52 per cent of votes. Whatever the secularist fears, the outcome was a victory for democracy in Egypt and a vote for change. Morsi was Egypt's first civilian president and the sight of a Muslim Brotherhood member being sworn in to the country's highest office would have been unimaginable just two years earlier. Winning by such a narrow margin, Morsi was now under pressure to prove his credentials. His first major step was to retire the generals. It was not clear if Tantawi and his deputy, Sami Annan, had agreed to step aside. But both Islamist and military sources indicated that a deal had been reached with lower-ranking officers to sacrifice the generals in return for guarantees that the military would not be investigated for its transgressions during the transition period and would remain shielded from parliamentary scrutiny. The apparent deal raised questions over the depth of reform the Egyptian system could now undergo, but it rid the country of ageing men who had hitherto sought to hold the process back. Of all the military men who could have led the transition, Tantawi was one of the least likely to take bold steps, to encourage debate over the future of the country, or to nurture a younger generation of political leaders with grand ambitions. According to a leaked US diplomatic cable from 2008, the Egyptian military had declined under Tantawi's tutelage. He was unpopular with mid-ranking officers who complained that he valued loyalty over merit. Ambitious, young officers with new ideas were considered to be a threat and effectively sidelined.[61] Derided as 'Mubarak's poodle', the cable claimed that Tantawi was also unpopular for his dictatorial style, discouraging criticism in a way that led younger cadres to feel the military had atrophied and lost touch with the nation, much as Mubarak himself had done. With the army back in its barracks, it was left to Egyptians to decide what kind of country they would now build.

Islamic Egypt

It was meant to be the 'Friday of Unity and Popular Will', when Egypt's diverse opposition groups would show their strength in a message to the country's military rulers. It was meant to call for an end to military trials of civilians, justice for the families of dead protesters, and the creation of special courts to try Mubarak and his cronies – common goals that all groups, Islamist and secular, left and liberal, could agree on. More than twenty-six groups were taking part in what was expected to be one of the biggest mass mobilizations since Mubarak vacated the presidency.[68] Instead, 29 July 2011 turned into a show of force by the full spectrum of Egypt's Islamists, who filled Tahrir Square calling for an Islamic state. Secular activists and youth groups, vastly outnumbered by a mostly male crowd sporting beards and carrying banners calling for the imposition of *sharia*, or Islamic law, were eventually forced to withdraw from the demonstration.[62]

In stark contrast to the February uprising, where Muslims and Christians had prayed side by side and protesters were unified by the slogan of the Arab Spring – 'The people want the fall of the regime' – the Islamists now shouted 'the people want God's law'.[63] In a direct challenge to liberals and leftists pushing to limit the role of religion in legislation Islamists carried placards declaring 'The Koran is our constitution'. In a parody of the banners reading 'Hold your head up, you're Egyptian' Islamist placards enjoined readers to 'Hold your head up, you're a Muslim'. Except, of course, not all Egyptians are Muslims. What was a Christian protester to make of this?

The protest was a turning point. It exposed the fault line that had divided Islamist and secular activists all along, but had been pushed beneath the surface by the unifying clamour to bring down Mubarak. It also left no room for doubt that the Islamists, in their various guises, were both more numerous and more organized than their woefully fragmented opponents. Buffeted by a rising tide of religious conservatism that had swept through Egyptian society, secular liberals and leftists had already been in retreat for decades, shifting the entire political debate to the right. Whereas a division emerged in Tunisia between secularists who wanted no role for religion in politics, and Islamists who have made concessions on alcohol, the veil, Islamic banking and family law, in Egypt the debate was not about whether religion should play a role in public life, but about how far its role should extend.

Flush from his success in helping to end the crisis in Gaza, on 22 November 2012 Morsi issued a decree that seemed to confirm fears among its opponents that the Muslim Brotherhood would never truly accept democracy. In it, Morsi replaced the prosecutor general, ordered a retrial for Mubarak and stripped the judiciary – which many Egyptians believed was still stuffed with Mubarak loyalists – of the authority to challenge any of his decisions. At the heart of the decree appeared to lie a fear that the courts could yet issue a ruling voiding the election that brought Morsi to victory, much as they had done with earlier elections that saw Islamists take more than two-thirds of the seats in the new parliament and much as they were now threatening to do with the constituent assembly. The controversial decree meant that in addition to his own executive powers, Morsi also held legislative power in place of the dissolved parliament and was now placing himself above judicial oversight. Even Mubarak had not attempted to seize direct control of all branches of government in this way.

Now, with the constitutional court due to rule on the legitimacy of the constituent assembly, Morsi asked the Islamist-led panel to complete a draft first. Christians, secularists and others who had walked out or threatened to boycott an assembly they said had been hijacked by the Islamists were now faced with a choice: return and try to influence the document or resist in the hope that the Islamists would not complete a draft in time. Working around the clock and in the face of widespread opposition, the Islamist-dominated assembly rushed through a draft and Morsi announced that a referendum would be held on 15 December.

Morsi had promised that his extraordinary powers would be given up with the passage of the new constitution and new legislative elections, but the decree raised the very real danger that, having amassed this level of authority, any leader might be loath to give it up. The Muslim Brotherhood had already reneged on some important pre-election pledges. It had promised not to field a candidate for president, yet here Morsi was. And for all the claims that Islam was the solution, protesters still filled the streets complaining about the slow pace of change. Morsi's political opponents immediately demanded new demonstrations to force him to rescind the decree, and a group of activists eventually set up protest tents outside the presidential palace.

Morsi's move had served to unite a fractious opposition that now saw Nobel peace laureate Mohammed ElBaradei, former foreign minister Amr Moussa and former Muslim Brother Abdel Monem Aboul Futouh close ranks with youth activists. On 5 December, the demonstrators were attacked by groups of Islamists. Clashes ensued, lives were lost and in the space of a few weeks several of Morsi's top aides, including the only Christian, resigned, blaming him for the escalation and for failing to consult them on his decree in advance. It was not clear if the attackers were Muslim Brothers or whose orders they were following, but for the opposition, the scenes bore worrying similarities to Mubarak's use of *baltagiya* in Tahrir Square. Finally, with violence spiralling and protesters demanding his resignation, Morsi backed down. On 9 December he dropped his expanded powers but kept his new prosecutor general and refused to postpone the referendum.

The contents of the constitution were not as alarming as many liberals and leftists had feared, but the document was rushed and, instead of thrashing out controversial points, its authors either omitted them to save time or skirted over them with ambiguous language that left many articles open to interpretation. Despite secular accusations that the Muslim Brotherhood would use the constitution to seize power, the document enshrined the principles of democracy and the rotation of powers and limited any individual to two four-year terms as president. That was a significant change from the 1971 constitution, which allowed the same individual to run an unlimited number of times. The new constitution also enshrined freedom of speech, but did not explain how this would be balanced against another article that protected individuals and prophets from 'insults', a provision that could make it incredibly difficult to criticize religion or mock the president. The constitution enshrined freedom of worship but only for monotheistic religions. It declared that all citizens were equal but did not make specific provisions on women's rights, as demanded by some activists.

It named *sharia* as the principal source of legislation, but that provision was not new. However, to placate conservative Salafist Islamists, the document added a vague definition of *sharia* as being in accordance with Sunni Muslim schools and identified Al Azhar, a respected seat of Islamic learning, as the authority whose advice could be sought on matters related to *sharia*. It did not specify, however, if this advice was binding. The constitution did not ban alcohol or force women to wear the veil, though an appeal to *sharia* could see such laws passed if the next parliament is also dominated by Islamists. For some observers, the flexibility contained within the document was positive, allowing the new constitution to serve regardless of which groups and individuals win future elections. In the event and despite the 'no' campaign, 64 per cent of voters chose to accept the constitution, many of them persuaded that a yes vote was a vote for stability and for Islam.

But the context in which the constitution was passed was more troubling for many than its content. Rather than seeing the constitution as a new founding document for a new Egypt, and thus one that required the widest possible buy-in to enable it to last, the Muslim Brotherhood took a majoritarian approach, seeing its electoral victories as a mandate to push through the draft against widespread opposition. The result was a document that, whilst winning a clear majority of votes, did so on a turnout of 33 per cent of eligible voters, casting doubts on its legitimacy and exposing it to future attack. Rather than serving as an anchor in the turbulent times Egypt will no doubt face, the constitution could instead become a source of division. And as the Muslim Brotherhood's relations with rival currents broke down, it turned increasingly inward and by the end of 2012 relied almost exclusively on Islamists for political support. The Muslim Brotherhood's failure to reassure its critics, along with a sometimes obstinate opposition too quick to resort to boycotts and reject dialogue, has polarized Egypt's political scene. The Muslim Brotherhood had come to power, but it struggled to leave behind many of the insecurities born of decades underground and in opposition.

The Muslim Brotherhood was Egypt's largest and most organized opposition group long before its Freedom and Justice party won both parliamentary and presidential elections. Established in 1928 by schoolteacher Hassan al-Banna, the Brotherhood is one of the oldest Islamic organizations in the world. In keeping with Banna's view that Islam offered a comprehensive way of life, the Muslim Brotherhood was at once involved in teaching, prayer, political activism and social welfare, offering healthcare and aid to the needy. Within a few years of its creation it boasted hundreds of thousands of members.

As early as the 1930s, a debate raged inside the group about whether violence was a legitimate means of achieving its aims of reforming society to prepare it for the ultimate creation of an Islamic state. For Banna, the emphasis was on changing society before seizing political power, but in 1948 a member of the Muslim Brotherhood assassinated the Egyptian prime minister. The following year, Banna himself was assassinated, probably in retaliation, and the Muslim Brotherhood was officially suppressed.[64] These were turbulent times, and Egypt was heading for the revolution that came in 1952.

Nasser clamped down on the Muslim Brotherhood, imprisoning and even executing members and driving the movement underground. The repression was to backfire. It was inside one of Nasser's jails that Sayyid Qutb wrote *Maalim fi al-Tarik*, or *Milestones*, which became the handbook of *jihad*. The Muslim Brotherhood renounced violence in the 1970s.[65] But some militants split away to form their own organizations, such as the Gamaa Islamiya, or Islamic Group, some of whose members were later involved in the 1981 assassination of Sadat and which mounted violent attacks including the 1997 slaughter of sixty-two people at a Pharaonic temple in Luxor. Reeling from public disgust at the assault, the group was rehabilitated and later renounced violence. Another offshoot was the Egyptian Jihad, whose leader Ayman al-Zawahri merged it with the late Osama bin Laden's Al-Qaeda just three months before 9/11.[66]

For many of its older generation, the Muslim Brotherhood had already come a long way by 2011. It now positioned itself as the antithesis of what

Al-Qaeda stood for, even though it acted as an early incubator of the radical ideas that still dominate *jihadi* thinking. It has sought to define itself as a moderate group that embraces democracy and the rule of law. It has never ceased to defend its commitment to *sharia*, but has persistently avoided commitment on the specifics.[67] Unlike Tunisia's Ennahda, which clarified its position on controversial issues such as the veil and the permissibility of alcohol, the Muslim Brotherhood proffered contradictory opinions before, during and after the elections and it was unclear how its policies might differ on specifics from those of more conservative Salafists.

Such ambiguity on the details was partly a matter of political expedience, allowing the Muslim Brotherhood the flexibility to hone its policy depending on the situation. It also helped the group to carry all of its members. Like any large organization, the Muslim Brotherhood embodies a spectrum of opinion, and while it has famously emphasized discipline in its ranks, long-standing internal divisions burst into the open after the fall of Mubarak. The group shed supporters from its left and right fringes, partly because it banned its members from joining any political party other than the FJP, and partly because it contains various generations that sit uneasily together and often vie for influence.

As far back as 1996, one member had split off to form the more moderate Al Wasat, or Centre, Party, which competed independently in the 2011 elections. Some of the most recent tensions can perhaps be seen in the younger generation, those in their twenties and thirties who do not share the same bitter experience of prison as older Brothers. Frustrated by the Muslim Brotherhood's strict hierarchy and top-down approach, and keen to engage with other aspects of civil society, a few younger members have begun to drift away. The Egyptian Current, for instance, was co-founded in 2011 by a former Brother who was involved in the uprising and ran in the elections as part of a coalition of revolutionary youth and socialist activists, shunning the two Islamist-led coalitions.[68]

At the other end of the spectrum, Salafist ideas have spread rapidly in Egypt in recent decades, particularly among young men looking for meaning and dignity in lives otherwise subsumed by the struggle to make ends meet. Their opponents accuse the Salafists, whose men sport beards and whose women wear the *niqab* or face veil, of rigid thinking and of seeking to turn the clock back to the Middle Ages. Yet the Salafists' influence has increased greatly in rural areas, including the Nile Delta and

Upper Egypt, where some zealots have clashed with the southern region's sizeable Coptic community.

The Salafists went head-to-head with the Muslim Brotherhood's coalition in the 2011–12 elections and won more than a quarter of seats in parliament, a performance that startled many Egyptians. While they are splintered into different groups and lack the political experience and organization of the Muslim Brotherhood, the Salafists' rise puts the Brotherhood in a tricky position. The more the Brotherhood struggles with the challenges and necessary compromises of government, the more these Salafists, with their simple call for an Islamic state, could present themselves as standing for the 'real' Islam. Indeed, while the Muslim Brotherhood has clashed more openly with liberals, secularists and leftists since Mubarak's departure, its biggest challenge arguably comes from the right. The popularity of Abu Ismail, the Salafist preacher who was excluded from the 2012 presidential race, was felt as a real threat by his Islamist rivals as well as by Christians and women, who have secured scant gains since the uprising.

Minority Voices

It began, by the accounts of the protesters themselves, as a peaceful gathering outside Cairo's Maspero building to demand justice over a church attack in the southern province of Aswan. By midnight on 9 October 2011, at least twenty-five people were dead and more than two hundred wounded.[69]

Protesters who were running back and forth from Maspero armed with small rocks, exhausted, sweating, eyes red from tear gas, said the violence started when a demonstration coming from the Shubra area of northern Cairo, where many Christians live, was attacked first by thugs, then by the army, sparking pitched street battles. Gunshots rang out in downtown Cairo, tyres and vehicles were set on fire, shops were closed. 'I came in the big protest from Shubra this evening and we were attacked three times on the way,' said Andrew Sarwa, a young protester who was holding on to an icon. 'Then, outside Maspero, they drove tanks over people and crushed them and shot at people with live bullets. The protest from Shubra had Muslims and Christians in it but they first attacked it in Shubra, before we got here. We wanted justice over the church that was burned. We want the people behind it brought to justice, that is all.'[70]

Another man came forward to explain that it was not just about the church in Marinab, 700 kilometres to the south. It was about discrimination against the country's Coptic Christians. It was about the licencing process that hampered church-building, forcing Copts to break the law while mosques sprang up on every corner. It was about puritanical Salafists who attacked not just Christian churches but Muslim shrines they considered idolatrous, and about the government's reluctance to stand up to them. It was about pushing Copts out of the country which they had inhabited long before the seventh-century arrival of Islam.

But for all the Muslims, many of them secular youth activists, who came out to support the Coptic protesters on 9 October, there were others who came out to attack them. A group of bearded men came out shouting 'Islamic, Islamic'. Suspicions abounded. One young protester with a bleeding leg limped to a hospital for help but was brusquely told by the staff standing outside that this was a private hospital. No one would help him. In a nearby street, a man complained to his friend that Copts had held the protest because they were religious extremists.[71]

'No one burnt their church. It is a lie. These Copts want their own state. They want to divide Egypt and have their own state in the south,' said one man, who described himself as a journalist. When the Muslim Brotherhood finally made a statement, it blamed the violence on regime remnants, side-stepping the question of why soldiers, in that case, had not protected protesters.[72]

What came to be known by activists as the 'Maspero massacre' high-lighted not only the dangerous nature of the standoff between the military and the youth activists, but the deteriorating state of communal relations in Egypt. Coptic Christians make up at least 10 per cent of Egypt's 80 million-strong population, and are spread across the country. Though they comprise a larger proportion of the population in Upper Egypt, their relatively small overall numbers and lack of political clout mean Muslim fears over church-building or secessionism are largely unfounded.

Rows over places of worship have long been central to Coptic complaints in Egypt, but a spike in attacks since the uprising that overthrew Mubarak raised sectarian tensions to new levels and heightened Christian fears that a more Islamic Egypt which would be less tolerant of religious differences was emerging from the turmoil. Only three weeks before the uprising, on New Year's Eve, a suicide bomber had attacked a church in Alexandria, killing twenty-three people and igniting sectarian riots.[73] In March 2011, a romance between a Christian man and a Muslim woman prompted an attack on a church in Helwan and subsequent clashes that killed 13 people and wounded 140.[74] In May, several people were killed when sectarian riots broke out in the working-class Cairo neighbourhood of Imbaba, after Muslims attacked a church because of a rumour that a convert to Islam was being held against her will.[75] Rumours seem often to be at the centre of sectarian clashes, with Christians quick to believe churches have been attacked and Muslims reacting to whispers about women converting or eloping. As with any mob, it is always difficult to discern who is inciting the violence.

Whatever the case, the fall of Mubarak had emboldened the myriad Islamist groups in Egypt, a more overtly conservative place today than it was half a century ago. The veil, which was not so common among the middle classes up to the 1960s, was so pervasive by 2011 that an unveiled woman in form-fitting or flesh-revealing clothing could expect to be harassed in the street. A large number of Egyptian men proudly sport the *zbiba*, or raisin, a dark callous that forms on the forehead of fervent worshippers. Outward markers of religion have also created a more visible distinction between Muslims and Christians. So many Muslim women wear the *hijab*, or head covering, that Christian women stand out in a crowd more than they once did.

More generally, the national identity had been transformed over the past century from an Egyptian identity under the monarchy, to a broader Arab one under Nasser, to an increasingly Islamic one by the early 2000s. The Egyptian and Arab identities were religiously inclusive, emphasizing national and socio-linguistic loyalties over religious belief. There was no contradiction between being a pious Copt and an ardent Egyptian nationalist. Nasser's socialist policies had an adverse affect on Egypt's wealthy Christian families, but he also repressed the Muslim Brotherhood and his rhetoric was nationalistic rather than religious in tenor and content. The Islamic identity gained ground under Sadat and was in the ascendant by 2011.

The divisions are clearer in classrooms, playgrounds and offices, and Christians increasingly view themselves as a victimized minority.[76] Like other Middle Eastern Christians, many feel they no longer have a place in Egypt, while Coptic NGOs suggest that emigration, which began in the 1950s, has increased since the uprising. It is an assertion supported by anecdotal evidence, though accurate figures are hard to come by.

The upheaval that began in 2011 has also left the Coptic church in an uncomfortable position and threatened to undermine its leadership. While many young Copts felt the revolution was the perfect time to push for equal rights under a civil state, and held successive protests, the church was more cautious, walking a fine line between defending the flock and provoking an Islamist backlash. Like many Middle Eastern minorities, the Copts had tended to offer political acquiescence in return for protection from Mubarak's nominally secular regime. With that equation now changed, Copts have been outspoken in their demands for equality and some now speak of a new politicization and growing activism in the Christian community.

It was not just Christians who were forced to rethink their position in light of the uprising. Women played an equal role in the protests but have had their representation rolled back since. There were no women in the army and therefore no women on the military council that ruled until August 2012. The new electoral rules passed by the SCAF removed a quota of sixty-four parliamentary seats for women introduced in 2010. No other system was devised to ensure that women were well represented, as the results sadly showed. Only nine women won seats in the 508-seat lower house in the 2011–12 elections and two more were appointed by the military council.

Parties running in the elections were forced to include only one woman on each list but these were closed lists, which meant that those at the top were more likely to win seats, and they were mostly men. The decision to force the parties to run even one woman faced opposition from the Salafist Noor Party. During the election campaign, the Noor Party prompted online controversy by replacing the campaign photos of its female candidate first with a flower and then with a picture of her husband, so that voters were asked to cast their ballot for the wife of so-and-so, raising questions about how full a role she could play in a parliament dominated by men. In the lead-up to elections, Salafists also prompted ridicule when they veiled a public fountain in Alexandria, offended by the bare-breasted mermaids that adorned it.[77] Salafists have been unequivocal in their view that a woman or a Christian cannot hold the position of president.

Bouthaina Kamel, a television newsreader and veteran activist, announced after the uprising that she would run for president, making her the first woman candidate for Egypt's top job. Speaking in 2011, before she was forced to drop out of the race after failing to secure enough nominations, Kamel said:

Women are marginalized so when a woman reaches the level of running for president it is a message to all marginalized sectors of society, from Copts to Bedouins to Nubians to the disabled. The right to run is the same as the right to vote. This is a message to all Egyptians, that you do have a chance in this nation, you have an opportunity in your revolution. I am fearful for Egypt, not fearful, but concerned because, to be honest, I will fight for democracy my whole life, for a democratic, free, modern and civil state in which all citizens are respected equally by the constitution. Citizenship is what decides rights and responsibilities and it makes us all equal, minorities, majorities. We are citizens and not subjects.[78]

When women's rights activists held a protest in downtown Cairo in March 2011 to mark International Women's Day, they were attacked by thugs who sexually harassed, molested and hit them.[79] When the military arrested protesters in Tahrir Square, they took away seven unmarried women who were later subjected to virginity tests in a country where any doubt over a woman's chastity will blight her reputation and marriage prospects. So traumatic was the experience that only one woman, Samira Ibrahim, an unmarried virgin, sued the military over the tests describing the crude examination, which was carried out by a man in full view of other soldiers, as sexual assault. She lost the case. Many women were now too scared to protest, which women's rights activists say was the ultimate goal of using shame and sexual violence as a deterrent to political action.[80]

Unfortunately for the women, the Christians, the moderate Muslims and the secular Egyptians who protested side by side in Tahrir Square, even if the Egypt that emerges from the turmoil is more democratic, it is unlikely to be more liberal. It is instead likely to be a more religious, more conservative place where Christians feel excluded from an increasingly Islamic national narrative and identity. The position of women in the new Egypt could become more precarious, at least in the short term, as their rights come under assault from conservative religious groups with a new-found voice in law-making.

Yet many activists say that despite the difficulties they have faced in the first years since the uprising, the changes have opened up new spaces for discussion and action and have encouraged grass-roots movements, as opposed, for instance, to the ostensibly pro-women laws that were passed under Mubarak while independent women's groups were sidelined. 'It was not possible in 2010 to talk about establishing a movement for women's issues, not laws, a movement, but this idea is open now. In 2010, it was not even possible to talk about setting up a political party. Whether you like what has happened or not, there has been an experience with political parties now,' said Mozn Hassan, director of feminist studies group Nazra, in late 2011. 'It could fail, it could be stolen but there are spaces and there are subjects that are open now that you could not discuss in 2010.'[81]

The Road from Tahrir

Even before the pyramids come into view, the touts have spotted the car. At the bottom of the uphill road to the entrance, young boys crowd around, dragging it to a near standstill. As one breaks away, another suddenly leaps out, forcing the driver to swerve, then jumps on the side and slithers through the window to promote his services as a guide. Inside the site itself, no more than a few dozen foreign sightseers pick their way around the sand, each looking harassed and unhappy at the centre of a scrum of touts, one carrying their tickets, another trying to sell them over-priced trinkets, another promoting camel and horse rides. Egyptian touts have long been notorious pests, wont to ruin the holidays of even the most relaxed visitors, but the phenomenon has only intensified since the uprising. This was the start of Egypt's peak tourist season, which runs from October to May, and tourists were outnumbered by increasingly desperate hawkers.

Nearly 15 million people visited Egypt in 2010, generating about $12.5 billion in earnings.[82] The sector, which directly or indirectly employs some 12 per cent of Egypt's workforce, took a serious hit in the wake of Mubarak's departure, with arrivals dropping by 41 per cent between March and June 2011.[83] The all-important tour operators that pulled their customers out when the revolt erupted in the middle the season have been slow to return and visitor numbers were up just 20 per cent near the end of 2012. With so much to offer, from Pharaonic temples to Nile cruises, deserts, beaches and diving, Egypt's tourism industry will recover, just as it did from a spree of attacks in the 1990s and a spate of suicide bombings at Red Sea resorts in the 2000s. But the protracted nature of the unrest has taken its toll not just on tourism, but on the wider economy. Whether Egypt becomes more liberal or conservative, democratic or authoritarian, its leadership will face the same daunting socio-economic challenges.

Real GDP growth, a robust 5.1 per cent in the 2009/10 fiscal year, fell to 1.9 per cent in 2010/11,[84] not nearly enough to create sufficient jobs, and remained sluggish through 2012. Unemployment in the third quarter of 2011 was at 11.9 per cent, its highest level in ten years.[85] A year later, it had risen to 12.6 per cent. And despite the flagging growth, inflation of between 8 and 12 per cent in the first six months of 2011 squeezed household budgets while food prices remained susceptible to periodic spikes.[86] All the while, strikes have continued apace. From factory workers to bus drivers to teachers, all have pushed for higher wages, better conditions and for the removal of Mubarak-era appointees. Over 500 independent unions sprang up in the eight months after the uprising, some of them representing single factories or industrial towns and others whole sectors, a growth in grass-roots activism that bodes well for Egypt's budding democracy but could complicate economic recovery.[87]

In some ways, Gamal Mubarak, acquitted in 2012 on charges of corruption but still facing other charges, may have been on the right course in privatizing state-owned companies. But how those companies were privatized is of huge importance. The public perception of corruption on a grand scale has undermined privatization efforts around the region when economists say reviving the private sector is vital to growth and job creation. There is great pressure from unions and activists to change course and offer national industries more protection from competition, even though these provide poorly paid jobs with little prospect of progression. Both unions and political parties are pushing for the imposition of minimum and maximum wages, which may cut income inequalities on paper but will do little to root out the corruption that has rotted the system.

Mismanagement, waste and underemployment are so pervasive that the whole system needs reform, but few politicians will be brave enough to undertake painful structural adjustments, or streamline the public sector, for fear of renewed protests or of tipping many more Egyptians below the breadline. In its first few months in power, the Muslim Brotherhood gave little indication it would make any radical change of course on the economy, yet it seemed reluctant to pay the political price of the structural reforms required to avert a looming financial crisis.

With national finances deteriorating, the government clinched a preliminary deal with the IMF in November 2012 for a $4.8 billion loan to shore up national finances. The IMF deal was important not just for the cash it would provide to support Egypt's economy through transition. IMF negotiations had been repeatedly delayed during the period of military rule and investors saw the agreement as a sign that the new administration was willing to push through policies that could include unpopular tax hikes and cuts in subsidies on which millions of poor Egyptians rely. But Morsi would quickly discover just how tough it would be to secure political and public support for such measures.

When he announced a raft of changes to the tax structure in early December, the political reception was hostile. Already battling to push through the constitution in the face of mass protests, the president realized he could ill afford such an unpopular move and quickly put the reforms on hold. And just as the IMF deal had begun to restore confidence, Morsi's government announced that talks to finalize the loan would be postponed. With the economy in limbo, pressure on the Egyptian pound was growing and the central bank announced that the foreign reserves it had used to defend the currency since Mubarak's departure had reached a critical low. In a country increasingly dependent on imports, notably of oil, a disorderly devaluation could have a disastrous effect on spending power.

To avert crisis, Egypt borrowed $2 billion from Qatar in December 2012 but the cash, which followed a previous $500 million loan, was spent almost immediately. Qatar has supported Islamist governments in the wake of the Arab Spring, but reliance on cash from the Gulf may only postpone the inevitable. While the media chooses to focus on the Muslim Brotherhood's social and religious policies, ordinary Egyptians are focused on the struggle to make ends meet. After just a few short months in power, Morsi's personal popularity, along with that of the Muslim Brotherhood as a whole, was already on the wane. It was clear that in Egypt, as elsewhere in the region, power and its compromises would strip the Muslim Brothers of some of the appeal they had in opposition. And failure to deal with bread and butter issues could ultimately undermine the credibility of an organization that partly built its reputation on charitable works to support the poor.

Genuine efforts by an elected government to reform Egypt's economic and political system could also come up against the vested interests of the army, whose role in the coming months and years is central to whether the 2011 uprising will be defined by historians as a revolution. Unlike the Tunisian army, a relatively lean and professional institution, the Egyptian military was an entrenched part of the atrophied economic and political system which the protesters had sought to remove. The army had returned to its barracks in 2012, leaving the controversies of daily politics to elected civilians, but its withdrawal from the front lines of government came at a cost to Egyptians. Egypt's new constitution protects the military budget from parliamentary oversight. It is a national defence council comprising the military's top brass and presided over by the president that has the final say in the military budget and all laws that affect the armed forces. To complete their revolution, Egyptians need to minimize the influence of the army on policy and unpick its business holdings – changes that may require buy-in from the military establishment itself and will necessarily move slowly.

If the first stage of the revolution took eighteen days, the next will take years, if not decades. In the meantime, Egypt may move slowly towards a hybrid system that includes an end to the rigged elections of the past, a more empowered and accountable government and relatively free competition among political parties, but involves some level of military influence over strategic policies. Economic reforms may be tolerated by the military as long as they do not encroach too deeply or too quickly on its own vested interests or threaten to tip the country into hunger and chaos. Political reforms may be accepted as long as they do not threaten Egypt's peace deal with Israel, its friendly ties with the United States, or the US military aid and training that the army values so much.

For the United States, worries that a Muslim Brotherhood government would seek to scrap the peace treaty with Israel or play a destabilizing role in the region were soothed with the Gaza crisis of November 2012. Morsi indirectly mediated a deal aimed at ending the violence and averting future flare-ups. Washington thanked Morsi for his personal leadership and it soon transpired that he had been in close contact with President Barack Obama throughout the crisis. The experience bolstered Morsi's regional stature and no doubt reassured the United States that it could work with the Muslim Brotherhood as did with Mubarak and other Arab leaders on matters of strategic importance.

The Muslim Brotherhood's handling of its newfound power will be central to Egypt's future. Politics means compromise, and realistic policies backed by actions, all of which could inflame new tensions within the organization just as it faces increasing competition from Salafists to its right and opposition from secular groups with a socialist, liberal or nationalist agenda. As these divisions come to the fore and a new era of multi-party politics opens up, the Islamist camp could increasingly fragment into different groups, much as the secular camp already has.

For many Egyptians, the more important changes that have taken place in Egypt are not at the institutional level but within society itself.

Egyptians, once too apathetic to vote, have embraced democracy and no longer shy away from street protests as a means of expressing their opposition to unpopular policies and unfair judicial rulings. In this way, the Egyptian people are slowly defining the acceptable limits of political and judicial power. Though grass-roots activists have faced arrests and violence, more people have the courage to speak out after the uprising. More Egyptians believe they can change their country, even if it does take decades. That is the real revolution in Egypt. 'The continuation of the revolution is a given. It is not an option. The real change that happened is that people are ready to act and have courage. People do not feel desperate and alone,' argued Amal Bakry, who had never joined a protest before the 2011 uprising but one year on was a member of a pressure group demanding an end to military trials for civilians.[88]

Yet, just as the Egyptian people's success in overthrowing Mubarak inspired revolutionaries from Tripoli to Manama, any failure to transform those gains into a prosperous and stable democracy could also ripple outwards across the region. There are plenty of foreign powers – not least Israel and Saudi Arabia – that would prefer stability to further upheaval, even if that upheaval is the only way that Egypt can complete its lurch towards democracy.

That desire to retain the status quo may have been strong in Egypt, but in Bahrain, where another protest movement was gathering pace in early 2011, it was overwhelming.

CHAPTER 6

Bahrain: An Island Divided

My conclusions have convinced me that the overwhelming majority of the people of Bahrain wish to gain recognition of their identity in a fully independent and sovereign state free to decide for itself its relations with other states.

– Vittorio Winspeare Guicciardi, Representative of the UN Secretary General to Bahrain, May 1971[1]

In the alleys of Bilad al-Qadim, the mourners had begun to gather. On the tattered walls, anti-government graffiti had been painted over by police, but fresh slogans had appeared. 'No to dialogue' was scrawled on the closed metal shutter of a shop in this Shi'ite Muslim village, long since consumed by the urban sprawl that is Bahrain's capital city of Manama. Further down the road, someone had sprayed the words 'Down with the 2002 constitution'. It was shortly after noon and worshippers were making their way back from the nearby suburb of Draz. There, Bahrain's most senior Shi'ite cleric, Sheikh Issa Qasim, called on the faithful who filled the mosque and the streets outside to remain peaceful and to reject sectarian divisions on this majority Shi'ite island ruled since the eighteenth century by a Sunni Muslim family.[2]

By early afternoon, thousands were crowded together in the March sunshine for the funeral of thirty-three-year-old Hani Abdulaziz, who had been chased by police from outside his home and hit by several rounds of buckshot as he hid in an unfinished building.[3] His coffin, wrapped in a Bahraini flag and strewn with flowers and sweet-smelling herbs, was finally driven to a nearby cemetery. On the way, a procession of friends, family members and well-wishers called loudly for the fall of Bahrain's King Hamad bin Isa Al Khalifa and for the expulsion of the Peninsula Shield, the joint Gulf Arab military force sent in after a month of protests focused around the country's Pearl roundabout had brought the island close to a standstill.

Over a week had passed since 14 March 2011, when the first 1,000 troops rumbled across a causeway that joins Bahrain to Saudi Arabia, the region's economic and political powerhouse and bastion of Sunni Islam. Opposition activists said more than 100 people were missing and believed to be in custody.[4] Many more activists had gone into hiding or fled into exile. By the end of the month another twenty-four people would be dead, including four security officers and seven bystanders. It was a drop in the lake of blood that would soon be spilt in Libya and Syria, but a national crisis in a country of just 1.2 million people that is six times smaller than the US state of Rhode Island.[5]

Abdulaziz had bled to death because his neighbours were too scared to take him to Bahrain's main public hospital, Salmaniya Medical Complex, where security forces had arrested wounded protesters and rounded up the doctors who had treated them or spoken out against the state's violent handling of the crisis.[6] They had instead taken Abdulaziz to a private hospital where he was picked up alive by Bahraini security forces and returned to his family as a corpse six days later, the day of his funeral.[7]

In the ensuing weeks and months, thousands of Shi'ite Bahrainis who went on strike during the uprising were fired or suspended from their jobs. Bahrain's top Shi'ite athletes were replaced. Two stars of the Bahraini national soccer squad faced trial for taking part in the protests.[8] The senior editors of *Al-Wasat*, Bahrain's leading independent newspaper, were forced to resign and face trial. Two of them, both Iraqi Shi'ites, were summarily deported along with their families.[9] A co-founder of the newspaper died in custody.[10]

If the departure of Tunisia's Zine al-Abidine Ben Ali and Egypt's Hosni Mubarak in January and February 2011 had raised popular hopes that a new Middle East was in the making, Bahrain's crackdown the following month blew the first distinctly chill breeze through the Arab Spring. Despite the hopes of so many Arabs watching the protests spread from one country to another, their rulers would not fall like dominoes. In Bahrain, the Arab Spring came up against the cold, hard interests of larger neighbours and global superpowers. In Libya, an early revolt had not spread and was about to be crushed by Muammar Gaddafi's forces. In Yemen, dozens of peaceful youth protesters had been shot already, their calls for political reform over-shadowed by an unfolding elite power struggle.

The relatively professional army that was able to stand on the sidelines during the Tunisian uprising, the relative religious homogeneity in that country, the weakness of tribal ties in Tunisia and Egypt and their largely unarmed populations had allowed them so far to weather remarkable and sudden change with relatively little bloodshed.

The circumstances were altogether less favourable in Bahrain. Its 2011 uprising may have been inspired by Tunisia and Egypt, but its roots go back far longer and are bound up in a regional conflict that has complicated the historical tussle over power on the island.

Like all small states, Bahrain is hostage to its geography and to the wider regional power struggle between Shi'ite Muslim but non-Arab Iran and Saudi Arabia, zealous proponent of the particularly puritanical *Wahhabi* brand of Sunni Islam. With Bahrain's Sunni ruling family relying on Saudi support, the reforms they could offer found their limits in Riyadh. Bahrain also remained closely tied up with the strategic interests of the United States, keen to maintain stability in the world's largest oil-exporting region and keep the US Fifth Fleet based on the island.

While activists have long called for political reforms that appeal to all, carefully couching demands in terms of equal citizenship and broader participation in politics for all Bahrainis, the biggest grievances lie with the country's Shi'ites, who have more to be disgruntled about and less to lose. The divides in Bahrain were not religious in nature – they revolved around universal calls for the Al Khalifa family to relinquish some political power to the people, to empower the elected parliament, to boost transparency and to end discrimination – but by the close of the year divisions were being couched in increasingly sectarian terms.

Bahrain would end 2011 a more polarized society than it started the year, with suspicions between Sunni and Shi'ite running higher than they had even during an earlier uprising in the 1990s. A decade of painstaking efforts by the opposition and the monarchy to rebuild trust and open up the political space would be lost. Sunnis who began 2011 believing reform could resolve political tensions, ended it believing the Shi'ites would only be satisfied with the overthrow of the monarchy. Shi'ites who began 2011 believing reform was enough, ended it believing the Al Khalifa monarchy had to go.

'After this, we want to bring down the regime. We want nothing else,' said Abdulaziz's cousin, walking back from the cemetery. 'Hani had twins under one year old. What a shame to take their father away at that age, but we have no weapons to defend ourselves and our lives ... How can they ask the

Peninsula Shield in and then accuse Iran of meddling? Did you see anyone with a gun?'[11]

The dynamics of Bahrain's uprising and its role in the Arab Spring are bound up in the history of activism in the country, in how a majority Shi'ite country came to be ruled by the Sunni Al Khalifa monarchy, and in the regional rivalries and imperial ambitions that have coloured politics for centuries in this vulnerable state. What happened in 2011 was the latest episode in a long and bleak cycle of uprisings and crackdowns that would continue long after the Pearl roundabout was demolished.

A History of Divisions

Up two flights of rough concrete steps, past a basic kitchen that had seen better days and a small living room where a dozen or so children played on the floor, the roof offered a sheltered view of the main road in Jidhafs, a Shi'ite suburb of Manama. It was just before dusk and the call to prayer was punctuated by the occasional pop of tear gas being fired. A clutch of riot police swung round a corner and into sight, but the youths who had been loitering on the street slipped silently into rundown houses whose front doors opened directly onto the road. The police looked around, buckshot rifles at the ready for any sign of protest, then ran down a side alley. Balaclavas and helmets obscured faces and muffled voices, disguising the identity of these security forces who, according to Shi'ite Bahrainis, were Sunnis recruited from Syria, Jordan, Yemen or even Pakistan.[12]

Inside, on a wall of the rooftop annex, was a small picture of Hassan Nasrallah, leader of Lebanon's Hezbollah, a Shi'ite political group that receives Iranian military and political support. On the other wall was a larger framed photograph of an elderly man with a turban and white beard. The Shi'ite cleric was the deceased father of the eleven siblings who grew up in this narrow three-storey home, and a member of Bahrain's first parliament, which was established in 1973 and suspended two years later.

The scene in Jidhafs was not simply one of disempowered civilians demanding more political rights and coming up against the armed might of the state. It was also a microcosm of the overlapping sectarian, ethnic and national loyalties, the glaring social, economic and political disparities, and the conflicting regional ambitions that complicate the uprising in Bahrain.

Huddled in the roof annex with his siblings, waiting for the tensions to calm down, Jaafar explained his alarm at the sudden escalation in sectarian tensions and the intervention of Gulf troops. 'There is no sectarian problem in Bahrain. We hear on television that our Sunni brothers are guarding their homes and we wonder why. We don't even teach our children anything sectarian. The government has lied to the Sunnis, and said these Shi'ites want to take your rights, but whenever a Sunni would join us at the Pearl roundabout, we were proud,' he said, offering a glass of fruit juice and turning on the air conditioning against the still spring air. 'This is our country. We don't accept Iran or anyone else to touch or violate the sovereignty of our country.'[13]

That is not how the ruling Al Khalifa family or many Sunnis see it. Like the other Sunni rulers in the Gulf, Bahrain's monarchy has long painted Bahraini Shi'ites as a potential fifth column, more loyal to their co-religionists in the Gulf's Shi'ite power Iran, than they were to Sunni fellow Arabs.[14]

These insinuations are vehemently denied by Bahraini Shi'ites, the majority of whom identify themselves as Baharna, people of Arab descent and adherents of Shi'ism since the early days of Islam, long before Iran adopted the Shi'ite creed around 1501.[15] It is not just their religious sect that differentiates the Baharna from their Sunni compatriots and rulers. It is also their historical narrative, which identifies them as the settled natives of a territory that once encompassed not only today's archipelago of thirty-three islands, but also stretched from the Qatar peninsula to southern Iraq.[16]

This historical Bahrain has not existed for 500 years. The sixteenth-century Portuguese invasion of the Bahraini islands severed political ties to the mainland. That divide was cemented when the Iranian Safavids expelled the Portuguese in 1602 and ruled Bahrain until the eighteenth-century arrival of the Sunni Al Khalifa family, who were still in power when the 2011 revolt broke out.

Yet the notion of belonging to a territory that predated the modern borders imposed on them by successive conquerors is a cornerstone of the Baharna narrative of an oppressed native identity that is inherently hostile towards the established Sunni dynastic rulers.[17] It is everyone else, the Baharna contend, who hail from elsewhere and whose loyalties are in question.

Arriving from Qatar, the Al Khalifa family had a tribal background, dialect and historical narrative that differed significantly from that of the Baharna, whose family and social relationships revolved around sedentary farming communities and whose villages retain that character despite being swallowed up by the city.[18] Like their predecessors, the Al Khalifa family faced consistent external and internal threats to their rule and may not have survived as long as they did without the support of Britain, which had brought the islands under its protection in 1861 and subsequently made the country an administrative centre for its interests in the Gulf.[19, 20]

Over the ensuing century, Britain received and rejected several Iranian claims to Bahrain, which Iran declared in 1957 to be its fourteenth province.[21] Iran did not drop its assertion until 1970, a year before Britain finally left Bahrain and ended its *Pax Britannica* in the Gulf.

Already advanced among its Gulf Arab neighbours, Bahrain enjoyed a long history not only of trade but of political and cultural vibrancy. Its people were among the first in the Gulf to be formally educated, and Bahrain was producing doctors, bankers and engineers when many Gulf natives still lived in palm frond shacks. It was the third Gulf country to strike oil, in 1932, and the first to start running out of oil and diversifying its economy. From the mid–1970s, when Dubai was still a small port, Bahrain was the Middle East's financial capital, taking on the mantle lost by Lebanon as it slipped into civil war.

Bahrainis have a long history of political and labour activism. Uprisings, strikes, clashes or protests broke out virtually every decade throughout the twentieth century, so, by the region's standards, Bahrain could boast an established and resilient civil society and widespread political awareness.[22]

Invited to join a nascent federation of Gulf states by Abu Dhabi ruler Sheikh Zayed Al Nahyan in the aftermath of Britain's retreat from the region, Bahrain's rulers felt confident enough to go it alone despite their lack of oil wealth. In 1973, Sheikh Isa bin Salman Al Khalifa, then the ruler of Bahrain, promulgated a constitution that allowed for a powerful elected parliament and raised hopes of increased political participation by Bahrainis. But the first elections in 1973 ushered in outspoken politicians, alarming Sheikh Isa, who set about clamping down on dissent.

In 1975, just two years after Bahrain's experiment with parliamentary politics, Sheikh Isa dissolved the assembly, suspended the constitution and imposed a State Security Law that severely curbed political freedoms. Through the ensuing decades, thousands of Bahrainis were jailed, the media was tightly controlled, and the ruler concentrated absolute authority in his own hands.

With the British gone, it quickly became clear that the Al Khalifa family lacked the financial and political clout to survive against a politically active population without Saudi help. Despite its poverty, relative to the vast hydrocarbon wealth of its neighbours, its negligible land mass, small population and diminished strategic importance as an oil, pearl, trading or administrative centre, Bahrain's unusual position as a majority Shi'ite country ruled by a Sunni family saw it once more become a proxy battle-field in the struggle between Saudi Arabia and Iran.

When Saudi troops crossed the causeway linking the two countries in March 2011, they highlighted the historical web of regional and international ambitions that complicate Bahrain's crisis and make it extraordinarily difficult for any uprising to either topple the Al Khalifa monarchy or secure deep political reform. The intervention also exposed the limits of Bahrain's sovereignty and of any internal efforts to resolve the political crisis without the blessing of Saudi Arabia.

The Al Khalifa monarchy was not financially independent. More than 75 per cent of Bahrain's oil comes from the Abu Safa field, which is under Saudi sovereignty and administration but whose revenues are shared as part of a contract that has left the Bahraini monarchy beholden to its wealthier neighbour.[23] While Bahrain's government had worked hard to diversify its economy over the years – the financial sector alone comprised a quarter of GDP – oil still provided 80 per cent of government revenues on the eve of revolt.[24]

In 1986, the 25-kilometre King Fahd Causeway joined Bahrain to Saudi Arabia's Eastern Province and highlighted just how close the island was to the Arab littoral. The opening of the bridge was not just a practical or commercial venture, but consolidated Riyadh's strategic and economic influence over its tiny neighbour and sent a strong message to Iran. Bahrain was literally no longer an island.

By 2008, an average 50,000 vehicles were crossing the bridge each day.[25] With bars, clubs and even cinemas banned in Saudi Arabia, and shopping centres, coffee shops and fast food outlets gender-segregated, Bahrain became a regular weekend haunt for Saudis, making regional tourism a mainstay of its economy. Though Saudi Arabia had not, like Iran, laid claim to Bahrain as a lost province, in the four decades since independence it had exploited the financial weaknesses and political insecurities of its ruling family to bring the island firmly into its sphere of influence.

Adding to the confusion over the divergent identities of Bahrainis, and central to the wider tensions in the whole region, is the transnational nature of Shi'ite religious affiliation and its relationship to politics. The split within Islam goes back to the struggle for succession that followed the seventh-century death of the Prophet Mohamed. Most Muslims accepted the election of the next four caliphs from among the senior leaders of the Muslim community. These were followed by a series of dynastic sultan-caliphs. The Shi'ites believed the succession should have passed directly through a line of the prophet's descendants beginning with Ali, the Prophet's cousin and trusted associate and the husband of his daughter Fatima. The Shi'ites became a permanent community in Islam who followed a hereditary line of what they believed to be infallible imams who could guide Muslims. With the disappearance of the twelfth imam as a young boy in ninth-century Iraq, these so-called Twelver Shi'ites became a messianic sect who believed that this 'Hidden Imam' would return at the End of Days to bring justice to the earth.

In the absence of this imam, the faithful choose a senior scholar or jurist as their *marjaa al-taqleed*, or source of emulation, to whom they turn for spiritual guidance. Given that a source of emulation is usually an ayatollah or a grand ayatollah, meaning he has reached the highest ranks in the Shi'ite hierarchy of religious learning, only a few men qualify at any one point. With so few scholars to choose from, a Bahraini Shi'ite might emulate an Iraqi or Iranian jurist.

And to the chagrin of Sunni political leaders, some Shi'ite clerics do not limit themselves to issuing *fatawa*, or edicts, on matters of religion, family or social affairs, but issue them on political affairs too, advising followers on questions such as whether to vote in or boycott elections.[26] For Sunnis, including those in Bahrain, the Shi'ites could not be trusted because they recognized an authority, often a foreigner, above the political leadership in their own country.[27]

There is also little doubt that Iran's 1979 Islamic Revolution, which allowed Grand Ayatollah Ruhollah Khomeini to transform his theory of *wilayet al-faqih*, or the vice-regency of the jurist, into an experiment in direct political rule by religious clerics, both emboldened Shi'ite activists in Arab countries and alarmed Sunni political leaders. Khomeini set about trying to export his revolution – and many Arab Shi'ites were keen to import it.

Whereas Gulf governments were previously focused on suppressing leftist and Arab nationalist activists, in the 1980s their attention turned to this new threat. In 1981, Bahrain's government uncovered what it said was an Iranian-backed plot to overthrow the monarchy and install a theocratic state.[28] Most of the seventy-three people eventually sentenced over the failed coup were Bahraini, and none was Iranian. But the coup attempt along with a spate of attacks by Iranian-inspired Shi'ite groups in the Gulf and Lebanon during the 1980s, were serious enough to encourage the nascent Gulf Cooperation Council, a six-member economic and political bloc of Sunni-ruled Arab countries, to push ahead with joint security arrangements and move towards setting up the joint defence force that was dispatched to Bahrain in 2011.[29]

Tensions with the new Shi'ite Islamic Republic across the Gulf inflamed sectarian feeling around the region, not least in Bahrain, where Shi'ites comprised, depending on which statistics you believe, a larger proportion of the population than in any other Arab country. Sectarian sensitivities were such that breakdowns of Bahrain's demographic balance had not been published since 1941, when a survey conducted under British auspices estimated that Shi'ites comprised 53 per cent of the population and Sunnis 47 per cent. The population of Bahrain was less than 90,000 that year and had grown to more than 1.2 million on the eve of revolt, though half of them were expatriate workers.[30] Of the Bahraini nationals, estimates vary from claims by Shi'ite activists that their community accounts for 75 per cent, to claims by establishment Sunnis that the population is split broadly in half. The truth, as is often the case, probably lies somewhere in between.[31]

Divisions in Bahrain were further inflamed by the fact that the sectarian divide was broadly mirrored by the class divide. Most of Bahrain's Shi'ites are descended from peasant farmers and have tended to occupy the lower socio-economic classes, suffering disproportionately from unemployment and low incomes compared to other communities, who tend to hail from wealthier merchant families or be tied to powerful tribes or landowners.[32]

Of course, this is a generalization. There are also struggling Sunni families and wealthy Shi'ite families. Big-business families such as Jawad, who own a chain of supermarkets, and Hawwaj, who are behind the country's foremost chain of cosmetics and pharmaceuticals stores, are Shi'ite multi-millionaires. Shi'ite doctors, engineers and architects have built large, gated villas on the edges of their villages. Bahrainis are well-educated in general, and Shi'ite professionals are well-represented in the private sector. But the overall economic divisions exacerbate feelings of discrimination among Bahrain's Shi'ites, who point to the dilapidated roads in their villages and the poor state of housing as evidence of institutional preference for their Sunni compatriots.

Such institutional bias is difficult to prove or quantify, but a drive around Bahrain reveals a glaring contrast between the manicured lawns and well-lit streets of Sunni towns and the dilapidated warrens of ramshackle housing in some Shi'ite areas.

It was in the midst of rising unemployment and falling incomes that the 1990s uprising broke out. The suspension of the constitution and the crackdown on freedoms had been painfully felt by all Bahrainis and the economy had suffered. Leading Bahraini clerics and opposition leaders, including leftists and nationalists, had begun in 1992 to petition the then ruler, Sheikh Isa, to restore the constitution and hold elections. They had been ignored and the 1994 arrest of three Shi'ite clerics, accused by the government of being ringleaders in an attack on scantily-clad runners in a relay race, inflamed Shi'ite anger.[33] Their arrest came as unemployed Shi'ites picketed the labour ministry demanding jobs and that protest swelled in size as demands escalated. Security forces cracked down heavily on the protest and a new cycle of violence was sparked that would wrack Bahrain for the rest of the decade.

While the worst unrest and the most violent crackdowns of the 1990s took place in the Shi'ite villages, the end of emergency rule and the restoration of elections and political freedoms were demands that resonated among religious leaders, political activists, intellectuals and beleaguered businessmen across both religious communities.[34] Bahrain's constitutional movement was a national one, involving several high-profile Sunnis, but it was fiercely resisted by the Al Khalifa family who feared losing power after two centuries of treating Bahrain largely as a personal fiefdom.

A Decade of Hope and Frustration

The 2000s had been a decade of both hope and frustration for Bahrainis. On the death of his father in 1999, the new emir, soon to rename himself king, had promised an era of reform. In 2000, Hamad bin Isa Al Khalifa stunned the people of Sitra with a visit to the Shi'ite area that had been a hotbed of rebellion during the1990s uprising. Sitra, home to most of Bahrain's oil facilities, was paradoxically one of the poorest parts of the country, with youth unemployment rampant and schools and health services lacking.

Here was a king who was mixing with ordinary people, listening to their needs, and who appeared genuinely determined to turn a page on the bitter past. The people of Sitra and Shi'ites around Bahrain were jubilant. To many Bahrainis, it seemed the new king was serious about implementing reforms that would restore political life to the country and address the grievances of Shi'ites.[35]

In 2001, Hamad put forward the National Action Charter. This constitutional declaration promised to protect individual freedoms and equality, to restore the rule of law and to work towards a constitutional monarchy with a bicameral parliament and separation of powers.[36] Following assurances to Shi'ite religious leaders that the elected parliament would be empowered, an extraordinary 98.4 per cent of Bahraini voters approved the document.[37]

The new ruler lifted the State Security Law that had been in force since 1975 and had effectively suspended the political freedoms and constitutional rights of Bahrainis. Political prisoners and exiles were pardoned and the State Security Court, used to try political opponents in the 1990s, was closed down.[38] It seemed the country really was changing and Bahraini society was buoyed up by a genuine excitement about what the future might bring.

Political parties remained banned, but opposition activists were allowed to form political societies that effectively played the same role. In 2002 alone, sixty-five civil society organizations were set up, including eleven political groups and thirteen professional associations. By the end of 2003, more than 300 NGOs had been created, including independent human rights groups.[39]

Among the significant political groups established was Al Wefaq, or Harmony. Al Wefaq brought together several mainly Shi'ite Islamist opposition groups and figures under the leadership of the youthful cleric Sheikh Ali Salman. Another prominent group was Waad, or Promise, a secular leftist group that was led from 2005 by the Sunni opposition activist Ibrahim Sharif. These groups devised political programmes and began to hold meetings that openly discussed their vision for the future of Bahrain.

King Hamad allowed the establishment of the country's first opposition newspaper, *Al-Wasat*, or the Centre, in 2002. Its editor-in-chief Mansoor al-Jamri was the son of the late Sheikh Abdul Amir al-Jamri, who had been the country's top Shi'ite cleric, an MP in the dissolved 1973 parliament and a leader of the 1990s uprising who had spent years in detention. Over the ensuing decade, *Al-Wasat* played an important role in opening up political debate, criticizing ministerial policies, breaking taboos and publishing investigative features almost unheard of in the hitherto staid and loyalist Bahraini press.

The new reforms were not limited to politics either. Crown Prince Salman bin Hamad Al Khalifa, educated in Washington and at Cambridge

University, was little older than thirty when his father became king, and was put in charge of implementing the new reforms, which stretched to housing and urban development. The crown prince began a programme of economic reforms that sought to encourage foreign investment, to increase transparency and to break the stranglehold of old patronage networks run by his uncle, the prime minister.

Hopes were high, so when the king finally promulgated a new constitution in 2002, as promised by the National Action Charter, many Bahrainis were disappointed by what appeared to be an effort to concentrate power in the ruler's hands behind a facade of elections to a disempowered parliament. While the charter had stipulated a bicameral system, many were dismayed that the appointed upper house would have the same legislative powers as the elected house and would be able to block its laws. Any laws would have to be passed by a majority in both houses and be approved by the king, who could also pass his own rulings by decree.[40] The shape of the new constitution, and the way it was issued by unilateral decree and without further consultation, revived a deep-seated mistrust of the monarchy's intentions among politically active Bahrainis. Many opposition groups now felt that, despite the new assurances of broader political participation, power over the judicial, legislative and executive branches of government, and the resources of the country, would remain firmly in the hands of the Al Khalifa family.[41]

Despite the disappointment over the new constitution, life in Bahrain improved for many. After boycotting the 2002 elections, Al Wefaq and its allies ran in both the 2006 and the 2010 elections. Al Wefaq won seventeen and eighteen seats respectively in the forty-seat chamber, cementing its place as the most popular opposition group and the single largest representative of Bahraini Shi'ites.

Once inside parliament, Al Wefaq raised sensitive corruption cases and led a groundbreaking parliamentary probe into land deals that appeared to blur the line between private- and public-sector property. The outspoken and combative attitude of Al Wefaq and other opposition groups broadened the scope of public discussion in Bahrain.[42] Politics was back and the media became more outspoken, taking advantage of the new opening that now made Bahrain the most politically vibrant Gulf country after Kuwait.

The economy was also booming. Riding a wave of oil price rises that had enriched the Gulf Arab region, Bahrain built hotels and luxury apartment blocks, reclaiming land to use for new developments. The crown prince was instrumental in bringing Formula One motor racing to the island. The inaugural Grand Prix was held in 2004, putting Bahrain on the map and attracting thousands of visitors with cash to splash each year.

Yet eight years after elections were reintroduced, it felt to some that participation in the electoral process would not translate into influence on state policy. While almost half the elected parliament was Shi'ite, only a handful of Shi'ites had been appointed to the cabinet since the introduction of the 2002 constitution. This reinforced the impression of a systematic effort to keep them from high office and a growing sense that elections were just democratic window-dressing for what remained a near-absolute monarchy.

The monarchy's domination of government also raised the ire of prominent Sunni families, who felt they too were being locked out of politics. Of twenty-five ministerial portfolios, twelve were held by members of the Al Khalifa family in 2010. These predictably included all the important ministries such as interior, defence, foreign affairs, finance and justice. The prime minister, Khalifa bin Salman Al Khalifa, was the king's uncle and had been premier since before independence in 1971. A conservative with close ties to Saudi Arabia and a vast web of businesses that the opposition believed posed serious conflicts of interest, Khalifa saw the new reforms as a threat.[43]

The king and the crown prince faced pressure from opposition groups and the Shi'ite community to speed up their political reforms, but at the same time were encountering strong resistance from Khalifa and other conservatives inside the royal family. Bahrain's new ruler was also facing resistance from Saudi Arabia, which was concerned that Bahrain's reforms were moving too fast and could awaken political ambitions among nationals across the Gulf region, who lived largely under absolute and hereditary rulers.[44]

The limits of Bahrain's ability to pursue such dramatic policy shifts without Saudi blessing, came into stark relief when it signed a free trade agreement with the United States in 2004 without the consent of its neighbour. Bahrain, part of the Gulf Cooperation Council, already enjoyed free trade with the six members of that economic and political bloc. Outraged by this display of independence, Saudi Arabia cut the 50,000 barrels-per-day donation of additional oil it granted to Bahrain from the shared Abu Safa field.[45]

Bahrain's experiment with political reform was also taking place in a tense regional atmosphere that complicated what may otherwise have been seen as largely domestic policies. Sectarian tension had already increased across the Middle East with the invasion of Iraq, which toppled a Sunni ruler and ushered in a new era in which the Shi'ite community, would dominate government. From the point of view of Saudi Arabia, the biggest winner from the 2003 invasion was Iran, which enjoyed good relations with the Baghdad government, and influence among Shi'ite Islamist groups it had supported during years in exile. In 2004, Jordan's King Abdullah spoke with concern about the rise of what he described as a 'Shi'ite crescent' stretching from Iran through Iraq all the way to Lebanon on the Mediterranean coast.

Al-Qaeda and other Sunni extremists reacted to this Shi'ite resurgence with violence, recruiting suicide bombers from around the Arab world. Huge car bombs began to go off in Iraq's Shi'ite neighbourhoods and outside Shi'ite mosques on festival days, while Shi'ite militias ran amok as sectarian violence reached new highs.

It was not just Iraq that became a proxy battleground in the rivalry between Saudi Arabia and Iran, but Lebanon too. A standoff between Saudi-backed Sunnis and Iranian-backed Shi'ites pushed that country from one political crisis to the next in the late 2000s. Tiny Bahrain could not escape this new regional context.

For Saudi Arabia, political reform in Bahrain posed an additional threat. Successful reforms could raise expectations among Saudi Arabia's own Shi'ite Muslims, who were clustered in the Eastern Province, home to most of the country's oil facilities, and were linked to their co-religionists in Bahrain by the King Fahd Causeway.

By the mid-2000s, in a regional atmosphere of growing sectarian tension, and faced with serious opposition to reform from inside the royal camp, trust was beginning to erode. The 'Bandargate' scandal that erupted in 2006 appeared to confirm the worst fears of Bahrain's Shi'ites. Salah Bandar, a British-Sudanese government adviser, blew the whistle on a secret five-year plan by a senior royal to exacerbate sectarian tensions and minimize the representation of Shi'ite groups who had decided to run in the 2006 elections.[46] The report was never substantiated and opposition groups went on to perform respectably in the polls, but it is widely seen by Shi'ites as proof that behind the facade of reform, there was a conspiracy to keep their community down.

Increasingly, Bahraini Shi'ites complained that non-Bahraini Sunnis were being encouraged to immigrate for work and apply for citizenship in a systematic effort to alter the country's religious, national and social fabric. State officials said foreigners were naturalized in accordance with the law, which requires that Arabs live in Bahrain for fifteen years, and non-Arabs for twenty-five years. However, the law makes allowances for Arabs who have offered unspecified 'great services', and it gives the king the right to grant citizenship to whomsoever he pleases.

In 2008, the government announced that it had naturalized just 7,012 people in the previous five years, including nearly 3,600 Asians and over 3,300 Arabs.[47] It did not give their religions, but their nationalities suggest they are likely to have been Sunni. In 2001, the government naturalized 8,000 Saudi members of the Dawasir tribe, who continued to hold Saudi passports and live across the bridge, while also giving citizenship to about 1,000 stateless Shi'ites.[48]

Activists complained that the real numbers were far larger and accused the monarchy of diluting any opening-up of the political arena with 'political naturalization' of Sunnis. By 2007, estimates cited in a subsequently leaked US embassy cable suggested that almost 40,000 people had received Bahraini passports, with controversy surrounding some 5,000 applications apparently rushed through ahead of the 2006 elections.[49] By 2009, the issue had become such a point of antagonism that MPs from the main Shi'ite opposition group, Al Wefaq, wore 'No to political naturalization' buttons on their clothing and held regular demonstrations against the practice.[50]

Whatever the sectarian balance in Bahrain, Shi'ites complained that their numbers were not reflected accurately at the ballot box because of gerrymandering. They said electoral constituencies were drawn up to give a disproportionate number of seats in parliament to sparsely-populated areas that were mainly Sunni, compared to densely-populated regions that were Shi'ite-dominated. This effectively meant that a Shi'ite vote was not worth as much as a Sunni vote. As Bahrainis have tended to broadly vote along sectarian lines since the country's first election in 1973,[51] the effect was to give Sunnis a slight majority in the elected house, even though Shi'ites are widely believed to outnumber them.[52]

Some Shi'ite activists also claimed that efforts were afoot to segregate Bahrain by refusing to sell land in some Sunni-majority areas to Shi'ites. In 2007, a Shi'ite cleric complained to the US embassy that Shi'ites had been banned from buying land in the old town of Muharraq, a mostly Sunni island where he lived.[53] Others complain that they have not been able to buy land in the Rifaa area, home to a royal palace and to large numbers of Sunnis, since the mid-1990s. For Shi'ites living in nearby Sitra, being kept out of affluent and well-maintained Rifaa appeared to represent a deliberate obstacle to class mobility.[54]

1 Tanks and soldiers behind barbed wire in front of the Interior Ministry on Avenue Habib Bourguiba in central Tunis, January 2011, as protests continued following the departure of President Ben Ali.

2 Graffiti reading 'Merci le peuple! Merci Facebook!' on Rue de Rome, off Avenue Habib Bourguiba in Tunis, just after the ousting of Ben Ali in January 2011. Social media and the internet played an important role in mobilizing protests and raising awareness in Tunisia.

3 Protesters pray in Cairo's Tahrir Square on 31 January 2011, during the 18 days of rallies and protests that would end with President Hosni Mubarak stepping down from power.

4 A junction on Misrata's Tripoli Street shortly after the rebels broke a Gaddafi siege, May 2011. Misrata experienced amongst the worst damage of any Libyan city during the 2011 conflict.

5 Bahraini protesters chant slogans at the Pearl roundabout in the Bahraini capital Manama on 19 February 2011. The roundabout became a focal point for anti-government demonstrations.

6 Following a widespread crackdown on protests, the imposition of martial law and the arrival of GCC troops, the Pearl monument was demolished by the Bahraini authorities on 19 March 2011.

7 Thousands of Syrians attend a rally in support of President Bashar al-Assad in central Damascus, 29 March 2011. Earlier that month, anti-regime demonstrations had begun to spread from the southern town of Deraa.

8 Yemeni president Ali Abdullah Saleh greets Saudi Arabia's King Abdullah on 23 November 2011, shortly before signing the power transfer deal that saw him step down after 33 years in power. Riyadh played a central role in brokering the agreement.

9 Yemen's Tawakul Karman, a prominent figure in the 2011 anti-government demonstrations and the first female Arab winner of the Nobel peace prize, shows her ink-stained thumb after voting in Sana'a on 21 February 2012. The election saw Abed Rabah Mansoor al-Hadi, the only candidate, voted in to replace Ali Abdullah Saleh.

10 A member of the Free Syrian Army, with his face covered with the pre-Ba'ath Syrian flag, in Idlib, north-western Syria on 18 February 2012 as the armed rebellion against Bashar al-Assad gathered pace.

11 A caricature of Muammar Gaddafi and rebel fighters on a wall in the Ras Hassan area of Tripoli, January 2012.

12 US Secretary of State Hillary Clinton poses with Libyan soldiers in Tripoli on 18 October 2011. Two days later, the death of Muammar Gaddafi marked the end of a conflict in which the US played a vital political and military role.

13 At a huge rally in Cairo's Tahrir Square on 25 January 2012, Egyptian protesters hold an obelisk with the names of those killed during the uprising that began exactly a year earlier and toppled President Hosni Mubarak.

Even assuming there was no systematic effort to boost the ranks of the Sunni community, the rapid pace of population growth and the pattern of property development and land use pushed prices beyond the reach of lower-income citizens. The country's population doubled in the decade before 2011 and the number of Bahrainis, though increasingly overtaken by foreign workers, rose by 28 per cent, creating more competition for state benefits such as subsidised housing.[55]

Dissatisfaction with access to adequate housing was repeatedly raised as a major concern by protesters in 2011. A Gallup poll in late 2010 found that 41 per cent of Bahrainis and Arab expatriates had had problems paying for adequate shelter at least once in the previous twelve months, a sharp increase from a year earlier and higher than the seventeen other Arab countries surveyed.[56]

The issue of housing had become such a political hot potato that a Shi'ite housing minister was appointed early in the crisis in an effort to appease demonstrators. In February 2011, the minister said that more than 46,000 families were on the waiting list for subsidised property.[57] It was not clear what proportion of them were Sunni or Shi'ite, but a drive around Bahrain revealed major disparities in the quality of housing enjoyed by the two groups.

Jaafar's home was a case in point. 'I live with my brother and our wives on the second floor. On the ground floor, my three brothers have a room next to my mother's room ... If my six sisters had not gotten married and moved out, I don't know where we'd all sleep,' he said.[58]

Jaafar's sister, who was visiting with her children, agreed: 'I've been married eleven years and I'm living with my in-laws. We have had four children since then and the naturalized just get a key on arrival.'[59]

Shi'ites also complained increasingly of discrimination in security-related and senior diplomatic jobs, with the most common grievance related to the Bahrain Defence Force, the National Guard and various branches of the police, whose ranks they believe the ruling family had bolstered with Sunni Muslims imported from Jordan, Syria, Yemen or Pakistan.

Bahraini Shi'ites widely see these forces as little more than mercenaries hired to protect the royal family, having less compunction about firing at protesters than a Shi'ite soldier might, and believe they are fast-tracked into acquiring Bahraini citizenship. In the midst of the 2011 uprising, a trust with close links to the Pakistani army had taken out advertisements in Pakistani newspapers to recruit former soldiers for Bahrain's National

Guard.[60] Bahraini officials do not declare the number of non-Bahrainis or naturalized Bahrainis working for the security forces, but it is not uncommon to come across police who do not speak Arabic or who speak non-Gulf dialects of the language, adding anecdotal evidence that the practice is widespread.

By the time the Arab Spring brought people onto the streets in Tunis and Cairo, Bahrain's fragile political experiment was already threatening to unravel. Both the regional powerhouse Saudi Arabia and influential figures inside the royal family opposed change. It is difficult to gauge the true extent of King Hamad's personal commitment to reforms, but it was clear on the eve of the Arab Spring that opposition to greater liberalization had rendered him unable to fully satisfy all the hopes he had awakened on inheriting the throne.

For the Shi'ites, reforms had been bestowed as royal privileges, not as formal rights, and democracy had not been enshrined in the constitution. In the years leading up to the 2011 uprising, Bahrain witnessed repeated outbreaks of rioting that saw young Shi'ite protesters burn tyres in the streets. The number of activists and bloggers in jail or exile was mounting again.

With political freedoms once more being curtailed, Al Wefaq's position as representative of the Shi'ite community was being undermined. Increasing numbers of Shi'ites saw their participation in elections as part of a meaningless charade. Once in the assembly, they could raise issues of importance to the opposition, but they could not change the law. More and more Shi'ites were being drawn to more radical groups, such as Al-Haq, or The Right, which had rejected the elections and were calling for more fundamental changes.

Al Wefaq was campaigning for a full constitutional monarchy, but even this demand was too much for the royal family, which knew it would bring in a parliament dominated by Shi'ite opposition groups that could destabilize its rule and further bolster the regional influence of Iran.

The sensitivities inflamed by Iraq were further exacerbated by the speed with which the Tunisian and Egyptian leaders had apparently been abandoned by the United States. The North African experience suggested that the Al Saud family, who had provided a stable supply of oil to the world market and had operated beneath the US security umbrella since the Second World War, might not be able to rely on its old ally in the face of any serious domestic crisis.[61] The political ties cemented by Bahrain's decision to host the US Fifth Fleet, and the Gulf monarchies' status as a regional network of US allies and a bulwark against Iran, no longer seemed a watertight guarantee of US support. Even before the Arab Spring had brought a single person onto the streets of Manama, it was clear to the Gulf's Sunni rulers that a repeat of Tunisia or Cairo could not be allowed on their doorstep.

The Pearl Revolt

In the aftermath of Hosni Mubarak's departure in Egypt, revolutionary groups sprang up around the Arab world. In Libya, many coalesced around the 17 February protests in Benghazi. In Morocco, it was the 20 February youth movement. Bahrain's youths chose 14 February, a date which held the significance of being a full decade since the National Action Charter was approved. Calling for peaceful protests, the 14 February youth movement demanded a rewrite of the constitution that had proved such a disappointment nine years earlier, and an investigation into claims of high-level corruption and political naturalization, and allegations that activists who had been rounded up in recent years had been tortured in jail.

Uncomfortable with the sweeping scope of those demands, the king sought to sap the momentum of protesters by ordering that each family receive $1,000 to celebrate the anniversary of the charter. His gesture misread both the depth of frustration in Bahrain and the spirit of revolution that had by now infected the entire region and spread beyond it.

When 14 February came, the demonstrators only numbered in the hundreds but the ensuing crackdown inflamed anger and encouraged opposition. One protester was killed in the first day of demonstrations, and another police clampdown at his funeral procession the following day saw a second person lose their life. With the death toll mounting and public sympathy swelling, Al Wefaq, which had not been involved in organizing the demonstrations, swung behind the movement and withdrew from parliament. Angered by the deaths and emboldened by Al Wefaq's support, thousands of protesters stormed the Pearl roundabout, a traffic island ironically adorned by a monument to the GCC, and set up camp. The statue comprised six dhow sails, representing each of the members of the GCC, holding up a giant concrete pearl, a symbol of the region's pearl fishing heritage before the discovery of oil. On the grass beneath it, a sea of red and white flags fluttered in a conscious emulation of Tahrir Square. The scene alarmed the royals.

In the early hours of 17 February, Bahraini security forces attacked and cleared the site. Five people were killed and tanks filled the streets as the area went into lockdown. With images of the crackdown flashing across the world's television screens, the United States pressured Bahrain to withdraw its troops. Protesters were allowed to return and the crown prince offered talks. With the king's backing, he was given three or four weeks to deliver a political solution. If he failed, hardliners within the royal family would be allowed to push ahead with a military solution.[62] The head of the armed forces, Sheikh Khalifa bin Ahmed, and his brother, the royal court minister Sheikh Khaled bin Ahmed, were close to Saudi Arabia and agitating for a crackdown. The crown prince was in a delicate position.

So was Al Wefaq. The deaths had infuriated Bahrainis and hardened attitudes on the street. Fearing that any talks that did not secure concrete gains would cost them grass-roots support, Al Wefaq and its six opposition allies set a list of pre-conditions for talks that the crown prince could not publicly accept. The Crown Prince and the opposition immediately launched intensive secret contacts aimed at finding a way out of the crisis. Meanwhile, hardliners on both sides worked to polarize Bahraini society.

Less than a month after Bahrain's protesters had taken over the Pearl roundabout, tents filled the grassy verge and makeshift kitchens served kebabs and tea to the thousands who showed up each night to socialize and listen to the speakers on a central stage. Gory photographs of the seven Bahrainis killed in the first phase of the uprising were on display, along with demands for justice. Banners sought to calm fears of sectarian divisions. 'Sunni and Shi'ite are siblings in one nation,' they read. But with the middle ground increasingly squeezed, efforts to bring the crisis to the negotiating table were on the brink of failure.

By staying on the Pearl roundabout, protesters risked becoming irrelevant. Foreign journalists had already drifted away to cover faster-moving events in Yemen and Libya. The numbers converging on the roundabout each night had dwindled, sometimes amounting to only a few hundred. They either had to escalate or to accept talks.

On 8 March 2011, three groups – Al-Haq, the closely related Wafa, or Fidelity, and the London-based Bahrain Islamic Freedom Movement – held a news conference at the Pearl roundabout calling for the overthrow of the monarchy and the creation of a democratic republic. Two days later, a group of some 200 mostly Shi'ite protesters marched on the royal palace in Rifaa, an area that was home to royals, members of the armed forces and other establishment Sunnis. The protest did not attract many followers, largely because Al Wefaq had warned against escalation, and it caused splits inside the 14 February youth movement.

Undeterred, the following Sunday, the first day of the working week, protesters tried to stop employees from entering the Bahrain Financial Harbour, two modern towers that had become the symbol both of Bahrain's painstakingly-cultivated 'business-friendly' image and of top-level corruption. The protesters cut off the capital's main highway with tyres, rocks and other debris, disabling the road that connected Bahrain International Airport, on the mostly Sunni island of Muharraq, not only to the financial district but to the country's main shopping centres and ultimately to the King Fahd Causeway that runs across to Saudi Arabia. It was a clear provocation.

Efforts to clear protesters and reopen the highway descended into pitched battles that lasted hours. Hundreds of riot police were able to push the protesters from the Financial Harbour to the Pearl roundabout, but were met there by rock-throwing youths who disabled police tear gas cans by burying them in the sand. Eventually running out of tear gas, the police gave up and retreated, leaving the highway blocked and in the control of protesters as dusk fell. The next morning, youths had rolled barrels and bins onto the streets around the Pearl roundabout, setting up their own makeshift checkpoints that waved cars through.[63]

This was a turning point. Bahrain was no stranger to riots and clashes but this was the first time that the protesters had taken over a central zone and frozen the financial heart of the country. Sectarian clashes broke out at Bahrain University. Fights erupted between Sunni and Shi'ite schoolchildren. Misunderstandings about parking spaces and other trivial conflicts were quickly escalating. Bloggers and commentators began to warn that the country was on the brink of civil war.[64]

For the Al Saud family, which had united and ruled over a country of 28 million stretching from the holy cities of Mecca and Medina near the Red Sea to the vital Gulf oilfields, the risks were simply too great to be left to chance. An absolute monarchy, Saudi Arabia suffered from many of the same problems that afflicted other Arab countries. It was flush from a prolonged oil price boom, but had unemployment of above 40 per cent in some age brackets and a youthful, quick-growing population.[65] Billions of riyals in stipends and other benefits were distributed each year among the royal family, which included thousands of princes and princesses, while many Saudis lived on low incomes or in areas with dilapidated infrastructure and inadequate housing.[66]

Even before the Arab Spring, Saudi Arabia had been facing an uncertain future. Those waiting in line to the Saudi throne were now in their eighties. Even if the ruling family succeeded in subduing unrest and sidelining any serious opposition from within the royal family, it could expect a turbulent decade ahead as more of its members passed away, resulting in frequent changes at the top.

Inspired by events in Tunisia and Egypt, Shi'ites in the Eastern Province had already been holding small-scale regular protests. Calls on Facebook for a 'Day of Rage' in March had been met with warnings that protests would not be tolerated, while an overwhelming security presence had emerged on the streets of Riyadh and Saudi clerics issued a *fatwa* labelling protests un-Islamic. In the event, there was no unrest in the capital, but the Arab Spring had heightened political awareness and raised expectations. King Abdullah was now forced to buy off dissent with a massive package of pay rises, benefit increases and promises to ease unemployment and a housing crunch.

Protests had also broken out in Oman which, like Bahrain, was running out of oil and was short on cash. Shortly before the crackdown, the GCC had promised Oman and Bahrain $10 billion each to help maintain order. But in Bahrain, the crisis only seemed to escalate.

Riyadh was not willing to stand by and let the United States try to steer a middle course that could threaten the Al Khalifa, embolden Shi'ite protesters in Saudi Arabia itself and risk the kind of domino effect in the Gulf that would see off three North African leaders in a single year. Revolution, or even serious reform, in Bahrain would send a signal to activists everywhere that Saudi Arabia was willing to stand aside under popular pressure. From Riyadh's point of view, a strong signal was necessary to show that it would defend its allies.

The United States was reluctant to jeopardize its historically-close relations with Saudi Arabia. It was also loath to upset the Bahraini royal family and see the US Navy's Fifth Fleet, whose aircraft carriers were used for airstrikes on Iraq and Afghanistan, evicted from an island that lay just across the water from Iran. Its presence in the Gulf had taken on added importance as the last US combat troops prepared to leave Iraq. The US approach to the Bahrain crisis appears to have involved pushing for faster top-down reforms to sap the momentum of protesters and limit the chances of full-scale revolution that would destabilize the region and shake oil markets.

While criticizing the crackdown in Bahrain, the United States knew that the overthrow of the Al Khalifa family by Shi'ite-led protesters would be a foreign policy win for Iran, and that it had good customers with deep pockets in Sunni allies that were seeking to deter the Islamic Republic. Notwithstanding regular claims of meddling by Bahrain's rulers, Tehran was unlikely to risk a conflagration with the United States or Saudi Arabia by arming Shi'ite protesters in Bahrain. For the United States, the best outcome would be one that defused the crisis by coaxing both sides to agree on reforms. With tensions rising on the streets of Bahrain, however, it seemed that the Saudis were in no mood to listen.

On 12 March, US Secretary of State Robert Gates' planned visit to Saudi Arabia was cancelled with just a few days' notice by Riyadh. Gates went straight to Bahrain instead, where he told the king that 'baby steps' on reform would not be enough.

With the crisis worsening, the crown prince renewed his call for national dialogue. In a new bid to lure them into talks, he now set out seven points of importance to the opposition that were open to serious discussion. The talks would address demands to bolster the power of the elected parliament and to redraw the electoral districts that the Shi'ites complained were deliberately skewed against them. The composition of the government would also be up for debate, as would complaints of corruption, sectarian discrimination and accusations about Sunni naturalization. The reforms agreed through dialogue would then be put to a referendum, the crown prince promised.

Moments after his call was read out on Bahrain TV, a speaker at the Pearl roundabout shouted 'No to dialogue, no to dialogue'. The crowd cheered. The opposition parties were in a difficult position, caught between this confrontational sentiment on the street and their instinct to avert a new crackdown. Al Wefaq decided to reject the talks.

The next day, 1,000 Saudi troops rolled across the causeway in an advance party that included tanks and armoured personnel carriers, and would be bolstered over the ensuing days. The intervention, whose participants grew to include the UAE and Kuwait, sent the message that any attack on one Gulf Arab ruling family would be considered an attack on all. While the forces sent to Bahrain were only there to protect strategic locations, the symbolism was not lost on protesters around the region who thought that popular action alone could bring down any regime.

Assistant US Secretary of State Jeffrey Feltman arrived in Bahrain the same day to push for a peaceful resolution to the crisis. In what looked like an eleventh-hour deal, the opposition announced that it had met the crown prince and agreed a mechanism for national dialogue. It appeared, however, to have come too late. [67]

By the time martial law was declared on 15 March 2011, power had already been transferred to Sheikh Khalifa bin Ahmed, the commander of the Bahrain Defence Forces, and the royal reformers had been effectively sidelined.[68] Early the next morning, the Pearl roundabout encampment was cleared in a hail of tear gas and over the ensuing days, the Pearl monument would be demolished and replaced by a traffic interchange, in what the foreign minister described as an effort to erase 'bad memories'. A night-time curfew was imposed. Tanks surrounded the former Pearl roundabout and checkpoints were set up all over the main roads. Security forces launched a systematic crackdown against anyone associated with the uprising. Bahrain had returned to its bleak cycle of protests, violent crackdowns and funeral processions.

Even before the crackdown had begun, the information war was in full flow, inflaming sectarian tensions in a way that alarmed and tainted the largely peaceful demonstrators who had been meticulous in their focus on political demands that would appeal to both Sunni and Shi'ite. Bahraini TV spoke of Sunni patients being denied medical attention at Salmaniya hospital. When scuffles broke out at schools and universities between Sunni and Shi'ite students, Bahrain TV accused Shi'ites of running riot, prompting Sunni vigilantes to set up checkpoints to protect their neighbourhoods from imaginary attack.

The channel accused Shi'ite protesters of loyalty to Iran, and of planning to set up a Bahraini Hezbollah, akin to the Lebanese armed group that answers to Tehran. Despite scant evidence, the Bahraini government repeatedly accused Iran and Hezbollah of interference during the 2011 uprising, though most of this meddling appeared to come in the form of media statements and solidarity protests.[69] Iran and Bahrain engaged in tit-for-tat diplomatic expulsions and registered complaints with the United Nations, Tehran criticizing the crackdown that drew a muted Western response and Bahrain criticizing Iran's interference in its affairs.[70]

But at the same time, Iran's Arabic-language Alalam channel was painting a picture of a Saudi invasion to crush the Bahraini people. As Bahraini security forces backed by helicopters cleared the protest camp on 16 March 2011, mainly using tear gas and military vehicles, Alalam was reporting that Saudi fighter jets were hovering above the Pearl roundabout. The Iraqi Shi'ite channel Ahlulbayt painted the crackdown as sectarian cleansing, causing alarm among Shi'ites who were increasingly incited to view Sunnis as their enemies.[71] Lebanon's Hezbollah-owned Al Manar also weighed in and when its leader Hassan Nasrallah gave a speech supporting the Bahraini protesters, it only appeared to prove government accusations that this was an Iranian-backed plot. In response, Bahrain suspended flights to Lebanon and expelled some Lebanese from the country. Meanwhile, the frequent appearance of Shi'ite opposition activists on pro-Iranian channels appalled Sunnis, who saw this as evidence of the protesters' divided loyalties and of Iranian meddling.

Qatari-owned Al-Jazeera, which had given wall-to-wall coverage to the uprisings in Tunisia and Egypt, providing some of the momentum they needed to succeed, was more muted on Bahrain. The protests were covered, but as routine events rather than revolutions-in-the-making. Neither Qatar nor Saudi Arabia, who own the major Arab satellite news networks, were interested in spreading the unrest to the shores of the Gulf.

Carried away by what they saw as a historic opportunity to ride the wave of revolution sweeping Arab countries, Bahrain's protesters had overplayed their hand, undermining reformers inside the ruling family, antagonizing Saudi Arabia and ending 2011 in a far worse position than they had begun it. Both in the royal camp and in the opposition camp, hardliners had won the day.

The crisis had quickly taken on more of a sectarian dimension than the 1990s uprising. Some Sunnis such as Sheikh Abdel Latif Mahmood, who had been in the opposition camp in the 1990s and made efforts to expand the a middle ground early in 2011, ended up staunchly in the monarchist camp and blamed the Shi'ites for escalating the conflict and turning it sectarian. Some Sunni opposition leaders, such as Waad's Ibrahim Sharif, were arrested in the crackdown, but the vast majority of those rounded up were Shi'ites.

Martial law was lifted in June and many of those who had been detained were freed or put on trial. Through the summer, however, it increasingly appeared that reformists within the royal family had lost ground. When the king made a speech in August 2011, pardoning protesters, promising to investigate abuses and ordering the reinstatement of those expelled from their jobs or universities for taking part in protests, his orders were not immediately implemented. The episode suggested some personal loss of authority for the king. Both he and the crown prince were sounding a more conciliatory note than many ordinary Sunnis who had welcomed the Gulf troops and had come to see the protesters as little more than traitors.

For many Shi'ites, it was too late for reform anyway. 'For Hani's mother, no reform will bring her son back. He was not even killed at a protest. So are the Shi'ites not people?' said Khadija, a mourner at the funeral in Bilad al-Qadim in March 2011. Zahra, a neighbour of Abdelaziz, agreed: 'Al Wefaq are scared for their seats and we don't care. People have got to the stage where they don't want dialogue. They want these people out.'[72] But that was unlikely to happen without an equally monumental shift in Bahrain's neighbour.

Saudi Arabia's decision to give shelter to Ben Ali, its outrage at the ouster of Mubarak, and its bold decision to intervene in Bahrain has seen it labelled as the main counter-revolutionary force to emerge in 2011. To simply call it counter-revolutionary, as the final section of this book argues, oversimplifies its role. But the Gulf has certainly emerged as a red line for Saudi Arabia in a year that would see protests spread from the Mediterranean to the Red Sea.

The Immovable Object

Efforts at healing the wounds opened up by the crackdown and the Gulf intervention had floundered by the end of 2011. A National Dialogue held by the king in July did not come across to dissidents as a serious effort to address the grievances of opposition parties. It involved some 300 participants from all walks of Bahraini society and the political opposition received just thirty-five seats, drowning out their voices. Participants eventually agreed to give the elected parliament a greater degree of scrutiny over government, reforms that were approved by the king. They were unable, however, to agree on measures to empower the elected lower house vis-à-vis the appointed upper chamber.[73]

Al Wefaq at first joined the dialogue, but withdrew when it realized that no major concessions were on the table. After taking part in 2006 and 2010 elections, it refused to participate in the September 2011 by-elections to fill the eighteen seats vacated by MPs who had resigned during the February uprising. Amid opposition calls for a boycott, turnout was a dire 17 per cent. The result, predictably, was a lower house with a dismal number of Shi'ite representatives and no opposition deputies at all.[74]

Gone were the days when Al Wefaq and its allies took part in a lopsided political process in the hope of building trust and effecting gradual change from within. In October 2011, Bahrain's alliance of opposition parties issued the Manama Document, which called once more for direct negotiations between the opposition parties and the royal family. Up for discussion would be reforms to empower the elected house and bring in an elected government, but this time the parties also warned that the alternative to talks was more unrest.

The bilateral dialogue the opposition had demanded from the start was not to be. Instead, the government placed enormous emphasis on an independent investigation it had commissioned in June into whether security forces had violated international human rights law during the crackdowns.

The calibre of the investigating team, led by respected Egyptian-American human rights lawyer Cherif Bassiouni, went some way to inspiring trust in the Bahrain Independent Commission of Inquiry (BICI), and its findings made for grim reading. The commission found that Bahrain's security forces had used excessive force to suppress protests. It said a total of thirty-five people had been killed, including five security personnel, and that five people had died as a result of torture in custody. It also charged that the security services and interior ministry followed 'a systematic practice of physical and psychological mistreatment, which amounted in many cases to torture, with respect to a large number of detainees'.[75]

In light of the findings, Bahrain referred to the public prosecutor all cases of abuse involving the police. It also hired senior US policeman John Timoney, and John Yates, a former Assistant Commissioner of the UK Metropolitan Police, to help reform the police force and establish a code of conduct.[76] King Hamad set up a commission to lead reforms and stopped all cases against the country's athletes. But to those in the opposition camp, the BICI report smacked too much of an effort by the state to draw a line under the crisis that had shaken the economy and badly damaged Bahrain's overseas image.[77]

Seeing the BICI as little more than a publicity stunt aimed at proving to the international community that the government was accountable and transparent, Al Wefaq and other opposition parties remained unconvinced. The problem for Bahrain's opposition was the government's effort to treat the 2011 uprising as an unfortunate incident, a blip in an otherwise smooth trajectory of reform, reconciliation and growth, a problem that could be resolved by sacking a few police officers, releasing some prisoners and improving its rights record. For them, none of those measures addressed the political grievances that had precipitated the uprising and that still festered unresolved.

While it has never called for the overthrow of the monarchy and has consistently pushed for more meaningful and speedier reforms, Al Wefaq's constituency remains angry over the deaths, the arrests, the beatings and torture that took place in jail, the mass redundancies suffered by Shi'ites and the clampdowns on protests that felt increasingly like collective punishment.

Government supporters, meanwhile, have been persistently told that the Shi'ites are partners in an Iranian plot to bring down the whole system, though the BICI report found no evidence of Iranian meddling. Many Sunnis no longer believe that the Shi'ites will be content with reforms alone. Many are convinced that the more the royal family gives, the more the Shi'ites will demand and the weaker the regime will appear. The king and the crown prince have faced severe pressure from inside the royal family and from the wider Sunni community not to appear soft and not to give away more concessions. Their true commitment to change was unclear. They were willing to offer enough reforms to ease unrest and placate the Shi'ites and other opponents, but it now appeared they would stop short of ceding any real power to ordinary Bahrainis, whatever their religious beliefs.

The sectarian dimension taken on by the conflict poisoned Bahraini society in 2011, even though divisions in the country had not been simply sectarian in nature. Demands for more political rights had crossed religious divides. Historically, both Sunnis and Shi'ites had been involved in union and nationalist movements.

But in the battle for the aftermath of Bahrain's own spring, people who had previously called for unity found themselves pressured to join one or another camp. Though the Al Khalifa family has not attempted to legitimize its rule using any religious rationale and has generally not attempted to suppress Shi'ite religious practices,[78] a campaign to knock down unlicenced *Husseiniat*, small Shi'ite mosques, or *ma'atim*, the funeral halls used during the commemoration of 'Ashura and other Shi'ite holidays, could only have been felt as a collective punishment by the Shi'ite community.[79]

Even before thousands of Shi'ites had been expelled from jobs and universities, the hope that had marked King Hamad's ascension to the throne had faded. The curfews and crackdowns on Shi'ite villages, along with the information war, created two different experiences and narratives of the uprising, and widened divisions.

The intervention of Gulf personnel, particularly from Saudi Arabia, complicated efforts to find a middle ground. Bahrain's Shi'ites, saw the intervention as an attack by a Sunni royal family in Riyadh that had survived largely through its pact with a group of religious zealots who would not tolerate any kind of diversity at home and were holding back change in their neighbours. In reality, Bahrain's sovereignty was materially compromised even before the Gulf intervention. Its financial reliance on Saudi Arabia meant that its monarchy could not always act independently and the economic impact of the 2011 uprising, which saw companies decamp to Dubai and the Formula One Grand Prix cancelled for the year, only reinforced Bahrain's dependence on oil and on Saudi largesse.

Yet Bahraini grievances cannot be resolved with armed force. Major popular movements for reform and rights have taken place throughout the past century and are likely to continue as long as the current regime monopolizes power.

Bahrain has been spared armed conflict by the simple fact that its people are unarmed, resorting to rock-throwing and petrol bombs when faced with police. Unlike countries with porous borders like Libya, Yemen or even Egypt, Bahrainis who wish to turn to more violent means of pushing for change will face huge difficulties getting their hands on weapons. Instead, violence has taken the form of makeshift bombs. Five blasts rocked the country in November 2012, killing two migrant workers. The government blamed Shi'ite activists it claimed were trained by Hezbollah and acting in Iranian interests. The Lebanese group accused the Bahraini government of staging the attacks to justify its crackdown on opponents. The incident seemed merely to reinforce the chasm that has opened up in Bahraini society.

Even if the fight does become militarized, protesters will be no match for Gulf forces equipped by the United States and funded with oil wealth. Bahrain's opposition cannot rely on international help. US President Barack Obama's advice to the Al Khalifa family to engage Al Wefaq directly in serious talks was well received by the opposition, but Washington is unlikely to take action against its old ally nor further undermine its relationship with Saudi Arabia. With Iran's nuclear programme persistently near the top of the foreign policy agenda, the US is unlikely to endanger its naval presence in the Gulf and its close ties with Saudi Arabia.

By the end of 2011, trust between the Al Khalifa family and the Shi'ites had broken down, and trust between the Shi'ite and Sunni communities had reached a new low. What happened in 2011 and 2012 has set Bahrain's political process back years, and it will take major concessions from both sides to restore the trust that had already begun to fade before the Pearl revolt. In the meantime, the country appears set for a period of prolonged unrest that risks further polarizing society and radicalizing increasing sections of the opposition. Those Bahrainis seeking meaningful reforms were increasingly coming to realize they were unlikely to see their wishes fulfilled until there was major change in Saudi Arabia and a monumental shift in Western foreign policy. Libyans, in contrast, faced no such hurdles in toppling their own leader.

CHAPTER 7

Libya's Revolution from Above

Be generous to the soldiers, and take no heed of anyone else.
          – Roman emperor Septimus Severus,
              born in Leptis Magna, Libya, AD 145

A portrait of Muammar Gaddafi used to hang in the customs hall at Tripoli International Airport, head wrapped in traditional cloth and eyes masked behind reflective sunglasses. 'Partners not wage workers', read a nearby sign. A mute line of newly-arrived Korean or Chinese construction workers, already in shiny overalls and orange hard hats, waited to have their passports processed by customs officials who wielded a stamp in one hand and a cigarette in another. Young families returning from a holiday in Europe breezed through the desks reserved for Libyans only, while sweating Western businessmen in the queue marked 'foreigners' muttered expletives under their breath.

Endearingly amateurish posters on the back wall advertised Libya's world-class archaeological sites like Leptis Magna or Sabratha. Nearby, a glass cabinet displayed the dusty wares of the local duty-free company, including an inauspicious male aftershave called 'Surge' and some antique-looking packs of Lego. A faded billboard showing a Green Book emitting rays of sunshine across the world, circa 1978, stood over the baggage reclaim belts downstairs.

In the waiting hall, cockroaches occasionally scuttled under metal chairs occupied by transit passengers from Bamako, Conakry or Cotonou bound for London, Paris or Brussels. It was rumoured that drug mules flying in from sub-Saharan Africa would secrete their stash in the ceiling panels of the toilets, where corrupt airport officials would later collect them. A desk in the corner of the hall sold more legitimate products, including colourful sheets of postage stamps extolling various aspects of life in Gaddafi's Libya. They ranged from light-hearted pieces, such as 'Flora and Fauna of the Jamahiriya', to others with a graver political slant like 'American Aggression 1986', an arty tableau of images telling the story of Ronald Reagan's Operation Eldorado Canyon.

Outside on the tarmac lay sparkling new Airbus planes sporting the insignia of Afriqiyah Airways, their interiors decked out in green synthetic leather and tailfins decorated with the 9.9.99 date of the Sirte Declaration that called for the formation of the African Union. Next to the dilapidated terminal, a fleet of cranes and cement mixers were thumping away at what was planned to be one of Africa's biggest new airports. Like many of the major projects that Libya embarked upon in the mid-2000s, it was given the hopelessly ambitious deadline of 1 September 2009, the fortieth anniversary of the *'fateh* revolution'. By the time the 2011 uprising began it was already about four years behind schedule.

This was Gaddafi's Libya in the final years of his marathon rule. A bizarre mishmash of new and old, sinister and comic, rich and poor, mundane and unique. A hall of mirrors in which no one really knew what was happening, or who was in charge. A country with breathtaking scenery whose people are among the friendliest in the region. A canvas for competing global interests and a must-visit destination for those seeking cash at a time when funds were drying up almost everywhere else. The diversity of individuals who passed through Tripoli in those years ranged from Steven Schwartzman, CEO of Blackstone, one of the world's largest private equity firms, to Omar Hassan al-Bashir, the Sudanese president wanted by the International Criminal Court (ICC) for crimes against humanity.[1] With so many high-profile courtiers, it was not surprising that Gaddafi and his sons seemed shocked to find themselves almost totally friendless in their hour of need.

That hour would not have come – at least not in 2011 – without the dramatic events unfolding in Tunisia and Egypt, whose successful uprisings inspired disillusioned groups in Libya with various axes to grind. But even they would have failed to tear down the Gaddafi regime without a controversial military intervention that has been variously described as everything from a neo-imperial regime change to a humanitarian rescue mission. It moved Libya's revolt and the entire Arab Spring into a new phase. Over a long, hot summer, the ensuing conflict killed tens of thousands of people, armed hundreds of thousands more, and eventually found closure shortly after a bloodied man was dragged out of a concrete drainpipe in Sirte on 20 October.

That conflict could be best defined by a simple faultline. It was waged between those who fought for Gaddafi, and those who fought against him. But with that question answered by the end of 2011, it broke down into a cacophony of other battles as different domestic groups staked their claim to power and perks in the new Libya. Simmering racial and tribal tensions, bottled up for decades, reared their heads in the absence of a strong central state and the presence of abundant weapons. Islamic extremists, crushed or watched carefully by Gaddafi, were free to make their voices heard. Other, more subtle hostilities divided international powers who sought their own rewards for supporting the uprising.

On one level, Libya has achieved the most far-reaching and surprising change of any country in the Arab Spring. By the end of 2012, it had held free and fair elections, sworn in a new government and restored oil output to pre-conflict levels. But that same change has brought lawlessness, violence and a penchant for devouring its children - or at least its midwives. Unlike Tunisia or Egypt, the battle over the role of religion has not been the central one in the aftermath of Libya's revolution. Understanding the battle for the future of Libya requires going back to consider how Gaddafi was removed in the first place, and what the country has inherited from a man whose legacy will take decades to dissipate.

The Man who Came in from the Cold

On 29 May 2007, with a grinning Tony Blair by his side, BP chief executive Tony Hayward signed a landmark agreement with Shukri Ghanem, the chairman of Libya's National Oil Corporation (NOC). Under its terms, the British energy company would invest a minimum of $900m to prospect for oil in what BP called its 'single largest exploration commitment'.[2] One of the concession blocks it had secured was as big as Kuwait, and the deal was noteworthy not just for its size but for its political message. Libya was open for business, and even its former enemies were scrambling to get through the door.

The agreement came three years after Blair had first visited Gaddafi in Tripoli and shaken his hand to end two decades of diplomatic warfare. For London and Washington, rehabilitating the Libyan leader from malevolent pariah to cooperative autocrat involved a controversial rapprochement with a man they considered responsible for numerous acts of overseas terrorism. But it was also hailed as a triumph for years of patient diplomacy designed to engage, not overthrow, a regime that almost from its very creation had stirred up international trouble.

That regime was born on 1 September 1969, when a group of young army officers took control of strategic buildings in what was then Libya's capital city, Benghazi. Their declaration of a Libyan Arab Republic meant that King Idris, the country's first and last monarch, who was in Turkey at the time, would never again set foot on Libyan soil.

The twenty-seven-year-old, charismatic and handsome Muammar Gaddafi declared himself Commander-in-Chief of the Armed Forces and de facto leader of Libya. He and his colleagues took their inspiration from the anti-colonialist, nationalist and socialist tenets that were so in vogue at the time and that formed the ideological backbone of Hafez al-Assad's Syria and Gamal Abdel Nasser's Egypt. But as the idea of pan-Arab unity soured in the 1970s, Gaddafi dreamed up his own odd, utopian philosophy of governance that became the subject of his multi-volume *Green Book*, completed in 1976. In theory, his political system meant the direct rule of the masses, an ultimate democracy that Gaddafi described as a *jamahiriya*, or a 'collection of republics', comprising people's congresses at the local and national level and in which virtually the entire economy would be nationalized.

The ensuing political, social and economic experiment was partly built on fear, with a pervasive military and security apparatus suppressing opposition and publicly executing those behind the many failed attempts on Gaddafi's life over the years. It was also funded by oil. Flush with cash during the 1970s price spikes, Gaddafi spent billions on the military and on grandiose projects like the Great Man-Made River, a system of giant underground tunnels designed to pump water from desert aquifers to the populous coastal towns. Oil allowed Gaddafi to aggressively assert his independence and helped set his regime on a course to international isolation.

Within a year of his coup, he had evicted the US and British military from Libya and nationalized the Libyan branch of Barclays bank. His right-hand man, Major Abdul Salam Jalloud, had renegotiated oil production agreements with Western firms and, in the process, revolutionized the way that oil-rich countries around the world agreed terms with foreign energy companies. Gaddafi funded political factions and guerrilla groups from Lebanon to Latin America, running an often inept campaign of assassination against his own political opponents abroad and intensifying his enmity towards the West in the charged Cold War environment of the 1980s.

This culminated in Ronald Reagan's decision to launch air strikes on Libya in 1986 after the bombing of a Berlin disco that killed two US servicemen. A few years later, Gaddafi stood accused of the December 1998 bombing of Pan Am flight 103 over the Scottish town of Lockerbie, which killed 270 people, most of whom were US citizens. By now, wide-ranging political and economic sanctions were in place, effectively cutting off Libya from much of the outside world for a decade. Gaddafi became the global face of rogue leadership and these were dark days for Libyans themselves, trapped in an oppressive cage that restricted their travels and fed on an insipid diet of state propaganda, while their shops were left devoid of foreign products.

The *Green Book* experiment was in bad shape by the 1990s. Low oil prices had curtailed Gaddafi's main source of income, while the heavily national-ized economy, denied international expertise and supplies, was creaking. The collapse of the Soviet Union and its ideology suggested that Gaddafi might best serve his interests by moving into the orbit of the world's now-unopposed superpower, whose stance in the post–9/11 world threatened rogue regimes from Iraq to North Korea. The interception in December 2003 of a Tripoli-bound ship carrying nuclear centrifuge parts put further pressure on Gaddafi, his apparent plans to develop a nuclear programme now out in the open.

By the late 1990s, back-door diplomatic channels to end Libyan isolation were beginning to bear fruit. As part of the deal that took shape, Gaddafi was required to give up unconventional weapons programmes and settle damages for past crimes. After protracted wrangling, a $2.7 billion compen-sation package was agreed in 2004 for Lockerbie, and its payment tied to the progressive lifting of economic sanctions. Tripoli also agreed to pay $1 million each to the families of passengers on a French airliner blown up over Niger in 1989.[3] The UN and the United States eased sanctions from the early 2000s, and warming diplomatic relations were exemplified by Blair's visit in 2004.

Libya became a member of the UN Security Council in 2007 and a year later took on its rotating two-year presidency. It was even elected to the UN Human Rights Council in 2010, a status that was hurriedly revoked in 2011. Gaddafi became president of the African Union in February 2009 and, in the process, persuaded 200 tribal leaders to anoint him as the 'King of Kings', much to the unease of many African heads of state.

Italy, Libya's old colonial foe and its main trading partner, formally renewed ties in August 2008 with a 'Treaty of Friendship', and Gaddafi's relationship with Italian President Silvio Berlusconi developed to such an extent that by 2009 he had even begun to appear next to Gaddafi on giant posters in Tripoli. Relations with Washington were warmer than before, if still tepid. In 2006, the US representative office in Tripoli was upgraded to a full embassy and the Pentagon removed Libya from its list of state sponsors of terror. In September 2008, Secretary of State Condoleezza Rice's visit brought the highest-level US diplomatic presence in Tripoli for more than half a century.

In 2007, the newly-elected French premier Nicolas Sarkozy had helped secure the release of five Bulgarian nurses and a Palestinian doctor sentenced to death for allegedly infecting Libyan children with HIV. Shortly afterwards, Sarkozy announced that France would cooperate with Libya on nuclear power generation. Gaddafi's visit to Paris later that year resulted in more deals, including a major order for Airbus and an expression of interest in buying France's Rafale fighter jets – an aircraft that would ironically unleash the first strikes against his tanks in March 2011.[4]

These deals hinted at the alluring economic rewards of reintegrating Gaddafi. In the mid-2000s Libya was seen as an unopened treasure chest, boasting Africa's largest proven oil reserves but suffering from a lack of investment and expertise that meant it was pumping less crude than it had in 1969. Rising oil prices were generating bumper surpluses for Tripoli, and Libya's disconnected economy was well insulated from the economic crisis buffeting the rest of the world, making it an even more appealing catch for governments and companies in dire financial straits.

In 2006, a year before the BP deal, three US oil companies had restarted their joint venture with Libya's NOC and other US firms picked up major contracts in Libya. Construction giants from Brazil, Korea, China and India sought to capitalize on a gigantic investment programme that planned to build hundreds of thousands of new houses, as well as overhaul roads, bridges, airports, ports, universities, and sewage, water and electricity networks. The Libyan Investment Authority (LIA) was successfully wooed by Wall Street and invested hundreds of millions with Goldman Sachs, JP Morgan and the Carlyle Group.

The Corinthia Bab Africa – Tripoli's first international five-star hotel – was booked up months in advance, while dilapidated towers in the capital boasted long waiting lists for office space.[5] International brands signed deals to manage new hotels, while European retailers like Marks and Spencer, Mango, BHS and Next started to open up in Tripoli's upmarket districts. Property prices went through the roof as years of latent demand flooded onto the market.[6]

Inbound foreign investment rose from $143 million in 2003 to $4.7 billion in 2008,[7] outstripping Algeria, Morocco and Tunisia, with new legislation offering tax incentives. Even tourism was picking up. Libya had been off-limits to all but the most determined of travellers until the early 2000s, but visitor numbers rose more than fivefold between 2003 and 2006 as Europeans began to explore the country's world-class Greek, Roman and Saharan attractions, and Tripoli even became a port of call for Mediterranean cruise liners.[8] New rules on private business offered customs and tax benefits for investment in tourism and services, and were eagerly taken up by local entrepreneurs keen to profit from this economic spring.

Libya was no longer the ultra-socialist economy of the 1980s, when private individuals could not own shops, hotels or more than one piece of property. It was now a bizarre combination of laissez-faire rule-bending, in which anything could be done if you knew the right people or paid them enough, and anachronistic nationalist regulations, such as the requirement that all external signs on shops or hotels be in Arabic only. No one appeared to have told that to the new operators of the refurbished Al Mahary hotel in Tripoli, where a prominent Western brand name was abruptly sheathed in tarpaulin soon after it reopened.

Politically, too, there was optimism. Libya seemed to set an example for what could be achieved through international diplomacy rather than force, especially with the emergence of Saif al-Islam Gaddafi as a possible reformist successor to his father. Educated in Austria and seemingly more bookish than his militaristic or playboy siblings, Saif completed a PhD at the London School of Economics (LSE) in 2007 that would later ignite scandal, but then bolstered his credentials as the reform-minded, Western-friendly face of the Libyan regime.

At home, Saif led a counter-terrorism initiative that released several hundred members of the Libyan Islamic Fighting Group (LIFG), the Al-Qaeda affiliate formed in the 1990s whose former members would play a leading role in the 2011 revolt. He also fronted a programme of economic liberalization. His Economic Development Board (EDB) paid astronomical fees to US consultancies who advised on Libya's development and introduced senior Libyans to movers and shakers in the West. Saif was also outspoken in calling for political reform. 'Society needs to have independent media to highlight corruption, cheating and falsification ... Libya must have an independent civic society and independent bodies,' he said in an August 2007 speech which one British newspaper said underlined Libya's 'transformation from a pariah state into a Western ally'.[9]

That was overstating the case, but there was certainly debate behind the scenes about how far change should go. On one side was the old guard, which included Saif's brother Mo'atassim and Prime Minister al-Baghdadi Ali al-Mahmoudi, and on the other, reformist elements championed by Saif and technocrats like NOC chief Shukri Ghanem and the US-educated Mahmoud Jibril, head of the EDB. The struggle was manifested most publicly in the media sector, when in early 2009 newspapers and TV stations belonging to Saif's media company, Al-Ghad, or 'Tomorrow', began to criticize Egypt's quiescent approach to the Israeli bombardment of Gaza. One of his channels was quasi-nationalized a couple of months later, and in November 2010, while Saif was out of the country, some sixteen journalists from Al-Ghad were arrested by the internal security forces. Its flagship newspaper, *Oea*, was subsequently closed before being reopened with new management.

Was all of this simply manufactured to convince the Libyan public and the wider world that Saif was a genuine reformer? Perhaps, but there were very real splits over what direction Libya should now take. Gaddafi's woolly ideology had been overtaken by economic liberalization and renewed friendliness with the West, raising questions about where Libya might go after he was dead or had retreated from the front lines of power. Those opposing Saif's outlook saw him as a rival to their own long-entrenched interests and were irritated at being openly criticized over issues like the lack of economic reform, corruption and the overly-powerful military.[10] As far as Saif harboured any genuine desire to reform Libya's political system, the old guard seemed determined to stop him. It was also extremely difficult for Saif or anyone else to alter power structures that had been in place for decades, based on a system of tribal and family loyalties that favoured some groups and deliberately marginalized others.

Gaddafi shuffled the same ministers around different portfolios, not allowing any one power base to become too entrenched. Positions in government or at the head of public companies were essentially ways of bestowing favours, allowing senior figures to milk their positions for financial perks that would filter down to their extended families. People could and did get rich independently of government positions, but the ultimate source of all wealth was the oil revenues, erratically controlled by the ruling family. 'It's like a tap,' said one local businessman. 'Whenever it gets switched on, everyone crowds round to get a drink before it gets switched off again.'[11]

Gaddafi's approach overseas was also shifting. Tripoli still funded rebel groups in Africa and further afield, but its campaign to assassinate exiled political opponents had been abandoned. Human rights abuses were frequent and brutal, there was no rule of law, and many thousands of prisoners still languished in sub-human conditions, but this was not the same regime of door-to-door terror that Hisham Matar described in his bleak novel about 1980s Libya, *In the Country of Men*. A Human Rights Watch report from 2010 even described a number of 'breakthroughs' in Tripoli:

> We first noted a shift in the Libyan winds during a research trip in April when journalists and lawyers spoke openly to us about the restrictions they faced, a startling break from previous visits. The families of [the] 1996 Abu Salim massacre – an event never publicly acknowledged by the government – were demonstrating in the streets, refusing to accept the compensation they were offered to stop demanding justice. Journalists from two newspapers and foreign-based Libyan websites wrote critically about government failings ... There was open dissent among the ruling elite, and a public struggle to control the lawless security forces.[12]

Though Gaddafi still could, and often did, exert control over the most mundane details of life in the country, his power had been diluted by Libya's international reintegration, the rise of the internet and satellite television, and the burgeoning private sector. He had hardcore opponents and hardcore supporters, as 2011 would show, but for many Libyans he had become something of an embarrassing irrelevance, an ever-present face that loomed over streets and appeared on television in outlandish robes and sunglasses, but who had little direct involvement in their everyday lives. True, the *Green Book* was still required reading in schools, but few took much notice of it and even fewer bothered to attend the local councils that it proclaimed to be the bedrock of popular rule.

Gaddafi's regime was not monolithic or totalitarian. Nor was Libya a hermit kingdom like North Korea. It had cracks, splits and disagreements that led to volatility and confusion, and made for little meaningful progress on political reform. But after the initial post-sanctions optimism about Libya, there were more and more signs that although Gaddafi had come in from the cold, he was still only willing to play by his own rules.

The Failed Reintegration

In August 2009, some British expatriates in Tripoli decided to leave the country for a long weekend. Others, away on their summer holidays, delayed their return for a few days. No one quite knew how the Libyan regime might react if the Scottish authorities decided not to release Abdulbasset Ali al-Megrahi, the only man ever convicted for the Lockerbie bombing. A month earlier, a doctor's report had given him less than three months to live, prompting a debate on whether he should be released on compassionate grounds or left in prison. To the palpable relief of British expatriates and companies in Libya, Kenny MacAskill, the Scottish Justice Minister, decided that Megrahi could be freed.

His release was hugely sensitive, and openly opposed by Washington and many British parliamentarians. But what made matters immediately worse was Megrahi's arrival in Tripoli, where he and Saif al-Islam provoked international fury when they were greeted at the airport by a stage-managed group of cheering supporters. Tripoli was not prepared to hide the fact that it saw Megrahi as a wrongly-accused hero, whatever the international sensitivities involved. The issue refused to go away, with leaked cables claiming that British diplomats had written to the Libyan authorities with legal advice on Megrahi's release, or that Libyan ministers had met Kenny MacAskill shortly before the release.

The row was overtaken by the events of 2011, but it was one of several episodes that highlighted Gaddafi's refusal to abide by international norms and forge relationships that might ultimately have saved his regime. That defiance was illustrated again just a month after Megrahi's release, when Libya's leader flew to New York to address the United Nations. Despite being one of the world's wealthiest men, its longest-serving head of state, and president of the African Union, Gaddafi could find no one willing to rent him land to pitch his tent.

But arguably the most damaging affair was a prolonged standoff with Switzerland, triggered in July 2008 when Swiss police arrested and briefly jailed Hannibal Gaddafi, one of the Libyan leader's sons, and his wife, who were accused of beating their domestic staff in a Geneva hotel. Infuriated, the regime withdrew an estimated $7 billion from Swiss banks and boycotted all Swiss companies and citizens.[13] To make sure everyone got the point, police toured shops in Tripoli to remove bars of Swiss chocolate and rows of Swiss watches. Swiss companies had their offices closed and

Libya stopped shipping oil to Switzerland, which responded by blacklisting and freezing the assets of 186 senior Libyan officials.

The spat escalated. Tripoli jailed two Swiss nationals whom it had prevented from leaving Libya due to 'visa irregularities'. Gaddafi even called for *jihad* against the land of cheese and cuckoo clocks, urging Muslims to 'go to all airports in the Islamic world and prevent any Swiss plane landing, to all harbours and prevent any Swiss ships docking, inspect all shops and markets to stop any Swiss goods being sold'.[14] Then in March 2010 foreign minister Moussa Koussa announced that all nationals of the 26 countries in Europe's Schengen zone were now banned from entering Libya. The travel ban was lifted after mediation by other EU parties, but relations with Switzerland, and other European countries that had been dragged into what was essentially a bilateral dispute, were permanently soured.

The whole episode highlighted how Gaddafi's regime was failing to build real bridges with the international community. Either it did not understand, or did not care about, the norms of international diplomacy, instead insisting on a self-destructive pride that meant foreign diplomats had to approach Libya with the softest of kid gloves. It was the same attitude that prompted Gaddafi, on his first-ever official visit to Rome in 2009, to pin on his uniform a photo of the popular Libyan resistance hero, Omar al-Mukhtar, being arrested by Italian colonial forces in 1931.

Meanwhile, Libya was turning out to be a great commercial disappointment. Many foreign firms had simply lost patience with the opaque bureaucracy, unpredictable government policies, corruption and unpaid bills. Nor was the all-important energy sector the treasure trove that many had hoped for, refuting the argument that the 2011 intervention was all about oil. Several international firms chose not to extend their exploration licences in 2009 and 2010 after poor results, focusing on other countries with friendlier business environments and less draconian terms. Almost four years after signing its landmark deal in 2007, BP was only just starting its exploratory drilling in early 2011.

Foreign companies had also been dismayed by what happened to Verenex, a Canadian wildcatter that struck oil in Libya in 2008 and earned a buyout offer from the state-owned Chinese National Petroleum Company (CNPC) the following year. The sale required the approval of Libya's NOC, which dragged its feet for five months before finally deciding to block the sale, upon which CNPC withdrew its offer. The Libyan Investment Authority (LIA) later made its own bid for Verenex that was 37 per cent lower than the Chinese offer. Verenex shareholders, effectively having to take whatever they could get, accepted the sale.[15]

The episode further eroded commercial trust, suggesting that the Gaddafi regime was not a trustworthy business partner and that Libya was not a reliable place to invest. On the ground, there was disquiet among foreign firms and even rumours that oil explorers were now keeping discoveries secret from the authorities. Tripoli had bullied its way into getting what it wanted, but this was a Pyrrhic victory.

Tourism was faring even worse than energy. New rules introduced in 2007 required all non-Arab nationals to carry a certified Arabic translation of their passport details, and by 2009 visitor numbers had almost dwindled back to their pre-sanctions levels. When asked in 2010 for the latest figures, a government official said they had been told not to release them because they were so bad.[16] Tourist guides started looking for other work, while hotels in peripheral towns like Ghadames, a UNESCO world heritage site, were starting to shut their doors.[17] British Airways had cut one of its two daily flights to Heathrow, while another airline, BMI, endured months of delays and red tape to launch its own London-Tripoli route, eventually beginning flights on 21 February 2011. It completed only one return trip before the uprising escalated and the route was deemed too unsafe to operate.[18]

Grandiose schemes to build marinas, hotels, hospitals, towers, airports, roads, factories and golf courses mostly failed to get moving, often due to infighting over money. In October 2010, several Libyan newspapers reported a scandal at the Economic and Social Development Fund (ESDF), one of the largest public-sector institutions with subsidiaries across various sectors, claiming that tens of millions of dollars had been siphoned off by senior management. The scandal prompted unusually strident criticism in the media – especially as the ESDF was theoretically meant to be owned by lower-income families. Senior officials, some of whom were jailed, stood accused of forging the minutes of meetings, transferring money to their own accounts, and colluding with foreign companies to take bribes.

There had been efforts to clean up corruption. Some state companies or funds were given new management, sometimes appointed directly by Saif, and told to clamp down on a culture of graft. But that culture was an intrinsic part of Libya's odd politico-economic structure. It allowed oil wealth to trickle down without the need to implement any formal distribution mechanism and enforce 'rules', a practice in which Libya was not especially accomplished. Bribes and commissions paid on transactions large and small helped to offset the insultingly low salaries in the public sector, which employed some 40 per cent of the workforce on average wages of about $250 per month. It was a system aided and abetted by the cash economy, with most purchases – even of big-ticket items like cars – conducted in bags of notes rather than bank transfers.

But corruption was one of the most corrosive elements of Gaddafi's Libya, hindering genuine economic development, providing no incentive for a long-term approach, widening divides and depressing swathes of young Libyans without the connections to get jobs or run successful businesses. Government policies had failed to meet the expectations of people who were aware of their country's oil wealth, and were beginning to wonder where it had all gone. Many compared themselves not with Tunisians or Egyptians, but rather with Qataris, Emiratis or Kuwaitis. There was such low trust in local healthcare, for instance, that most Tripoli residents would drive to Tunisia for even the most basic medical treatment.

Infrastructure had failed to keep up with urban growth, with new areas of cities lacking paved roads and housing developments years behind schedule. And towards the end of 2010 there were unusual signs that patience was becoming seriously frayed. Local families took over a number of nearly-complete housing projects on Tripoli's Airport Road, angry that their promised new apartments were still unfinished and that they were still living in run-down districts. Others even attacked the site offices of foreign construction firms who were building the schemes. Their actions were not a serious threat to the regime but, coming on the eve of the uprising, showed that frustration was already starting to boil over.

Around the same time, the US ambassador in Tripoli became one of WikiLeaks' biggest casualties. For the most part, Gene Cretz's reports from Tripoli seemed to confirm what people already suspected: US-Libya relations were still hugely uneasy, with much suspicion on both sides. The reports also contained plenty of juicy gossip on Gaddafi himself, who could go nowhere without his 'voluptuous' Ukrainian nurse and employed an aide to summarize Barack Obama's books for him. The cables mocked the comic ineptitude of the regime, one anecdote recounting how a Libyan 'frogman' sent to Italy for specialist diving training could not even swim. Cretz was forced to leave Libya in January 2011.

Yet despite diplomatic hostilities, open popular frustration and splits within the regime, Gaddafi's rule was not on the verge of collapse in late 2010. He faced no serious Islamist threat and no organized and unified political opposition, and was awash with money. Despite the less oppressive political and media atmosphere, political apathy was far more common than political activism. Just as the removal of Mubarak would not have happened in 2011 without the Tunisian revolution, so the Libyan uprising would not have taken place without the success of demonstrators in its two neighbours.

The Cyrene Uprising

Gaddafi was initially blind to the implications of both of the monumental events that had cleared out his neighbours. 'You have suffered a great loss,' he told Tunisians in an ill-judged speech made shortly after Zine al-Abidine Ben Ali had fled to Saudi Arabia. 'There is none better than Zine to govern Tunisia.' Like other Arab leaders at this time, he seemed to regard his country as immune to protests. Perhaps, like Bashar al-Assad in Syria, Libya's leader felt comfortable because he was not aligned with Western interests in the same way that Ben Ali and Hosni Mubarak had been. He also seemed to believe that his *jamahiriya* had long ago delivered what protesters elsewhere were seeking, and advised Tunisians to seek 'the final destination for the peoples' quest for democracy'.[19]

That opinion was not universally shared by Libyans, especially those with deep-seated antagonism towards Gaddafi. It was no coincidence that the uprising was initially most successful in the north-east, home to Libya's second city, Benghazi, the seat of King Idris and historically a more important centre of learning and business than Tripoli. After the UN-brokered unification of the three historical provinces of Libya in the early 1950s, the official capital had alternated every two years between Tripoli in the north-west and Benghazi in the north-east, reflecting the long rivalry between the two cities.

There was also a legacy of resistance in the north-east. Cyrenaica, or Barqa, as the eastern province was called prior to unification, was the home of Omar al-Mukhtar, one of Libya's few genuine popular heroes. He had led a campaign of guerrilla warfare against the Italians in the 1920s and 1930s, and was immortalized on film by Anthony Quinn in the (Gaddafi-funded) *Lion of the Desert*, which depicted the European colonial power in such a bad light that it was not shown on Italian television until 2009.

Omar al-Mukhtar may have been an anti-colonialist, but he was also an Islamic fundamentalist who fought in the name of God. The north-east was Libya's religious heartland, the spiritual home of the Senussi order which rose to prominence in the mid-nineteenth century. Named after the Algerian scholar who founded it, the movement followed an ascetic brand of mystical Sufi Islam and opened up religious centres or *zawiyas* around Libya. The first, called the White Monastery or *zawiya al-bayda*, gave its name to the town of al-Bayda, where Saif accused residents of wanting to set up an 'Islamic emirate' in February 2011.[20]

The north-east remained the most conservative region in a conservative country. In the final years of Gaddafi's rule, for instance, you would see far fewer women on the streets of Benghazi than in Tripoli. It was also a breeding-ground for Islamic militants, supplying hundreds of fighters to Iraq or Afghanistan and producing several senior and influential members of Al-Qaeda. The Libyan Islamic Fighting Group made several attempts on Gaddafi's life in the 1990s and was met with unforgiving repression; its jailed members were among the estimated 1,600 who were killed in the 1996 Abu Salim prison massacre in Tripoli. Gaddafi also cooperated with Western intelligence services to provide information on suspected militants. One former commander of the LIFG, Abdel Hakim Belhadj, claimed to have been arrested in Malaysia in 2004 and secretly sent to Tripoli by the CIA, where he was put in jail.[21] In 2010, he was pardoned and a year later was leading former LIFG members who were among the best-trained of those fighting pro-Gaddafi forces.

Gaddafi himself had deliberately neglected Benghazi, relocating ministries and public company headquarters to Tripoli in the early years of his rule. A top-level push in the late 2000s had tried to stem the economic marginalization of the region, planning new projects that ranged from housing, hotels, sports stadiums and even a Benghazi metro. Several state-owned entities had been told to make quicker progress on projects in the north-east, but many – just like elsewhere in Libya – were inevitably mired in delays.[22] Some were also a useless waste of money. A monument to commemorate Benghazi victims of a plane crash in Egypt in 1973 seemed to be making quicker progress than new housing, while another unresolved sore point was a decades-old and malodorous sewage problem in Benghazi's lakes.[23]

In the years leading up to 2011, open criticism of Gaddafi was more common in Benghazi than in Tripoli, and state propaganda on the streets was rarer. In February 2006, protesters in Benghazi had attacked the Italian consulate after an Italian politician had suggested that T-shirts should be made of the Prophet Mohamed cartoons that had appeared in Danish newspapers. The demonstrations broadened into a general protest against the regime, which responded with a mix of force – police killed at least ten people – and conciliation, with dozens of political prisoners released from jail.[24] The 2006 protests began on 17 February, a date that would be invoked five years later to mark the launch of a much more serious disturbance.

It had started with small-scale protests in January 2011, as local residents in some towns followed the lead of Tripoli and broke into half-finished housing developments that were meant to be completed years ago. The protests gathered pace after the departure of Egypt's Mubarak on 11 February. A local lawyer, Fathi Terbil, was briefly arrested and then released in Benghazi on 15 February after a small demonstration. At this stage, the regime's response was still muted. It allowed rallies to go ahead and made pledges to improve housing and raise salaries.

On 17 February, residents in Benghazi and other north-eastern towns like Derna and Tobruk took to the streets on the anniversary of the 2006 protests. The rallies were biggest in Benghazi but other places also saw unrest. A TV station called Libya Al-Hurra, or Free Libya, was set up by Mohammed Nabbous, a Benghazi activist, and streamed live footage out of the country. Nabbous was shot by snipers in March, but his role in covering those early moments was considered instrumental in influencing local and international opinion.

It is still difficult to piece together the sequence of events but the peaceful protests descended, relatively quickly, into an armed insurrection. Rank-and-file soldiers, often from the towns where they were supposed to be quelling protests, defected or fled. They left behind unprotected garrisons and triggered a monumental spree of weapons looting that would go on all year. Towns like Tobruk and Bayda were among the first to fall from Gaddafi's grip. A week later Benghazi was in rebel hands. Around the same time, the drawn-out and destructive battle over Misrata, Libya's third-largest city and an important business and logistics centre, was beginning. Protests had turned into an armed insurgency as Gaddafi's forces tried to retake territory and key locations, including the airport, which had been captured by rebels. Months of shelling, fierce street-fighting and a siege would leave parts of the city in ruins by mid-summer.

Meanwhile, senior figures had started to defect. Among the most important would be Mustafa Abdel Jalil, the Minister of Justice, and Mahmoud Jibril, the head of the Economic Development Board. They emerged as the two leading figures in the National Transitional Council (NTC) that was formed in Benghazi in late February, sending a bold and brave message to the rest of the country. The NTC boasted a powerful symbol in the old monarchical flag, which was soon flying across the north-east, and had the vital advantage of controlling – however loosely – a piece of Libyan territory.

A mixture of terror, apathy and popular support kept Gaddafi in control of Tripoli and much of the surrounding area, where pro-government forces and alleged African mercenaries shot or arrested demonstrators and restricted any large-scale rallies. Regime support remained solid in strongholds like Sirte, Gaddafi's birthplace, and in Sebha, Libya's fourth-largest city and the place where he had gone to school. And despite the rash of defections, it soon became clear that the disorganized rebels had neither the firepower nor the nationwide support to hold off the advance of the better-trained, better-equipped and still loyal military brigades which by early March were on the outskirts of Benghazi.

With hindsight, perhaps Gaddafi's biggest error was the language he used to threaten the rebels. His now-infamous pledge to go *'zanga zanga, dar dar'* or from 'alley to alley, house to house' to 'cleanse' the 'rats' and 'cockroaches' carried echoes of the 1994 genocide in Rwanda, when Hutus described the Tutsis in similarly insect-like terms. Saif al-Islam's calls for dialogue and a 'general assembly' were ignored by both the opposition and the outside world. His rambling speech threatening 'rivers of blood' prompted Western politicians to fall over each other in their rush to distance themselves from Libya's heir apparent. International calls for a ceasefire were ignored by Gaddafi, whose forces were engaged in what they saw as an existential standoff with armed rebels. Though Gaddafi promised an amnesty to those who gave up their weapons, threats of 'no mercy' to those who resisted suggested that a terrible vengeance would soon be visited upon Libya's second city.

On 21 February, two Libyan pilots flew to Malta and defected, claiming that they had disobeyed orders to bomb protesters in Benghazi. The opposition claimed that a massacre was about to be perpetrated. Some warned it would be 'another Hama', referring to Hafez al-Assad's assault on that Syrian city in 1982, which killed somewhere between 5,000 and 25,000 people. The arguments for and against such a scenario are too complex to discuss here, but the crucial point is that the humanitarian threat was considered great enough to justify a military intervention that would also serve the ulterior motives of those who led it. From the start, UN Resolution 1973 was about much more than just protecting civilians.

A unique convergence of factors brought it about. The first was the humanitarian threat. Another was the curious role played by Bernard-Henri Levy, a wealthy French philosopher whom even the Parisian elite regarded as narcissistic. BHL, as he is known in the French media, met the new NTC leaders in Benghazi in the first week of March, then flew to Paris where he apparently persuaded President Sarkozy to unexpectedly recognize the council as the legitimate Libyan government. This took place on 10 March, without the knowledge of foreign minister Alain Juppé and just a day after senior officials had said France recognized 'states, not parties'.[25] 'It will be very difficult now to make the blow jobs to dictators in the Arab world,' Levy told Al-Jazeera a few days later. 'The world has changed.'[26]

At the time, Sarkozy's world also needed changing. A poll had just rated him less popular than the far-right National Front leader Marine Le Pen, while he faced a potentially formidable adversary, Dominique Strauss-Kahn, in the 2012 presidential elections.[27] France's dreadful handling of the Tunisian uprising meant the Elysée had already lost leverage over one North African government. Spearheading an intervention in Libya – as he would end up doing – could help Sarkozy's image at home and salvage something from the Arab Spring.

The intervention also took place at a time when it felt as if the entire Arab world might be on the verge of revolution. In early March there was talk of a domino effect, a Berlin Wall moment that would sweep away Arab rulers from the Atlantic to the Gulf. So far the West had been largely behind the curve, fence-sitting in Tunisia and Egypt until it became clear which way the tide was turning, while staying quiet on the Bahraini uprising. Libya presented an opportunity to join a battle that appeared to pit popular will against evil regime, and to emerge on the right side of history.

Washington, Paris and London had effectively burned their bridges with Tripoli by this time, with all three calling for the Libyan leader to 'go' – if he had not already gone to Venezuela, as British Foreign Secretary William Hague claimed in February. Doing nothing would allow Gaddafi to regain control of the country and emerge isolated but dangerously hostile towards those countries that had abandoned him during the crisis.

A Western intervention in the region so soon after Iraq would require Arab support. That too was on the table, but again was driven by more than just humanitarian considerations. It is hard to think of a case other than Libya, and a moment in time other than March 2011, where so many Arab countries would have either supported, or abstained from objecting to, Western-led action in a Muslim and Arab country.

The largest bloc in the Lebanese government, which co-sponsored Resolution 1973, included the two Shi'ite Muslim parties of Hezbollah and Amal. The latter's founder and spiritual guide, Imam Moussa Sadr, had notoriously vanished while visiting Libya in 1978, something that the party had always blamed on Gaddafi. In 2008, Lebanon had even issued an arrest warrant for the Libyan leader and other senior regime members. 'Let no one think that we will forget or make any compromise,' warned Nabih Berri, the speaker of the Lebanese parliament and Amal's long-standing leader, at a rally marking the 30th anniversary of the Imam's disappearance.[28]

Libya's neighbours in Tunisia and Egypt were too preoccupied with their own internal strife to get heavily involved, and did not recognize the NTC until later in the year. In contrast, the two Gulf states of the United Arab Emirates and Qatar were ambitious, stable, wealthy and in pursuit of political and commercial influence beyond their own tiny borders. There was evidence that both countries, but Qatar in particular, provided military, financial and logistical support to the NTC from an early stage. Saudi Arabia's King Abdullah had a long-running spat with Gaddafi, who had funded a bungled plot to assassinate the Gulf monarch in 2004. In 2009, he had stormed out of an Arab League meeting after denouncing King Abdullah as a Western stooge – a rant that only ended when the emir of Qatar switched off his microphone.

Riyadh would not mourn the demise of Gaddafi, and a war in Libya might divert attention from events closer to home. Two days after the Arab League voted in favour of a no-fly zone over Libya, Gulf forces entered Bahrain to help quell protests. Nascent signs of unrest in eastern Saudi Arabia even suggested, at that point, that the kingdom might be the next Arab country to be overrun by mass demonstrations. If that happened, a bloody crackdown seemed inevitable, and would put Riyadh's Western allies in an uncomfortable position. Another argument had it that Western involvement was all about oil, an unlikely motivation given the lacklustre success of exploration in recent years and the fact that British and US oil firms were already active in the country.

In reality, Libya was a unique case at a unique time, and there could so easily have never been an intervention at all. Had Gaddafi not used such emotive language, had Bernard-Henri Levy not persuaded Sarkozy to recognize the NTC, had the Libyan regime courted more Arab friends, then Resolution 1973 might never have been tabled at all. Cynics, and there were plenty of them, say the protection of civilians provided an insurance policy for sponsors whose real goal was regime change. If their aims appeared fuzzy or the campaign went off course, which it did, then they could always fall back on the humanitarian angle and the deliberately vague wording of the resolution, which allowed 'member states to take all necessary means'. Even so, Germany, South Africa, Russia, China, India and Brazil all abstained from voting, making clear that this was very much a US-, British- and French-led affair.

It began on 18 March when French jets launched air strikes on Gaddafi forces outside Benghazi. Other armed forces soon joined in the coalition, with the US and British militaries bombing military depots, enforcing a no-fly zone and setting up a naval blockade. Washington played a lower-key role than Britain or France, who had to strongly twist Obama's arm to support intervention at all, but its moral and logistical backing was vital in sparing European blushes. 'The mightiest military alliance in history is only eleven weeks into an operation against a poorly armed regime in a sparsely populated country – yet many allies are beginning to run short of munitions, requiring the US, once more, to make up the difference,' complained Robert Gates, the former US Defence Secretary.[29]

After a week, NATO took command of the campaign and led it through the spring and summer as Gaddafi's arsenals of tanks and artillery, as well as his aircraft and command and control centres, were battered from above. Anything seen as threatening to civilians was fair game, with the idea being to create the vital momentum needed to bring Libyans out onto the streets to topple the weakened regime. It was hoped this would happen in a matter of weeks. But as the months rolled on, the country was effectively divided into two parts – areas that were under Gaddafi's control, and areas that were not.

Only a week after the intervention began, then Arab League secretary-general Amr Moussa said that he 'deplored' the bombing campaign: 'What happened in Libya is different from the intended aim of imposing the no-fly zone. We want to protect civilians, not the bombing of more civilians.'[30] Russia and China slammed NATO, accusing it of pursuing regime change by another name. African nations, including South Africa, pushed for diplomatic solutions and continued to criticize the intervention. From almost all quarters there were misgivings about the bending of the UN resolution, what exactly constituted a legitimate target, and how the intervention's success would actually be measured.

A NATO air strike in April on what appeared to be a residential villa killed Saif al-Arab, a lesser-known Gaddafi son. On a tour of the destroyed compound hours after the attack, government minders pointed to furniture, a table football set and other innocuous paraphernalia of domestic life that appeared to indicate that this was not a military target. Gaddafi and his wife had been there hours earlier for a get-together with their children and grand-children, they said, accusing NATO of deliberately trying to assassinate a head of state.[31] In December 2011, however, Saif al-Islam claimed that the house had been used as a secret meeting-place between Gaddafi and Moussa Koussa, who had dramatically defected a month earlier, and that Libya's leader had been there moments before the air strike.[32] 'We are not targeting Gaddafi directly, but if it happened that he was in a command and control centre that was hit by NATO and he was killed, then that is within the rules,' was how General Sir David Richards, the head of the British Armed Forces, put it in May.[33]

Nocturnal bombing raids were frequent in and around Tripoli, but life appeared relatively normal on the surface. Traffic was quieter than usual, but shops were open, informal markets were bustling and some companies were still working. Trying to talk to people about what was happening elsewhere in the country, however, elicited little response in a climate of almost tangible fear. A shopkeeper near the Rixos Hotel, where foreign journalists were effectively kept under lock and key, openly criticized Gaddafi and his family before suddenly going quiet whenever a car pulled up outside or someone entered the shop. A television behind the counter was showing Al-Arabiya, whose coverage of the Libyan uprising was heavily anti-regime.[34]

At a roundabout close to the city centre, minders excitedly showed journalists a small protest camp where dozens of African nationals were half-heartedly declaring their support for the Gaddafi regime and extolling the virtues of life in Libya. Other stage-managed trips included visits to 'training camps' outside of the capital, where groups of people, including some children, were receiving instructions in how to take apart machine guns or to fire rocket-propelled grenades.

One young government minder at the hotel, wearing a smart jacket with a picture of Gaddafi on his lapel, was philosophical about the upheaval. 'My mother showed me an old dress made out of the colours of the old flag,' he said, 'but I told her to put it away for now and we would get it out if Gaddafi goes. I'm wearing the Gaddafi pin for now because this is the guy in charge. If that changes I have the other flag at home as well.'[35]

The Endgame

Somewhere between 30,000 and 50,000 Libyans had been killed by early September, six months after the intervention was launched.[36] When measured as a percentage of Libya's population, and in that time period, this was a bloodier death toll than Iraq. As the situation on the ground appeared to have reached a stalemate, the intervention grew increasingly active rather than protective. There was evidence that on-the-ground 'spotters' from Western special forces were working with rebels to identify targets.[37] In the Jebel Nafusa mountains, south-west of the capital, the French had airlifted weapons to rebel groups, violating the terms of the UN resolution. And it would later emerge that Qatar had shipped in hundreds of its soldiers to train and assist in the fighting.[38] The only way of defending civilians, it now seemed, was to attack Gaddafi.

As the war struggled into a long, hot August, several groups of rebels, now better-organized but still suffering huge casualties, were moving towards Tripoli with increasingly robust air support from NATO. In Misrata, a largely home-grown resistance, often made up of civilians rather than army defectors and based on local resources rather than external help, had managed to break Gaddafi's siege in mid-May. It was a hugely symbolic victory and one that gave the opposition a vital strategic foothold in the centre of the Libyan coastline. By the late summer several brigades from the city were on the offensive and beginning to take territory of their own.

A stalemate persisted along the front in the north-east between Sirte and Benghazi, with towns like Brega and Ras Lanuf frequently changing hands. In Jebel Nafusa, armed rebel groups were making gains and moving in on towns to the west of Tripoli. The western areas were vital in bringing in supplies and fighters across the Tunisian borders, with the town of Nalut becoming something of an operations base. Qatari special forces were training rebels in the area, as the opposition grew in both quantity and quality.[39] Among the most prominent militia was that from the small town of Zintan, also in the western mountains, which had played an important role in the opposition's military effort and whose airstrip would be vital in receiving and controlling money and weapons flown in from the east.[40]

Zintanis also helped break the deadlock in mid-August. Key to this breakthrough was the seizure of Zawiya and its oil refinery, which brought the main road between Tripoli and the Tunisian border under opposition control and denied the capital its main supply line. This meant that the capital could now be encircled. A long-planned operation to storm Tripoli, dubbed Mermaid Dawn, rolled into action slightly earlier than expected. Opposition cells inside the city were activated. Some rebels moved in by road from the west and others by sea.

Dramatic scenes were captured on television during the night of 21 August, when rebels began entering Tripoli through its western suburbs. They were met not with resistance but with burnt-out cars, abandoned jeeps and the discarded uniforms of soldiers who had given up the fight and blended into the masses of people who cheered and waved the new Libyan flag. The next day, Tripoli residents walked freely around the newly-renamed Martyrs' Square, having consigned its predecessor, Green Square, to the dustbin of history.

A concentrated assault on the Bab al-Aziziyah compound, Gaddafi's sprawling headquarters in central Tripoli, now began. If the capital was to fall into rebel hands, then Bab al-Aziziyah had to be taken, and many suspected the Libyan leader himself was holed up there with his inner circle. A combination of NATO air cover and ground attacks by Libyan fighters and foreign special forces made swift progress, and on 23 August the first rebels began streaming into the warren-like complex, originally a royal barracks, that was thought to hold so many secrets. After killing or capturing the remaining pro-Gaddafi soldiers, rebel fighters – and the world's media – began to explore the compound that for decades had been a symbol of state power.

They found the golf buggy that Gaddafi had driven around in his bizarre television appearances earlier in the year. They climbed on the giant bronze fist that crushed an American fighter jet, a symbol of Libyan resistance to the Reagan bombing of 1986. One man was delighted by finding Gaddafi's military hat in the former leader's bedroom. Others unearthed family photo albums and decades-old home videos showing the former leader playing with his children. Many more concentrated on looting as much ammunition and weaponry as they could find, loading boxes of bullets, rocket-powered grenades and rifles into jeeps that were hastily driven off.

But Gaddafi himself was not among the secrets that Bab al-Aziziyah offered up to its conquerors. It would later emerge that he and his family had left Tripoli by car days before the capital fell, and now seemed to have vanished into thin air. Wild jubilation and celebratory gunfire erupted in Tripoli at the start of the *Eid al-Fitr* holiday in late August, but a shadow still hung over their victory.

In the meantime, little semblance of authority had emerged in the capital. The NTC leadership remained in Benghazi and seemed hesitant to visit Tripoli, let alone decamp there. Local councils and committees began to emerge in the absence of any central power, and in the fear that outsiders might try to take power. Old regional rivalries came to the fore again, particularly that between Tripoli and Benghazi. Tensions rose as individual militias asserted their authority and their claims to the roles they had played in helping to free the capital. The shortcomings of the NTC became glaringly obvious as it was thrust from being a symbol of anti-Gaddafi resistance and a vehicle for mobilizing international intervention into its new role as a makeshift government. Yet despite some inevitable looting and lawlessness, there was surprisingly little chaos and bloodshed at this early stage, as Tripoli breathed again after effectively being under siege for six months.

And finally, in late October, the shadow that still hung over the country was lifted. It was not until the pictures started appearing that anyone believed it was true. There had been so many false alarms, rumours and lies over the past two months that only hard proof would be enough. Mahmoud Jibril had claimed that Gaddafi was in the south of Libya, moving across borders with Algeria or Niger and protected by loyal tribesmen. Other ill-defined 'NTC officials' or 'senior military commanders' quoted in the media were confident that Gaddafi's movements in the desert were being tracked by satellite. All were wrong.

The first image was posted online around lunchtime on 20 October. Taken at knee-height, it showed the top half of a man with bedraggled hair, drenched in blood, being dragged along by his shoulder. More photos followed, and then the inevitable videos, recorded shakily on mobile phones, were uploaded. Some showed Gaddafi mumbling incoherently while being slapped or beaten. Others showed the concrete sewer in which he and his bodyguards had sheltered after their convoy, trying to flee the besieged and ruined city of Sirte, had been hit by an air strike. Later, more graphic footage appeared to show one rebel fighter sodomizing Gaddafi with a stick.[41]

'What did I do to you?' were among his last words, according to eye-witnesses. It was reportedly an eighteen-year-old from Misrata who fired the fatal shot into the side of Gaddafi's head. But it did not really matter who the executioner was. After nine months, the first phase of the battle for Libya was finally over.

Yet even in death Gaddafi inspired fascination and controversy. The ultimate piece of booty, his body, was driven to Misrata and laid out on a plastic sheet in a meat freezer. Still not completely convinced it could be true, many Libyans travelled hundreds of miles to see the corpse of the man who had loomed over their country for forty-two years. Lying next to his rotting body was that of his son, Mo'atassim, who had also been captured alive. A video had shown him sitting on a chair, calmly smoking a cigarette and talking to his captors. At some point in the ensuing few hours, he was executed.

For the Libyans who had fought for so many months, perhaps Mo'atassim and his father deserved nothing better. Gaddafi lived by the sword and died by it, and in some ways this was a fitting end. But while most Libyans welcomed his demise and cared little about its method, others were also keen to see him held accountable in the dock. Had the NTC missed a chance to demonstrate that they wanted to leave behind the practices of the past and embrace the rule of law, beginning the new era as they would presumably wish to continue it?

This misses the point. The NTC never wielded enough authority to control the manner of Gaddafi's death, even if they had wanted to. Their leaders had international legitimacy but not domestic legitimacy. The people in charge were rebel fighters who were largely free to take matters into their own hands, as they had been since the beginning of the uprising. That freedom was highlighted a month later, when militia members stopped a car that was driving out of the southern desert town of Ubari. They questioned a bearded man dressed in Tuareg robes who called himself Abdelsalam, but who on further inspection turned out to be none other than Saif al-Islam, on the run since the fall of Tripoli in August.

The former darling of the West was swiftly flown to Zintan, where he essentially became a bargaining chip in the jostling for post-revolutionary power. He was still there by the end of 2012.

Out of the Cycle

A few Libyans may still remember the set of elections in 1952 that followed unification and the appointment of King Idris as monarch. Dogged by accusations of vote-rigging, the ballot triggered unrest that ultimately led to political parties being banned and left behind a weak government structure that was eventually overturned by Gaddafi in 1969. By the end of

2012, there were hopeful signs that the first Libyan elections for more than sixty years might produce something longer-lasting.

More than 1.7 million voters, a turnout of 62 per cent, had gone to the polls in July to choose the 200 members of the General National Congress (GNC), the new Libyan parliament. Although they were delayed, the elections were a success and fostered a relatively smooth transition from the self-appointed interim government, in place since 2011, to one that could claim popular legitimacy.

Unlike in Tunisia or Egypt, the vote produced a fractured parliament with no single dominant group. This was partly because of how the GNC was structured, with 120 seats set aside for independent members and the remaining 80 for political parties, but also because Libyan voters were not polarized along the same lines as their neighbours. For better or worse, Gaddafi left little or no ideological legacy to shape politics after he had gone.

Mahmoud Jibril's National Forces Alliance, a loose collection of smaller parties, took almost half of the seats allocated for parties but still lacked a majority to force through decisions. The Justice and Construction Party, which was affiliated to Libya's Muslim Brotherhood, won seventeen seats, while Abdelhakim Belhadj's more conservative party, Al Watan, failed to win a single one.

On the one hand, a dispersed parliament means that no single group can railroad decisions – as Egypt's Muslim Brotherhood was increasingly accused of doing by late 2012. On the other, it may be a recipe for sluggish decision-making, as the formation of a new cabinet in the autumn seemed to suggest. The new parliament rejected two cabinets put forward by Mustafa Abu Shagour, who narrowly defeated Jibril to become prime minister. Parliamentarians then removed Abu Shagour through a no-confidence vote before finally giving the green light to a government line-up presented by his successor, former lawyer and diplomat Ali Zeidan.

The new government's task of navigating the next phase of the Libyan transition will not be easy. An elected government theoretically holds the reins of power, but its control over the country is in practice tenuous. That was highlighted in dramatic fashion on 11 September 2012, when US ambassador Christopher Stephens was killed during the storming of an American diplomatic building in Benghazi. Whether the attack was premeditated by an Al-Qaeda affiliate on the anniversary of 9/11, or was the unforeseen result of a more spontaneous protest over an Islamophobic film called *The Innocence of Muslims*, produced by a US-based Egyptian Copt, it highlighted the deeply precarious security situation in Libya. It also carried more than a tinge of tragic irony, given Benghazi's status as the birthplace of the 2011 uprising and the pivotal role that Washington played in bringing down Gaddafi.

The attack, as well as other incidents including an attempt on the life of the British ambassador, suggested that extremist Islamist groups such as Ansar al-Sharia had free rein in the post-revolutionary power vacuum. Reports suggested links between Libyan extremist groups and Al-Qaeda in the Islamic Maghreb (AQIM), which operates in the lawless parts of the Sahara that straddle Algeria, Mali, Niger and Chad, and whose borders with Libya are even more porous now than they were under Gaddafi.

In the south-west, semi-nomadic Libyan Tuareg have long wandered freely from country to country. Not all are or were pro-Gaddafi, but he had some success in winning loyalty by supporting their campaign for greater autonomy in Niger and Mali, or by naturalization or recruitment into the military. Some Tuareg assisted Gaddafi's inner circle during 2011. With his defeat, they moved out of Libya, taking large numbers of looted weapons to help spark a crisis in northern Mali in spring 2012. It was another unforeseen consequence of the intervention, and one with disastrous effects for Libya's poorer southern neighbours.

Localised clashes flared up inside Libya itself throughout 2012, often over control of lucrative cross-border smuggling routes. The most serious was in Bani Walid, which in October was besieged and then attacked by militias who were essentially wreaking vengeance for the town's pro-Gaddafi stance during the conflict. The interim government was virtually powerless to halt the battle.

Even in Tripoli, crime and lawlessness appeared to be on the rise, with more frequent reports of abductions, car-jackings and break-ins. The ominous-sounding Supreme Security Council (SSC), essentially a militia put in charge of securing Tripoli after Gaddafi fled in August 2011, had become a law unto itself, and many residents were increasingly fed up and fearful. Several attacks by ultra-conservative Salafists on Sufi shrines caused widespread anger, especially when a mosque containing the shrine of a fifteenth-century Islamic scholar was bulldozed in broad daylight, with no police or army able to stop it.

If imposing state authority was the most urgent of the tasks confronting the new government by the end of 2012, another was deciding how much political and financial power to devolve to the local level, and reverse the damaging centralisation that Gaddafi had pushed through during his rule.

This issue has historical overtones. Back in 1950, Adrian Pelt, a Dutchman assigned by the UN to help forge a new political structure for unified Libya, invited seven representatives from Tripolitania in the west, Cyrenaica in the east, and the Fezzan in the south to form a new national assembly. The provinces were arguably a colonial-era invention that allowed France, the UK and Italy to carve up Libya for their own interests; it would be a mistake to imagine today that there are three distinct zones within Libya, each with their own coherent desires, identities and outlooks. The current reality is far more fractured, something which actually bodes well. Throughout 2012 Libya was effectively composed of *de facto* self-governing towns and cities, many of which organized their own local council elections, overseen by a weak central authority with a short-term remit. Importantly, this self-rule takes place at town level, not regional level, and individual towns within a specific region often have greater antagonisms with one another than with places hundreds of miles away.

This system has partly developed due to the top-level power void since the end of the 2011 conflict, but also dates further back. The Gaddafi regime was not a totalitarian structure that could effectively control every corner of Libya through a system of local offices or branches. That would be giving far too much credit to its organizational ability. In truth it was a patronage network, co-opting different extended families or towns and often devolving some local powers – although it always had a veto and could always impose its will by force.

On the positive side, this means that there are no regional armies or regional governments to fight one another. Clashes and disputes may be all too common, but they will be waged between smaller communities rather than larger units. For that reason it is hard to see a major civil war developing in Libya, or any discernible 'front' between warring parties of a significant size.

Money will also play both a stabilising and destabilising role. Comparisons have been made between Libya and other post-conflict countries that have suffered from freely-circulating weapons and a weak central authority, such as Lebanon, Iraq or Yemen. None of these comparisons is particularly accurate, but one fundamental difference in Libya, aside from the lack of sectarian divides, is the combination of a wealthy government and a tiny population. On the one hand this means there is more to fight over. On the other, it means that the state can theoretically afford to buy stability, whether by integrating former fighters into the armed forces or simply by purchasing their weapons.

But to persuade people to give up their guns, the government will first have to prove it can provide security. Crucially, it must also deliver what Gaddafi did not: good-quality housing, schools, hospitals, roads, universities, utilities and other basic public services. This might sound straightforward for a country with no debt and plenty of oil, but there is a huge risk that ministries and funds will be treated as private fiefdoms and run through patronage networks, much as they were under the old regime. But any system that fails to use oil revenues in a more efficient and distributive way than its predecessor will not last long. Unemployment is high, especially amongst young people, and outlying areas that were previously marginalised – including Benghazi and the north-east – will need winning over in order to ease discontent.

Libya's wealth helped it get through the fragile post-revolutionary period, and oil output returned to normal much more swiftly than expected, but the country is not as rich as it seems. The revolution has saddled state finances with enormous bills: in the first ten months of 2012, for instance, the government was spending an average of $71m every day on public-sector wages and subsidies on basic foods, fuel and services. Petrol prices were slashed in 2011 to just $0.12 a litre, making them just about the lowest in the world. Unless those costs can be streamlined, Libya will need external sources of finance if it wants to build everything that its people will expect.

Foreign contractors, who were undertaking the bulk of construction in Libya prior to the revolution, remained reluctant to resume work without receiving old outstanding payments and without an improvement in the security situation. At the same time, the government was reviewing all contracts signed under the Gaddafi regime, a process which could theoretically take years.

Libya will not be transformed overnight from one of the world's most difficult places to do business into an efficient, transparent and investor-friendly haven. Some problems, like bureaucracy, corruption and infighting, are unlikely to get better quickly, and others may get worse. By the end of her tenure in November 2012, the interim health minister, Fatima Hamrouch, was forced to travel with eight armed bodyguards and live in a hotel because she feared for her life after attempting to expose widespread misuse of public finances since the revolution.

Similarly, while a new government might play less hardball than Gaddafi on contracts with international oil companies, it will also face popular pressure to safeguard national resources and sovereignty. Issues of trust between Libya and the international community will have to be overcome, a job made more difficult by a surge of post-revolutionary nationalism.

Having its own source of wealth means that Libya need not be in financial hock to overseas patrons, but many foreign parties are jostling to win contracts, attract Libyan investment and gain local influence to help justify the financial, military and moral support they provided in 2011. While feelings towards the West have certainly warmed in many quarters, general suspicion of overseas interference has deepened in others – and the legacy of the past four decades will take time to dissipate.

Whether democratic legitimacy trumps revolutionary legitimacy will be central to whether Libya really has moved on. It will take years to know the answer, and so far the picture is mixed. The process of integrating all the diverse local interests into a new political and economic structure will be volatile, with sticking points about representation in the national assembly, decentralisation and – as with Tunisia and Egypt – the role of religion. Writing all that into a new constitution, which the transitional timetable hopes to achieve in 2013, will be a spiky process.

Another obvious question, and one with particular relevance for Syria, is whether the NATO-led intervention was ultimately a success or a failure. Many commentators have unhelpfully analyzed Libya's post-revolutionary progress through the prism of this question, seeking to make a bigger argument about Western foreign policy. One side has cherry-picked evidence to argue that military interventions tend to be disastrous, the other has used the same technique to propose the opposite. Both sometimes overlook what is arguably the most troubling aspect of the 2011 intervention: the fact that a major military action can be approved by the UN but then outsourced to a small number of countries who are effectively free to direct it as they wish.

Was the Libya of late 2012 a better place to live than that of late 2010? On a day-to-day level, probably not. Crime was on the rise, corruption was still commonplace, more trash littered the streets of Tripoli, power cuts were more frequent, the rule of law remained weak, and if the revolution had not happened, thousands of new apartments and houses under construction in 2010 would have been finished by now.

But are Libya's long-term prospects now better than they were under Gaddafi? The answer, surely, is yes. A bright future is there for the taking, and it is up to Libyans alone to either seize or squander it. For all its pitfalls and problems, the country enjoys many natural advantages that Yemen, another Arab state having to confront the legacy of a longstanding leader in 2012, sorely lacked.

CHAPTER 8

Disintegrating Yemen

He who fills our hands with coins is our Sultan.

– Yemeni saying

The civilian and military mingle almost seamlessly in Yemen, a country where open conflict never lurked far beneath the surface before 2011, erupted during it, and will persist long afterwards. At Sana'a International Airport, whose terminal looks and feels more like a bus station than the international gateway for a capital city, passenger aircraft take off and land from the same runway as Soviet-era Mig–29s whose parachutes puff up as they touch down. The curved *jambiya* dagger that Yemeni men, young and old, tuck into their belts are not just for decoration; they are kept sharp. Outside the cities, in the north of the country, it was not so rare to see men carrying AK47s slung over their backs, despite government efforts to stop guns being so openly carried in public. Yemen is reckoned to be the world's most heavily armed country after the United States – although it might well have lost ground to Libya after 2011.[1]

More than a century's worth of conflict is commemorated in often uncompromising detail in the National War Museum in central Sana'a. Outside the front entrance near Tahrir Square – renamed Taghyeer, or Change, Square by the demonstrators who gathered there in 2011 – are several Ottoman-era cannons, the husk of a torpedo and what looks like a very early version of a tank. Inside, blurry black-and-white photos from the first half of the twentieth century show a series of grim executions. Parked in an interior courtyard at the back of the building is a purple limousine which, according to the endearingly misspelled sign next to it, was an 'Armour Cadillac American cr used by the forst president after revolution'.

An old fighter jet stood redundant nearby, its tail fin still adorned with the North Yemen flag in a reminder of the period between 1967 and 1990 when the country was split into two, and which it may be once more in the future.[2]

Given this volatile heritage, it was somewhat surprising that Ali Abdullah Saleh, who became president of North Yemen in 1978 after his predecessor was assassinated, had not just managed to stay in office for more than three decades, but had actually remained alive for that long. Many had thought his political career was over in June 2011, after a rocket attack left him severely burned and temporarily exiled him to Saudi Arabia for medical treatment. But the diminutive, moustachioed Saleh was nothing if not a survivor. His return in September would add fresh drama to a complex and often tragic tale in which the Arab Spring had penned only the latest chapter.

If the removal of authoritarian leaders in Libya, Egypt or Tunisia unleashed battles that had been festering for decades, then those battles were bursting violently above the surface in Yemen long before 2011. A sustained uprising in the north-west, a resurgent separatist movement in the south, an increasingly ambitious Al-Qaeda franchise, a looming succession crisis, myriad tribal rivalries and persistent deadlock over constitutional reform were already hammering cracks in a brittle national unity. Add a collapsing economy, dwindling oil and water resources, rampant demographic growth and the worst living standards in the Arabic-speaking world, and the picture gets even bleaker.

Yemen has long been Arabia's anomaly. It is the only country on the peninsula to hold meaningful elections, however dysfunctional they might be, and the only one to permit political parties. Its heritage, culture and concept as a specific geographical place date back much further than those of its *arriviste* Arabian neighbours. 'When Yemen was civilization, the House of Saud was still a tent,' was how one observer put it.[3] But Arabia Felix is less happy now than it was in the first century after Christ, when Pliny the Elder described it as the richest land in the world. Behind the facade of democratic institutions, political parties and elections lies a complex system of tribal, religious and regional affiliations that have long prevented the emergence of a strong state. Managing them is what Saleh once likened to 'dancing on the heads of snakes' – although some would say he was the biggest snake of them all.

Tens of thousands of young Yemenis marched and occupied the streets of the country's largest cities in 2011, inspired by events in Tunisia and

Egypt, to demand a wholesale overhaul of their own political system. For a brief moment, they were joined together with other groups to share what seemed to be a vision of a unified, democratic country that involved neither their long-standing president nor the system he oversaw. They were tired of being neglected, not only by a regime bent on extending its own longevity, but also by international powers that seemed to interact with Yemen only in terms of their own interests.

But that moment proved to be fleeting. Those seeking to achieve what their counterparts had managed in Tunisia were facing a hopeless task in a country that shared few traits with the birthplace of the Arab Spring. They would soon be figuratively and literally caught up in the crossfire of conflicts being waged between more powerful forces that despite removing Saleh as president, would in 2012 would take the country down a depressingly familiar path.

Divided, not Conquered

As remarkable as Saleh's ability to cling to power over the years was Yemen's ability to hold together in the two decades following the 1990 unification that rejoined north and south. Understanding the many different fractures that dislocated the country in 2011 requires going back to their roots. Yemen is a place that has always existed more as a concept than as a state. Its forbidding but beautiful landscapes, its mountains and deserts, highlands and lowlands, isolated valleys and remote plains had long thwarted the attempts of national or foreign powers to extend their control over tribal fiefdoms that fiercely defended themselves against outside parties they saw as suspicious and ephemeral interlopers.

Yemeni civilization can be traced back to antiquity, but much of its twentieth-century history – and perhaps its immediate future – was characterized by the divide that split the country into two very different states. This divide was nothing new. Since the middle of the nineteenth century, the British had established themselves in the strategic deepwater port of Aden, signing loose agreements with tribal sheikhs throughout the south but never really trying to impinge on their local autonomy. The more populous north-west had lived under a religious Imamate that until the First World War had vied with the Ottomans for the control of territory. A succession crisis in 1962 triggered a bloody civil war that drew in Gamal Abdel Nasser's Egypt on one side, and Saudi Arabia and Britain on the other. The Egypt-backed military regime emerged victorious, giving birth to the Yemen Arab Republic (YAR), with its capital in the highland town of Sana'a.

Britain's 1967 withdrawal from Aden led to the creation of the People's Democratic Republic of Yemen (PDRY) in the south, a distinctly odd entity that was the only self-declared Marxist state in the Arabic-speaking world, marrying the unlikely bedfellows of urban socialism and rural tribalism. Troubled by internal conflict throughout its short history, the PDRY lost its financial and ideological *raison d'être* with the collapse of the Soviet Union in 1990, and merged with Saleh's north. But many south Yemenis, as 2011 would again show, had never come to terms with unification.

Other tectonic plates were also grinding against each other. Since 2004, Saleh's military had battled at least six rounds of rebellion in the mountainous north-west province of Sa'ada, which shares a long and porous border with Saudi Arabia. This was a many-layered conflict that spanned religious, tribal and political issues, but at its heart was a local Zaydi community that felt economically marginalized and vulnerable to political and religious interference from Sana'a and further afield.

The population of Sa'ada is mostly Zaydi, members of an offshoot of Shi'ite Islam who are estimated to make up slightly less than half of all Yemenis – including Saleh's own tribe. In the 1990s, Zaydis in Sa'ada had set up a group called the 'Believing Youth' as a means to protect their religious and regional identity against external influence, especially the puritanical *Wahhabi* form of Sunni Islam that is practised and promoted by Saudi Arabia. After local protests in 2004, the authorities tried to arrest Hussein al-Houthi, a Believing Youth leader and an outspoken member of a prominent local family. Saleh subsequently sent forces into the province to quell what had become an armed rebellion, killing Houthi in September 2004 but triggering several confused bouts of war over the next five years that would again come to the fore in 2011.

Sa'ada had an international narrative too, with Saudi Arabia launching a military intervention after the fighting spilled across its border in 2009. Saleh had long stoked fears in Riyadh, claiming from an early stage that the Houthis were backed by Iran, and sought to establish a new Imamate in the north-west while also linking them variously to Al-Qaeda, Gaddafi's Libya and Lebanon's Hezbollah.

Another narrative, which only later became clearer, was an apparent proxy war between different Yemeni military units and their commanders. Rumours spread that General Ali Mohsin al-Ahmar, a member of the president's Sanhan tribe, who headed the army's First Armoured Division in the Sa'ada wars, was at increasingly bitter odds with Saleh's eldest son, Ahmed Ali, who headed the elite Republican Guard. Mohsin, a powerful potential rival to Saleh in his own right, was against the idea of Ahmed Ali inheriting power. A WikiLeaks cable released in 2010 suggested that Saleh officials had, a year earlier, provided the Saudi military with bombing coordinates that were centred on Mohsin's headquarters in Sa'ada. According to the document, it was only when Saudi pilots raised doubts about their target that the bombing raid was called off.[4] Other rumours claimed that Saleh had deliberately supplied the Houthis with anti-tank missiles in a bid to weaken the military units under Mohsin's command. These tensions would blow up into open warfare in 2011.

The Houthi rebellion highlighted not only Yemen's political, regional and tribal strains, but also its economic fragility. The total direct cost of the Sa'ada wars was estimated at over $1 billion, and even if Riyadh stumped up some of the bill, it was nonetheless enormously expensive for a country that was rapidly running out of money. Oil exports had been the backbone of the economy since unification, but Yemen's energy resources are expected to dry up completely some time in the 2020s.[5] Oil production declined from 450,000 barrels per day (b/d) in 2000 to about 260,000 b/d in 2010, equivalent to just three per cent of Saudi Arabia's output, but nonetheless the source of about three-quarters of Yemen's government revenue and 90 per cent of its exports.

Nor was oil the only commodity in short supply. Yemen's annual renewable water supplies per capita are barely more than 10 per cent of the Middle East and North Africa average, with its groundwater supplies being rapidly depleted by a 24 million-strong population that is easily the quickest-growing in the region. The state has lacked the resources and the authority to manage its water resources, failing to prevent illegal wells, mass wastage and inefficient forms of irrigation that are drying up stocks at an alarming rate. Resource scarcity has also incurred a sizeable human cost, one study estimating that armed disputes over land and water kill 4,000 Yemenis each year.[6]

About a third of the country's groundwater is guzzled by a single crop, *qat*, whose narcotic, chewable leaves have contributed in no small way to Yemen's woes. In one of the world's most impoverished countries, a depressingly large proportion of household income is set aside for daily purchases of the plant. A World Bank survey in 2007 found that 72 per cent of men and 33 per cent of women were regular users, with more than half of male consumers spending at least four hours every day chewing the bright green leaf.[7] From the early afternoon, pick-up trucks roll into markets across Sana'a to meet the ever-reliable stream of customers eager to stuff their cheeks with snooker ball-sized clumps of the plant. Various government and international campaigns have tried to wean Yemenis off their habit, especially in the north, where it is much more prevalent, but with little apparent success.

The socio-economic curse of *qat* is one reason why Yemen was ranked 154th out of 187 countries in the UN's 2011 Human Development Index, which measures indicators like poverty, inequality, education and health, and noted that more than a third of Yemenis are illiterate and almost a fifth live on less than $1.25 a day.[8] Schools, hospitals and basic infrastructure are hopelessly inadequate in a country where, outside the cities, you can drive for hours without seeing many obvious signs of the state.

Even before the Arab Spring, Yemen's fragile political structure was in a state of stagnation, if not outright crisis. In early 2009, Yemen's political parties had agreed to delay parliamentary elections to allow time for dialogue on reforming the electoral and constitutional framework that Saleh and the General People's Congress (GPC), the apparatus he had formed in 1982 to rule the YAR, had moulded to their own needs since 1990. Yemen's first post-unification presidential elections were in 1999, with Saleh essentially running unopposed and winning 96 per cent of the vote. A second poll in 2006, deemed to be freer and fairer, saw Saleh win a second seven-year term with 77 per cent of votes.

The GPC had dominated the Yemeni parliament since unification, and in 2009 held 235 out of 301 seats. The largest opposition party was Islah, or Reform, a tribal-Islamist alliance headed by one of the north's most powerful families, which in 2002 had loosely coalesced with the four other main parties to form the Joint Meeting Parties (JMP). With a long-held conviction that political institutions were tilted so steeply towards Saleh's power bases that democracy in Yemen had become the flimsiest of veneers, the JMP had lobbied for electoral and constitutional reform to level the playing field. On the eve of the revolt, however, talks with Saleh and the GPC were at an impasse.

On top of all this, Islamic militants were attempting increasingly bold and frequent attacks, both inside Yemen and internationally, that had long provided another snake's head for Saleh to dance on – and some would say deliberately charm. Their rising ambitions in the years before the Arab Spring had become most associated with Al-Qaeda in the Arabian Peninsula (AQAP), an entity that developed from a small and fairly ragtag group of fighters returning from the Afghan *jihad* in the 1990s and was formed in early 2009 with the merger of the Saudi and Yemeni Al-Qaeda franchises.

Shortly after being appointed head of the CIA in summer 2011, General David Petraeus labelled AQAP as the 'most dangerous regional node in the global *jihad*'.[9] Opinions were divided on whether that was true or not, but they were certainly another layer in the quagmire of a country that, even before 2011, was already defined by its conflicts. Southern separatists were gaining traction, Houthi rebels were battling Saleh's forces and formal political institutions were paralysed by disagreements between the main clans that controlled them. Now, a surge of popular protests would add a new ingredient to the mix.

Springtime in Arabia

Like their counterparts around the region, a younger generation of Yemenis was inspired by events in Tunisia to take to the streets in early 2011. The JMP, frustrated by the meagre progress in reforming the dysfunctional political system, had organized licenced rallies in January to demand reform within the system, rather than the removal of the president. From the very start, however, youth activists and more strident elements of the formal political parties, like Tawakul Karman – an Islah party member who would share the Nobel Peace Prize later that year – were calling for Saleh to step down.

But it was the electrifying news of Hosni Mubarak's departure on 11 February that began to transform the organized, relatively moderate rallies into much more organic, spontaneous and large-scale demonstrations calling for Saleh's downfall. Mimicking the slogans used in North Africa, like *irhal*, or 'get out', and *al-sha'ab yurid isqat al-nizam*, or 'the people want the fall of the regime', what started as small-scale rallies soon gathered their own momentum. Thousands of demonstrators marched in several major cities, including Sana'a, Aden, Ibb and especially Ta'iz, the country's industrial and intellectual capital and considered to be more secular than other Yemeni cities.

At this stage, protesters appeared to be united under the banner of removing Saleh and ensuring that Yemen did not miss out on a historic wave of change that, in mid-February, seemed like the start of a domino effect that might bring down governments from Morocco to Bahrain. Students in Sana'a, separatists in the south and even some elements of the Houthis in Sa'ada, were discussing ways to work together and, for the time being, putting aside the fact that they had divergent goals and aspirations. An estimated 100,000 people took part in a demonstration in Ta'iz on 25 February, with tens of thousands coming out in Sana'a and Aden as the JMP, which had been overtaken by organic, unorganized marches, also announced their support for the movement.

Saleh appeared to be on the back foot. His forces had already killed a number of demonstrators, and had initially dealt most harshly with the surge of pro-secession protests in the south that repeated calls for a referendum on independence. Between nine and eighteen people were killed in the south in late February and many others disappeared, including leading figures from the southern separatist movement.[10] Several GPC members resigned over the violence and, faced with increasing pressure, Saleh announced that he would not run in the 2013 presidential election, nor hand over power to his eldest son, Ahmed. For the protesters, 2013 was two years too long and would give Saleh the time to reassert control and roll back on his promises.

In the background was the escalating enmity between Saleh's family and its biggest rival, the Ahmar clan. Both were part of Yemen's largest tribal confederation, the Hashid, which had been led for many years by Sheikh Abdullah bin Hussein al-Ahmar, who was also the speaker of the Yemeni parliament and leader of the Islah party. He acted as a vital and influential counterweight to Saleh's own family, and his death in 2007 provided another catalyst for the unstable chemical reaction that would bubble over in 2011. He left behind several powerful sons who grew openly antagonistic towards Saleh and his own family, which now began to exhibit more open signs of autocracy. 'After Sheikh Abdullah's death, you began to see the state media refer to Saleh as "His Excellency" whereas before they would call him "brother", observed one expert in Yemeni tribes. 'He tried to portray a different image to before.'[11]

The most powerful of Sheikh Abdullah's nine sons publicly broke ranks with Saleh early on during the protests. After initially sitting on the fence, the fifty-five-year-old Sadiq al-Ahmar, who had inherited the Islah leadership, issued a statement in March calling on Saleh to respect popular demands and step down. Hameed al-Ahmar, a billionaire businessman who ran one of Yemen's mobile phone operators, told the *New York Times* in the same month that 'there is no more government now, just gangs'.[12] Another son, Hussein al-Ahmar, had resigned from the GPC in late February and began encouraging his tribal supporters and other disparate groups to put aside their differences and help topple the regime.

A turning point in this power struggle, and in the broader disintegration of the country, came on 18 March, when snipers shot and killed some fifty-four demonstrators, mainly youth protesters, at a peaceful march close to Sana'a University. Saleh subsequently declared a state of emergency and blamed the deaths on armed groups acting outside of his control.[13] The incident ignited popular fury and prompted one of the largest rallies of 2011, with an estimated 150,000 marching in Sana'a and tens of thousands across other cities. Whereas resignations had previously been a trickle, they now became a wave. Dozens of civil servants and politicians rushed to dissociate themselves from the regime. Tourism minister Nabil al-Faqih became the first cabinet member to resign, and for many more the massacre, known as the *jumaa al-karama*, or the Friday of Dignity, was a point of no return in their willingness to negotiate with Saleh.

But the most important defections in March were military. General Ali Mohsin announced on 21 March that he would deploy units under his command to protect the protesters, signalling a split with Saleh that amounted to a declaration of armed opposition, if not outright war. It triggered a series of further defections in the military and pitted Mohsin's loyal troops, including his First Armoured Division, against the elite units, like the Presidential and the Republican Guards, which were directly controlled by Saleh's family. Mohsin had effectively joined forces with the al-Ahmar family, although there was limited physical cooperation between the two, and had taken the lid off a pressure cooker that had been simmering over the preceding years.

The defections would have mixed effects. On the one hand they offered clear evidence that the protests were changing the status quo, and seemed to bolster the strength, numbers and resolve of the anti-Saleh opposition. But on the other, it was the moment when the pattern of the protest movement was overshadowed by bigger forces. Some independent youth groups already resented the formal political parties for piggy-backing on the activist movement for their own ends, and now what had previously been a cold war between two of north Yemen's most powerful tribal clans was becoming an open conflict. While the defections meant that Saleh had lost significant allies, it raised the possibility that even if his regime or his family were ousted, they would be replaced not by a real democracy but by a similar tribal power structure. The disparate protest groups kept up the momentum of cooperation into April, but the longer the Ahmar-Saleh conflict dragged on in Sana'a and the surrounding regions, and the more the flow of defections slowed, the more likely different sections of the opposition were to retreat back into their own specific demands.

Meanwhile, top-down efforts were also under way to push Saleh out. In April, the Gulf Cooperation Council (GCC), dominated by Saudi Arabia, had drafted a transition proposal in which the Yemeni president would step down within thirty days and give way to a new president, who would be elected within two months. But recent efforts at external mediation in Yemen – like Qatar's efforts to broker a ceasefire in Sa'ada – had borne few fruits.

Over the years, Washington and Riyadh had poured funds into Saleh's coffers in return for his dubious support in tackling Islamic militants. That gave him the breathing space to nurture other internal crises and argue that, for all his faults, he was the only man able to ward off chaos. Insofar as any coherent Saudi policy on Yemen could be identified, Riyadh seemed to be adhering to the approach that Abdulaziz ibn Saud, the kingdom's founder, had recommended when he apocryphally told his sons to 'keep Yemen weak'. Riyadh had regularly meddled in its neighbour, seeing it as a threat to its own stability, but also had little desire for Yemen to become a strong, democratic and independent state.

As part of the GCC deal, which was the only plan put forward by the international community to find a solution to the impasse, Saleh's family would also be given immunity from any future prosecution. Towards the end of the month Saleh announced that the terms were agreeable, but later refused to sign the document, stalling by demanding that the leaders of the opposition parties should have to sign the deal in his presidential palace. 'Are we going to deal over the phone? Why don't they come?' he complained. The frustrated GCC envoy gave up and went back to Riyadh, announcing that mediation efforts were now suspended.

Others took matters into their own hands. On 3 June, a rocket attack on Saleh's compound in Sana'a struck a mosque where the president was praying, killing at least ten officials and advisers. The assault came a few days after Saleh's units had shelled the compound of Hameed al-Ahmar, suggesting that this was a retaliatory attack by his rivals, for whom Saleh had recently issued arrest warrants on charges of leading an 'armed rebellion'.[14] Government spokespeople initially played down Saleh's wounds, but it soon became clear that they were serious. Two days later he flew to Riyadh for medical treatment, leaving behind more violent clashes but new hope among his opponents that they had perhaps seen the last of their president. Saleh then made no public appearance for another month, until a short televized speech from Riyadh on 7 July that showed him weakened and heavily bandaged, claiming to have undergone eight operations and calling for dialogue to solve Yemen's problems.

A renewed bout of violence erupted in mid-September, with an attack on mainly peaceful protesters in Sana'a that was thought to be the work of units under the command of Saleh's family. Some seventy-five protesters were killed in the space of three days as forces used anti-aircraft guns, rocket launchers and shells against protesters trying to move from Taghyeer Square into other areas of the capital. The airport closed for the first time that year, while basic utilities like electricity and water were cut down to a minimum. 'There is genuine support for both sides, but for the regime it has probably now increased because it has manipulated fears and made the conditions harsher, so people seek a return to normality at all costs, which they think only the regime can do,' said Abdel-Ghani al-Iryani, a Yemeni political analyst who was in Sana'a at the time.[15]

Transition plans continued to stall. In early September, Saleh's deputy, Abed Rabah Mansoor al-Hadi, promised to sign the GCC deal on his behalf, but then stalled. A few weeks later, an official photo showed Saleh sitting alongside King Abdullah, reinforcing a belief among many Yemenis that Saudi Arabia was complicit in abandoning them to their fate and the rapidly deteriorating conditions in the country. Then, on the morning of 23 September, Yemeni state TV dramatically announced that a private jet carrying the wounded president had landed in Sana'a at dawn. Saleh's return was met with anger and despair by his opponents, jubilation by his supporters, and a renewed burst of clashes between the rival military units in and around Sana'a. Many expected it to fling Yemen further down the track of confused civil war that it already appeared to be set on.

A Failing State

The tribal power struggle in the north had distracted and divided the strength of government military forces, weakening the state's already precarious control over many other areas of the country. While the Ahmars and the Salehs fought each other in the suburbs of Sana'a, the breakdown in law and order elsewhere persuaded a number of other powerful groups that now was the time to play their hand. 'Sana'a is weaker, and there is a sense that the rest of the country is not looking towards the capital but rather towards self-government,' was how Ali Saif Hassan, a

Yemeni political analyst and activist, saw it in September.[16] Many signs suggested that the Arab Spring could trigger the disintegration of the country.

Among those with a hand to play were Islamic militant groups, operating in what were now increasingly lawless and opaque southern regions. The size, influence and capabilities of these groups remained unclear, but some AQAP-linked individuals could certainly boast an impressive portfolio of both successful and failed exploits. They included the 2000 attack on the USS *Cole* in Aden, which killed seventeen US sailors, and a 2002 assault on the French oil tanker *Limburg*. In 2006, some twenty-three Al-Qaeda-linked militants, several of whom were involved in planning the USS *Cole* bombing, tunnelled out of a prison in Sana'a.

In September 2008, AQAP had claimed responsibility for a bomb at the US embassy in Sana'a that killed sixteen people, all Yemenis, and had also organized several fatal attacks on European tourists inside Yemen. The group admitted to planning the failed bombing of a Detroit-bound plane on Christmas Day in 2009, attempting to kill the British ambassador in Sana'a in April 2010, and planting a series of explosive devices on cargo planes destined for the United States in October of the same year. It had also dispatched a suicide bomber to Riyadh in August 2009 in a failed attempt to assassinate Mohammed bin Nayef, Saudi Arabia's counter-terrorism chief and the son of the man who would become the kingdom's crown prince in October 2011.[17]

To Western eyes, one of the most high-profile and dangerous of the Islamic extremists in Yemen was Anwar al-Awlaki, a cleric who had lived much of his life in the United States, held American citizenship and spoke fluent English. Among those who claimed to have been inspired by Awlaki were Nidal Hussein, the US army officer who shot dead thirteen people at the Fort Hood base in Texas in November 2009, and Faisal Shahzad, the Pakistani who planned a failed car-bomb attack in Times Square in May 2010. Awlaki had earned the dubious honour of being the first US citizen ever to be placed on the CIA's hit list, and his killing by a US drone in September 2011 certainly mattered more to Washington than it did to most Yemenis.

It had long suited Saleh to tar as many people as possible, especially in the south, with the brush of Islamic militancy. While that label probably applied to a relatively small hardcore group, the breakdown of centralized military power over 2011 appeared to have emboldened them. Most accounts from the confused frontlines reported widespread clashes between Islamic fighters and government forces.

In April a senior member of AQAP, Adel al-Abab, had given an interview in which he claimed that the group, which he said was also known as Ansar al-Sharia, or Partisans of Islamic Law, had made gains in many provinces throughout the south, and was urging fighters to take the battle to the Houthis in the north.[18] In May, reports claimed that Islamic fighters had taken over the southern town of Zinjibar, defeating central government forces and disrupting the whole region. Many Zinjibar residents fled, some painting a grim picture of the town they had left behind, characterized by 'destroyed homes and shuttered shops, with dogs eating corpses on the streets'.[19] By June, according to the UN, the conflict across the southern Abyan governorate had created 20,000 new Yemeni refugees as confused and sporadic fighting persisted.[20] It would be another year before government forces could drive out Ansar al-Sharia from Abyan, in the process creating what a December 2012 Amnesty International report called a 'human rights catastrophe'.

There were also accusations that Saleh had deliberately ceded some towns and cities to reinforce the perception – to the outside world, at least – that without him, Yemen would become another Somalia. This was a tried and tested strategy, and one holding mainly financial incentives. Security cooperation and financial support from Washington had intensified sharply in the aftermath of 9/11 during the hunt for suspected Al-Qaeda militants based in Yemen. Those interests were aligned closely with the Al Saud in Riyadh, who were equally concerned about threats to their own power. In 2010, US secretary of state Robert Gates had approved an increase of official US military aid to Yemen from $67 million to $150 million, in addition to an unknown sum for covert assistance. In the same year, King Abdullah paid Saleh a grant of $700 million, despite opposition from some of the Saudi monarch's siblings. In the context of dwindling oil revenues, these handouts had become a vital source of income for the Yemeni president. To keep receiving them, he had to convince his foreign allies that AQAP did indeed pose a serious threat.

The lack of central control had also allowed the southern movement to gain traction. Ever since reunification, many in the south bitterly resented what they felt was a deliberate marginalization by the north. In the mid-2000s, a range of groups including civil society organizations and professional associations formed an umbrella entity called Al-Hirak Al-Jnoubi, or the Southern Movement. They had different ideas about what exactly the south should be, and how to achieve their various aspirations, but their broad general demands included greater local autonomy, a more equal distribution of state resources and better access to benefits and jobs. Saleh's regime had responded with a mix of repression and dialogue that ultimately proved fruitless and, if anything, convinced southerners that working within the framework of national unity could not produce the results they wanted.

'The civil war was the referendum,' had been Saleh's response to those calling for a public poll on southern independence. Clashes, arrests and pro-secession protests had intensified in 2009 and 2010 but the movement lacked unity and, critically, any real support from the outside world.[21] But Saleh still took it seriously enough to ask Saudi Arabia and Oman to extradite exiled senior leaders of the PDRY, including a former president, for allegedly stirring up sentiment that undermined Yemen's stability.

While the first few months of 2011 had seen some degree of cooperation between Hirak activists and the broader protest movement in the north, the southern interest groups had reverted back to their own specific demands over the summer and autumn. Many had lost faith that the protest movement in the north was genuinely supportive of southern independence, or even a federalist system, while disagreements with the official political parties over how the southern issue would be handled and prioritized in any post-Saleh era had also caused disillusionment. With events in Sana'a descending into a power struggle between rival northern tribes, southern activists became increasingly convinced that their fate would not necessarily be tied to what happened in the capital.

By the early summer, South Yemeni flags had already begun to fly above buildings in Aden as secessionists became bolder. In Sana'a, a group calling itself the 'Sons of the Southern Provinces in Sana'a' met in April, attracting more than 600 people to discuss plans for separatism or federalism.[22] Senior figures from the old PDRY, now exiled abroad, also became increasingly active as they saw a chance to press home their cause. They included the former president Ali Salim al-Beedh, who had been a proponent of unification in 1990 but was later exiled by Saleh after the failed secession attempt in 1994. Al-Beedh had since become one of the most vocal supporters of full independence for the south, but his views were not shared by other influential figures in the movement. In May, a group of southern supporters had met in Cairo and concluded that the best solution would be a two-state federal system, each with its own parliament and autonomy over internal affairs. That idea was backed by Ali Naser Mohammed and Haydar al-Attas, both former senior politicians from the PDRY, who argued that it was a more realistic goal than total autonomy.

But the absence of a clear, united stand by Hirak and the various strands it represents has doubtless limited its ability. The group has no strong organization or central leadership hierarchy, and many of its best-known figures have exhibited conflicting loyalties and shifting allegiances. The amount of leverage that its former leaders have on the ground is unclear. while the southern movement in general was an assortment of various groups often with different objectives. While the biggest divide lay between separatists and federalists, many south Yemenis simply want general improvements in their living standards rather than greater political representation. The support for different groups within Hirak varies from place to place around the south, and in many it appears to overlap with local tribal loyalties that take precedence above all else.

Those preferring separatism to federalism faced an uphill struggle for several reasons. First, the military forces they could muster would not be powerful enough to win any all-out civil war unless the army fell apart into different tribal and regional groups. Second, the largest political parties in the north, including Islah, did not support southern independence and would have little interest in devolving any more power to the south than they had to, even though some influential figures in the north do recognize that the current system is unsustainable. Third, there is little obvious foreign backing for the southern independence bid. Saudi support for Saleh had remained robust throughout the year, although Riyadh's hosting of several exiled PDRY leaders does suggest some hedging of bets. Neither the UK – the south's former colonial power – nor the United States have openly indicated any support for separation.

Another thorny issue in the southern question is Yemen's energy resources, which despite being rapidly depleted are nonetheless the financial underpinning of the state. They pose a geographic conundrum, with some oilfields straddling the pre-1990 borders between north and south and the majority of them located in southern areas themselves. The Yemen LNG project, a natural gas scheme that is the single largest investment in the country, draws on the Block 18 field in the province of Maarib, which also straddles the old borders, but the pipeline travels through south Yemen and its export terminal is on the Arabian Sea. Oil and gas revenues had been the source of several disputes during the 1990 unification process and would likely play the same role in any future debates over federalism or separatism.

Natural resources also played their part in another symptom of disintegrating state control in 2011. A council in the south-eastern Hadhramawt province, which covers more than a third of Yemen's entire territory, issued a statement in June demanding autonomy for the province as part of a wider federal system. They argued that Hadhramawt, which shares long borders with Oman and Saudi Arabia, should be allowed to maintain its own army and be granted the power to decide how the bulk of local revenues were spent. Hadhramawt is particularly important because of its oilfields, its long coastline and its powerful expatriate community, particularly in Saudi Arabia, where a number of billionaire merchant families – including the Bin Ladens – trace their origins to the Yemeni province. Some Yemenis fear that Riyadh has its own intentions in Hadhramawt, even seeking to annex the governorate or support its independence as a separatist state. Whatever the reality, the statement was another sign of how different regions were exploiting the weakness of Sana'a to assert their own identity and autonomy.

And this was not only happening in the south. In Sa'ada, which had attracted less international attention in the drama of 2011, the Houthis had been gaining even greater control over their territory and were also pushing outwards into other areas. 'The Houthis were the untold story of the uprising,' according to Dr April Alley, who writes and researches reports on Yemen for the International Crisis Group. 'They have come out of the turmoil as the most internally cohesive group.'[23]

Confused, sporadic fighting continued throughout the summer and autumn with attacks by Islamic militants and clashes between the Houthis and tribes loyal to the Islah party and extremist Salafist fighters. As 2011 began to draw to a close, these battles seemed to epitomize what had happened in Yemen during the course of the year. But there was still a twist in the tale.

Unhappy Arabia

In late October, the UN Security Council issued a resolution urging Saleh to accept the terms of the GCC proposal, under which he would step down. Saleh 'welcomed' the resolution and reiterated his commitment to 'the transition deal,' but said he would only hand over power to 'safe hands'. After delaying for weeks while the violence continued on the ground, he flew to Riyadh in mid-November and, much to the surprise of many Yemenis and international observers, inked the deal.

Under its terms, Saleh and his family were granted immunity from any future prosecution. He would retain the title of president, but power passed to his deputy, Abed Rabah al-Hadi, who organised elections in February

2012 in which he was the only candidate. Compared to the demise of Tunisia's Ben Ali, Libya's Gaddafi or Egypt's Mubarak, Saleh had secured by far the most favourable exit strategy of any Arab leader forced to relinquish power in 2011.

Youth groups rejected the deal, claiming that their revolution had been hijacked by the other political parties, especially Islah, that would use Saleh's departure to cement their own influence. Many also thought that Saleh, while alive and well and in the country, would continue to be president in practice if not in name. And other important constituencies, like the Hirak and the Houthis, were suspicious of a deal that seemed to be cooked up by the Sana'a based elites and their international powerbrokers.

It summed up the impact of the Arab Spring in Yemen, a country already in the grip of wrenching conflicts that shifted shapes several times throughout 2011. The successful removal of Egyptian and Tunisian leaders in January had inspired hundreds of thousands of mainly young, politically literate protesters to march against Saleh's regime in the hope of washing away a rotten political system and building a genuinely democratic new state. And for a time in March and April, Saleh faced a surprisingly united front of disparate interest groups that stuck together in the belief that they could find a solution that benefited all concerned. But that apparent unity did not last long.

Like the initial protesters in Tunisia or Egypt, who could articulate and galvanize negative sentiment but could not match the Islamists when it came to winning votes, so Yemen's peaceful demonstrators saw their hopes dashed. By breaking the fear barrier and drawing the elite military units into destructive infighting, they had opened up a window of opportunity that many other groups could exploit. Southern activists, who initially agreed to merge their demands with those of protesters in the north, concluded that their goals were best pursued alone, even though they also lacked a single voice. Quasi-autonomous tribes in the provinces saw that a distracted central government created an opportunity to establish an even greater control over their territories. Islamic militants saw a chance to make their own gains across and beyond the south, while Washington exploited the chaos to intensify its aerial strikes on suspected Al-Qaeda operatives that it felt posed an international threat.

And even a year after Saleh's exit deal went through, it seemed the reins of power had simply been passed between different elites rather than to the people, as what began as peaceful protests had been transformed into a battle between two powerful, well-armed and highly antagonistic clans.

European or other Arab powers that had helped remove Gaddafi or promised billions for democratic transitions in Tunisia or Egypt continued to view Yemen through the prism of their own issues, seeking to address the symptoms of the country's problems rather than a lasting solution to its causes. This is perhaps odd, given that Yemen occupies an important strategic location, sitting on one side of the Bab al-Mandab, or 'Gate of Grief', a narrow channel that links the Gulf of Aden with the Red Sea, the Suez Canal and ultimately the Mediterranean beyond. This is one of the world's most important shipping lanes, handling about 4 per cent of global oil production every year, and a vital trade route for the Mediterranean. It is also an obvious target for piracy and terrorism, particularly if cooperation between Yemen's Islamic fighters and those in nearby Somalia creates an arc of instability around the entrance to the Red Sea.

But Yemen was not Egypt, where Washington could pressure the army to force out Mubarak in the confidence that the country's military would be able to maintain some degree of continuity and stability after his departure. Power was in tribal rather than institutional hands. And Saleh was well aware that the turmoil in other Arab countries would distract the limited means and attention of the international community away from his own crisis.

Even though the transition deal avoided all-out war in 2011 and 2012, Yemen faces possible disintegration and an essentially non-existent central state. The country could split into north and south once more. Many southern independence groups are unwilling to accept anything less than full independence, and negotiating federalism will be a hugely complicated task given the political and economic issues that are involved. There is no obvious external mediator for Yemen's many conflicts. It took ten months of pressure to persuade Saleh to hand over power, a feat which may prove far easier than negotiating an end to the array of armed quarrels 'around the country' some of which are based on intractable grounds such as sectarianism.

But the biggest losers will be the silent majority of Yemenis who are far more concerned about finding the money for their next meal, or defending their land, than about reforming central political structures. Already living under an impoverished, weak state that was unable to even provide basic infrastructure, many might ask what Saleh's departure – the most obvious achievement of the 2011 maelstrom – had changed. The sad answer is that everyday life had simply become even more difficult.

Many could neither read or write, let alone access a computer or use Twitter. They wanted things to change, but suffocated under inflation that meant food and fuel prices were sometimes double what they were a year earlier. The economy, already barely functional, had collapsed further amid the unrest. Tourism and construction had ground to a halt. Oil output plummeted in the face of repeated attacks on pipelines and plants. The economy shrank by more than 10 per cent in 2011 and would contract again in 2012, while the UN's World Food Programme reported that the number of people receiving daily food rations more than tripled between January and September 2012.[24]

A fresh round of financial pledges in 2012 were intended to support the political transition process, with a total of more than $6bn promised from the World Bank, the US, various EU countries and Saudi Arabia – which remained by far Yemen's largest donor. Question marks hang over how effective that money will be, given the slow-moving, bureaucratic nature of government in Yemen, political fissures and the still-powerful patronage networks used by Saudi Arabia in particular to dispense informal largesse.

A National Dialogue Conference, intended to bring together all parties and groups – including the southern movement and the Houthis – had already been delayed by late 2012. The transition timetable plans a new set of elections for February 2014, by which time the Yemeni constitution is meant to have been amended, but already there are fears that this schedule is too ambitious. Real underlying reform of the economy will be impossible until the deeply engrained systems of patronage and corruption are eroded, and like other oil-poor Arab countries, Yemen will be caught between measures to win popular support, pleasing its international patrons, and taking painful long-term decisions to make its economy more viable. Attempting to curb the role of qat, for instance, will be complicated by the fact that it provides the main source of income for some 14 per cent of the population.[25]

By 2010 it was no secret that a perfect storm of crises loomed on the horizon. At the heart of Yemen's problem is the weakness of its state. Across this sprawling and beautiful land are dotted the relics of great and ancient civilizations, from the desert skyscrapers of Shibam to the postcard-perfect old city of Sana'a, yet you can drive for hours without seeing any sign of central government. Off the main road that links Sana'a to Aden, the streets are unpaved and children run around barefoot when they should be at school. Tribal and local allegiances outweigh loyalty to the central state, leading to a tragic situation where money and weapons, not political ideas, are the currency of power.

As the peaceful youth demonstrators discovered in 2011, Yemen inhabits a different world from Tunisia, even though the two countries shared grievances such as widespread unemployment, rampant corruption and a lack of change at the top. The prospect of any all-encompassing solution to Yemen's problems is unrealistic, and the rivalry between the Al-Ahmar and Saleh families risks flaring up into conflict at any moment. Neither, so far, appear to have lost much of their political and military clout as a result of the transition.

Yet Saleh's departure may still prove to be the first step of a longer-term revolution triggered by the Arab Spring, and the transition deal at least avoided the catastrophic civil war that was still ripping apart Syria more than a year after the Yemeni president agreed to leave his post. Bashar al-Assad, it seemed, would meet a different fate.

CHAPTER 9

The Struggle for Syria

Conspiracies are like germs, after all, multiplying every moment, everywhere. They cannot be eliminated, but we can strengthen the immunity of our bodies in order to protect ourselves against them. It doesn't require much analysis, based on what we heard from others and witnessed in the media, to prove that there is indeed a conspiracy. We should not waste time discussing it or being frightened by it.
— Bashar al-Assad, in a speech to Damascus University on 20 June 2011[1]

Close to dawn on 16 November 2011, a band of armed men mounted a daring raid on an Air Force Intelligence building on the outskirts of Damascus. It was the most audacious attack yet by the so-called Free Syrian Army, a group formed several months earlier by a rebel colonel who claimed at the time to command 15,000 former members of the armed forces.[2] Operating in the confused shadows of the wider uprising against the Syrian regime, they were filling their ranks with rising numbers of defected soldiers and smuggling in weapons across Syria's porous borders. The armed insurgency was becoming bolder, and the target of its latest attack could hardly have been more symbolic.

More than half a century earlier, a twenty-year-old Hafez al-Assad had been selected as a trainee pilot in the embryonic Syrian Air Force, beginning his career by flying British- and US-made propeller planes in the skies above north-west Syria and winning a prize for aerobatics when he graduated top of his class in 1955.[3] A few years later, Assad was stationed in Cairo during Syria's short-lived union with Gamal Abdel Nasser's Egypt, where he and four of his colleagues formed a secret committee of conspirators whose characteristics would be central to the future of the country.

All five were enthusiastic members of the Ba'ath, or 'Resurrection' party, formed in Damascus in 1947 around a secular, socialist Arab nationalism that aimed to rid Arab lands of foreign interference. They also hailed from minority communities. Three of them, including the future president himself, were Alawites, members of a sect whose opaque origins are usually traced back to a pupil of the eleventh Shi'ite Muslim imam, and who believe that Ali, the cousin and son-in-law of the Prophet Mohamed, was the truest embodiment of God on earth.[4] Then, as now, Syria was a country with a Sunni Arab majority and an overlapping mosaic of ethnic and religious minorities that included not just Alawites but also Kurds, Druze, Christians, Turkomen and Ismailis, another offshoot of Shi'ite Islam to which the other two members of Assad's secret committee belonged.

The Ba'ath party's secularizing ideas were particularly appealing to these minority communities, who risked being treated as second-class citizens in any conservative, Sunni-dominated state. They had largely been protected under the French mandate, which ran from 1920 until 1946 and had seen the old *bilad ash-sham*, or Greater Syria – comprised of modern-day Syria, Lebanon, Israel, Jordan and parts of Iraq – greatly diminished in size and then hewn into several distinct regions. In the west, the Alawites were granted a semi-autonomous state of some 278,000 people, while another slice of old Syrian territory was added to the Maronite Christian enclave of Mount Lebanon, creating the borders of present-day Lebanon.

Syrian independence in 1947 had given way to an unstable republican regime characterized by frequent coups. Back from Cairo in 1962, Assad's committee developed a network of allies and patrons that mounted their own takeover in March 1963, shortly after their Ba'athist counterparts in Baghdad had achieved the same feat. The coup propelled the ambitious young Assad into the leadership of the Air Force, a base from which he plotted a personal ascendance that culminated in 1970 with his appointment as president. Two years later, the other four members of his original Cairo committee were either dead, exiled or incarcerated.[5] Throughout the next three decades, Assad maintained an often unforgiving grip on power using three elements – the military-security complex, the Ba'ath party apparatus and a new Alawite elite – that were still at the core of the regime that his son and successor, Bashar, inherited in 2000 and fought to maintain in 2011 and beyond.

More was at stake in Syria than in any other country touched by the Arab Spring, a fact that mitigated both against the outbreak of protest and against a peaceful or speedy resolution once demonstrations had begun. A country of 24 million people located right at the sensitive heart of the Middle East, Syria borders Turkey, Lebanon, Israel, Jordan and Iraq and what happens in Damascus has long rippled far and wide. Syria's geography complicates its uprising, entangling all sides in a mesh of domestic and international conundrums that augur poorly for a resolution of the sort that saw Tunisia's Zine al-Abidine Ben Ali flee into exile after just weeks of protests, or Libya's Muammar Gaddafi die at the hands of foreign-backed rebels. The final result in Syria may eventually be the same, but the path towards it has already been longer, bloodier and fraught with more danger for Syria and all its neighbours. The clues to why Bashar al-Assad was still in Damascus by early 2013 lie in the make-up of the country which he inherited from his father and in its place at the nexus of the Middle East's most intractable conflicts.

From Father to Son

When he emerged as sole leader in 1970, Hafez al-Assad realized that striking a balance between Islam and Ba'athism, and between the various minorities and the Sunni majority, would be vital to managing Syria. The Ba'ath party's founders, one Sunni Muslim and one Greek Orthodox Christian, believed that all Arabs should stand on an equal footing, and considered Islam more of a cultural commonality than an all-guiding force.[6] This was reflected in the draft of Assad's new constitution, which in 1973 ignited protests by conservative Sunnis because it contained no clause requiring the president to be a Muslim. Islam was never recognized as the religion of state, but Assad amended the document after obtaining a *fatwa* from a Lebanese Shi'ite cleric stating that Alawites were indeed of the Islamic faith – though they were regarded as quasi-heretics by many other Muslims for shunning most mainstream beliefs and practices.[7, 8]

The constitution also noted that Syria would be a 'planned socialist economy', enshrining the round of nationalization that had already followed the 1963 Ba'athist coup. Private banks were shut down, the nascent Syrian stock exchange was closed and restrictions were placed on private-sector activities. The wealthy Sunni trading families that had historically domi-nated the economy suffered heavily, prompting many to move abroad, although Assad introduced some conciliatory measures when he became president, allowing trade and travel with Lebanon and reassuring busi-nessmen and merchants in the cities.[9] Nonetheless, Syria effectively became a monolithic command economy, run on five-year plans and reliant on modest oil production for state income.

Less than a decade after taking power, Assad faced what would be the regime's greatest domestic challenge prior to 2011. The secular tenets of Ba'athism were anathema to Syria's Muslim Brothers, whose early leaders were inspired by the eponymous Egyptian group and who were a rising political force in the post-independence years. A young Assad was even beaten up and knifed by a group of their supporters in 1948, adding a personal layer of enmity to his wider ideological conflict with the Islamists.

The Brotherhood was banned after the 1963 coup, but some elements organized underground resistance networks in conservative cities like Aleppo and Hama and, from the late 1970s, more radical groups began a campaign of suicide bombings, attacks on symbols of the regime and assassinations that included an attempt on the president's life. The insurgency prompted a vicious crackdown, led by Assad's brother, Rifaat. The assault reached its zenith with the Hama massacre of spring 1982, when government forces surrounded and shelled Syria's third-largest city in a month-long assault that left many thousands dead and razed historic districts where Islamist fighters had dug themselves in. The episode subsequently became taboo, banned from open discussion and referred to by the people of Hama simply as *al-ahdath*, or 'the incidents'. But it had certainly not been forgotten.

Assad's foreign policy, later passed down to his son, also revolved around maintaining domestic power. It tended to be more reactive than proactive, taking out insurance policies and hedging its bets to never entirely alienate any major external power. Although Syria had no comprehensive peace deal with Israel, the two countries had signed a ceasefire in 1974 after Assad had failed to regain the mountainous Golan Heights region, in Syria's extreme south-west, in the 1973 war. It left the two countries in a purgatory state of no peace, no war that would endure through several rounds of failed peace talks, including US-mediated negotiations that broke down just before Assad's death.

Damascus treated its other western neighbour, Lebanon, as a province in which it could act with almost total impunity, dispatching troops into the country in 1976, soon after the eruption of the Lebanese civil war, where they would remain for nearly three decades. As the conflict deepened, drawing in Israel and other foreign interests, Damascus cultivated numerous Lebanese allies. The most powerful of them would be Hezbollah, a Shi'ite group created in the early 1980s with Iranian ideological and military backing and which at the end of the civil war in 1990 was the only Lebanese faction allowed to keep its weapons as a means of national resistance to ongoing Israeli occupation. Although the Syrian president had no desire to see an Islamic state established in Lebanon – a goal that was theoretically among Hezbollah's aims – his relationship with the Shi'ite group would prove an invaluable bequest to his son.

Hafez al-Assad died, aged sixty-nine, on 10 June 2000. A few days later, tens of thousands of people gathered in the streets of Damascus to mark his funeral. Three men stood together in the crowds of mourners, sporting dark suits, five o'clock shadows and sunglasses in the manner of mafia dons paying their respects to a deceased *padrino*. The tallest of them was the thirty-four-year-old Bashar al-Assad, the second son of the late Syrian president, who would soon be elected secretary-general of the ruling Ba'ath party and receive 97 per cent support in a referendum to endorse him as leader.

At Bashar's side was his younger brother, Maher, rising quickly through the ranks of the elite Republican Guard and already gaining notoriety as a military commander. And standing nearby was a moustachioed older man, Assef Shawkat, who had risen to prominence through marrying Bushra al-Assad, Bashar and Maher's older sister and their father's favourite. By then, Shawkat was rising to the top of Syria's military intelligence apparatus and was considered one of the most influential men in the country.

Bashar was one of the new generation of Arab leaders that assumed power at the turn of the millennium. Yet unlike King Mohammed of Morocco and King Abdullah of Jordan, who had both succeeded their fathers in 1999 and were also in their mid-thirties, the young Syrian president was not a member of a royal family. He was the first and possibly the last Arab republican leader to inherit the presidency, a feat which Gamal Mubarak and Saif al-Islam Gaddafi were prevented from achieving by the events of 2011. Even so, Bashar al-Assad was never meant to rule Syria. Any plans that his father had to hand down power to his eldest son, Basil, were derailed in 1994 when he was killed in a car crash. The accident brought the more bookish Bashar home from London, where he was training as an eye doctor. He would spend the next six years being groomed as the future leader while his father assiduously worked to persuade both the wider public and his own generation of party and military officials, now in their sixties and seventies, to accept that hereditary rule was in their best interests.

Bashar kept on many of the old inner clique but he also sought a break from the past, trying to dilute the crushing cult of personality that had surrounded his father and allowing more generous political and media freedoms in a period that became known as the Damascus Spring. Activists were pardoned, political salons flourished and opposition figures began cautiously proposing reforms such as the lifting of the emergency law, which had been in place since 1963. Hostility from the powerful old guard and entrenched interests nipped the spring in its buds, however, starkly illustrating the limits of change for the new president.

Even the introduction of publicly-available internet, which only took place in 2000, had drawn opposition from hardliners who (rightly) feared it would erode the state's control over information. Bashar was a vocal proponent of the internet, and during his grooming period had been chairman of the Syrian Computer Society, a vehicle that helped establish his image as a reform-minded successor. But although he allowed a freer private-sector media than his father, selectively granting licences to new private-sector magazines and newspapers, Syria was ranked a miserable 173 out of 178 countries in the 2010 Press Freedom Index compiled by Reporters Without Borders.[10]

With serious political reform seemingly off the agenda, Assad adopted a 'Chinese model' that sought to allow economic liberalization without eroding the regime's monopoly on power. Syria's crude production was now on the wane, public finances needed preparing for the end of oil, and easing long-standing restrictions on trade and business would benefit some of the key pillars of his regime.[11] To implement his ambitious reforms, which one prominent Syrian banker likened to 're-engineering a whole country', Bashar brought in a clutch of Western-educated technocrats that included Abdullah Dardari, who as deputy prime minister and head of the State Planning Commission would earn a reputation as the champion of free-market reform.[12] New faces also appeared at the Ministry of Economy and Foreign Trade, the state-owned Industrial Bank and the Ministry of Tourism.[13] Another key figure in this technocratic clique was the first lady, Asma al-Assad, born and raised in west London, who had worked at Deutsche Bank and JP Morgan and was enrolled to study an MBA at Harvard when she married the new Syrian president.

When Hafez al-Assad died in 2000 there was not a single ATM in Syria.[14] But five years later, private banks and insurance companies were finally allowed to reopen after a decades-long hiatus during which much of the Syrian business community had routed its transactions through

Lebanon, Dubai or Cyprus. There was so much demand for their services that bank managers in Damascus recounted tales of customers turning up at newly opened branches hauling bags of cash that contained their life savings. In 2009, a long-planned stock exchange finally began trading and was generally considered a success, with the majority of share offerings healthily oversubscribed.[15]

Import tariffs and trade restrictions were progressively eased, rendering the streets of Damascus almost unrecognizable in 2010 from what they were in 2000. Gone were the elegant rusting Mercedes of the 1970s, or the ageing Dodges or Chevrolets put to work on the Beirut–Damascus taxi run. Replacing them were fleets of nondescript Kia, Seat, Nissan or Toyota saloons that lower customs tariffs had made cheaper and easier to import. Foreign retail outlets from coffee shops to shoe boutiques were cropping up in well-heeled Damascus neighbourhoods like Abu Romaneh and Malki. A kind of 'Beirutization' of the capital was taking place, as Syrians started to look more stylish and less drab than they had done a decade earlier, slowly catching up with their ultra-fashion-conscious Lebanese neighbours.

In the Old City, a UNESCO world heritage site, the Damascus authorities had granted new licences for hotels, restaurants and bars, often tastefully converted from beautiful Damascene houses with their elaborately-decorated interior courtyards and fountains. The white stone edifice of the Four Seasons hotel, funded by Saudi Prince Al Waleed bin Talal and opened in 2005, was now the go-to meeting place for the capital's political and business elite. Tourists were piling into a diverse country dotted with ancient covered markets, mediaeval castles and the stunning ruins of Roman cities. A total of 8.5 million foreigners arrived in Syria in 2010, 40 per cent more than a year earlier and a fourfold increase since 2000. The tourism sector was becoming a genuine success story, and by the end of the decade provided 13 per cent of Syria's jobs and a similar proportion of its GDP.[16]

Property prices were also on the up in the 2000s, thanks partly to an influx of wealthy Iraqi migrants who had fled the war, but also to greater private investment and to natural population growth as more and more Syrians migrated to the capital looking for work. It bolstered the wealth of the land-owning classes in the major cities, with real-estate development now a serious business for the new elite. Glitzy new projects in out-of-town suburbs like Ya'afour were sold out before they even broke ground; one developer planning a set of ultra-luxury towers on a hillside outside

Damascus said in 2010 that wealthy cash buyers close to the regime had already purchased all the as-yet-unbuilt penthouses and wanted more outlets for their money.[17]

Many landmark infrastructure and property projects had been mired in bureaucracy or infighting for years, but in 2010 local businessmen in Damascus talked with renewed optimism about things moving quicker. A major Gulf investor, Majid al-Futtaim, was about to break ground on an enormous shopping and hotel development that had been on the drawing board for at least five years. Controversially, a casino had even reopened on the outskirts of the capital, though it was hurriedly shut down in April 2011 as the government introduced measures to appease the more conservative Sunni community.

The leading local business families, often based in Damascus or Aleppo, joined forces to form new holding companies that were active in everything from banking to airlines and hotels. One, Souria Holding, was set up by wealthy Sunni shareholders and on the eve of the revolts was building a five-star hotel tower on the site of Damascus's old Baramkeh bus station. Another, Cham Holding, was set up in 2007 and had become Syria's largest company three years later. A joint venture between an investment vehicle controlled by Rami Makhlouf, the president's cousin, and dozens of wealthy Sunni families, it highlighted the two main groups who benefited most from Bashar's economic liberalization – the urban Sunni population and his own Alawite inner circle.

The most prominent of the latter were the family of Bashar's mother, Anisa Makhlouf, who had long put their privileged political status to lucrative commercial use. Their empire continued to expand under Rami and his brother Ihab, who among many other things were believed to control the Real Estate Bank, the shops at Syria's airports, ports and border crossings, the leading mobile phone operator, Syriatel, and a web of other investments, trading interests, oil concessions, land holdings and construction companies. Such was Rami's reputation for industrial-scale graft that Washington had gone as far as specifically labelling him a 'facilitator of state corruption' in February 2008.

Sons of senior figures from the Hafez era were also kept within the regime's sprawling network of patronage, oiled by government contracts or quasi-monopolies over particular industries. The system was not too different from Ben Ali's Tunisia, where the Trabelsi family had filled the Makhlouf role of the grasping, mega-rich in-laws who would become lightning conductors for public outrage when popular protests erupted. Unlike under the old regime, the *nouveau riche* elite in the late 2000s made little effort to hide a wealth that the more capitalistic climate allowed them to flaunt through cars, clothes and houses that were simply not available twenty years earlier. 'The big difference between Hafez al-Assad and Bashar al-Assad is that Hafez used money for political purposes, but Bashar al-Assad uses politics to make money. And this combination is a disaster,' said Saad Hariri, himself the billionaire politician son of the Lebanese prime minister, Rafik Hariri, who was assassinated in 2005.[18]

Yet while the Sunni urban business families and the Alawite elite were reaping the fruits of economic liberalization, others ploughed less fertile soils. Unlike his father, who was born and raised in an impoverished village with no paved roads, Bashar's lack of natural connection with the countryside became dangerously obvious in 2011. He grew up in the capital, studied medicine at an elite university and then went to London in the early 1990s. While many of Hafez al-Assad's close friends and advisors came from disadvantaged rural areas, Bashar's clique were far more urban-focused and internationalized. For much of his rule, Hafez had attempted to rebalance Syria's rural-urban divide, redistributing land from wealthy families to peasants and building infrastructure in the provinces. Yet Bashar effectively left those provinces behind in the free-market reform that favoured the cities and service industries. That bias would have grave repercussions.

Lower customs tariffs and fewer trade restrictions had enriched some but made it harder for locally-made and often inferior Syrian products to compete with imports. Corruption and vested interests prevented sectors with genuine potential, like food processing or textiles, from becoming competitive. Tourism was booming, but all taxis from Damascus International Airport were monopolized by a single company. Divides between urban and rural living standards widened. According to government figures, the average household in Damascus spent a total of $773 per month in 2009, almost double the $439 in rural parts of the Deir ez-Zour province, one of the more restive in 2011. A Damascus household allocated 35 per cent of its spending on food-related items, but in rural areas of the Aleppo province that figure was above 60 per cent. While the overall proportions spent on food had come down since 2004, the variations between the regions had become markedly deeper.[19]

Agriculture and water management remained inefficient and riddled with corruption, a disastrous state of affairs in a country whose population had more than trebled between 1970 and 2010 but which had suffered four successive years of drought from 2006.[20] Agriculture had comprised a third of national output at the Ba'athist coup in 1963, a quarter when Bashar came to power in 2000, and just 16 per cent ten years later.[21] And the provinces were essentially left in the hands of incompetent, often repressive local governors who saw their constituency as little more than a fiefdom for personal enrichment, an attitude that contributed so much to the outbreak of unrest in 2011.

The economic restructuring of the 2000s had not been a panacea for much of the population. Although inflation had fallen from an official rate of 15.2 per cent in 2008 to 4.5 per cent in 2010, price rises were still outpacing income growth for most people. A government poll of 15,000 families in 2009 found that the average monthly salary was just $194 in the private sector and $257 in the public sector. Soaring house prices benefited those who already owned land or property, but made it virtually impossible for young Syrians to rent or buy apartments in the cities, forcing many to delay their marriage plans. Government reforms tried to replace universal subsidies with targeted handouts to poor families, but were open to manipulation and caused unease. 'If diesel became any more expensive, then I'd start burning wood to heat my house,' said one Damascus shopkeeper in 2006.[22] 'The government tells us that electricity prices are the lowest in the region, but they forget to add that are our salaries are also the lowest.' Economic malaise was not the central cause of the Syrian uprising, but the skewed liberalization of the 2000s left some with much to lose and others with everything to gain.

Meanwhile, diplomats or analysts of Syria's foreign policy perennially described it as being 'at a crossroads', which was precisely the perception that its president wished to nurture. He fostered ties with Iran while never turning his back completely on Europe; he kept alive hopes of peace with Israel but supplied and supported Hezbollah and several Palestinian factions that rejected the 1993 peace deal with Israel; he shared intelligence on Islamic militants with Washington but also facilitated the insurgency in post-Saddam Iraq. It was a construction where no one was a pure ally and no one a pure enemy, but anyone could be pushed into either camp depending on the circumstances. When 2011 came around, regional and international powers had to weigh up their actions on Syria by playing out the myriad possible implications elsewhere.

Although the 9/11 attacks and the invasion of Iraq had transformed regional dynamics and brought war to Syria's doorstep, Bashar's greatest crisis had come in Lebanon. Even after the end of the Lebanese civil war in

1990, Damascus controlled a pervasive intelligence apparatus and maintained thousands of troops in the country, while Syria's military-political elite continued to milk networks of corrupt Lebanese politicians and businessmen. This was despite international pressure on Assad to reduce his military presence in Lebanon after Israel, which had first sent in troops to southern Lebanon in 1982, had withdrawn just weeks before Bashar came to power in the summer of 2000.

The Syrian leader overplayed his hand in the autumn of 2004, when against the better advice of many, including some of his inner circle, he rode roughshod over what little sovereignty Lebanon had by forcing through a constitutional amendment that extended the term of the pro-Syrian president, Emile Lahoud. It prompted the United States and France to co-sponsor a UN resolution calling for the withdrawal of all foreign forces and the disarming of militias, including Hezbollah.[23]

Bashar's uncompromising approach put him at loggerheads with Rafik Hariri, the billionaire Sunni businessman who resigned as Lebanon's prime minister in October 2004 after the extension of Lahoud's term and, on Valentine's Day 2005, was killed by a colossal bomb on the Beirut seafront. Nightly vigils around his tomb snowballed into huge anti-Syrian protests. Amid intense pressure, Bashar was forced to withdraw his remaining troops over the following months in what amounted to a humiliating defeat.

He became increasingly isolated. The UN launched a high-profile international investigation into Hariri's death, which Damascus denied ordering. Bashar's relations with the Al Sauds, who were close to Hariri, were severely damaged. The Syrian vice president and a stalwart of the Assad inner circle, Abdelhalim Khaddam, defected and fled to Paris. Bush's Freedom Agenda had put regime change on Washington's lips. A spree of bombings in Lebanon started to kill off anti-Syrian politicians and journalists.

Bashar's fortunes were partly revived by time – simply playing the long game and grinding down his adversaries – and partly by the six-week war between Israel and Hezbollah in the summer of 2006. Hezbollah's performance earned it popular admiration around the Arab world, some of which rubbed off on its Syrian and Iranian backers and allowed Damascus to portray itself as one of the few Arab governments still offering concrete resistance to Israel. Throughout that summer, street vendors in the Syrian capital did a roaring trade in posters, banners, flags and T-shirts portraying Bashar and his father alongside the grinning, bespectacled face of Hassan Nasrallah, Hezbollah's leader. Assad claimed that sentiment explained why Western-allied leaders in Tunis or Cairo were under such pressure. 'We have more difficult circumstances than most of the Arab countries, but in spite of that Syria is stable,' he said in January 2011. 'Why? Because you have to be very closely linked to the beliefs of the people.'[24]

Over a decade in power, the unlikely Syrian president had been through a string of internal and external tests that were stern by any standards. Yet on the eve of the Arab Spring, Bashar held a stronger deck of domestic and international cards than any other Arab republican leader. His liberalization of the business environment had benefited the country's powerful Sunni merchant families and enriched a crony elite loath to lose its perks. Damascus had a powerful ally in Hezbollah, a major force in Lebanon's parliament, the most potent military group in that country and a thorn in Israel's side. Syria's continued hosting of several Palestinian groups that rejected peace with Israel kept alive its tired claim of being a hub of resistance to the Jewish state. Bashar nurtured a friendship with Tehran while never entirely alienating the Europeans or the Americans. The fragmented domestic opposition, including the Islamists, had been militarily crushed, jailed, co-opted or exiled.

Syrians were also mindful of the sectarian violence that had ripped apart their Lebanese and Iraqi neighbours, then the Arab world's only two democratic states, and many valued the stability offered by the Assads against the threat of communal strife. The country may be home to a Sunni Arab majority, but its patchwork of ethnic and religious minorities fear that the fall of the Assads may also spell the end of the secular ideals that have governed Syria for fifty years, perhaps bringing political Islam to power. That struggle over the role of religion in state and society could pit not just Islamists against secularists, but Christian and Alawite against Muslim, Kurd against Arab. A protracted rebellion in Syria might well suck in Iraq and Lebanon, themselves divided along sectarian lines and over government support for Assad.

With so much at risk, and with Syria initially so quiet, how did Assad find himself confronting open and armed revolt only months after boasting that his foreign policy would keep him immune?

The Delayed Uprising

At first it seemed as if there might be no Arab Spring in Syria, let alone a battle for its aftermath. Within days and even hours of Mubarak's departure on 11 February, the ongoing protests in Libya, Yemen and Bahrain shifted up a gear. Syria, by comparison, seemed quiet. A 'Day of

Rage' organized through Facebook for 4 February was a non-event, a combination of fear and lacklustre enthusiasm keeping people at home. Syrians might have been glued to television screens showing the celebrations in Bourguiba Avenue or Tahrir Square, but they were not going out *en masse* in pursuit of the same goal.

Yet the Arab Spring had clearly changed the atmosphere. When a man was reportedly insulted and beaten by traffic police near Damascus's ancient roofed market of Souk al-Hamidiyah on 17 February, an angry crowd of about 1,500 people gathered. Men stood on cars and balconies of nearby apartment buildings chanting slogans like 'Thieves, thieves,' and 'The Syrian people will not be humiliated'.[25] Although nothing in comparison to the open revolt that was now going on in Libya or Bahrain, this was still highly unusual by Syrian standards. It also carried ominous echoes of Mohammed Bouazizi, the street vendor allegedly slapped by a policewoman in December 2010. It was a spark, but for now it was successfully extinguished by the minister of the interior, who arrived in a car to calm the crowd and take away the offending officer.

If the authorities had adopted a similarly non-confrontational approach a month later, in the town of Deraa, then perhaps the Arab Spring might have turned out differently for Bashar. It was not too late by early March, though it soon would be. For if Tunisia's revolt could trace its roots to Sidi Bouzid and Libya's to Benghazi, then Syria's uprising was conceived in an undistinguished southern town close to the Jordanian border. The Deraa revolt began after a handful of local boys, some no more than ten years old, were arrested by police for daubing walls with graffiti that included what had become the slogan of the Arab Spring: 'The people want the fall of the regime'. According to their own accounts, the children were beaten and tortured by the local security services.[26]

After failing to secure their release, hundreds of Deraa residents took to the streets to voice their anger at the children's treatment. They also aired grievances over other local issues, demanding the removal of the provincial governor and the notorious head of local security. On 18 March, the security forces opened fire and killed several demonstrators, further enraging sentiment and escalating the protests. Bashar dispatched a delegation from Damascus to meet local representatives in an effort to calm the situation, as well as firing the governor and releasing the mistreated children, but the conflict had now started to rotate through a familiar and vicious circle. Protests were met with a deadly response, therefore sparking even greater protests, and so on, until divisions became irreconcilable.

The focus of the demonstrators' chants quickly escalated from local issues, like the removal of an unpopular governor, to call for an end to emergency law, to finally demand the ouster of Assad. The local Ba'ath party offices were smashed and a statue of Hafez al-Assad was torn down as protesters attacked the symbols of the regime – a huge escalation that would draw much harsher punishment in Syria than it would have done in Egypt or Tunisia. By the last week of April, activists claimed that 130 people had been killed in Deraa alone, while Syrian state media said attacks by protesters had killed seventeen security personnel.[27]

Deraa was the torch that set light to uprisings in other provinces, as people across the country took to the streets in solidarity with those in the southern border town. In most cases, the same destructive pattern of escalation occurred. By late spring, there were regular protests and clashes in provincial towns like Deir ez-Zour, Idlib and Baniyas, but also in major population centres like Homs and Hama, as well as Duma, a suburb of Damascus. From a relatively early stage there was evidence suggesting that the protesters were fighting back using weapons, though the arrest and expulsion of independent journalists from March made details impossible to verify until many returned later in the year.

Rami Makhlouf had become an early target of public anger. In Deraa, angry mobs had trashed the local Syriatel offices and burned its SIM cards in a gesture of disgust with the cronies of the Assad regime. In May, Makhlouf had sold his duty-free shops to Kuwaiti investors and now promised to sell his 40-per-cent stake in Syriatel.[28] In mid-June, he promised that he would 'no more run any projects for personal profit' and would henceforth 'dedicate himself for charity, development and humanitarian work'.[29] It made no difference and few believed him anyway.

Bashar made a much-anticipated speech on 30 March, his first since the protests had snowballed. In a televised address to the Syrian parliament, he blamed the unrest on foreign agents, declaring that Syria faced a 'great conspiracy whose tentacles extend to some nearby countries and faraway countries, with some inside the country'. While he acknowledged that not all of the protesters were conspirators, he said the opposition was waging a 'virtual war using the media and the internet'. Explaining how and why economic reforms had taken priority over political change in the past decade, Bashar made vague promises to 'study' the lifting of the emergency law – in place continuously since 1963 – and to open up the political arena. A week earlier, he had dismissed the government and announced the formation of a National Dialogue Committee. There were also some early economic concessions: subsidy cuts were shelved, state salaries raised, fuel prices lowered and a long-planned introduction of VAT put off indefinitely. In a token gesture in February, direct internet access to Facebook and YouTube had been permitted for the first time, even though Syrians had long become adept at using proxies to access the plethora of blocked websites.[30]

The speech was a chance to recognize the real issues at the root of popular anger, but it struck many as being out of tune with the acute levels of tension and political awareness that both the domestic protests and the regional situation had created. His audience in parliament, a body run by the Ba'ath party since the 1960s, cheered any significant point and gave a standing ovation, but Bashar's effort to seem unperturbed, by grinning, giggling and joking, did not match the sombre public mood. Insinuating that the protests were driven by foreign agendas seemed an insult to the intelligence of Syrians. Even those who harboured goodwill towards the president and had expected solutions from his speech were disappointed, even if they were not angry. It was a squandered chance for Bashar to rescue the situation while he still retained some popular credibility.

But the president could still muster impressive support on the streets, whether through mild coercion or genuine backing. A rally on 29 March, a day before his first speech to parliament, gathered tens of thousands of people in Damascus and other major cities, while another, two weeks later, involved a 2.3-kilometre Syrian flag being carried down the Mezze highway in the capital. State media claimed that hundreds of thousands attended the rally, and accused foreign media of ignoring it.[31]

The information war was raging, just as it had in other countries, making it difficult to determine the real level of support for each side. But the mismatch between words and deeds, the rising death toll and Bashar's mounting international isolation meant many Syrians had already lost faith in their leader. 'It's like faith in God,' said one local businessman. 'Once you stop believing, you can't go back.'[32]

By the time he delivered another lengthy speech on 20 June, rights groups said the national death toll had risen above 1,300.[33] 'Conspiracies are like germs, after all, multiplying every moment everywhere,' said Bashar, claiming that the opposition possessed sophisticated weapons and communication systems. Promises of political reform and pardons now rang hollow. Bashar called on those who had fled to Turkey during a violent battle in the border town of Jisr al-Shughur, to return, promising that the army was 'there for their security and the security of their children'. Few took the president at his word. Others speculated that the harder-line elements of his regime, particularly his brother Maher, were really in charge. His loyal military brigades were sweeping from city to city to put down the protests, spreading fear and anger.

Those elite army squads were exhausted but still holding together late in the year. Syria's more than 400,000-strong armed forces were thought to include up to 300,000 conscripts drawn largely from the Sunni community.[34] A majority of the career soldiers, however, are believed to be Alawites.[35] Maher controlled the Alawite-dominated Republican Guard, the country's most elite division, as well as the Alawite-dominated Fourth Division. The so-called *shabbiha*, a word derived from the Arabic for ghost, were armed pro-regime thugs who opponents say were involved in beatings, drive-by shootings, executions, sectarian killings and intimidation. They were named after the organized crime gangs that ran amok in the town of Lattakia in the 1980s. It is not clear who the *shabbiha* are and who they answer to, but it is clear they have been used to rebuild the barrier of fear that kept Syrians off the streets for so long, allowing the regime to deny involvement in some of the most vicious attacks. Together with the *shabbiha*, these two elite military units were at the heart of a security apparatus whose ultimate goal was to ensure loyalty and enforce domestic control rather than fight foreign wars.[36]

Most of Syria's air force pilots were Sunni, for instance, but the air defence force which controlled logistics and communications is mainly Alawite, preventing the pilots from making a play for power.[37] The Alawite community's long history of internal divisions should not be underestimated, and past challenges have come from the inside, but by the end of 2011 their techniques had been effective in averting a military coup.

The sectarian nature of Syria's military structure also illustrated how religion would be central to what comes after the Assads, and could determine how they fall. Assad's Alawite elite had much to lose if the regime collapsed, but they had not yet calculated that their interests were best served by turning on the Assads. Their fate, it seemed, was tied to that of the leader and his family. Those who had joined the ranks of the Free Syrian Army would be likely to encounter a well-armed, well-trained and highly motivated core of Alawite military brigades who would fight to the death, even if Alawites themselves were less than a tenth of the 24-million strong population.[38]

By early 2012 many Syrian towns were in open revolt. An Arab League monitoring mission begun in December had provided cover for more demonstrators to come out on the streets, especially in Homs and Hama, but had served little other purpose and lost credibility. 'Even I am trying to leave on Friday. I'm going to Cairo or elsewhere… because the mission is unclear…. It does not serve the citizens,' one Arab League observer told Reuters. 'It does not serve anything. The Syrian authorities have exploited the weakness in the performance of the delegation to not respond. There is no real response on the ground.'[39]

Nor did any direct foreign intervention appear imminent, however, and many sections of Syrian society had not yet actively stood up to fight against Bashar – even if they had privately lost faith in him long ago – because they had too much at stake. The domestic and international cards that Assad had inherited from his father, and which gave him the protection that Gaddafi had so sorely lacked, had come into play.

Trumps in the Deck

As 2012 moved grimly on, localized protests and clashes were becoming ever more common in Damascus or Aleppo, the two largest cities in Syria, whose combined population of around 9.5 million comprised more than 40 per cent of the national total.[40] Yet the urban middle and upper classes, mainly Sunni, had not come out in great numbers, partly because the large, wealthy trading families to which they belonged stood to lose much from escalating the situation into all-out war. Albert Hourani's observation about a 'recurrent pattern in Middle Eastern history' was particularly relevant for Syria. 'The classes which dominated the structures of state and social power in the cities wanted peace, order and freedom of economic activity,' he wrote in his seminal *History of the Arab Peoples*, 'and would support a regime so long as it seemed to be giving them what they wanted; but they would not lift a finger to save it, and would accept its successor if it seemed likely to follow a similar policy.'[41] By now, many members of those classes realized Assad's days were numbered, and some were secretly funnelling cash to his opponents, though with the streets filled with security forces many had not risked their lives to rise up against him. This was not just about religion – many in the poorer provinces were Sunnis and indeed Alawites – but it is one reason why the rebellion would not draw out an overwhelming mass of people.

Another was Syria's collage of minorities, who will be at the heart of any future battle over the role of religion. Like the wider population, the majority of the opposition was Sunni Arab but it historically included large numbers of Christians, Kurds and even Alawite intellectuals, including some high-profile activists, who supported the uprising. The minorities were a card in Bashar's deck and his regime regularly warned of a potential civil war as it sought to fan popular fears and discourage protests.

For the same reasons that Syria's Muslim Brotherhood was naturally opposed to the Alawite-Ba'athist axis, many in the Christian community felt protected by it. Making up around a tenth of the population, Syria's Christians encompass Maronites, Greek Orthodox, Syriac Orthodox and Armenians, and are mostly clustered in Damascus, Aleppo, Homs and western areas close to the Lebanese border. Their religious freedoms had been protected under the Assads and Christians lived side by side with Muslims, in relative harmony. Within a brisk stroll in Old Damascus, you could walk from the stunning seventh-century Umayyad Mosque, where hundreds of cloaked Iranian pilgrims wept at the shrine of the Shi'ite imam Hussein, to the Bab Touma quarter with its churches, Christian icons, liquor stores and unveiled women wearing body-hugging clothes.

Just as the death of Hafez al-Assad in 2000 had caused anxiety among Christians, fearful of their status should the transition give way to a conservative Sunni regime, so the weakening of his son stoked similar concerns. In the intervening period, those concerns had been exacerbated by the persecution and exodus of Christians in post-Saddam Hussein Iraq and, in 2011 itself, by the sharp tensions between Muslims and Copts that followed the ousting of Hosni Mubarak in Egypt. With the protest movement now gathering steam, Christian leaders in both Syria and neighbouring Lebanon – where Christians made up a much larger proportion of the population – pointed to a dangerously unknown future which stood little chance of being more favourable to their community than the present.

The Maronite Patriarch of Lebanon, Bechara al-Ra'i, feared that a Ba'athist demise 'could lead the way to the birth of a fundamentalist Sunni regime and this could lead the way to sectarian violence or even the division of the country into three or four parts based on sectarian differences. These are scenarios that are deadly for the future of Christians in Syria.'[42] Yet there were also splits within the Christian community itself, from which many veteran and high-profile Assad opponents hailed. Many Christians believed that no Syrian could be free under the current system, and that a democratic regime would guarantee freedom to all. Appearing too cosy towards Bashar also raised the risk that, should he fall, his successors might take deliberate retribution on those who had failed to publicly support the uprising. It was a delicate balancing act.

Divided loyalties of a different kind could be found among Syria's Kurds. Reckoned to number about 10 to 15 per cent of the population, and concentrated in the impoverished and largely rural north-east, this was a group long marginalized by Damascus. A 'special census' in 1962 had decreed that many had crossed into Syria illegally from neighbouring Turkey, thus depriving them of Syrian citizenship and effectively leaving them stateless. Damascus had deliberately underinvested in Kurdish areas, paid Arab families to settle in the region, and restricted expressions of Kurdish cultural identity like its language or its celebration of *Nowruz*, the Persian New Year. Riots had erupted in March 2004 after a football match in the city of Qamishli, where local residents brought out a Kurdish flag and clashed with police. They later burned down the local office of the Ba'ath Party and toppled a statue of Hafez al-Assad, provoking a bloody response that killed dozens.

But here, too, the Assads had insurance policies to complicate the situation. In the late 1990s, Syrian support for outlawed Kurdish groups like the Kurdistan Workers Party (PKK) had brought it to the brink of war with Turkey before Bashar improved relations with Ankara by extraditing a prominent PKK leader and adopting a harder line towards militant Kurdish groups. Kurdish involvement in Syria's 2011 protests was at first muted. In the early summer, Bashar held talks with leaders of Kurdish organizations and promised, not for the first time, to grant Syrian citizenship to the stateless population. Later in the year, though, the killing of a prominent activist, Mashal Tammo, ignited an all-too-familiar pattern of escalating anti-regime protests.[43]

Yet while Syria's Kurds were doubtless antagonistic towards Damascus, like the Christians they were also concerned about the future – and especially one that continued to exclude them as non-Arabs or that brought Turkey greater influence in Syrian internal affairs. From the start, Kurdish political groups were decidedly lukewarm towards the opposition groups being formed overseas, including the Syrian National Council, and their hesitancy diluted the strength and unity of the anti-Assad movement. While Syrian Kurds say they do not seek a separate state inside Syria, their cause is enmeshed with the wider struggle for an independent state on a contiguous Kurdish-dominated area that transcends the borders of Iraq, Syria and Turkey. Assad played on that notion - and Turkish fears - by essentially ceding control of the north-east region in the summer of 2012.

The threat of ethnic and sectarian conflict seemed to loom over the Syrian uprising, particularly given what had happened in Iraq and Lebanon. For many of those who were part of the opposition, especially in the early days of the uprising, religion had little to do with it. Although their tactics and end goals differed, theirs was a fight against a dictatorship from which all Syrians suffered and from which they would all be relieved. But as the conflict deepened, sectarian faultlines started to open up and foreign *jihadis* - who were often better organized and trained than other opposition groups - began to exploit the power void in the country.

The more hardline Islamists had every reason to fight for Assad's downfall, just as they had done in the 1970s and 1980s, and became increasingly prominent on the front lines through 2012 as Syria descended into full-blown civil war. In hot spots like Jisr al-Shughur, a town close to the Turkish border that was the scene of a violent battle between Assad forces and Islamist militants in both 1980 and in the summer of 2011, Bashar claimed that he faced a sophisticated and organized enemy. While many car bombs, kidnappings or summary executions bore hallmarks of the Syrian security services, it became difficult to deny by early 2013 that *jihadi* groups were carrying out the types of attacks more commonly associated with Iraq.

Syria's Muslim Brotherhood, meanwhile, had been banned for decades and its organization, support base and logistics on the ground remained unclear. Like the main Islamist parties in Egypt and Tunisia, it would likely benefit more than any other group from any elections in the future, but its supporters may have deliberately stood back to avoid becoming associated with the Al-Qaeda-style extremism that was beginning to print its stamp on the fight against Assad, and which might discourage secular or minority Syrians from supporting the wider opposition effort. There were also ambiguities about the group's position. A senior member of the Brotherhood, exiled in Saudi Arabia, drew controversy in November by appearing to support the idea of a Turkish military intervention, something which other opposition elements were then opposed to.[44]

Worried that they might inadvertently escalate the domestic conflict and destabilize the whole region, external powers, including Turkey, were far less gung-ho about intervening in Syria than in Libya, with its religiously homogenous Sunni population. After all, the Assad regime had long capitalized on its location at the heart of the Middle East to cultivate overseas friends who could come to its aid or stir up trouble elsewhere. 'Strike Syria and the world will shake,' warned Bashar in late November, a threat that had not been tested by early 2013.[45]

'If there is no stability here, there's no way there will be stability in Israel,' threatened Rami Makhlouf in May 2011 highlighting one card that Damascus reckoned it could play.[46] There was little danger of war between Syria and Israel and, for all their firebrand rhetoric, the Assads had effectively kept peace with their neighbours for almost four decades.

Nonetheless, Bashar could cause disruption by deliberately removing restrictions on access to the UN-monitored Golan border from the Syrian side, permitting raids or rocket attacks by militants. On the 15 May anniversary of the *nakba*, or 'disaster', that commemorates the displacement of Palestinians during the creation of Israel in 1948, more than a dozen pro-Palestinian protesters were killed near the village of Majdal al-Shams on the Syria-Golan border. Washington accused Damascus of a 'cynical use of the Palestinian cause to encourage violence along its border as it continues to repress its own people...'[47]

Several days later, on the anniversary of the 1967 war, Syrian state media reported that twenty-three people were killed by Israeli forces as they tried to cross into the Golan, another incident that could not have happened without the express wish of Damascus.[48] Instability in the Golan, however, was less of a deterrent to foreign intervention than an effort to distract attention away from state repression and, in the process, remind Syrians of Assad's support for the Palestinian cause. That support had previously paid some dividends. In 2005, with Bashar under great international pressure over Lebanon, the exiled leader of the Muslim Brotherhood, Ali Bayanouni, had formed an uneasy alliance with the defected vice president Abdelhalim Khaddam. But it ended in May 2009, when Bayanouni announced that he supported Syria's stance in the 2008–9 Israeli bombardment of Gaza and considered Khaddam's position to be too pro-Western.[49]

Hamas, effectively the Palestinian franchise of the Muslim Brotherhood, was another factor in Syrian-Palestinian links. Damascus had hosted the political bureau of the group since the 1980s, and its leader Khaled Meshaal since 2001, but the Sunni Islamist group found itself in a sensitive position in 2011, unable to openly back the uprising against their long-standing hosts yet unwilling to criticize a popular movement against a minority regime. In February 2012 Hamas leaders in Gaza openly turned against Assad, and relocated to Cairo and Doha.

A far more worrying prospect was Lebanon. By now, Hezbollah was not just the single most powerful military force in the country, but also part of a powerful bloc in Beirut's parliament, which included other broadly pro-Syrian political groups. Lebanon, along with Algeria and Iraq, voted against the Arab League plan in November 2011 to temporarily suspend Syria unless it complied with demands to withdraw its forces from the streets. Yet Hezbollah and its allies stood to be some of the biggest losers from any major upheaval in Syria, whether that means the fall of the Assads or a conflict that threatened their supply lines into Lebanon.

How the group responds to any imminent collapse in Syria could well depend more on the wishes of Tehran, its principal backer, than on Damascus. One scenario envisages the group asserting its military capabilities inside Lebanon and sparking armed clashes, or worse, if its Sunni and Christian adversaries find support from any new Syrian regime. Another sees it mounting diversionary raids on the Israeli border, with dangerous consequences. Both could be extremely messy. A further possibility sees Hezbollah adapting to the new reality, the terminal decline of the Assads persuading it to focus on domestic politics. Whatever its actions, Damascus controlled other cells in Lebanon that were more than capable of causing serious trouble, and by early 2013 the relative calm there - despite clashes in the northern city of Tripoli and an October 2012 bomb that killed a security chief in Beirut - indicated that Bashar had perhaps not yet used all the tools at his disposal. Yet tensions were running high, and it seemed inconceivable that Lebanon would escape unharmed from the unfolding civil war in Syria if the Assads came close to the brink.

Iran, which continued to support Damascus throughout 2012, presented another risk. Links between the two governments had become closer in the wake of 2005, which saw Bashar increasingly isolated by the West, prompting a European effort in 2008 to 'peel' him away from the Iranian orbit. French premier Nicolas Sarkozy controversially gave the Syrian president a front row seat at the Bastille Day military parade in July, then visited Damascus later in the year, as did UK Foreign Secretary David Miliband. The diplomatic seduction achieved little, but was another example of Bashar's strategy of keeping fingers in different pies, especially as Turkish-mediated peace talks between Syria and Israel were going on at the time.

The prospect of eroding Iran's influence in the Levant might have encouraged Sunni-ruled Gulf Arab states, especially Saudi Arabia, to try to weaken Assad, but his links to Tehran also ensured that they stopped short of a direct military intervention for fear of exacerbating a Shi'ite-Sunni conflict that could also destabilize the Gulf. If any uprising pushed Bashar to the brink of collapse, then Tehran's reaction would test how strong its support for its Syrian ally really was. Would it sacrifice Assad and hold back Hezbollah as a weapon in another battle, such as a US or Israeli strike on its nuclear facilities? Or would it risk everything and seek to activate Hezbollah in some way? If so, would Hezbollah's Lebanese Shi'ite fighters put their Iranian or Syrian patrons before their national interests? Could the group survive such a choice or would they irreversibly lose public support and spark a new civil war in Lebanon? It was a complex calculation that extended far beyond the borders of Syria and by early 2013 was still in flux.

Bashar had burned most of his other international cards by the end of 2012. The Turkish government, which had previously sought to cultivate friendlier ties with Damascus, had progressively hardened its stance as the violence escalated. 'For the welfare of your own people and the region, just leave that seat,' said prime minister Recep Tayyip Erdogan in November 2011 reminding Assad of Gaddafi's recent fate. Turkey also mooted the idea of creating humanitarian corridors or 'buffer zones' to protect civilians, though Ankara also needed to take into account the Kurdish population in both Turkey and Syria, whose dislike of Assad was at least matched by their dislike of the Turkish government.

Qatar, another former ally, had initiated the Arab isolation of Assad as part of its proactive role in the Arab Spring. In July 2011, Doha withdrew its ambassador and closed its embassy in Damascus after it said it had been attacked by regime-hired thugs.[50] Riyadh pulled out its envoy a few weeks later, with Bahrain and Kuwait quickly following suit, and throughout 2012 several Gulf states became increasingly vocal in calling for outside intervention in Syria. Some observers saw in this an increased Arab intolerance for state brutality against citizens. In reality, the tightening pressure on Bashar aimed to weaken his regime and in turn tilt the balance of power against the Gulf Arab countries' own nemesis, Iran. For the Saudis, a Sunni-led Syrian government within Riyadh's orbit would be the ideal outcome of the conflict, and even a weak state, as long as Iran had reduced influence over it, would be better than a regime that aligned itself with Tehran.

Waiting for Assad

In January 2013, the UN published a bleak new death toll which estimated that 60,000 people had been killed in Syria since the beginning of the uprising in March 2011 – far more than previously thought. Lakhdar Brahimi, the former Algerian diplomat who had inherited Kofi Annan's unenviable role as UN envoy to Syria, reckoned that a further 100,000 might die in the year ahead if the conflict carried on in its current direction.

Despite Brahimi's efforts to foster peace talks, both the Assad regime and the main opposition groups had so far refused to seriously discuss a political solution. Both had lost too much and still seemingly believed that they could achieve a military victory without having to negotiate an end to the fighting. The rebels could not stomach a transition agreement which left Bashar in power, while the Syrian leader was hardly likely to leave of his own accord, at least not until the last, most desperate moment.

During three decades under Hafez al-Assad and a decade under his son, the ruling clique had constructed a web of external allies and domestic pillars that had kept it in power far longer than its counterparts in North Africa. By the time that Tunisians were marking the second anniversary of their January 2011 revolution, that web meant Bashar, though weakened, was still in Damascus.

By early 2013, Assad's strategy appeared to have involved letting large parts of rural Syria, especially in the north, fall out of central control, while concentrating on key strategic points like ports, airports, military bases and certain land borders. Although skirmishes around such locations were becoming more common, the regime still retained control of the airports in Damascus and Aleppo, and of the border crossings with Lebanon and Jordan. Crucially, it also commanded the skies – something which Gaddafi had failed to do from the very start of his attempted defence – and could effectively pummel entire neighbourhoods or rebel positions.

Yet the regime's finances, and indeed the wider economy, were increasingly decrepit. Many private businessmen had long since left the country, taking their money with them and setting up shop in the Gulf, Lebanon or Europe. Sanctions had crippled trade, along with sources of income for the embattled government, while foreign oil firms including Shell and Total had abandoned their joint ventures in late 2011.[51] Foreign currency reserves were running low, while by the end of 2012 the Syrian pound was worth around half of its pre-war value against the US dollar. Inflation, even by official figures, had reached 50 per cent by the start of 2013, and families were struggling to make ends meet and survive the harsh winter in northern areas.

Various timelines were put forward for the bankruptcy of the Assads; if the regime could no longer pay soldiers or power its military campaign then its collapse would be inevitable. Syria is not an oil-rich country, and Damascus did not hold gigantic stockpiles of cash or gold. But it did have wealthy supporters in Russia and Iran, both of whom were willing to provide loans, supplies and even fuel to keep the president going. How long that funding could continue, especially as the tide inched slowly against the Assads, would help shape the course of the conflict.

One factor that augured against a short, sharp resolution to the war was the unlikelihood of any direct military action by external forces, for the reasons explained earlier in this chapter. There would be no Libya-style intervention to remove Assad, but neither would there be a Bahrain-style intervention to defend him in the same way that the Saudis had shielded the Al Khalifa monarchy in March 2011. The one exception to that calculation would be any use of chemical weapons, which the US and others had suggested would trigger immediate action.

Instead, a situation had developed in which a blurred mix of governments, groups and even wealthy individuals from countries like Lebanon, Iraq, Turkey, Iran, Qatar or Saudi Arabia were arming and supplying their respective proxies in Syria. Foreign intervention was taking place, just not the type that removed Gaddafi in what now seemed a comparatively brief conflict in 2011. The evidence instead pointed to Syria becoming a long-term and bloody battleground for competing regional and global interests.

Other scenarios did still remain possible. One was an internal coup within Assad's inner circle, perhaps by hardliners who believed that Bashar was not the right person to see the fight through. Rumours had regularly spread about a power struggle at the very top, and some questioned whether the young president was really calling the shots or had simply been retained as a figurehead. Yet such a coup would arguably have been more likely earlier in the uprising, rather than when the violence had already spiralled out of control.

Another possibility was a rebellion within the broader Alawite community, if some of its members decided that their long-term survival would be best served by joining the uprising and disavowing Assad. Such a development would mean the Alawites would be less likely to suffer mass retribution than if the regime fell at the end of a long and bloody war. It might also involve a retreat to the sect's historic heartlands in western Syria, where they had effectively run their own affairs during the mandate era.

The opposition could also make a decisive breakthrough, but the level of organisation, funding and coordination between the diverse range of different anti-regime groups still appeared limited. They neither spoke with a single voice, nor agreed on tactics, nor adhered to a coherent future vision, while only a tenuous connection existed between the groups fighting on the ground and those being formed outside the country as a kind of government-in-waiting.

The most high-profile group to emerge during the first year of the uprising was the Syrian National Council (SNC), which was officially launched from Istanbul in October 2011. The council did not claim to represent the entire Syrian people, but presented itself as a temporary body to help coordinate the transition process. It was plagued with infighting and disagreement from the start, especially over the issues of foreign military intervention and of dialogue with Bashar, displaying a lack of unity that frustrated external powers who might otherwise have given it greater support.

In November 2012 the increasingly defunct SNC decided to join a new National Coalition of Syrian Revolutionary and Opposition Forces, formed in Doha, which by the end of the year had been recognized by France, the GCC, Turkey, the US and the UK as the legitimate representative of the Syrian people. The new group incorporated a military council, which included the Free Syrian Army, and, significantly, also had representation from prominent Kurdish councils and parties. Moaz al-Khatib, a Sunni cleric elected to lead the coalition in late 2012, was careful to appeal to all sects and ethnic groups, and the fact that he had fled the country only in July made him more credible than the many senior figures in the SNC who had been exiled for years.

But unlike Libya's interim national council, whose recognition by France paved the way for military intervention against Gaddafi, the coalition was not based inside Syria and its control over opposition fighters on the ground appeared to be limited. Plenty of plans were being drawn up for post-Assad Syria, ranging from post-conflict justice to new economic programmes, but there was little clarity on how his regime would actually be dismantled.

With every day that passed, it was becoming harder to reverse a pattern of growing disintegration and lawlessness, as well as the flourishing of well-organized *jihadi* groups whose vision for a new Syria was distinctly at odds with that of the overseas-based coalition. One such faction was Jabhat al-Nusra, which Washington blacklisted in 2012 and described as an affiliate of Al-Qaeda in Iraq. The opposition coalition rejected the US decision, which caused consternation amongst some rebel fighters on the ground who accused outside parties of doing nothing concrete to help their cause.

The episode illustrated the ethnic, religious and geopolitical tightrope that any future leaders in Syria will have to walk. As in Egypt or Tunisia, a more democratic Syria – assuming that such a system does eventually emerge from the rubble – will probably be far more coloured by political Islam than it was before 2011. The influence of religion on policy will depend partly on which opposition groups – and which of their backers – come out of the conflict on top, but the emergence of a new Islamist regime would be anathema not only to minorities like the Christians or Alawites, but also to the more moderate Muslim population.

Will Syria retain a secular identity that protects its ethnic and religious minorities? Or will it see Christians or Alawites flee the threat of persecution in a power vacuum that would inevitably follow the fall of the regime? The majority of Syrian society may well be religiously tolerant, but many groups that wield hard power on the ground and can claim to have sacrificed much in the conflict are decidedly more extreme in their outlook. And how will a new Syria deal with the demands of Kurdish groups in the north-east, who had increasingly been running their own affairs as the power of the central state dwindled through 2012?

By early 2013, despite the fog of civil war, it seemed the Assads would take the fight to the bitter end. The prognosis was grim. Syria could disintegrate, at least temporarily, into mini-fiefdoms based on sectarian or ethnic lines while the regime retreated back to its strongholds. The conflict could plunge Lebanon into yet more internal strife. It could destabilize the border with Israel. It could draw in foreign powers like Iran, Turkey or Saudi Arabia and escalate the situation into something far graver.

Syria is still fighting the first round of a battle that Egypt, Tunisia and Libya completed in 2011. That round that has now gone on for so long, with so much already lost and so much still at stake, that Assad's departure will not provide closure but simply open a new chapter. Far more so than elsewhere in the region, that new chapter has the potential to resolve or exacerbate wider issues and to redraw the physical and political map of the Middle East.

A change in Damascus would be a powerful blow to Iran and a boon for its main rival Saudi Arabia, potentially altering the regional balance of powers. It could bring a lasting peace with Israel and allow Lebanon to do the same. It might rob Hezbollah of an ally but also resolve the latter's status within the country. The resurgence of Kurdish nationalism in Syria could spell trouble for Turkey, which has long struggled with its own Kurdish minority and its desire for autonomy. It could unleash Syria's own undoubted economic potential and allow it to regain its 1950s status as the financial capital of the Middle East. It will keep the battle for the Arab Spring burning long beyond 2012 and will itself be shaped by the more ominous tussles in the region, some of which involved Gulf monarchies that had not escaped unscathed from the upheavals elsewhere.

PART 3

THE NEW ARAB POLITICS

CHAPTER 10

The Kings' Dilemma

Unless we ourselves take a hand now, they will foist a republic on us. If we want things to stay as they are, things will have to change.
– Prince Tancredi Falconieri, in Giuseppi Lampedusa's *Il Gattopardo*

In the winter of 2006, the United Arab Emirates was gearing up for its first ever elections. It would be wrong to call them free or universal because, of the 403,000 Emiratis aged twenty or older, less than 2 per cent would be given the privilege of a vote, and all of them would be chosen by the rulers of each emirate.[1] In fact, less than 0.25 per cent of the entire 3 million-strong population of UAE residents aged over twenty, including both Emiratis and foreigners, would be going to the ballot box.[2] And they would elect half the members to the Federal National Council, an assembly whose role was not to legislate but to advise an existing council of ruling sheikhs that hold ultimate policy-making power.

The elections were held as the oil-fuelled boom neared its peak. Dubai, then the poster child of a new economic and political model that sought to attract labour and capital from all corners of the world, was growing at breakneck pace. Despite the twenty-four-hour construction that had become the thudding soundtrack to life in the city, the emirate was struggling to keep up with the influx of new arrivals. Apartments viewed in the morning would be snapped up by lunchtime, and prices were rising so swiftly that the authorities imposed a series of caps on annual rent increases.[3] Both Dubai and Abu Dhabi, the UAE's capital and its largest emirate, were bursting at the seams.

Some Emiratis struggled to adapt to the pace of change in a country where the older generation could remember living in palm frond shacks. A few privately expressed alarm about a development policy that saw them become a tiny minority in their own country within three decades of its formation in 1971. But they were arguably the biggest beneficiaries of the boom, receiving generous financial benefits from the government while state subsidies shielded them from the worst effects of rampant inflation. Working largely in the public sector, Emiratis enjoyed job security and high salaries that were regularly upped to keep pace with the cost of living. A government survey in 2009 found that the average annual income for an Emirati household in Dubai was $210,400, compared to $150,000 for Europeans, $89,100 for other Arab nationalities, and a mere $6,800 for 'collective labourers', the hundreds of thousands of migrant construction workers.[4] Emiratis might not have enjoyed many political or media freedoms, but few openly demanded change.

A month before the polls, at a meeting with Anwar Gergash, the UAE minister of state in charge of organizing the elections, the disdain for the Arab world's efforts at introducing democracy was palpable. His media advisor froze, eyes dropping to the exquisite Persian rug, when the minister was asked if UAE nationals would ever be able to vote out their ruling families. 'We are not talking about democracy. What we are talking about is political participation,' said Gergash, a mild-mannered former politics professor and the scion of one of Dubai's big merchant families. 'I don't see the process in any way moving toward political parties or fundamentally questioning the dynastic nature of the state.'[5] He motioned to the enormous window that framed the hubbub of Dubai's cranes. Why would the UAE want to exchange this for the painful experience that other Arab countries have had with multi-party or, for that matter, one-party politics? Why would the UAE want to be like Lebanon or Iraq, where sectarian, ethnic or tribal loyalties trump policy considerations at the ballot box?

Why indeed. Monarchies around the region had long pointed to such troubled Arab experiments with democracy to remind the world and their own nationals of just how good they had it. They could point to how the removal of kings in Egypt, Iraq, Syria or Libya ultimately gave rise to military regimes coated in a veneer of republicanism and iced with leaders like Saddam Hussein, Muammar Gaddafi or Hosni Mubarak who all hoped to create their own dynasties. Political repression, mass jailings and heavy-handed surveillance had failed to protect those men from the upheaval of 2011, providing more evidence for Arab ruling families to argue that their islands of apparent stability, for all their restrictions, were preferable to the frothing sea of sectarian strife or military republicanism that surrounded them.

Yet absolute monarchs are an increasingly endangered species in the twenty-first century. With so few examples outside the Arab world, it is difficult to imagine that these families, and those who rely on their patronage, do not feel vulnerable to the winds of change. In most cases, too, the states they control have existed for but a fleeting historical moment. The Al Sauds forged their kingdom through twentieth-century conquest, Jordan was a European colonial creation, and only Morocco and Oman can trace a much older heritage of continuous family rule over a territory still in existence today.

The eight kingdoms or emirates in Jordan, Morocco, Kuwait, Qatar, Oman, the UAE, Saudi Arabia and Bahrain all survived 2011, but things had clearly changed. The sight of Mubarak in a courtroom cage and Gaddafi's rotting corpse on display to the snap-happy masses offered a gory glimpse of what might await them if revolution spread to their shores. Each faced different internal and external challenges that the Arab Spring and its aftermath exacerbated, activating grievances that might otherwise have remained subdued and forcing rulers to respond. The uprisings also encouraged the Gulf dynasties, particularly those of Saudi Arabia and Qatar, to pursue more proactive policies in the wider region rather than rely on Washington's lead. Aware that they could not push back the tide of change, they sought to harness it to serve their own interests.

Whether these ruling families can retain their grip on power in such a turbulent regional and global climate will hinge on several factors, including their reserves of legitimacy and goodwill, the strength of domestic demands for change, the depth of their pockets, the external pressures they face, and how the new-look republics shape up. Like all the authoritarian regimes that fell in 2011, the Arab monarchies suffer underlying social, economic and political imbalances that have the potential to tip over into serious upheaval unless handled with the utmost care.

Some countries felt compelled to make political concessions in 2011, allowing freer and fairer elections or transferring limited powers from kings to elected parliaments and deflating, for now, the swelling demands for change. Others used money and fear to suppress unrest, but have done little to deal with bottled-up tensions that threaten to detonate in the future. In the short term, all the Arab monarchies look well placed to avoid revolution. But for some, a storm is brewing on the horizon, and the Arab Spring has only blown it closer to their shores.

Buying Stability

In the decade before 2011, most Arab ruling families had tweaked their political systems to give the public more say in policymaking. At one end of the spectrum was Morocco, which permitted political parties and held elections for a parliament with limited powers. At the other was Saudi Arabia, whose only experiment with voting had been a 2005 poll for municipal councils in which women were not allowed to participate. In the absence of unified and broad-based opposition movements, reform everywhere was hesitant, cautious and initiated from above.

2011 changed all that. Inspired by the success of the Tunisian and Egyptian uprisings and the wave of change that appeared to be spreading across the region, youths and intellectuals began to air their demands. Protests broke out not just in Bahrain (discussed in an earlier chapter) but in Morocco, Jordan, Kuwait, Oman and even Saudi Arabia. For the most part, these were mild in intensity and their participants were largely unarmed. They called not for wholesale revolution but for political reform and economic concessions. None snowballed into mass uprisings or threatened to immediately topple the ruling families.

Yet these were unusual levels of domestic unrest for the Gulf, and in the context of the revolutionary fervour that had gripped the region, they were serious enough to prompt major financial concessions. Meeting the economic expectations of their citizens will be crucial if Arab dynasties are to sap the momentum of any future protest movements and limit the depth of political reform they could be forced to implement. The Arab Spring has already been a pricey affair for all the Arab monarchies and emirates, but some have much deeper pockets than others.

Kuwait, Qatar and the UAE are in the strongest financial position to provide high living standards for their citizens. From their very emergence as independent states, several common traits have enabled their ruling families to maintain power.

The first is their tiny populations. A census in 1970, a year before its independence, counted just 111,133 permanent residents in Qatar, of whom less than half were classified as Qatari nationals.[6] Dubai's first-ever census in 1968, three years before the formation of the UAE, recorded just 58,971 residents, with another 74,880 across the five northern emirates and 46,375 in Abu Dhabi. Kuwait was more populous, with 321,621 residents at independence in 1961, and also had a sizeable Shi'ite population.[7]

From the start, these minuscule constituencies meant that ruling families could physically consult with their subjects, maintain personal contact with the patriarchs of local families and, if they chose, pursue a relatively democratic rule through regular consultation and without the need for formal institutions to represent popular opinion.

By 2011, Qatari nationals made up around 15 per cent of a total population of 1.7 million, Emiratis barely 13 per cent of 7.3 million, and Kuwaitis roughly 30 per cent of around 3.5 million.[8] While the greater numbers of nationals created difficulties for the old form of personalized rule, which lacked the institutions to channel popular will to the government, their minority status meant that they could effectively be moulded into an elite that received a rich host of benefits denied to the majority of the population, made up of foreigners. These countries exhibited huge rich-poor divides, but the local populations, whose support was vital to the ruling families, were on the favoured side of that divide. Unlike nationals of Egypt, Tunisia or Libya, there was little reason for Qataris or Emiratis to complain about inequality or marginalization.

This divide was made possible by energy resources that in the space of a few decades had allowed these sheikhdoms to grow from primitive economies based on pearling, fishing and trading into some of the richest countries in the world, in per capita terms. In 2010, Qatar's hydrocarbons sector earned the equivalent of $281,593 for each one of its citizens.[9] In Kuwait, income from crude oil sales was equivalent to about $57,677 per Kuwaiti.[10] Energy wealth provided the ink for a long-established ruling bargain in which the rulers provided for the ruled, but demanded loyalty and political acquiescence in return.

Governments made little or no other demands on their nationals. None of the six states of the Gulf Cooperation Council (GCC) imposed personal income tax, and most nationals receive free housing, education, healthcare and soft loans. When inflation soared in 2007, the Dubai government increased its public-sector salaries by 70 per cent, while the Qatari government approved pay rises throughout the late 2000s, plus another of 60 per cent in September 2011.[11] Ostensibly to celebrate the fiftieth anniversary of independence and the twentieth anniversary of liberation from Iraq Kuwait's emir granted about $3,500 to every Kuwaiti in February 2011 and announced that basic foodstuffs would be free until March 2013.

The way these countries manage their oil and gas revenues is still riddled with inefficiencies. None is yet properly equipped for the post-oil era. But they have nonetheless used their natural wealth to provide significantly higher living standards than some other energy-rich regimes, not least that of Muammar Gaddafi in Libya. Their spending patterns are not sustainable in the long run, but the oil bonanza that began in the 2000s has so far allowed wealthier Gulf countries like the UAE to meet the economic demands of local populations while imposing a zero-tolerance policy on minority voices calling for a quicker pace of change.

In March 2011, five Emiratis, including Ahmed Mansour, a member of the Middle East advisory committee of Human Rights Watch,[12] and Nasser bin Ghaith, an economist and lecturer at the Abu Dhabi branch of the Sorbonne University, drafted a petition to Sheikh Khalifa bin Zayed Al Nahyan, the UAE president, urging greater freedoms. They referred to the country's original 1971 constitution, which called for 'progressing by steps towards a comprehensive, representative, democratic regime in an Islamic and Arab society free from fear and anxiety'.[13]

The document acquired the signatures of more than 130 Emiratis and was described by one local political scientist as 'probably the first ever political petition in the history of the UAE'.[14] But it crossed a line. Its authors were arrested and charged with 'instigation, breaking laws and perpetrating acts that pose [a] threat to state security, undermining the public order, opposing the government system, and insulting the leadership'.[15] They were sentenced to three years in jail after a trial that was described as 'grossly unfair' by independent observers, but were pardoned by Sheikh Khalifa one day later.[16]

Any other signs of an 'Emirati awakening' were nipped in the bud. In 2012, the UAE arrested sixty Islamists, members of a group called Islah or Reform, and revoked the citizenship of seven men who had previously been naturalized. The Islamists were accused of running an organization loyal to the Muslim Brotherhood, which came to power in Egypt that year, and plotting to destabilize the state. In response, Islah claimed it had no links to foreign groups and was seeking not to overthrow the royal family but to push for peaceful reforms, such as greater powers for the semi-elected FNC. However, many Emiratis felt that any lurch towards political Islam would destabilize the delicate balance of powers and endanger their financial security, undermining the model that had seen immigrants from around the world set up home in the country.

Media censorship, already strict, tightened further. And despite raising the number of Emiratis selected to vote from 7,000 to 129,000, or about

12 per cent of all UAE nationals, turnout for the second-ever FNC elections in September 2011 was a miserable 28 per cent, suggesting that most Emiratis were either not interested in political participation or considered the advisory body meaningless. It was a similar story in Qatar, where in May turnout was just 40 per cent in the first elections for its twenty-nine-member Central Municipal Council, a consultative body with very limited powers. But the Emir, Sheikh Hamad bin Khalifa Al Thani, surprised many in November 2011 by announcing that in 2013 he would hold universal elections for a new council with legislative powers. Although there was no obvious domestic pressure for such a move, it sent a clear message that the ruling family would set its own pace of political reform.

The other Gulf monarchies face more challenging situations, either because they lack the wealth needed to buy political allegiance or, in the case of Kuwait, because a system that seeks to marry hereditary rule with a relatively empowered parliament is beginning to crack. Kuwait's constitution allows for an elected parliament with legislative powers, but it is the emir, Sheikh Sabah al-Ahmed al-Sabah, who chooses the government, which has traditionally been led by a royal and packed with loyalists. Since 2006, opposition MPs, mainly Islamists, have insisted on their right to supervise government activities, repeatedly raising allegations of corruption and mismanagement and seeking to remove the prime minister, a nephew of the emir. There is little doubt that Kuwait's substantial wealth could be better managed, but the stalemate itself has paralyzed infrastructure, development and economic plans. The result is a wealthy country with ageing infrastructure and a stagnant economy that remains almost entirely dependent on oil.

The Arab Spring has only accelerated demands that Kuwait move closer towards a constitutional monarchy. A protest movement that culminated in October 2011 with the storming of parliament prompted the emir to dissolve the body and call a general election. The vote, held in early 2012, saw Islamists consolidate their hold on the chamber, from which they have pushed for increasing social conservatism as well as seeking to weaken the royal hold on government. Alarmed, the emir used emergency powers to amend the electoral law, prompting clashes between protesters and police almost unheard of in Kuwait. The opposition boycotted further elections in December, resulting, predictably, in a loyalist chamber. Though protests have continued, the opposition has struggled to maintain a united front, with differences between Islamists, tribal elements, liberals and young people undermining their campaign.

The Kuwaiti experience has proven both instructive and alarming for similarly wealthy rulers in the UAE, Qatar and Saudi Arabia. It suggested that, given any political opening, nationals may cease to be content with state payoffs and begin to openly question the principle of royal control over hydrocarbon resources. It also showed that genuine elections would probably see Islamists gain prominence and push for conservative social policies that discourage Western expatriates. And as in Bahrain, the Kuwaiti experience suggested that democratic reforms, no matter how halting, could prompt sectarian and tribal bickering that would destabilize Gulf economies and might open the door to the end of hereditary rule. For wealthier Gulf rulers, the Kuwaiti crisis seemed to debunk the view that democratic reforms would defuse criticism and fend off sudden, major change. Poorer monarchies and sultanates, however, had little choice but to offer reforms, however limited, to calm the demands for change.

Oman, which is expected to drain its remaining 5.5 billion barrels of crude some time in the 2020s, must prepare much sooner for a post-oil era.[17] High energy prices in the 2000s and better-than-expected production have postponed the problem. The Sultanate sold its crude at an average price of $77 per barrel in 2010 compared to $57 a year earlier, helping to cut its budget deficit.[18] But oil and gas still accounted for four-fifths of state earnings and exports in 2010, while government expenditure had jumped by 61 per cent since 2006. And the measures that Sultan Qaboos enacted after the 2011 protests added another $2.6 billion to an annual budget that was already expected to be the biggest ever.[19]

Providing jobs will be the pre-eminent challenge. Since 2007 more Omanis have been employed by the private sector than by the state, but its labour markets remain deeply skewed: 84 per cent of private-sector workers are expatriates, while 86 per cent of all public-sector workers are Omanis. Copying the Emirati or Qatari model of a privileged national elite is far more difficult in Oman, where only 28 per cent of the population are foreigners, and where unemployment and inflation could be disruptive if the state lacks the money to feather its citizens' nests.[20] Oman was forced to make political concessions.

The Sultanate's advisory body, the Shura Council, was granted additional powers in 2011 after protests in February saw roads blocked, shops burned and rallies held in several cities.[21, 22] The complaints aired by protesters focused on unemployment, rising prices and corruption and were met mainly with economic measures, like a 43 per cent rise in minimum private-sector wages and a promise of 50,000 new state jobs.[23]

But Sultan Qaboos, who celebrated his seventy-first birthday in 2011, also sacked many members of his cabinet, including the powerful ministers of the interior and the economy, and pledged to give legislative powers to the Shura Council, the only elected body in the country. He also promised that, for the first time, some of those elected from the council would be appointed as government ministers. These were not insignificant changes in an Arab monarchy where power is theoretically more personalized than in any other.

The sultan has no children or full brothers, and tussles over succession could become messy. Old religious tensions could re-emerge. It was only in the 1950s that the conservative interior was ruled by a religious imamate. Omanis seem in no rush to remove their leader and the succession may be smooth, but underlying conflicts that remained latent during his rule risk erupting with his death, especially in an era of declining oil revenues.

Oil-poor Jordan and Morocco are even more financially pinched. Jordan's outstanding domestic debt had reached 35 per cent of GDP in 2010, compared to 23 per cent three years earlier, and its finances remained reliant on foreign aid.[24] Desperate for income, the government had cut food and fuel subsidies as part of a wider free-market push aimed at reducing a record budget deficit of $2.1 billion in 2009.[25] In 2010, it had raised taxes on mobile phones, border crossings, gasoline, tobacco, hybrid cars and coffee, among other things.[26] But the 2011 protests forced a change of direction, with large-scale spending to cover the new concessions pushing the budget deficit far above initial targets. Signs of disquiet were already rearing up before 2011 as economic growth faltered, inflation jumped to 5 per cent, and unemployment remained stubbornly high.[27] Strikes were on the increase, while small-scale demonstrations railed against elite corruption and called for the resignation of the prime minister. The Arab Spring stepped those up a gear.

Lacking the cash to offer endless handouts, Jordan's King Abdullah faces a dilemma. If he allows greater political participation by the six-million-strong population as a means to ease political unrest, he risks irking his traditional supporters instead. Responding to public pressure to accelerate change, the king dissolved parliament halfway through its term in 2012 and promulgated a new election law as part of reforms that would see the prime minister picked from among elected MPs. But the changes pleased no one. They worried native Jordanians, the king's tribal support base, who fear that reform will erode their privileged position. But they also disappointed opposition groups who argued the new election law would continue to marginalize Palestinian Jordanians, who comprise over half the population. The Islamic Action Front, the political wing of Jordan's Muslim Brotherhood, said it would boycott elections set for early 2013 unless its long-running demands for freer and fairer polls are pushed through. If the electoral playing field does eventually become flatter then in Jordan, as elsewhere in the region, it will be an Islamist party that makes the biggest gains. But while the IAF might be the single most popular opposition group, many of the youth movements are disconnected from the old political parties. New forces will emerge in the years ahead and the role of religion is just one element in a more complex web of social, political, economic and demographic dynamics.

It was a similar story in Morocco, which could ill afford the economic concessions made in the wake of the protests. In August, the government announced that its compensation fund, which subsidizes the prices of basic commodities on the local market, would require a budget of $5.9 billion for 2011, more than four times as much as initially estimated. Lacking oil wealth and faced with some of the highest poverty rates in the region, Morocco's King Mohamed could only offer limited financial concessions.

Instead, he oversaw proposals for reforms that gave new powers to the prime minister, who would now come from the party with the most seats in parliament rather than be appointed directly by the monarch. But the palace would retain control over security, defence and foreign policy and the monarch remained head of the religious establishment, even though his position would now be described in the constitution as 'inviolable' rather than 'sacred'. The reforms won 98 per cent approval in a July referendum. Given calls for a boycott by the youth movement, turnout for the general elections held in October was 45 per cent of Moroccans who registered to vote, a modest figure but better than the record low of 37 per cent at the last parliamentary polls in 2007.

Though the new government was led by the Islamist group that won the elections, Moroccans suspected that the king and his close advisers still made all major policy and there have been continued protests demanding that funds directed to the monarchy be spent on the people instead. Morocco has inevitably suffered from the crisis in the Eurozone, its most important trading and tourism partner, and in 2012 the country secured a $6.2 billion line of credit from the IMF, a precautionary measure in case a sudden surge in unrest required increased spending. Lacking the money for Gulf-style handouts, the rulers of Jordan and Morocco could be forced to make ever greater political concessions and borrow ever more from Gulf allies to keep revolution at bay.

Yet the most dangerously unsustainable spending pattern can arguably be found in Saudi Arabia. Although it is the world's largest oil exporter, the kingdom's expenses bill is growing at a precarious pace. Annual government spending doubled between 2004 and 2009, while the public-sector wage bill rose by over three-quarters between 2003 and 2009.[28] The oil price required for the state to balance its books had doubled between 2005 and 2010, and stood at around $84 per barrel in the summer of 2011.[29] Domestic consumption of oil is rising faster than production, and for every barrel consumed at home at heavily subsidized prices, the state makes a paper loss from not selling it on the international market.[30]

The Arab Spring was more expensive for Saudi Arabia than for any other state. In February, King Abdullah announced a $130 billion package that included salary rises, tens of thousands of new jobs, and bigger housing loans. And this was before counting the overseas commitments that Saudi Arabia made, with the GCC promising $10 billion each for Oman and Bahrain over the coming decade, plus multi-billion dollar grants to Tunisia and Egypt and payments to politicians in Yemen.

Despite this, there is no urgency for the Al Saud family to cut spending. One study estimated in 2010 that the kingdom could run a deficit worth 10 per cent of GDP every year for a decade without having to issue any debt, and would still hold reserves above $110 billion.[31] Although the break-even oil price had soared it was still below the average market price in 2011, and still generating healthy budget surpluses.

But if left unchecked, these imbalances could trigger a future crisis. The turmoil of 2011 has set back Riyadh's halting efforts to prepare its economy and population for a time when the state will no longer be able to demand so little of its citizens, however distant that time may be. In practical terms, that may mean reducing fuel subsidies limiting state jobs and salaries or even introducing taxes. That would fundamentally change the social compact in the kingdom. When it happens partly hinges on oil prices, but most Saudis may well see drastic changes to their country within their own lifetimes. And whether it comes in 2020 or 2040, change in Saudi Arabia will bring regional repercussions that can be partly traced back to the Arab Spring.

Shaping Change

Drivers making the journey between central Amman and Queen Alia international airport in the autumn of 2011 followed a road that twisted around construction work on a new motorway. The $115 million project would not be complete until the following year, but Jordan's cash-strapped government had recently announced that motorists would be charged a fee, making it the first toll road in the country and one of only a handful across the region.[32] As the road continued into the affluent Abdoun area, cars passed the white stone walls of the new Saudi embassy, looming over one of the city's many valleys. It was a neat juxtaposition of Jordan's own precarious financial position and the oil wealth that extended its influence beyond the Arabian Peninsula.

The geopolitical concerns discussed in the first section of this book – oil, Israel and Iran – will continue to shape change as Arab monarchies reposition themselves in light of regional turbulence. Saudi Arabia may be unwilling to empower the Shi'ites in Bahrain because of its wider cold war with Iran; meaningful reform in Jordan is linked to the fate of the Palestinians; and no one, from Washington to Beijing, wants to see uncontrolled unrest in the world's biggest oil-exporting region that could further batter the fragile global economy.

But 2011 created a new external threat for Arab kings and emirs, one that might blow the seeds of political activism to their own shores. This was a serious concern for regimes that have not forgotten how Arab nationalism and Ba'athism filtered across their borders in the 1950s and 1960s, prompting what Malcolm Kerr called the Arab Cold War. The monarchies were seeking to control and limit change at home, but they were also trying to shape the impact of the Arab Spring outside their own borders. This was particularly true for two Gulf countries – Saudi Arabia and Qatar.

Riyadh has always been in a position of regional influence as the wealthiest Arab state, the most populous in the Gulf, the key US ally in that region and the birthplace of Islam. Its foreign policy has been principally aimed at retaining its own domestic power, whose basis was at odds with many of the ideas and aspirations voiced by the Arab Spring, and at exploiting the regional turmoil to weaken its biggest enemy, Shi'ite Iran. As far as any strategy was discernible, the kingdom has tried to protect other monarchies from revolution, and to ensure that political forces emerging in the new-look republics were not threatening to its own regional and international interests.

Qatar's tiny population, religious homogeneity and immense wealth mean that its motivations overseas are more about extending its political and commercial clout and acting as a rival to Riyadh. Through its ownership of Al-Jazeera, Doha clearly played a pro-revolutionary role in Egypt and Tunisia, essentially supporting the removal of leaders which Riyadh was loath to see go. Qatar has widely been seen as supporting the Muslim Brotherhood and similar groups that have won elections since 2011, which have been treated with much more suspicion in Riyadh and Abu Dhabi.

On other conflicts, Saudi and Qatari interests have converged and both opposed the upheaval in Bahrain while ramping up pressure on Assad in Syria. None of the Gulf rulers wanted to see kings in Jordan or Morocco overthrown, or even downgraded by popular pressure. However unlikely that possibility was in the short term, there were signs that Sunni monarchies were closing ranks.

Jordanians may have been surprised to read in May 2011 that their country might become a member of the GCC, the six-member economic and political bloc dominated by Saudi Arabia. Even more surprising was the news that Morocco, whose capital city is as close to Boston as it is to Riyadh, could also join. By September, talks had begun on how the council could incorporate the two newcomers, and a five-year financial support plan was mooted.[33]

The expansion plan suggested that Arab monarchies, spearheaded by Riyadh, were seeking to form a counter-revolutionary club of kings to insulate themselves against a future league of pro-democratic republics and their dangerous ideas. That is simplistic for several reasons. The monarchies may have some things in common – they are all Sunni Arab, for instance – but they do not have a unified strategy or speak with a single voice. Rifts and rivalries among the Gulf states go back far into history and partly explain a frequent tendency for the GCC to announce grand plans, such as a single currency, that never get implemented. The expansion plan may meet the same fate.

Nor is there a homogenous band of republics to face up to. The future of Egypt, Libya and Syria was so uncertain by early 2013 that any potential pro-democratic league of republics could only count diminutive Tunisia as a member. Even though its foreign policy had become more proactive – Tunis took a strong stance against the Assad regime for instance – that policy was hardly likely to include fomenting revolution in the monarchies as one of its main goals. Indeed, the Islamist-led government that came to power after the revolution soon turned to Qatar for loans it needed to quell economic discontent and sought cordial ties with Saudi Arabia though that country has sheltered Tunisia's ousted president.

Saudi Arabia and Qatar were not counter-revolutionary in the sense of trying to turn back the clock in Egypt, Tunisia or Libya, but they sought to exploit the momentum to further their own ends. Without their backing, the foreign intervention in Libya may never have happened. Qatar and the UAE were among the Arab combatants in that war to remove a fellow Arab head of state. Saudi Arabia and Qatar led the charge against Assad, raising international pressure on an Arab leader who has allied himself with Riyadh's greatest rival Iran.

Both countries, but particularly Saudi Arabia, also sought to ensure that the new forces emerging from the uprisings did not pose a threat to their own domestic grip on power. Riyadh must fear a scenario whereby a major domestic uprising requires such brutal repression that it isolates the Al Sauds in the same way that Gaddafi and Assad had been isolated in 2011. If the Arab League were to become a more relevant body in the future – its endorsement of a no-fly zone in Libya was a major part of the Western decision to attack Gaddafi – then having powerful friends in the new democratic republics would reduce the chance of external sanctions or intervention.

The worst case for them would arguably be the rise of an aggressively pro-democratic Arab government that supported or armed anti-regime groups in other countries, in the same way that Libyan militias had reportedly done with the Free Syrian Army in late 2011, or one that rallied other Arab countries and the international community against authoritarian monarchies clinging to power. Those scenarios are hypothetical, but the Arab Spring certainly demonstrated how quickly things could change and UAE fears over the growing confidence of local Islamist activists strained ties with the new Muslim Brotherhood leadership in Cairo in 2012.

Money was at the heart of how the Gulf sought to influence what happened in North Africa. Prominent Islamist leaders in Libya had been living for years in Qatar and it later emerged that Doha had been directly funding armed Islamist groups.[34] The Saudis have been accused of funding the ultra-conservative Salafists in Egypt, although no concrete proof has come to light. With Tunisia and Egypt facing troubled economic times, new governments led by Islamist parties will not be inclined to turn down financial support from Qatar or other Gulf states.

It is impossible to know the real level of this financial support, but the perception of Gulf interference was already provoking resentment, particularly against Qatar. Protesters in Tunis held a demonstration outside the Qatari embassy in November 2011 while across the region Al-Jazeera is now tarnished by its association with Qatari foreign policy. In Morocco and Jordan, the younger generation of activists are sceptical about GCC membership, fearing that the oil-rich Gulf would hold back a popular desire for change by subsidizing cheap commodities or funding thousands of well-paid government jobs. Many North Africans and Levantines, boasting ancient cultures and civilizations, still ask what they can learn from Gulf countries they consider to be *nouveau riche* desert tribes with little to offer beyond oil money and a particularly zealous form of Islam.

Abdel Rahman Shalgam, Libya's former ambassador to the UN who defected from the Gaddafi regime at the very start of the February uprising, provided the most colourful backlash against the tiny Gulf state. 'Qatar isn't neutral with all parties,' he said in November 2011. 'Qatar will gather these weapons and give them to others... we will not accept to be used by Qatar. We will not accept to be a new emirate that belongs to the new "Emir of the Believers" in Qatar... I do not rule out Qatar setting up a Hezbollah party in Libya. We don't want a foreign country to interfere.'[35]

Given a choice, Riyadh might well have taken Ben Ali over Ennahda and Mubarak over the Muslim Brotherhood. But if there had to be a democracy, then better a Sunni Islamist one that could bolster the Gulf's stand against Shi'ite Iran. And the more hierarchical structure of Islamist parties, with their older generation of leadership, also made them easier to interact with than the often nebulous secular youth movements.

For that reason, any regional pro-democratic movement is more likely to come from non-state actors than the new post-revolutionary governments. The type of secular, liberal youth activists who did so much to organize the occupation of Tahrir Square or the removal of Ben Ali in Tunisia might try to export their ideas, using Cairo or Tunis as their base of operations and the internet as their weapon. But, two years later, those forces looked weak. They were struggling to make any impact at the ballot box in their own countries, let alone elsewhere, and were hopelessly outgunned financially by the big budgets of Gulf countries.

Nor will activists find much support from Western powers, which have neither the means nor the inclination to facilitate popular action in the monarchies.

Washington and London no doubt realize that the current political and economic structures in the Arab monarchies are ultimately unsustainable, particularly with the decline of oil, but no Western government working to its own short-term electoral timetable wishes to see unrest that could push up energy prices or play into the hands of Iran. By gently pushing for gradual, top-down change, or remaining silent, they add to the risk that suppressed volatility in several countries, particularly Saudi Arabia and Bahrain, will eventually crash violently to the surface.

This does not mean that ruling families will not adapt to their rapidly changing circumstances, as they have so far proven adept at doing, but the point is that they will face little external pressure to move at anything other than their own pace and on anything other than their own terms. All this is possible with money, which the Gulf states have in abundance for at least the next decade. But beyond that, some, particularly Saudi Arabia, look vulnerable to upheaval. And if other players in the region have become reliant on Gulf financial support, then the impact of that upheaval could be huge.

Much also hinges on the mindset of individual kings, emirs and their families, a factor that is difficult to assess from outside the corridors of power. Some leaders claim to be committed to the idea of constitutional monarchies, gradually transferring power from the palace to elected institutions. '[The] Arab Spring actually gave me, in a way, the opportunity that I've been looking for the past eleven years,' said Jordan's King Abdullah in August 2011. 'Once you open the floodgates, that's it. Now the challenge, I'll be quite honest with you, is that the political reform is done in the right way.'[36]

But whatever the will and intentions of an individual man might be, many other political, social and business interests rely on his retention of power. A ruling family that decides its long-term survival is best guaranteed by shifting towards a constitutional monarchy will meet stiff resistance from those groups who stand to lose the most from change.

Lines of succession, and the credibility of future monarchs, will also be crucial. Jordan's King Abdullah may try to draw on his Hashemite lineage, which traces itself back to the family of the Prophet Mohamed, as does the dynasty of King Mohamed in Morocco. Their successors are likely to harness similar claims to legitimacy in the future, though their effectiveness is uncertain. The Al Sauds successfully managed a reshuffle of senior members after the long-expected death of Crown Prince Sultan in late 2011 was followed the next year by the passing of his successor, Prince Nayef. The changes confirmed that there were power structures and processes in place to guide the distribution of power. But the decision to replace the deceased heirs with ageing half-brothers, rather than shift to a younger generation of princes, highlighted the potentially explosive tensions within the sprawling ruling family and the country at large. Even allowing for a shift to the next generation, Saudis can look forward to a succession of geriatric leaders who may lack the vision and energy to prepare their country for the post-oil period and all it entails.

Meanwhile, broader generational shifts continue to alter political dynamics. Many Moroccans and Jordanians still remember the more oppressive rules of King Hassan and King Hussein respectively. Similarly, the new generation in the UAE or Qatar did not grow up during the process of state-building. They do not remember the hardships of the pre-oil era. With more of them exposed to and often educated in the West and wired into the Twittersphere, the future is likely to bring greater bottom-up pressure for change.

But all of the Arab monarchies are likely to survive in the short term. The GCC possesses the collective financial strength to appease its own populations and, if necessary, fund Morocco and Jordan to do the same. Any youth or Shi'ite-led uprising in Saudi Arabia will likely be met with a potent combination of religious decrees, suppression and money. The UAE and Qatar face little organized domestic opposition and can afford to nurture their privileged national elite. Kuwait may move more quickly towards a constitutional monarchy. But other Gulf states will be reluctant to see the Kuwaiti emir's power eroded.

While significant constitutional reform has taken place in Morocco, the palace is unlikely to give up its power any more quickly than the pace required to get protesters off the streets. In Jordan, the delicate dynamic between 'original' East Bank Jordanians, who are broadly pro-monarchy and have traditionally been economically favoured by the state, and the Jordanian Palestinians who hail from the West Bank, complicates change. But as with Morocco the system has constitutional safety valves to release pent-up pressure, and both countries are ruled by relatively young monarchs who enjoy at least some reserves of popular goodwill. Their battle to fend off both economic and political discontent is likely to see them accept greater assistance from the Gulf states, whether or not they ever join the GCC.

But the longer term, as always, is far less certain. Oil will run out at some point, and when it does, the entire structures of some of the Gulf states will be called into question. The relative lack of visible volatility in Saudi Arabia in 2011 masked dangerous imbalances, not least a jobless and disenfranchised youth and a marginalized Shi'ite population, which carry serious risks for the future.

In every monarchy there are bigger questions at stake. All had been within the US sphere of influence since the end of the Second World War, whether that meant security or military alliances, importing Western-style economic models, or cooperating in the 'war on terror'. The Arab Spring was a milestone in the disintegration of that old order, opening the stage for new regional powers, including the Gulf monarchies, to fill the gap that US decline was beginning to leave behind. And for them, the victory of Islamist parties in the first post-uprising elections carried both advantages and disadvantages.

CHAPTER 11

The Islamist Resurgence

The flaws inherent in the liberal democratic system should never be used as a pretext for rejecting it, for there is no alternative out there to democracy except dictatorship. An incomplete freedom is always better than no freedom at all, and to be governed by an imperfect democratic order is better than being governed by a despotic order, that is the whims and desires of a tyrant.

Rachid Ghannouchi, leader of Tunisia's Ennahda[1]

Anger was rising in Algeria. In the slums, young men prowled the streets with nothing to do, the unemployed legions produced by one of the fastest-growing populations in the world. Economic liberalization plans aimed at boosting the economy had only bred corruption as senior officials lined their pockets at the people's expense. Black-market profiteering meant staples such as cooking oil, flour and semolina were missing from the shops. The disenfranchised younger generation was born after independence and could not remember the sacrifices the nationalists, spearheaded by the Front de Libération National (FLN), had made to rid Algeria of the French. All they could see was bribery, a monopoly on power, and their country's diminished place in the world. When jobless youths ran amok in Algiers, burning and looting FLN offices or the upmarket shops frequented by the francophone children of corrupt officials, they were demanding work, justice and dignity.[2]

This was not 2011, but 1988. Alarmed, President Chadli Benjedid announced reforms, freeing up the press, allowing the formation of rival political parties, and promising elections that would ease the FLN's hold on power. Dozens of parties were formed and political debate was lively, but within three years it was clear that the Islamists, led by an umbrella organization called the Front Islamique du Salut (FIS), the Islamic Salvation Front, were gaining ground. Benjedid had encouraged the Islamists in the 1980s as a bulwark against the greater threat he saw from left-wing rivals, but they now threatened to overpower the FLN itself. The leader of the FIS, Abbessi Madani, had openly stated in 1991 that any election that brought the Islamists to power would be Algeria's last.[3] The group would declare an Islamic state with the Koran as its constitution and women, who emerged as the main battle line in competing visions for a new Algeria, would be banned from secondary education and placed under the control of male relatives. In just three years, the number of veiled women had already swung from a minority to a majority in Algeria. If the Islamists did not win elections, some FIS members were ready to take power by force.

The FIS gained a majority in council elections in 1990 and in the following year won the first round of general elections by a landslide. With the group apparently set to take two-thirds of the assembly, enough to lead the government and amend or annul the constitution, the army forced Benjedid to resign. It effectively took control of the country and cancelled the second round of polling. Already, some FIS fighters were hiding out in the mountains, preparing for the years of war that the coup would usher in and that at its height in the late 1990s saw armed gangs massacre entire villages. Some 200,000 Algerians would be killed in the conflict. A new generation grew up knowing nothing but violence in a country ignored by a world that had lost interest since the French exit in the early 1960s.

The tragedy that befell Algeria, blessed with hydrocarbon reserves and a diverse, enormous territory that should have made it one of the most prosperous states in Africa, was not far from the lips of secular and religious politicians in neighbouring Tunisia in the weeks before the October 2011 elections. Its echoes could be heard in the Egyptian military's assurances to its Western allies that an elected government would not have full control over the armed might of the state, at once a guarantee that Islamists would not take over and a limit to the democratic aspirations of Egyptians who had taken part in the uprising.[4]

A year after the Arab Spring began, religious parties of different stripes had won more than two-thirds of the seats in the lower house of parliament in Egypt's first elections after the overthrow of Hosni Mubarak. In Tunisia, the Islamist Ennahda party took 42 per cent of seats in the new constituent assembly. In Morocco, the Islamist Justice and Development Party (PJD) became the single biggest group in the new parliament formed in November 2011. In Libya, former members of the Al-Qaeda-affiliated Libyan Islamic

Fighting Group were prominent in the uprising and influential after it. By early 2013 hardline Islamist groups with foreign jihadis in their ranks were on the front lines of the Syrian civil war. In Jordan and in Bahrain, the main opposition forces were religious in outlook. In Yemen, too, the main opposition party was the Islamist-oriented Islah, or Reform, and it has played an important role in the post-Ali Abdullah Saleh era.

Some commentators in the Western media were already lamenting the speed with which Arab Spring had turned to Islamist winter.[5] The young secular protesters who had lit up televisions screens from London to New York earlier in the year had been hijacked, they said, by religious zealots who would now build oppressive theocracies. In the Arab Spring, some saw not just echoes of Algeria, but of the Iranian revolution which had, after all, begun with protesters of various hues coming together to remove the corrupt and authoritarian Shah. It had ended with the Islamists outmanoeuvring their former left-wing allies to declare an Islamic Republic.

The popularity of religious parties in 2011 and 2012 raised another terrifying spectre. Like the Nazis in 1932, some now argued, Islamists might embrace democracy until it brought them the desired number of seats in parliament, then they would cancel polls and declare an Islamic state, much as Madani had threatened to do in Algeria. After all, while Islamist parties differed in tone and emphasis, did they not all ultimately seek a state ruled by Islamic law, a state that would be naturally antagonistic to the West and to its models of liberal democratic rule? Might it not be better to have the old dictators back, who for all their faults were Western-friendly and not, at least, religious fundamentalists?

The notion that a win for the Islamist political parties necessarily equals a loss for democracy is false in the context of the Arab Spring. The ultimate fallout from rising Islamist influence is far from predetermined and will differ from country to country, but another Iran or Afghanistan did not, two years on, seem in the making. Indeed, while the Western media has focused on the dangers of Islamists taking power, their twentieth-century experience has left many Arabs more wary of secular rulers trying to monopolize power than of Islamists doing the same. There are indeed Islamists, as there are nationalists, socialists and various other secularists, who do not espouse democratic values and who would seek to impose oppressive restrictions on society. Not all Islamists fall into this category, though, just as not all nationalists or socialists do. The religious right has proven more popular than many expected, especially in Egypt, and some religious conservatives appear to have strong financial and political backing from wealthy Gulf patrons. Yet it is only by engaging with Islamist parties who win at the ballot box, and are the legitimate representatives of the voters, and by allowing them to be tainted by the same inevitable failures and criticisms that afflict every government, that post-uprising countries like Tunisia and Egypt can move beyond religion as a deciding factor in politics.

It is also the only way that some in the West can shed an often destructive view of Islam that allows little scope for nuance, compromise or evolution of position. With so many religious groups operating in the shadows for decades, it was easy for those looking in from the outside to lump them all in the same category of uncompromising violence and repression that Al-Qaeda and the Taliban had brought to be associated with Islam. Such extremist attitudes do indeed exist, but the Arab Spring has provided an opportunity to revise simplistic views, to engage with new democratically-elected Islamists and to allow their own constituents to test their skills in bringing the dignity, prosperity and freedom that so many protesters risked their lives for in 2011.

The Islamist Spectrum

The very term 'Islamist' incorporates such a wide variety of views that it can often be misleading. 'Islamism' views Islam as a framework for political and social action and rule, not just personal conduct or spiritual belief. Islamists use religion to achieve political goals, but those goals can differ as significantly as the tactics used to pursue them. Those who espouse the violent overthrow of governments and the re-establishment of the lapsed Islamic caliphate across all Muslim lands are Islamists, but so are those who have reconciled Islam with democracy, accept the principle of the rotation of power within the borders of individual states, and do not seek to enforce measures that grab headlines in the West, such as the wearing of the head-scarf or the banning of alcohol.

In Tunisia, Egypt, Libya, Morocco, Jordan and Syria the majority follow Sunni Islam, which has no clerical hierarchy or practice of emulating a religious authority that would lead to the kind of theocratic rule seen in Shi'ite Muslim Iran. An Islamic state in Sunni Islam is not a state ruled by clerics, but one ruled by laymen in strict accordance with Islamic law or simply in the spirit of Islamic values that emphasise family and community welfare. In any case, the interpretation of Islamic law differs significantly from one school of Islamic jurisprudence to another, and from one scholar to another. Some approaches are austere and puritanical, some seek a return to the daily practices of the earliest Muslims, but others are more flexible and dynamic and view Islam as constantly evolving and renewing to move with the times.

'Islamist' refers to so many different movements that its meaning has been eroded over the years and journalists are constantly forced to qualify the term with adjectives such as 'moderate' or 'militant' to distinguish between different groups with different visions. With Islamists now in parliaments across the region, both outside observers and people inside the region, many of whom are equally mistrustful of political Islam, increasingly need to distinguish between the radical and the moderate, the non-democratic and the democratic, the violent and the peaceful. The only way this can be done is by forcing different groups to reveal their hand, to be specific and concrete on issues from Islamic penal punishments to modern banking on which some groups have remained ambiguous in the past. Faced with the practicalities of governing day to day, Islamist groups will need to make tough decisions and will no longer be able to hide behind the abstract ideals of Islamic rule or simple slogans like 'Islam is the solution' that served them so well during their long years in opposition.

Only then can the more extreme strands be marginalized and the groups that are willing to make the compromises necessitated by parliamentary politics and embrace the majority of the people's demands, lose their undeserved association with violence and repression. That process has already started in Egypt and Tunisia, where freer and fairer elections have allowed Islamists to play a much greater role in politics and, in the process, revealed the stark variations in policy and outlook among the different parties.

In Tunisia, some Salafists have rejected democracy entirely and have therefore not been allowed to establish political parties. In contrast, Tunisia's Ennahda was one of the first Islamist movements to endorse democracy. Since its inception in 1979, it has been internally governed by elections to different bodies that balance each other and allow for new ideas to rise to the top. Its founder Rachid Ghannouchi is also a leader of a school of modern Islamic political thought that advocates democracy and pluralism. Written in 1993, his *Al-Hurriyat al-'Amma fid-Dawla al-Islamiyya*, or *Public Liberties in the Islamic State*, is little known in the West but is one of several important contributions to the debate about the compatibility of Islam and democracy. Ghannouchi sees democracy at its most basic level as little more than a practical mechanism that can be put to use in Muslim countries to avert the rise of new dictatorships, while leaving enough scope for Islamic values to flourish.

He opposes any government enforcement of outward markers of piety, such as the headscarf or the banning of alcohol, which he says must be left up to the individual. Ennahda has promised not to meddle with Tunisia's Personal Status Code, which bans polygamy and enshrines women's rights. It has forty-two women MPs in the constituent assembly. Yet a democracy in Ghannouchi's conception is not the same as the secular or liberal democracies born out of European traditions. It is a democracy bound together by the spirit and cultural values of Islam that are shared by so many Tunisians.

Egypt's Muslim Brotherhood, like Ennahda, also accepts democratic principles and again interprets them through the concepts of *shura* and *ijmaa*, or consultation and consensus, by which the early Islamic community was governed. Unlike Ennahda, however, the political platform of its Freedom and Justice Party, which won the most votes in the 2011-12 parliamentary elections, clearly calls for the extension of *sharia* law across all aspects of life, while the concepts of equality and freedom it espouses are qualified by Islamic rules governing the role of women and minorities.

Despite being officially banned from politics for decades, its candidates had long run as individuals in Hosni Mubarak's sham elections and, since winning parliamentary and presidential elections it has sent mixed messages. It has pushed through a constitution that, despite widespread opposition, enshrines the principles of democracy and rotation of power. At the same time, it has avoided taking a clear stand on women's rights while the the failed attempt by the new president, Mohammed Morsi, to place himself above the law, even temporarily, and the use of street violence by his supporters, suggested an authoritarian streak. Though the democratic credentials of some secularists are not beyond doubt, the Islamists' long and sometimes violent past is an indication that they cannot be trusted.

As an older organization, the Brotherhood not only inspired branches in other countries, like Syria and Jordan, but gave birth to several offshoots. Some of these have been decidedly more unbending and radical in their political vision and in the means they are willing to use to achieve their goals.

A leading Muslim Brother, Sayyid Qutb, espoused a new theory in the 1960s which argued that Muslims had a duty to fight for an Islamic state. Qutb argued that sovereignty and the right to legislate belonged to God alone, a repudiation of democratic systems that, like the new Egyptian constitution, vest sovereignty in the people. He articulated the concept of *takfir*, or declaring someone an unbeliever because they do not adhere to these strict precepts. His ideas set back earlier efforts by Islamic scholars to reinterpret Islam for modern life, and inspired a generation of militant groups.[6]

When the Muslim Brotherhood, under Hassan al-Hudaybi, renounced violence in the 1970s, several militant members split off to form the Gamaa Islamiya or Islamic Group. They mounted violent attacks, particularly on foreign tourists, culminating in the 1997 slaughter of sixty-two people, mostly sightseers, at a Pharaonic temple in Luxor. Reeling from public disgust at the attack, which hit Egypt's tourism sector hard, the group was rehabilitated and renounced violence.

Another offshoot was the Egyptian Jihad, whose leader Ayman al-Zawahri merged it with the late Osama bin Laden's Al-Qaeda just three months before 9/11.[7] Zawahri, who helped bring more militant members of Gamaa Islamiya into Al-Qaeda in 2006, now leads the latter itself after bin Laden's death in May 2011.[8] Both Al-Qaeda and its affiliates reject democracy as a Western import alien to Islam and seek to re-establish the lapsed Islamic caliphate, the empire which once ruled Muslim lands. They reject not only non-Muslims, but practise *takfir* and have encouraged violence against many fellow Muslims, chief among them the Shi'ites, who do not adhere to their own narrow interpretation of the religion.

Salafism is another conservative strain of Islamist thought that has spread in recent decades. Again, it encompasses a spectrum of views and the definition of the term has mutated over the years. In general, however, Salafists believe in returning to the fundamentals offered by the scriptures and in emulating the behaviour and appearance of the earliest Muslims, known as *al-salaf al-salih*, or the righteous predecessors. To this end, Salafist men usually grow a certain style of beard and wear shorter robes, in line with the fashions of the Prophet Mohamed's day, and Salafist women often wear the *niqab*, or full-face veil, in line with the separation of men and women prevalent in seventh-century Arabia.

Many Salafists seek the full implementation of *sharia*, down to punishments such as amputation and stoning, but they differ in how to achieve this. Some simply practise their beliefs in their own day-to-day lives, and others follow violent means. *Al-Salafiyya al-Jihadiyya*, or jihadist Salafism, is closely linked to Al-Qaeda and similar groups who reject as apostates those non-Muslims, Shi'ites and even Sunni Muslims who do not follow their narrow interpretation of Islamic scripture. Salafists took part in 2011/12 elections in Egypt and performed surprisingly well, winning about a third of seats in the lower house of parliament, which is now dominated by the religious right. But in Tunisia, they have tended to be more uncompromising, resorting quickly to rioting and joining what they see as the jihad in Syria.

Islamist parties are not only highly diverse but, like other political parties, they have also evolved over time. Many began seeking an Islamic state ruled by a modern-day caliph, but have since come to work within the confines of their own state. Some that once mounted violent campaigns to overthrow secular governments have since renounced violence. The shocking scale of the 9/11 attacks and the deep suspicion it heaped upon ordinary Muslims across the world prompted some organizations to publicly renounce the use of violence as a means to achieve their ends.

That does not convince everyone that even the more moderate Islamist parties have a genuine commitment to democracy. Secularists insist that the Islamists have not changed their beliefs but have simply improved their public relations. They worry that the Islamist groups are playing the long game, reassuring sceptics while they seek to slowly Islamize society with a view to eventually remaining in power permanently.

As of early 2013, Ennahda and the Muslim Brotherhood had not seized power and sought to impose their own vision, nor to violently eliminate their enemies. The new constitutions they oversaw in 2012 include - on paper at least - an acceptance of the rotation of power, the right of worship for Christians and Jews and the right to free speech. Street violence by supporters of Islamist governments in Egypt and Tunisia and Morsi's failed attempt at a power-grab have undermined trust, however. And the biggest test of their democratic commitment is not how Islamist parties behave when they win elections, but how they will respond when they eventually lose.

The Easy Winners

As soon as the leaders of Tunisia, Egypt and Libya were removed, there was a broad consensus that free and fair elections were the way forward, with little apparent disagreement over the need for a separation of powers to avoid a new dictatorship or the need to strengthen the rule of law. All but the most extreme of Islamist groups in post-uprising Tunisia and Egypt have taken part in elections, simply because they had the most to gain from them. In Egypt and Morocco, it was the more liberal youth who called for elections to be delayed or boycotted because many realised that they lacked the resources and the organization to win against much longer-established religious groups.

The debates that emerged in the vacuum left by the ouster of rulers in Tunisia and Egypt revolved around the role of religion in law-making and society, over the best way to remove the remnants of the *anciens régimes* and over economic policy, not over the principles of political pluralism or the right of the public to choose their leaders and representatives. Even in Libya, the draft constitution of the transitional council, born in the most conservative region of that country, enshrines the idea of free and fair elections. True, it was likely designed to appeal to an international audience, and it may be heavily rewritten in the years ahead, but those basic political freedoms were regarded as given from the beginning.

Aside from famous exceptions, such as the tragic trajectory of Germany after the 1932 elections which made the Nazis the largest party in parliament, parties that reach power by the ballot box are more likely to leave by the ballot box. Shi'ite Islamists have played a dominant role in Iraqi politics since the 2003 invasion and while that democracy is far from perfect and rights groups have complained of growing repression, there has been no effort to abrogate elections, or to institute the sort of clerical rule found next door in Iran.

Whereas Islamic slogans and anti-Western rhetoric were rife during the Iranian revolution of 1979, while Ayatollah Ruhollah Khomeini played a leading role in inspiring and encouraging the protests even from exile, this was not the case in the Arab Spring. In Tunisia and Egypt the slogans had universal appeal, and the Islamists did not play a leading role in toppling leaders. In Libya, Islamist fighters were on the front lines of the rebellion that ousted Gaddafi, and are highly influential in the fragile state that followed, but they claim to have renounced violence and to have embraced democratic principles.

While they were not the driving force of the initial uprisings, the subsequent popularity of Islamist parties in the first elections after the Arab Spring should come as no surprise. There are several explanations for their appeal, but none appear to include a mass desire to create Taliban states in North Africa, and much of that appeal will be less potent by the time the next round of elections begins.

First, Islamist parties are among some of the longest-established political groups in the region. Egypt's Muslim Brotherhood dates back to 1928 and Syria's to the 1930s. The predecessor to Tunisia's Ennahda was formally established in 1981 though it was informally active before that. These groups were hierarchical in structure and well-organized, and their members were disciplined. The only way they could survive repeated crackdowns by secular authoritarian rulers was through cohesion and in some cases secrecy – experience that would lubricate the wheels of their well-oiled electoral machines in 2011.

They also offered voters a strong vision of a just society. Islam seeks to provide not just spiritual guidance but an entire design for life, leading to the Muslim Brotherhood's rallying cry of 'Islam is the solution'. This was a simplistic motto and Islamist parties are notoriously short on detail when it comes to the nitty-gritty of economic policy, for instance, but it was as powerfully attractive to the disenfranchised and downtrodden as socialism or nationalism once were. Like Christian fundamentalist organizations in the United States, Islamists emphasize family values and social conservatism, attracting followers from different classes. In a region where most people are Muslims, they also offer the word of God. It is a value system with a wide reach and one that offers comfort and solace to millions who feel their very identity under attack from globalization and from secular rulers who for decades appeared more interested in pandering to their allies in the West.

Arab rulers reserved their harshest repression for the Islamists because they perceived them to be a genuine threat. Yet while closing down Communist Party offices or banning their newspaper could rob Communists of their means to reach the general public, the Islamists always had the mosque to gather in and spread their message. Their political activities might have been curbed by the state, but in some countries they were able to focus instead on charitable works. The extent of repression in the name of the quasi-secular state in Tunisia or Syria made this impossible. In Egypt, however, while the Muslim Brotherhood was banned as a political party, it was allowed to establish a vast charity network that operated clinics, helped educate poor children, and supported disadvantaged families.

Good deeds in the name of religion, particularly in countries such as Egypt, where the state bureaucracy was too poorly managed and funded to meet the demand for public services and welfare, are sure-fire vote winners. This did not matter for the government of Egypt as long as elections were meaningless, but it gave the Muslim Brotherhood – and the Salafists – a ready-made constituency in 2011 and 2012 when they could compete far more freely than before. It also meant they were already in contact with the ordinary person, allowing them to better gauge, respond to and influence the public mood.

For secular parties, which performed less well in the first post-uprising elections in Egypt and Tunisia, the situation was very different. Secular political groups were not linked to charities and were not able to buy backing through good works. The ruling parties in pre-2011 Egypt and Tunisia were secular and, as the upheavals suggest, failed to meet the aspirations of the people. In Syria and Iraq, Ba'athist ideology that sought to emphasize Arab nationalism over religion had appeal in the 1950s and 1960s, but was little more than a tool for oppressive one-party rule by the 2000s. Its exponents were failing to provide the new middle classes with meaningful jobs and adequate pay while their early socialist or nationalist values had been eroded by corruption and political stagnation. A vote for the Islamist parties was not simply or not always a vote for religious values, but a vote to reject the past and a general expression of new-found political freedom.

The young revolutionaries who led the protest movements of 2011 were often associated with neither the Islamist nor the established and discredited secular parties. Some of them were union members, though they acted at grass-roots level in trade syndicates that were controlled by the state. Others were bloggers, using new technology to feel their way around the stifling restrictions of state media. Some were involved in human rights NGOs, advocated for women's rights, or found other specific issues through which they subtly agitated for political change. Some had been able to set up new parties, though they faced sham trials or harassment. These activists were mostly young and had little to lose by taking action. They were not taken as seriously by the authorities as the Islamist parties, who were watched and repressed and forced to weigh up carefully any decision to act.

The focus of these activists on what they did not want – human rights abuses, martial law, one-man rule, high-level corruption – resonated far beyond their own ranks, allowing them to build broad coalitions with groups and activists with whom they did not share a world-view. These coalitions were effective in putting people out on the streets, but their negative demands could not act as a blueprint for government. Where they succeeded in overthrowing their rulers, as in Tunisia or Egypt, or securing reforms, as in Morocco, they were not geared up for elections. They were inexperienced and lacked the charitable networks, the money and the personnel needed to reach people at the local level, particularly outside the major cities. For the Islamists, cash was pouring in from domestic and foreign donors, particularly in the Gulf and from the fees or donations paid by their huge membership. Secularists simply could not compete.

Counterweights and Constitutions

The Islamists may be the most powerful electoral force in the new Arab world, but they are far from alone. In every country where they have made gains, counterweights to their influence will limit the Islamization of state and society, but could also become dangerous flashpoints.

One such limit will simply be the compromise and debate of parliamentary politics itself. The need to form alliances, to consult, to make unpalatable deals, to respond to popular demand but to balance this with economic realities and realistic foreign policies, will push Islamist parties towards increasing pragmatism.

It is easy, while in opposition, to call for measures like the banning of alcohol, for instance. In government, however, an Islamist party in Egypt or Tunisia must also consider the impact on jobs in the crucial tourism sector. Poor management of the economy and declining living standards do not tend to win votes for any party, religious or not. And in their first year in office, Islamist governments in Tunisia, Egypt or Morocco gave little indication that they were planning a radical departure from the policies of their predecessors. Being in government could also force Islamist groups to take concrete positions on issues such as relations with Israel, and go beyond vague populist railing against the Jewish state. The first test for the Muslim Brotherhood came with the Gaza crisis of 2012. Morsi's role in mediating an end to the violence won him plaudits from the United States, reassured that it could work with a Muslim Brotherhood president as it did with his predecessor. In fact, beyond headline issues such as *sharia*, there was little reason to believe Islamist-led governments in Egypt and North Africa would behave differently to any other.

In Tunisia, Ennahda faces a strong secular legacy that is already energetically opposing their influence. It may have won the single largest number of seats in the constituent assembly, but the majority were still controlled by largely non-religious parties. Ennahda exerted a strong influence on the new constitution, but was forced to make concessions under secular pressure; the document contains no mention at all of *sharia*. It has already promised not to enforce the *hijab* or to ban traditional banks, whose payment and receipt of interest is considered usury in Islam.

In Egypt, where society is more outwardly religious and where the term 'secularism' carries vote-losing connotations of being anti-God, the situation is more complex. The Muslim Brotherhood's closest rivals in the elections were not secular liberals but rather the Salafist Noor, or Light, party, which has effectively put the Muslim Brotherhood near the centre of a political spectrum that had been shifting to the right since the 1970s. The most obvious measure of increasing religiosity, or at least increased social pressure to conform to religiously prescribed dress codes, has been the growing prevalence of the *hijab*, to the extent that by 2011 the vast majority of Egyptian Muslim women covered their hair in public. So widespread has the veil become that Islamist politicians scarcely need to resort to law to enforce it.

The popularity of the Muslim Brotherhood was well known before 2011, but the Salafists were untested in elections and their strong performance at the polls came as a surprise to many observers, particularly in the first round, which covered more cosmopolitan parts of Egypt such as Cairo and Alexandria. Salafists have so far been less organized than the Muslim Brotherhood, but given their more recent arrival on the political scene their popularity has been striking.

Under pressure to deliver, the Muslim Brotherhood has already been forced to offer concessions to the military in return for staying out of daily politics and has made concessions to the social demands of Salafists, whose political support it regularly needs to call upon, as well as to non-religious groups and civil society activists who have kept up the pressure.

The main counterweights to Islamist influence in Morocco and Jordan will be the institutions of the monarchies. But, like Egypt's military, they will prefer to work with hierarchical mainstream political parties – even if they are Islamist – than the unpredictable youth who rejected constitutional reform measures in 2011 for not going far enough. Both monarchies may choose to promote and engage with more moderate Islamists in order to sideline extremist religious groups and the more determined secular liberals. Giving Islamist parties the freedom to operate and win elections – which in Jordan will require serious electoral reform – could go some way to sapping the appeal of violence as a means of achieving political change and encourage peaceful engagement.

External, as well as local, influences may also push Islamist groups towards increasing pragmatism. Had the Arab Spring taken place just two decades ago, there would have been no stable democracy in a majority-Muslim country for Arab countries to look to. By 2011, Turkey and

Indonesia both provided working – though flawed – examples demonstrating that majority-Muslim countries did not have to be monarchies, dictatorships or theocracies. Some Arab Islamist parties, such as Ennahda or Morocco's PJD, have said they look to Turkey's AKP in particular as an example of a moderate Islamist party which functions in a democratic framework and has overseen robust economic growth and eroded the power of the military. For others, Turkey is no model and its AK Party has made too many compromises to be counted as Islamist.

Turkey is far from perfect. The declining power of the army, especially in its role as guardian of the secular state, discomforts secular Turks. Some worry about what they see as Erdogan's increasingly authoritarian style, and point to rising numbers of arrested journalists and to constitutional amendments they say aim to keep power concentrated in his or his party's hands. But the point is that many mainstream Islamist parties – if not the more conservative Salafists – are leaning more towards a Turkish-style system than an Afghan one. A poll across five Arab countries in October 2011, including Egypt and Morocco, found that Turkey was overwhelmingly seen as having played the 'most constructive' role in the Arab Spring. When asked which world leader they admired most, respondents put Erdogan top.[9]

In Tunisia, Egypt and Libya, the most immediate battleground between the different Islamist groups and their various counterweights are the new constitutions. The extent to which those documents will be Islamized, or further Islamized, in the wake of the Arab Spring will differ from country to country.

But few Arab states had fully secular constitutions before 2011. Unlike Turkey, whose constitution explicitly defines the country as a secular state – even though Islamists have reached government and the presidency – most Arab constitutions refer directly to religion. Even in Tunisia, the country held up as one of the most secular in the region, the constitution identifies Islam as the religion of state. In Syria, protests broke out in 1973 when a new Ba'athist constitution failed to name Islam as the religion of state. This clause was never inserted, though the Syrian constitution does say that the president must be a Muslim and that Islam is a source of jurisprudence. In Egypt, the constitution has since 1980 described *sharia* as 'the principal source of legislation'. The new constitution, passed by referendum in 2012, keeps that clause. It also enshrined democracy and set a limit on presidential terms.

The main danger for democracy lies in how easily the new constitutions can be altered. Amendments are always necessary in any constitution, allowing them to evolve and initial mistakes to be corrected, but making it too easy to change key clauses could open the door for abuse. If a constitutional amendment required only majority parliamentary approval, for instance, popular parties or individual leaders might be tempted to change the rules to allow them to legally extend their terms, stay in power indefinitely, or circumvent elected bodies by going straight to a public referendum on key issues.

What would happen, for instance, if an Islamist government in Egypt held a referendum proposing that all non-Muslim parties should be banned? Or, even if a constitutional amendment required a two-thirds majority in both houses, it would be theoretically possible for immensely popular Islamists to push through an amendment that suspends elections. Both scenarios appeared unlikely by early 2013, but given that Islamist parties took up to 90 per cent of the vote in some parts of Egypt in the first elections, it is hypothetically possible.

In Arab countries which have a recent history of non-religious rulers practising these types of abuses, there appears to be a genuine desire to create constitutions that provide checks and balances against the rise of new dictatorships. Nevertheless, some constitutions may function more as 'showcase' documents, setting out utopian ideals to which the country aspires, rather than hard principles which it can hope to enforce practically. In countries where the independence of the judiciary has been routinely compromised for decades, it could take many years of concerted effort to foster a culture of integrity among judges and to build up public trust in the system. But these are challenges that governments will face regardless of whether Islamist parties are voted into power, and they pose a bigger risk to the establishment of stable and functioning democracies than the religious leanings of those in cabinet or parliament.

Those most likely to suffer from the introduction or extension of *sharia* law are women and minorities. Most Muslim countries tend to prioritize the application of *sharia* in family law, which governs issues such as marriage, divorce, custody and inheritance, over its implementation in criminal law, which might see thieves have their hands amputated. Even if Islamist groups do not pass headline-grabbing measures such as enforcing the veil, women could come under more social pressure to conform in their dress and behaviour. While women have the theoretical right to divorce in Islam, in practice their rights can be severely restricted by the rulings of the male-dominated *sharia* courts. Women do not have equal rights of inheritance in Islam. Polygamy, too, clearly goes against the concept of gender equality by giving men rights in marriage that are not available to women. In *sharia*, Muslim men may marry Jewish or Christian women, but Muslim women may not marry any kind of non-Muslim.

Mixing aspects of *sharia* with modern constitutions that declare all citizens equal before the law creates obvious contradictions. Which trumps the other – *sharia* or the equal rights enshrined in the constitution? Who decides? Is there a constitutional court that overrules the *sharia* court? In that case, would it be acceptable for a temporal court to overrule the law of God? Will regular courts face the difficult task of trying to apply both aspects of the law, or arbitrate between the two?

Tunisians do not confront most of these issues, as Ennahda has accepted the Personal Status Code, but such issues are already raising questions in Libya, where the interim government has declared that polygamy would be legal while at the same time assuring women that they would have equal rights with men.

In Egypt, the religious problem is more complex because the country is home to an ancient Christian minority that comprises some 10 per cent of the population. For some Islamists, it would be unacceptable for a Christian to be president. This is perhaps a moot point, since a Christian would stand almost no chance of winning in presidential elections in the current conservative climate prevailing in Egypt.

Yet even the hypothetical discussion raises a whole host of dilemmas for some countries in the post-Arab Spring era as they try to simultaneously superimpose several overlapping identities and ideologies: a national identity that does not always match a religious identity, and a democracy that does not always include equal citizenship.

Islam views the *umma* as the community of believers, which may include people of different nationalities but excludes people of different religions. Like most major religions, Islam predates the relatively recent creation of the nation-state and for those who wish to create an idealized Islamic community, as some Islamists do, it is not always easy to relinquish aspects of their religious tradition for the sake of creating a coherent national identity.

Consequently, the systems that have emerged from the Arab Spring in Tunisia, Egypt, Libya or Yemen are on their way to becoming democracies, but not the secular and liberal democracies that Westerners are accustomed to. Indeed, they may be illiberal or religious democracies in which the government is elected and there is a rotation of power but where, for instance, homosexuality remains banned and minorities and women lack the same rights as Muslim men.

Problematic as this may be, it must again be considered in its context. Family law already tended to be governed by *sharia* in many Arab countries before 2011, and the degree to which women will suffer differs from country to country. In Tunisia, where women's rights groups are long-established, high-profile and active, and where there is a powerful secularist movement, women have a higher chance of retaining their rights despite the election of Islamists to government. In some countries, women will be just as badly off as they were before. In other cases, such as Egypt's, where a parliamentary quota reserving sixty-four seats for women was scrapped after the Arab Spring, they may be worse off, at least in the immediate term.

While women often played an equal role with men in demonstrations from Cairo to Sana'a, an opportunity to improve their lot in the design of new constitutions and electoral rules have been largely squandered by religious conservatives who did not play a major role in overturning the old system but have since won the battle for votes. Such a monumental opportunity to legislate more progressive rights for women, and to enshrine genuine equality among citizens after so many years in which all citizens had their rights curbed by authoritarian rulers, may not present itself again for a long time.

Beyond the Backlash

In a functioning liberal and secular democracy, the rise of overtly religious groups could be construed as a step away from equality. In Tunisia and Egypt, however, where no democracy existed before, the elections of 2011 and 2012 were a first step towards establishing a system of rule that reflects the wishes of the majority of the people. It is tempting to hold up new democracies to the unrealistic standards which long-established Western democracies do not themselves meet, or have only met through centuries of gradual development. In the United States, the Christian right has a powerful impact on politics. Some areas are 'dry counties' where local residents, influenced by puritanical Christian teachings, have voted to ban alcohol. Abortion remains a divisive issue and a political hot potato, with the religious right broadly in the anti-abortion camp and the secular left broadly supporting the right to choice. The dollar bill still bears the words 'In God we trust' and when a president is voted into office, it is on the Bible that he swears his oath. Even in the United Kingdom, where the influence of religion on politics and day-to-day life is much diminished, twenty-six seats are reserved in the House of Lords for Anglican bishops. This may be symbolic, but it is a reminder of the powerful role that religion once played in politics.

It is unrealistic to expect Arab countries to establish in two years the separation of politics and religion that took centuries in Europe. In France, women did not win the vote until 1945 and in Switzerland women were not allowed a federal vote until 1971. Up until the 1960s, there were US states where black Americans were not allowed to mix with white Americans. Democracy does not function in a void, divorced from the history of the country or the identity of its inhabitants. A new political system can be installed in a short time, but social customs and prejudices are often much slower to change.

Groups with religion as their defining tenet are likely to continue to win the first elections held in countries where the Arab Spring has swept away old dictatorships. If King Abdullah of Jordan enacts meaningful electoral reform then the Muslim Brotherhood's party will be the main winner. The major opposition parties in countries that have survived the first phase of the Arab Spring, like Morocco, will continue to be Islamists. They are untried, the public wants to give them a chance, and they offer the solace of religion and identity to Arabs who feel rocked by globalization and by repeated Western political and military intervention in their lands.

Not all Islamists are democrats, but keeping such groups underground has worked neither for the Islamists themselves, who never got a taste of government, nor for the secular rulers who repressed them, nor for Western countries that became the target of attacks by militant groups.

Not only have some Islamists been radicalized in prison, but their suppression has given an air of legitimacy to their claims that the Muslim world's problems could be solved with a return to strict religion. Al-Qaeda and its affiliates have a narrow and oppressive vision of the Islamic world which they wished to create, seeing violence as the only way to unseat corrupt rulers. Egypt and Tunisia proved them wrong, and the subsequent elections there boosted the credibility of Islamist groups with a more pragmatic approach.

But to say that 2011 was a defeat for Al-Qaeda is to miss the point, and overstate its original appeal. Al-Qaeda's ideology had always thrived on the fringes of Arab society, and despite its headline-grabbing and deadly attacks, the network always relied on small bands of fanatics that could wreak havoc. It never presented a viable alternative for the vast majority of Arabs and Muslims.

Nevertheless, groups who subscribe to Al-Qaeda's vision have been able to exploit the post-2011 power void in several Arab countries. This goes for Yemen, where groups linked to Al-Qaeda in the Arabian Peninsula (AQAP) fought for control of large parts of Yemeni territory as the central state weakened ever further, and in Libya, where radical Islamist groups were believed to have carried out the attack on the US consulate in Benghazi in September 2012 which killed Ambassador Chris Stevens. Security and military structures have been weakened in Egypt and Tunisia in the aftermath of uprisings, while weapons from Libya have flooded across lawless borders on either side. This has been devastating in Mali, where an Islamist rebellion owed much of its success to arms and fighters that filtered out of Libya during and after the 2011 conflict. And in Syria, two years after the first popular protests, radical Islamist militias were now amongst the best-organized and equipped of any groups fighting to bring down the Assad regime. When the Taftanaz air base in northern Syria was overrun by rebels in January 2013, it was an Al-Qaeda flag – not that of Free Syria – that flew over its gate.

The dire economic situation across North Africa and the Levant will make it easier for such groups to recruit from the ranks of disgruntled and unemployed young men, while weakened state and security structures will provide more opportunities for attack. But such groups will appear increasingly detached not only from the parties like Ennahda, but from the Salafists, who despite their much more conservative outlook did nonetheless take part in elections in Egypt.

Political Islam is in the midst of a dramatic resurgence after a long period of suppression, but its appeal is already waning. In many ways, the groups that win the first elections after a revolution are sipping from a poisoned chalice. Expectations of what democracy and freedom can deliver are extremely high across the Arab region, and the challenges are many. Islamist parties are not known for their economic nous, and may face difficulties in formulating coherent policies that marry their tendency to support free trade and business with their focus on social justice and helping the impoverished. Egypt, where the Muslim Brotherhood-led administration was struggling to push through economic reforms in early

2013, was a case in point. Opposition parties in parliament will have ample material to criticize and undermine new governments, whoever leads them.

Long-established groups like Ennahda or the Muslim Brotherhood, which encompassed a spectrum of opinions, may see offshoots split away as they are forced to take concrete decisions that do not please everyone in their ranks. In Tunisia, Ennahda faces persistent protest both from secularists who accuse it of trying to Islamize the state and undermine women's rights, and from Salafists who accuse it of betraying Islam in the compromises it has made. Egypt's Muslim Brotherhood has already seen several members or factions branch off, unhappy with its majoritarian approach. They are keen to work with secular activists and take a more dynamic approach than the slow-moving and patient dinosaur that is the Muslim Brotherhood.

Established secular parties will have time to regroup, while new secular parties will have time to build a support base and gain valuable political experience. If Islamists overreach with their religious policies, or try to seize power, there may yet be a backlash against them, as we have already seen in Egypt. Once in power, tainted by the same failures and corruption scandals as other groups, they will lose support and become just another popular but compromised political group. More importantly, voters will begin to choose their parties not by their level of religious zeal but rather on the practical success of their policies, particularly in the economic sphere.

Nor can religious parties roll back the social changes and generational shifts that partly precipitated the Arab Spring. Women in Arab countries in 2010 gave birth to an average of less than three children each, down from an average of six a generation earlier. Female literacy rates are catching up with those of males, while the former practice of women being married off to their cousins is declining as women delay marriage and childbearing in favour of education and a career. An educated and employed mother is likely to ensure that her daughter also receives an education and enters the workplace.

Though Arab countries remain patriarchal, some more than others, patriarchal authority is weakening, along with traditional attitudes that see women as mothers and homemakers. The norms that govern the relations between men and women in the family and in the public sphere, and the relationship between religion and the lifestyle choices individuals make, are shifting. That is the real revolution, and, unlike the political upheavals of 2011, this far more fundamental change cannot be achieved in a matter of weeks.

In time, Islamist parties will lose some of their appeal as the most obvious way of rejecting the status quo. Indeed, we may already have seen the peak of their popularity. But by early 2013, it was not clear what new ideas would compete effectively with them.

CHAPTER 12

Embracing the Void

I don't care whether it's a white cat or a black cat.
It's a good cat as long as it catches mice.

– Deng Xiaoping

'A Marshall Plan is needed,' declared the Egyptian labour minister Hassan al-Boraei at a gathering of the World Economic Forum in Jordan in October 2011, outlining the economic challenges his country faced in the aftermath of the Arab Spring.[1] But the money would not come from the United States, which was in no position to recreate the massive financial package it had extended to war-ravaged Europe from the late 1940s. Nor was this post-1990 Eastern Europe, where politicians could adopt a ready-made blueprint for liberalized, free-market capitalism and realize it with the economic support and technical advice of a then triumphant West.

A catastrophic financial crisis, bloody wars in Iraq and Afghanistan, towering levels of debt and a loss of moral authority had since accelerated the decline of Western power and cast fresh doubts over the economic and political model it ostensibly stood for. The days of the United States standing out as the pre-eminent international power in the Middle East, and in the wider world, were coming to an end. But in the post-Cold War, post-credit crunch era, no new political or economic philosophy appeared readily available as a viable alternative for countries seeking a fresh start.

This had not been the case in the previous hundred years, a century in which the Arab world had been buffeted by the rise and fall of greater outside forces that had each left their imprint on, and in some cases drawn the boundaries of, modern Arab states. The collapse of the Ottoman

Empire after the First World War gave way to European protectorates and mandates. These were followed by the Ba'athist and Arab nationalist waves of the 1950s and 1960s, part of an anti-colonial, secular and socialist movement that was gaining popularity in many parts of the world. Inter-regional rivalries were then defined by the global struggle between two credible and competing ideologies promoted by the world's twin superpowers.

With the collapse of the Soviet Union in 1990–91, however, the modus operandi of its rival seemed to have emerged unopposed. Marxism was considered dead. As the United States exerted more and more political, economic and cultural clout in the second half of the twentieth century, it filled the gap that had been opened up in the Arab world by the decline of Ottoman, European and now Soviet power. It was Washington that had brokered Israel's peace deals, first with Egypt and later with Jordan. It was to the White House that the Middle East looked for a solution to the Israel-Palestine conflict. From the 1970s onwards, the Middle East, including Israel, received more US financial aid than any other region in the world. When the US military swiftly ejected Saddam Hussein's forces from Kuwait in 1990–91, it deepened a security alliance with the Gulf states that had begun with the relationship between President Franklin D. Roosevelt and Saudi Arabia's founder, Abdel Aziz Ibn Saud, and would be crucial to the dynamics of the region. And after the September 2001 attacks, or with the expected rise of a nuclear Iran, the Middle East waited to see how the world's only superpower would react.

In the economic sphere, the so-called Washington Consensus – a loose term coined in the late 1980s that favoured liberalization, privatization and globalization – had become the theoretical underpinning of institutions like the IMF and the stock solution in crisis-stricken countries from Eastern Europe to Asia to Latin America. In the former Soviet satellites the United States and Western Europe provided huge financial support for the transition towards market economies and multi-party democracies. India launched an IMF-linked programme of free-market reforms from 1991 onwards. Deng Xiaoping's 'southern tour' of China in 1992 would bring the winds of capitalism to what was one of the world's few remaining Communist one-party states. The Middle East was already moving in the same direction. In 1970s Egypt, Anwar Sadat's policies of *infitah*, or 'opening', had broken away from the state-dominated economy. In 1987, Tunisia took out loans from the World Bank and the IMF for the first time.[2] Morocco had adopted reform programmes supported by these two institutions in 1983, as did a near bankrupt Jordan in 1989, while a heavily-indebted Yemen began a structural adjustment programme under IMF supervision in 1995.[3]

Even the most enthusiastic Arab importers of socialist doctrine seemed to have reluctantly accepted that they might have got it wrong. In Syria, Bashar al-Assad mimicked the Chinese method of economic reform without political change.[4] In Libya, the vague and eccentric socialism dreamed up in Muammar Gaddafi's *Green Book* had created an economy that, by the 1990s, was arguably the most restrictive and isolated in the region. But alongside the political unfreezing of the early 2000s came economic liberalization and the end of sanctions. In what would be the twilight of the Gaddafi era, the government was actively, though not very successfully, pursuing a programme of privatization, while heir apparent Saif al-Islam had hired big-name US consultancies to help restructure the Libyan economy.

The full spectrum of US influence in the Arab world is too detailed to explore here, but it was a measure of how much power was attributed to the country that, when Barack Obama assumed office in early 2009, many observers thought it presented a unique opportunity for the entire Middle East to change direction. No other country, none of the BRICs, no European state, and not even any Arab country, was perceived to have the influence that Washington could bring to bear in the region.

Within the Arab world itself, the perception of an all-powerful United States had long been the grist for a rumour mill of conspiracy theories that – not always totally without reason – attributed any significant events to Washington's design. Such was the perception of its reach that, even in 2011, it was not so unusual to meet people who believed that an event as dramatic as the Arab Spring must surely have been devised in the Pentagon, a master plan to remove ageing and change-resistant leaders and cement long-term US influence among the new democratic forces in the region.

Yet by the beginning of the Arab Spring, the West's global hegemony had already peaked. The uprisings were played out against the backdrop of an accelerating transfer of power and wealth from the old economic power-houses of the twentieth century to the fast-growing emerging giants of Asia and Latin America, and indeed to the super-rich Gulf Arab states. The economic and political templates that the United States and Western Europe had long extolled were being seriously undermined by the dramatic financial crises in their own backyard and by the outcomes of their foreign policies. And it had not gone unnoticed.

A Multifaceted Bankruptcy

Throughout 2011, the latest drama in the Arab Spring competed for the front pages with a financial and economic calamity that had become global in scale but was Western in origin. More than four years on from the implosion of the US sub-prime housing market in 2007, the crisis was still lurching from one emergency to the next. In 2008, it had ripped through the banking sector and ravaged stock markets. In 2009, the world's economy had shrunk for the first time since the end of the Second World War. In 2011 and 2012, the virus mutated into a sovereign debt emergency as mismanaged European economies threatened to blow apart the continent's single currency and trigger another credit crunch.

If this was not a crisis of capitalism itself, then it was certainly a crisis of the particularly unfettered brand that had flourished since the 1980s and had its temples on Wall Street and in the City of London. It meant that more Americans than ever before – 15 per cent of the total population and 27 per cent of the black and Hispanic communities – were considered to be living in poverty.[5] While America's worst-off certainly enjoyed better living standards than the vast majority of Tunisians or Egyptians, the income inequalities between rich and poor were sharper, and getting ever more so.[6]

It was not just events at home that suggested something was seriously wrong. As the first section of this book outlined, the experiment with a Western economic model in Arab countries where reforms were not supported by the rule of law, independent courts and tribunals, or anything approaching a fair marketplace for goods and ideas, was deeply flawed. The attempt to graft trade liberalization or privatization programmes onto authoritarian regimes that simply twisted them in money-spinning schemes for their own cronies had widened divides, facilitated high-level corruption and fuelled public anger. And as 2011 drew to a close, arguably the most pressing challenge for new governments in countries like Tunisia, Morocco, Jordan and Egypt was to ease that anger by improving the lot of their citizens.

As in any revolutionary moment, when all sections of society try to extract as many gains as possible, governments faced rising popular pressure to implement knee-jerk measures such as raising subsidies and salaries that would take people off the streets but would ultimately be detrimental to the economy. Reverting to greater protectionism, maintaining or swelling the bloated ranks of the public sector or shunning the very idea of privatization would be deleterious to public finances and could not be credible long-term policies, particularly for countries that lacked the energy wealth to fund them. They would not provide the vital boost to the private sector, encouraging the entrepreneurs who could generate thousands of new jobs.

Three months into the Arab Spring, Robert Zoellick, the head of the World Bank, urged people to 'keep in mind, the late Mr. Bouazizi was basically driven to burn himself alive because he was harassed with red tape … one starting point is to quit harassing those people and let them have a chance to start some small businesses'.[7] Zoellick might have missed the larger point about the Tunisian vegetable seller's suicide, but he got the one about building small and medium-sized companies. In Tunisia, considered to be one of the region's more private sector-heavy economies, some 97 per cent of all private companies had less than six employees in 2010.[8] In the US, just 5 per cent of all private companies had fewer than five employees in 2008.[9] But in the aftermath of the Arab Spring, governments around the region took measures that risked saddling themselves with an even greater financial burden.

Free-market reforms now carried negative associations with the old regimes. High-level corruption and the blurred lines between private interests and the government had given big business a bad name. Policymakers associated with the past were sometimes shunted out. The governor of Jordan's Central Bank was removed in September 2011 due to his strong opposition to excessive social spending in the wake of the protests. Fares Sharaf had 'showed that he was not in tune with the special government orientation of social welfare economics as opposed to free market views he embraced', according to Prime Minister Marouf Bakhit.[10] In Egypt, Gamal Mubarak – now standing trial on charges of profiteering – had been a strong proponent of privatization and reform that mostly benefited the cohort of wealthy businessmen, but also generated healthy growth. In Syria, the government's latest five-year economic plan, due to run between 2011 and 2015, was reportedly hushed up early in 2011 because it contained so many measures to raise taxes and reduce subsidies, measures that were probably healthy for the economy in the long term but would now be unpalatable to an increasingly angry population.[11]

Some of the international institutions that had promoted pro-free-market reforms, whatever their merits, were similarly tainted. Many Tunisians had not forgotten that, barely a year earlier, then-IMF chief Dominique Strauss-Kahn had visited Tunis to be decorated as a Grand Officer of the Order of the Republic. State television showed President Ben Ali hanging a medal around the Frenchman's neck, before the two men hugged each other and Strauss-Kahn delivered a glowing report on the Tunisian economy.[12]

In June 2011, Egypt turned down a $3.2 billion loan from the IMF designed to help bridge the budget shortfall for that year. The terms of the loan were favourable, with an interest rate of just 1.5 per cent, but the connotations it carried were not. Under the slogan of 'Open Your Eyes, The Debt Comes Out of Your Pocket!' a group of Egyptian activists launched a campaign against taking on more debt. Many harked back to the spendthrift regime of Khedive Ismail, who by the 1870s had racked up such colossal arrears on a grand plan to modernize the country's infrastructure that Egypt was forced to sell its stake in the Suez Canal to Britain, and effectively lost its independence to foreign debtors. Later in 2011, the Egyptian government reopened negotiations with the IMF, and by the end of December 2012 had still not agreed a deal. Unrest and a constitutional crisis towards the end of the year meant ratings agencies were again considering downgrading Egyptian bonds and currency, having already done so in early 2011.[13]

The dilemma over accepting IMF help reflected how economic policy-makers in the non-oil countries seemed to be struggling for direction, clear that a change was needed but less clear on what should come next. 'In the past there were two models; the socialist and the capitalist,' said Bashar al-Assad in June 2011. 'Many people believe that these models have fallen. Now we do not have ready-made experiences to take and implement. We need to look for a model which suits Syria.'

There was no shortage of pledges from the international community. In May 2011 the G8 countries, plus other invitees including Turkey, Qatar and Saudi Arabia, established the 'Deauville Partnership' that aimed to provide billions of dollars for countries going through what were hoped to be democratic transitions.[14] Egypt and Tunisia were named as the first recipients, with Morocco and Jordan added later.

Yet by the end of 2012, relatively little of this promised money had materialized. Several loans had been signed off by the European Investment Bank (EIB), the Tunis-based African Development Bank and the European Bank for Reconstruction and Development (EBRD), but the US congress had failed to include in its 2011 budget the two aid programmes for Egypt and Tunisia that Obama had announced in May, partly due to concerns about what type of regime might emerge in both places.[15] By the time the G20 countries met in Cannes in November, the Arab Spring barely even featured on an agenda that was dominated by the eurozone crisis and an

IMF whose finances were stretched to the limit. It seemed that the economic stragglers in the Arab world, those who did not have the luxury of oil and gas, would have to look elsewhere for support.

But it was not just Western economic models that were in trouble. The political systems that nurtured them were also being questioned, often angrily. In the United States and Western Europe, the chummy links between corporate and political power had long blinded governments to the catastrophic bubbles that were inflating. Many saw the state-funded bank bailouts as an exercise in institutionalized fraud, designed to keep the powerful financial sector solvent and profitable while an increasingly destitute government, in thrall to the debt markets, slashed its budgets for education and healthcare and spent an ever-growing proportion of the national income on interest payments. Protesters in Greece railed against externally-imposed austerity measures that would shape their futures but in which they had no say. In Spain, where unemployment was higher than anywhere in North Africa, the *indignados* movement brought thousands of angry people onto the streets.

Europeans began to ask whether they lived in democracies or 'marketocracies', and people around the world asked whether their governments were really run by and in the interests of the people any more. Some pointed to how much money the financial services sector donated to Britain's Conservative Party, the dominant partner in the governing coalition after 2010, or why US presidential elections were funded by multi-billion-dollar campaigns that gave the wealthiest the biggest chance of victory. In India, the world's most populous democracy, hunger-striker Anna Hazare galvanized mass public anger against political corruption and widening divides. Around the world, it seemed that a tiny elite – increasingly described as the 'one per cent' – was gathering ever-greater power and wealth in its hands as the masses suffered.

If the US and Western Europe were the homes of democracy, embodying the values of freedom and equality more than any other, then it was hardly a shining beacon for others to copy, and left Arab activists who sought Western-style liberal democracies open to obvious criticism.

At the same time, the aura of power which had surrounded Western military might was also fading. By the late 2000s Iraq and Afghanistan had proven devastating to both the finances and reputation of the United States, and almost nine years after George W. Bush delivered his now notorious 'Mission Accomplished' speech from an aircraft carrier off the Californian coast, both had gone seriously awry. By the end of 2012, more than 2,000 US nationals had been killed in Afghanistan since the start of the war eleven years earlier, with little concrete achievement to show for all the losses. When the final US combat troops were withdrawn from Iraq in December 2011, they left behind a country where Tehran had become the main beneficiary of Saddam Hussein's removal. 'The myth about the unipolar world fell apart once and for all in Iraq,' was the blunt view of a policy document issued by the Kremlin back in 2007.

Both Iraq and Afghanistan had helped US government debt double between 2003 and 2010 and by late 2011 become larger than the country's GDP for the first time ever.[16] Coupled with the astronomical cost of the corporate rescue packages during the financial crisis, these potentially crippling arrears prompted major cutbacks in military spending by both Washington and London that threatened to undermine their overseas capabilities. The EU, meanwhile, needed all the money it could get if it was to rescue its Greek, Italian or Spanish laggards.

The war on terror also battered the moral authority of the West. The humiliation of Iraqi detainees at the Abu Ghraib prison near Baghdad, the camps at Guantanamo Bay in Cuba that denied its inmates the protections enshrined in the Geneva Convention, and the 'extraordinary rendition' of terror suspects to secret prisons and 'black sites' around the world, including within the Middle East, suggested that the United States and its allies had little respect for the values that they were ostensibly fighting for. In December 2012, the British government paid out £2.2m in compensation to a former Libyan opponent of Muammar Gaddafi who - along with his family – was forcibly rendered to Tripoli in 2004.

On top of all that, the Arab Spring once again illustrated to many the stark contradictions between what the Western world preached and what it practised. Washington, which had pledged its support for democratic transitions in Tunisia and Egypt, turned a comparatively blind eye to the crackdown in Bahrain. Virtually until the very eve of Ben Ali's departure, Paris had offered to sell the Tunisian president the equipment and expertise needed to contain the unrest, and for years had been trying to seal defence deals with Gaddafi before eagerly pummelling his hardware in 2011. In September, Washington's proclaimed backing for the freedom and dignity that so many people in the region were demanding rang hollow when it blocked Palestine's bid to become a full member of the United Nations. And in November 2012, shortly after Israel's bombardment of the Gaza Strip, the US was one of only a handful of countries to vote against Palestine's successful attempt to win permanent observer status at the UN.

Realists would argue that there is nothing fundamentally wrong or new about a foreign policy that prioritized national interests above wider principles, but it chafed to many when Washington, Paris or London tried to portray those national interests as being aligned with popular will in the Arab world. The outcome that Washington sought in Bahrain was not the one that most Bahrainis wanted, for instance, and trying to pretend otherwise simply did not wash with them.

Given that so many people from Rabat to Manama had demonstrated in favour of the values that were embodied more strongly in the US national psyche than any other, it was ironic that the reputation of the United States appeared to deteriorate during the course of 2011. Between 2009 and 2011, according to one poll, the proportion of respondents who held a favourable perception of the United States fell from 30 per cent to 5 per cent in Egypt, from 55 per cent to 12 per cent in Morocco, and from 41 per cent to 30 per cent in Saudi Arabia.Another poll from August 2012 found that 63 per cent of people polled in the Middle East and North Africa did not trust the US to 'act responsibly in the world'. The equivalent figures for China and Russia were 49 and 56 per cent.[17]

Was the United States still successfully projecting its soft power in the Middle East? The technological tools that so many Arab activists had harnessed in 2011 – Google, Facebook, Twitter – were all creations of American entrepreneurs, or of California's Silicon Valley. But social media was an inherently equalizing and interactive framework, a blank canvas that could be moulded according to the user's purpose, where they lived and what language they spoke. It did not so obviously advertise US power in the way that Coca Cola or MTV had done in the 1980s or 1990s, nor did it embody an overtly 'Made in America' brand. For the man on the street, the internet did not inspire the same awe as a NASA space shuttle (which, incidentally, was launched for the last time in July 2011 before the shuttle programme was shut down for being too expensive).

The perceptions of Arab leaders towards Washington had also shifted. While it was hard to argue that the United States was not still the single most powerful country in the world, its recent failures and its reaction to the uprisings had unnerved many authoritarian rulers. To a certain extent, of course, Obama could not please everybody. To openly back the wave of demonstrators in January and February 2011 might have given them the kiss of death. But to declare full and unwavering support for regimes facing a potentially successful uprising risked leaving Washington high and dry if they were overturned.

Sitting on the fence and hedging bets seemed to anger both the protesters – who decried what they saw as a hypocritical US stance and lacklustre moral and financial support for their cause – and authoritarian allies in the region, who felt Washington had abandoned Mubarak too easily or criticized Bahrain too strongly. 'We are astonished at what we see as the interference in the internal affairs of Egypt by some countries,' said Saudi Arabia's foreign minister in February 2011, referring to Obama's unambiguous calls for Mubarak to step aside.[18]

If the old global heavyweights, then, were seemingly unable to offer leadership in this uncertain new Arab world, then what about the rising ones, the emerging superpowers like China or Russia? And what about countries within the region that could also bring their political and economic weight to bear, countries like Turkey, Saudi Arabia or Qatar? All had their own interests in the Middle East, but none could provide a realistic model for any other Arab country to aspire to.

Filling the Gap

In 2009, for the first time ever, China bought more Saudi Arabian oil than the United States. Over the first decade of the new millennium, Saudi exports to China had risen by more than 21 times, while its imports from China had increased more than tenfold.[19] By 2010 Saudi Arabia was supplying about a quarter of Chinese and Indian oil imports, but sent just 16 per cent of its crude to the United States and 4 per cent to Europe.[20] The amount of oil that the United States imported from Saudi Arabia – its key strategic partner in the region – had fallen by more than a third in 2009 as the world's biggest economy struggled under the recession and financial crisis.[21] The global economy's centre of gravity was shifting.

Trade with China was not perfect, of course. Bilateral disputes were frequent and Chinese firms found doing business in the Middle East just as tricky as their Western counterparts. Nor were the US and Western Europe any longer important commercial partners to many countries in the region. But trade with the Chinese came with fewer complications. There was little question, for instance, of the Chinese media criticizing how dictators or kings ruled their countries, as the Western press was frequently wont to do. Nor was Beijing ever likely to launch an embarrassing investigation into corruption scandals or arms sales.

Yet it was precisely this 'no strings attached' approach that highlighted how the world's rising superpowers, who wielded the financial and commercial clout to enlarge their political influence in the Middle East, were failing to fill the gap left by a retreating United States. The West had preached a certain political and economic ideology, but there was no obvious alternative waiting in the wings. China, Russia and India still saw the region through a prism of commercial pragmatism and political survival – with a generous sprinkling of anti-Western sentiment thrown in for good measure.

In Beijing, where the Arab Spring came as an unwelcome shock and prompted a domestic crackdown, the overriding priority of the Communist regime was to secure its own power. Steering clear of complex Arab politics, China focused on securing the natural resources it needed to fuel economic growth that was so crucial to keeping its own people happy.

Russia was more proactive in the Middle East, and as the world's single-largest crude producer did not rely on the Gulf energy exporters. Moscow's attitude towards the Arab world might be best summarized as desiring to provide a counterweight to Western, and particularly US, influence, rather than seeking a leadership role. It, too, faced domestic uncertainties, as the nascent Russian protest movement of late 2011 showed.

India runs on different internal dynamics and takes a more cautious approach to the Arab world. Like China, it relies on the Gulf for energy imports and has little interest in seeing political instability threaten them. Around 5.5 million Indian nationals reside in the six GCC countries, part of a mutually beneficial relationship that provides abundant cheap labour for the oil-rich Gulf and generates colossal remittances for Indians. India's Muslim population, estimated at around 177 million people, also influences how the country deals with the region.

Reaction, rather than action, defined the stance of all three countries in 2011. India, China, Russia, Brazil and South Africa all abstained from voting on Resolution 1973 – which authorized the military intervention in Libya – then criticized it later. In September, Syria, China and Russia vetoed a proposed Security Council resolution that would have condemned the actions of Bashar al-Assad, with Russia in particular staunchly supporting the Syrian leader throughout 2012.

Beijing and Moscow have, in general, sought to discourage external intervention in, or sharp criticism of, authoritarian regimes embroiled in the messy business of restoring domestic order. For one thing, intervention or sanctions set a dangerous precedent should Russia or China ever be in that very position. For another, their opposition to intervention in the Arab world suggests to non-democratic rulers elsewhere that Russian or Chinese patronage is worth having.

Both countries will probably emerge from 2011 with diminished influence and a tarnished reputation in parts of the Arab world. They may not be unduly worried. Tunisia is too small to matter. In Libya, their companies may find it more difficult to win or renew government contracts. In Syria, they are likely to enjoy little favour with any replacement to Assad. But none of these countries is a major trading partner for Beijing or Moscow, and in reality, they need the emerging superpowers more than the superpowers need them.

So while the role of the West is on the wane, none of the new poles in the multi-polar world have yet shown the authority, credibility or willingness to play a leadership role in the Middle East. Instead, Arab countries undergoing transformations are more likely to look within the region itself for guidance. Here too there is no obvious model.

Turkey stands out as an example of a Muslim country that has managed to erode the political role of its military, build a functioning democracy, and generate decent economic growth. But it is hardly perfect. Rights groups complain about Turkey's human rights record, and Ankara has failed to resolve the issue of Kurdish separatism or recognize the Armenian genocide of 1915. The ruling AK Party is increasingly intolerant of dissent and its prime minister, Recep Tayyip Erdogan, is accused by critics of showing dangerous authoritarian tendencies. Media and academia operate under worrying restrictions. Yet of all the countries in the wider region, Turkey arguably has the most relevant experience to offer countries like Tunisia, Libya or Egypt as they look to learn from others.

As the previous chapter discussed, Iran's theocratic system does not translate to Sunni Islam. Saudi Arabia's unstable foundation of a monarchy allied with a religious establishment is no blueprint. The kingdom might be a source of funds and religious ideology, but it is not dynamic or secure enough to undertake policies that are not directly or indirectly linked to the goal of maintaining domestic power. Although they are more ambitious, stable and self-confident, the United Arab Emirates and Qatar can offer little besides money and moral support. Their economic, social and political models are vastly different from those in North Africa or the Levant, and are hardly transferable to them. Even oil-poor Dubai's state-driven capitalism had all but collapsed by 2009, and required colossal bailouts from its wealthier neighbour in Abu Dhabi to stay afloat. Dubai cannot provide direction for policymakers in Tunis or Cairo, although it can certainly demonstrate the long-term value of investing in infrastructure, free zones or tourism.

However much money Tunisia, Egypt, Syria or Morocco do receive from the Gulf over the coming years, it will fund short-term life support rather than build long-term solutions, addressing the symptoms of problems rather than their causes. Reforming Egypt's public sector, for instance, is akin to turning round an ocean liner travelling at full speed. Giving it fuel to keep steaming in the same direction simply makes the change more painful when it comes. This is an equally apt way to summarize how Gulf states responded to the 2011 uprisings, mollycoddling their citizens even more by offering financial perks that were much easier to give than they will be to take away. The Arab Spring may well have set back their efforts to prepare for the post-oil era, a day in the not too distant future when, as previous chapters discuss, the contract between state and citizens will have to be painfully rewritten.

Libya, with its small population and substantial energy wealth, shares some characteristics with Qatar and the UAE. It may learn something from the relatively successful way that these two states have distributed oil revenues to their citizens and built infrastructure, but an intrinsic element of that development model has been a family-run political system unencumbered by the bickering that pluralist politics always brings. In contrast, Libya now faces a period of violent squabbling in an enormous, unsecured country awash with weapons and ostensibly run by fragile new democratic institutions. Rulers in Doha or Abu Dhabi hardly boast the relevant experience to offer advice. Past Qatari efforts at mediating in Lebanon or Yemen, for instance, have involved large amounts of money and have not resolved underlying problems in either country.

Libya has a chance to cherry-pick the best aspects of other energy-rich countries around the world. It inherited no coherent ideology from Gaddafi, and like the Gulf states is wealthy enough to chart its own course without being dependent on external financial support. It has an opportunity to craft the relationship between state and citizens in a much more sustainable way than the Gulf states have done, and could avoid the mistake of nurturing a population that relies on artificial and overpaid public-sector jobs. What makes this unlikely to happen, of course, is that many Libyans will demand lasting post-revolution dividends to compensate them not only for the sacrifices of 2011, but also for decades of poorly managed oil wealth. The prospect of being heavily cosseted by the state is not unappealing.

There is no magic policy bullet to slay the demons of chronic unemployment or low incomes, particularly in Tunisia or Egypt, which do not even have Libya's luxury of oil revenues. When it comes to looking at possible models used by other countries, the challenge for new Arab governments will be to filter out what is relevant for their own unique circumstances. They do not need high-frequency stock trading, ultra-liberalized banking sectors or asset-stripping private equity firms, but nor should they discourage the type of entrepreneurship that in so many countries has been crushed by cronyism, corruption or oil wealth. Economic success must be judged not on growth, GDP per capita, state indebtedness or foreign investment levels, which reveal little about popular discontent, but rather on job creation, income distribution and regional inequalities. In the late 2000s Libya had zero debt, impressive economic growth, solid foreign investment and one of the highest GDPs per capita in Africa. Tunisia was long hailed as an economic miracle. Such advantages saved neither country from revolution in 2011.

The chances of long-term stability will be improved if no foreign country seeks to impose a specific economic or political blueprint. As they asserted their independence and made a break from the past, the new political forces in Tunisia, Egypt, Libya or elsewhere were in any case unlikely to embrace such a blueprint. This increases the likelihood of new structures being derived more from bottom-up popular agreement than from a top-down authoritarian regime or an ill-suited external concept.

In each of those places, a loose consensus had been formed about what should come next. No one in the mainstream was calling for a dictatorship, military rule, absolute theocracy or Soviet-style communism. They were not perfect, but the new constitutions being drafted in Tunisia, Egypt and Libya sought to enshrine the values that the majority of protesters were demanding, namely a stronger rule of law, greater economic equality and political accountability, and to realize them through the mechanism of meaningful elections to empowered parliaments that were answerable to the people. So did the draft programme of the Syrian National Coalition, the most prominent political opposition to Bashar al-Assad.

Broader context will be just as important in shaping outcomes as the politics of domestic constituencies. In the 1950s, when the previous wave of revolution spread through the Arab world, new regimes were joining a world in which one-party states were common. In 2011, only a handful of military dictatorships or absolute monarchies could be found outside of the Middle East. In the 1950s and 1960s, they were born into a Cold War that fought some of its proxy battles in the strategic and wealthy Arab world. But 2011 was a less polarized globe where even many of those living in established democracies had growing misgivings about their own systems.

Here is not the place to ask whether all this supports the theory that Western-style liberal democracy might be the end point of human political development. But that idea links the aftermath of the Arab Spring to the wider sense, in many countries, that something was not quite right. Did the increasingly flawed democracy in the West just need to be tweaked, rather than ripped up completely? Did the predatory, unproductive breed of capitalism in the United States or Britain simply need reform rather than replacement with a totally different system? The momentous events of 2011 have raised those questions anew, and they will not go away easily.

If democracy does take firm root in the Middle East, it will naturally bear the imprint of local circumstances. In Egypt it may be a hybrid between a military regime and a democratically elected parliament, with invisible but meaningful red lines between the two. In Libya it may be a democracy built along localism, with voting defined not by party manifestos but rather by home towns and extended families. In Tunisia it may be a democracy characterized by a tug-of-war between secularists and Islamists. Morocco and Jordan may become limited democracies overseen by a monarch whose absolute power is gradually eroded over time. In every case it will take years, and possibly another round of uprisings, for the dust to settle.

None may turn out to be particularly liberal democracies. Their political structures may enshrine the values that people had demanded in 2011 by introducing multi-party parliaments, universal suffrage and greater accountability for leaders, but nonetheless be subservient to a constitution that derives its ultimate authority from Islam. But for most of those who demanded change in 2011, even secularists, an illiberal democracy that can grow and change is an improvement on a dictatorship. And if society itself is conservative, then the most successful parties in such a democracy will be conservative too.

Yet it would be wishful thinking to imagine that local communities alone will shape future political systems. Foreign influences will be ever-present, particularly in those countries where much more is at stake than individual states. Bahrain will not be shaped by the will of the majority, but rather by the will of its monarchy and its allies in Riyadh and Washington. The new Libya may not be moulded by popular consensus but rather by those with the strongest revolutionary legitimacy and the most guns. Syria is too central to the future of the Middle East, and of the cold war with Iran, to be ignored by competing external forces. In contrast, Tunisia probably stands the best chance of success because it holds the least strategic importance to the region and the wider world. If it is lucky, it may largely be left alone.

Nor should the waning influence of the United States be exaggerated. Despite its costly floundering in Iraq and Afghanistan, that country still wields more political and military clout in the Arab world than any other international power. Despite its debt crisis, investors bought billions of dollars' worth of US treasury bills in 2011 and 2012. But the old belief that Washington could lead and control events in the Middle East, and that it was central to solving the region's biggest problems, is now defunct. The relationship between the West and the Arab world could now become much healthier, partly as the days of large-scale Western-led military intervention in Arab countries are over. Libya was a unique case under unique circumstances – widespread regional support, no major geopolitical knock-on effects and the looming risk of a humanitarian crisis – that will not be found elsewhere. This is not to say that interventions will not take place elsewhere in the region, but they are more likely to originate from within the Middle East itself, or to be more covert affairs rather than all-out invasions.

This new regional picture holds serious implications for Israel, which has watched and waited for most of 2011 and 2012. It would be unrealistic to imagine that 2011 will not affect Arab ties to the Jewish state in their midst, but those relationships will be recalibrated at a later stage. Its existing peace with Egypt and Jordan is unlikely to be threatened, though it may eventually be renegotiated. Based on the evidence so far, including from the November 2012 Gaza conflict, there is no reason to believe that a Muslim Brotherhood-led government in Cairo is any more likely to break the truce than Mubarak was, or have any more chance of winning a war. But Egypt's new leaders will need to reflect popular will in their policies, which is likely to mean more vocal condemnation of Israeli policies so unpopular on the Arab street.

Much also hinges on what happens in Syria, which has been in a purgatory state of 'no peace, no war' with Israel since 1974. Whoever emerges to lead that country will be in no military position to fight a war with Israel, but may be more willing to negotiate a peace deal that retrieves the Golan Heights. And if Hezbollah in south Lebanon is weakened by the fall of the Assad regime, it could alter the complicated connections between Lebanon,

Syria and Israel as well as recalibrating the internal dynamics of that fractured country.

Yet it would be dangerous to make predictions on such a seemingly intractable issue, which could get worse before it gets better. What we can say is that the process of change unleashed in 2011, if it is driven more by domestic rather than international constituencies, has the potential to resolve not only the festering tensions within individual states, but also the wider regional problems such as the Israel-Palestine conflict, the status of Hezbollah within Lebanon, or even the proxy battle between Saudi Arabia and Iran. That process will decades and, as our conclusion argues, the cacophony of overlapping battles described in this book will take different countries in different directions.

Afterword

On 17 December 2012, the local authorities in Sidi Bouzid organized a series of festivities and speeches to commemorate the anniversary of the event that would later be seen as the start of the Arab Spring. It was exactly two years since Mohamed Bouazizi, a vegetable seller who went on to become the town's most famous son, had set fire to himself.

A large red banner reading "Second International Festival of the December 17th Revolution" provided the backdrop to a podium from which president Moncef Marzouki delivered a speech to a restive crowd that had gathered in the town. 'I understand your legitimate and illegitimate anger and fear,' said Marzouki, 'but we are dealing with the aftermath of fifty years of dictatorship, and we cannot fix in only twelve months.'[1]

His words were partly drowned out by people shouting '*Dégage!*', or 'Get out!', the same phrase they had thrown at Zine al-Abidine Ben Ali two years ago. A handful of protesters then hurled stones and tomatoes at Mustafa Ben Jaafar, the speaker of the Tunisian parliament, before he could even address the crowd. Both he and Marzouki had to be ferried away to safety by the security services.

Two years on and much had changed in Tunisia, the country that had achieved a smoother post-uprising transition than any other. The fact that people were able to speak their minds to the country's leaders was a mark of how much freedom of expression had increased since Ben Ali's day. And the fact that those leaders – unlike their predecessor – had been democratically elected showed how far the political system had come.

But much remained depressingly familiar. Unemployment was higher than before the revolution. Prices had risen even quicker in 2011 than they had in 2010. Investors were just as nervous. For those in the central southern areas, the Petri dish of the protest movement, everyday life was even more difficult. Many old institutions and practices from Ben Ali's day remained embedded.

No country in the region could claim a total overhaul of the status quo by the end of 2012 and, in many, the Arab Spring had barely elicited a single piece of reform from unelected governments. The obliteration of the Gaddafi family had certainly created an opportunity for Libyans to construct a vastly improved political and economic structure. But that opportunity had not yet been fulfilled and might never be. Egyptians had removed Hosni Mubarak and voted in a more meaningful round of elections, yet two years on, the country remained bitterly divided and restive. In Morocco, there had been reform but not revolution. Yemenis had forced their president to step aside, but faced the same disheartening litany of political, humanitarian and economic crises as they had for decades. Bashar al-Assad still occupied the presidential palace that overlooked Damascus. Bahrain's uprising had only succeeded in polarizing its society.

'Rarely has revolution been more universally predicted, though not necessarily for the right countries or for the right dates,' was how historian Eric Hobsbawm described the years prior to the 1848 revolts in Europe. To a large extent, and with the same luxury of hindsight, the same had been true of the Arab world in the years leading up to 2011. It was clear that many countries were out of kilter, their creaking political and economic structures unable to meet the expectations of youthful societies and the shifting world around them. Change was overdue, but no one knew when it would come, where it would begin or how it would play out.

Like 1848, 2011 meant different things at different times in different places, and in some countries it meant very little at all. The fact that the events of that year have been variously described as uprisings, revolts, revolutions, protest movements, insurrections, rebellions, insurgencies or awakenings is partly why, for all its faults and inaccurate historical parallels, 'Arab Spring' gained traction as an umbrella term in both English and Arabic.

The phrase also reflects how the seeds of change had been growing underground long before shooting above the surface in 2011. What happened cannot be called an 'awakening' because the region had not been asleep. The uprisings capped a decade of political activism in which Arabic-language satellite television, mobile phones and the internet had already revolutionized media and communications. New media offset the lack of political freedoms, eroded the cults of personality and exposed the repression and the international conditions that had allowed unelected leaders, many of whom still remained in power one year on, to survive for so long. Authoritarian leaders and their systems of rule were unable to adapt to the social, economic and technological changes that were going on around them and the longer the decade wore on, the harder they had to work to keep burgeoning protest movements and labour unrest at bay.

When the floodgates did open, the course of the Arab Spring was determined not just by the different pre-existing conditions in each country, but by the various reactions of governments in 2011 itself. If Gaddafi had not used such unremittingly graphic language to threaten Benghazi, he might not have provided such a ready pretext for foreign military intervention. If Assad had dealt more forgivingly with grievances in Deraa, there might never have been a mass uprising in Syria. If King Mohamed had ordered his forces to fire on peaceful rallies in Morocco, he might have already been deposed. Just because the Al Sauds were still standing did not mean that underlying conditions in their kingdom were necessarily equipped to last for the long term. There was no natural selection that removed the most inept and repressive regimes in the region and left the more reform-minded and promising governments intact.

Some parallels have been drawn between 2011 and the 1989 revolutions that brought down the Berlin Wall and spelled the end of communism in Eastern Europe, but in that case a new ideology was waiting in the wings. People voted with their feet for democracy and capitalism. Others have compared the Arab Spring to the so-called colour revolutions that took place in the former Soviet states in the 2000s, which share some attributes in the non-violent techniques used by protesters in Egypt, Tunisia, Morocco, Bahrain and elsewhere. But the changes taking place in the Arab world, while they will disappoint many hoping for a speedy and all-encompassing transformation, are more significant.

Others have judged the Arab Spring against the great twentieth-century revolutions in Russia, Iran, China or even the Arab world itself, and found it lacking. In those upheavals the group that emerged with the reins of power possessed a new, coherent, often radical ideology that promised to transform state and society. The Bolsheviks had a clear vision of the country they wanted to forge after the demise of the Romanovs in 1917. Ayatollah Khomeini had spent years developing his concept of a theocratic Iran that could succeed the Shah. Even the Ba'athist takeover of Syria in 1963, Gamal Abdel Nasser's coup in Egypt in 1952 or Muammar Gaddafi's *fateh* revolution of 1969 were all based on specific and sometimes extreme visions, though many would later veer off-course.

In contrast, the Arab uprisings took place in a world where all of those ideologies, even including many elements of the Western-style blueprint that had gained so much influence after the Cold War, had lost their sheen. The protesters who squared up to riot police in Athens, occupied Zucotti Park in New York or camped on the flagstones outside St Paul's Cathedral in London had no shortage of discontent and anger with the current system, but struggled to articulate a lucid or inspiring vision of how they would do things differently. In the Arab world, based on election results in 2011 and 2012, many seemed to think that Islam might offer its long-vaunted solution.

The Arab Spring was not an Islamic Spring. That initial surge in early 2011 was not about religion but was an expression of anger over elite corruption, economic inequalities, widespread injustice and geriatric leaders who were out of touch with reality. Yet by early 2012 Islamist-oriented parties had exploited those early revolutionary gains to emerge triumphant from elections in Tunisia, Egypt and Morocco. They will play a major role in the future Syria, where they were crushed by Bashar al-Assad's father, and they are one of the most powerful forces in the new Libya. In virtually every country that underwent significant change in 2011, Islamists have undoubtedly been the biggest winners at the ballot box.

This should not have come as a surprise. What made the first round of protests successful – their use of social media to communicate and agitate, their absence of clear leaders and their suspicion of the political rhetoric that had so failed them in the past – carried the seeds of their later failure. Into the void leapt older, more ingrained and more powerful forces, adroitly exploiting these divisions to further their own interests.

Of all the established groups in the region, those with Islam as their guiding tenet were the only ones who had any hope of making major gains in the first free and fair elections after the Arab Spring. They were the only ones with a long-established organizational structure and a clear programme who had not been tainted by the corruption and compromise of government. For no matter how viciously they had been crushed by successive nationalist movements or military dictators, they always had the *minbar*, or pulpit, to claim as their own. They also had the word of God, so appealing to the bulging ranks of the disenfranchised and the downtrodden. Islamist views on women and minorities may be unpalatable to secularists, but in a region where the vast majority of people are Muslims and where secular nationalists had brought at best mismanagement and at worst oppression, they offered a return to old-fashioned family values, and they preached justice and honesty. Whether or not they can meet the expectations of those who voted for them is another question.

Yet it would be wrong to see the battle for the Arab Spring purely through the prism of religion. Other tensions, simmering below the surface in the 2000s, have also come to the fore. Policymakers are at odds over how best to tackle economic problems, which if left unaddressed will only trigger more revolts in the future. Old feuds have been reawakened and new battles over land and resources are breaking out.

Amid so much turbulence and uncertainty, can successful Arab democracies really emerge? People in the region had often, it seemed, been presented with an artificial choice between chaos and dictatorship by unelected rulers who liked to highlight failures in Arab democracy to justify their own existence. The idea of an Arab exception suited them just fine. But democracies need decades to take root, and in the turmoil that accompanies their delicate nurture, powerful international forces will try to shape change to their own ends, especially because far more than just the future of individual countries is at stake.

As the battle for the Arab Spring unfolds, prolonged instability or bouts of violence in the Gulf could heave up oil prices, and with them the worldwide cost of food, transportation or heating. At a time of deep economic malaise in so many countries around the world, this could have disastrous consequences. The struggle for Syria could suck in Iraq, Turkey and Lebanon. A change in Damascus could further isolate Iran and empower Saudi Arabia, both Islamist countries and arch rivals, and could have a profound effect on the Kurdish national struggle. The rise of former *jihadis* in Libya could raise questions over the wisdom of the NATO intervention and the friendly intentions of all Islamist governments in a region that produced the 9/11 hijackers.

Nor can what happens in the Middle East be separated from the context of shifting global power. Staggering from the fog of two wars in Iraq and Afghanistan that propelled its debt to stratospheric levels and undermined what moral authority it claimed in the eyes of Arabs, the United States lacks the means or the credibility to maintain its old influence in the Arab world. It will, of course, remain hugely influential, but the superpower left standing at the end of the Cold War can no longer give lessons to people tired of its support for their unpopular governments. Nor can it expect absolute loyalty from Arab rulers who have watched it abandon some of its long-standing allies. The stage is wide open for regional powers to buttress their influence and their own regimes.

The extraordinary events of 2011 suggested the end of an era for the Middle East. The withdrawal of US troops from Iraq in December provided one bookend to 9/11. The removal of old republican leaders waved goodbye to dinosaurs from another age. The resurgence of political Islam heralded a new period of religious conservatism but also of greater democratic representation. Even Al-Jazeera, the champion of the media revolution in the 2000s, had seemingly drawn a line under the past. Waddah Khanfar, the Palestinian who had led the channel's editorial operations, resigned in September and was replaced by a Qatari royal.

Yet many other factors suggested continuity. All the Arab monarchies survived and, despite feeling the ground move beneath their feet, are likely to be around for some time yet. Guantanamo Bay, a potent symbol of Bush's war on terror, remained open. Iran and the United States were still at loggerheads. The Israel-Palestine issue seemed further than ever from resolution, and the Gaza conflict of November 2012 suggested that little had fundamentally changed. Oil continued to flow abundantly from wells in Saudi Arabia or Kuwait and sold for more than $100 a barrel. And around the region, millions of young people might now have different leaders, but many remained unemployed, impoverished or illiterate.

Again, a comparison with the 1848 Spring of Nations is apt. Those revolts spread to some 50 countries, affecting most of Europe and even reaching Latin America. Their roots lay in widespread disaffection with existing rulers, demands for greater participation in politics, rising nationalist sentiment, crop failures and economic discontent among the urban working classes. Their ideas were distributed by the burgeoning popular press, raising expectations among people whose lives had already been improved by new technology. Conditions in each country were different and, in most cases, the coalitions that brought together diverse classes with diverse demands were defeated by a royalist counter-revolution led by powerful armies and aristocracies with vested interests to fight for.

Yet while gains were often limited, rolled back or crushed, the spirit of 1848 brought reforms over the ensuing generations that strengthened the political and economic power of the middle classes, eroded feudalism and laid the groundwork for future European democracies. Many Arab countries may suffer the same fate in the coming years as counter-revolutionary forces play their hand, but the seeds of change have been sown. In many places, a revolution in mindset has already torn down the barrier that for decades had stood between action and inaction, between protest and silence. Unions will become more potent forces in Tunisia, Egypt, Jordan and Morocco. People will speak up if they are unhappy with government policies. The people once again are a key combatant in the battle for power.

From liberals to nationalists to Islamists, old parties have recalibrated their positions and are trying to shape new constitutions in Tunisia and Egypt. In Bahrain, where an uprising has been suppressed, it will resurface. In Syria, it will rumble on. If reforms fall short in Morocco or Jordan, more demonstrations will surely follow. In Libya, despite the election of a government, much hard power lies with armed groups who are jostling for influence and money in the fragile post-Gaddafi era. Across the region, many who set aside differences to overthrow the old order have since retreated to the cosseted protection and comfort of tribe, family, religion or sect as the turbulent struggle for power unfolds.

After decades of suppressed volatility disguised as stability, the Arab Spring has kick-started a more prolonged period of change that may eventually bring down the Al Khalifa family in Bahrain, evict Egypt's military from the political arena, or downgrade Morocco's monarchy to constitutional status. It may even see revolution in Saudi Arabia, a kingdom that might have been too big to fail in 2011 but which has perhaps now been prodded further along the road to a major upheaval. The region now faces great instability as an array of tensions and conflicts bubble over. But only by allowing them to be played out, rather than bottled up, can they be resolved. Suppressing religion served only to breed extremism. Ignoring demands for better living standards or freer elections only led to the angry youth explosion of 2011. Giving one set of people preference over another only cultivated rage.

This new era will not be peaceful or pretty. There will be winners and losers, revolutionaries and counter-revolutionaries, bloodshed and truces, hope and despair. There may be war and another round of revolts before the dust settles in certain countries, and many in the region will privately wish that 2011 had never happened at all. The gusts of the Arab Spring have blown in new uncertainties to replace the certainties of old. In this new climate, anything now seems possible. For the people of the region, forced for so long to live out a pretence at stability, hopeless that they could change their world or shape its future, that is the biggest prize of all.

Endnotes

Introduction

1. 'Egyptian Election: Hosni Mubarak's NDP Sweeps Second Round', BBC, 7 December 2010,www.bbc.co.uk/news/world-middle-east–11935368 (accessed 15 September 2011); Human Rights Watch, 'Egypt: Elections Marred as Opposition Barred from Polls', 29 November 2010, www.hrw.org/news/2010/11/29/egypt-elections-marred-opposition-barred-polls (accessed 15 September 2011).
2. Human Rights Watch, 'Bahrain: Elections to Take Place Amid Crackdown', 20 October 2010, www.hrw.org/news/2010/10/20/bahrain-elections-take-place-amid-crackdown (accessed 15 September 2011).
3. 'Tunisian President in Fifth Win', BBC, 26 October 2009 (accessed 15 September 2011).
4. Catherine Goueset, 'Ben Ali et la liste des 65 flatteurs', *L'Express*, 20 January 2011, www.lexpress.fr/actualite/monde/afrique/ben-ali-et-la-liste-des–65-flatteurs_953972.html (accessed 15 September 2011).
5. UN population statistics for Middle East and North Africa in 2010.
6. Dhillon, Navtej and Yousef, Tarik, 'Generation in Waiting: The Unfulfilled Promise of Young People in the Middle East', Brookings Institution Press, 2009.
7. Arab Human Development Report 2002, pp. 27–9, www.arab-hdr.org (accessed 14 September 2011).
8. Ibid., pp. 52, 65 (accessed 15 September 2011).
9. Ibid., p. 78.
10. Kassir, Samir, *Being Arab*, London: Verso, 2006.
11. Gurr, Ted, *Why Men Rebel*, New Jersey: Princeton University Press, 1970.
12. Quinn, Andrew and Doherty, Regan E., 'Clinton Talks Tough to "Stagnant" Mideast Allies', Reuters, 13 January 2011.
13. 'Arab World Experiences Rapid Population Explosion', 23 March 2010, http://world-focus.org/blog/2010/03/23/arab-world-experiences-rapid-population-explosion/10090/ (accessed 29 October 2011).

Chapter 1: An Arab Malaise

1. Eurasia Group, 'Top Risks 2011', www.eurasiagroup.net/pages/top-risks (accessed 15 September 2011).
2. Huntington, Samuel P., 'Democracy's Third Wave', *Journal of Democracy* 2 (2), 1991.
3. Cole, Juan, 'Saad's Revolution', Truthdig, 1 February 2011. www.truthdig.com/report/item/saads_revolution_20110131/?utm_source=feedburner&utm_medium=feed&utm_

campaign=Feed%3A+Truthdig+Truthdig%3A+Drilling+Beneath+the+Headlines (accessed 15 September 2011).

4. Authors' calculations based on figures in 'The SPIRI Military Expenditure Database', Stockholm International Peace Research Institute, http://milexdata.sipri.org/ (accessed 20 September 2011).

5. 'Saudi Arabian National Guard', www.globalsecurity.org/military/world/gulf/sang. htm (accessed 20 September 2011).

6. Conversation with author in September 2010.

7. Heydemann, Steven, 'Upgrading Authoritarianism in the Arab World', Analysis Paper No. 13, October 2007, Saban Center for Middle East Policy, Brookings Institution, pp. 7–8, http://www.brookings.edu/~/media/Files/rc/papers/2007/10arabworld/10a rabworld.pdf (accessed 21 September 2011).

8. Sinjab, Lina, 'Is Syria ready to engage with NGOs?', BBC website, 24 January 2010, http://news.bbc.co.uk/1/hi/8477748.stm (accessed 21 September 2011).

9. 'Queen Rania: The 21st Century Queen', *Glamour*, 1 November 2010, www.glamour. com/women-of-the-year/2010/queen-rania (accessed 21 September 2011) and 'The World's 100 Most Powerful Women,' *Forbes*, www.forbes.com/wealth/power-women/ list (accessed 21 September 2011).

10. Malone, Noreen, 'The Middle East's Marie Antoinettes', Slate, 23 March 2011, www. slate.com/id/2289021 (accessed 21 September 2011).

11. Richard Nixon, Gerald Ford and Jimmy Carter all attended. Photos of all three posing with Ronald Reagan at the White House can be found at the Reagan Library in the University of Texas, www.reagan.utexas.edu/archives/photographs/four.html (accessed 15 September 2011).

12. Remarks made in an exclusive interview with Biden aired on PBS on 27 January 2011, www.pbs.org/newshour/bb/politics/jan-june11/biden_01–27.html

13. BP Statistical Yearbook.

14. Ibid.

15. Ibid.; includes the neutral zone shared with Kuwait.

16. 'US Energy Information Administration figures published 20 August 2011, http://205.254.135.24/dnav/pet/pet_move_impcus_a2_nus_ep00_im0_mbbl_m.htm (accessed 15 September 2011).

17. 'US says Syrians reportedly engage Moslem Brotherhood', Dow Jones Newswires, 11 February 1982.

18. Friedman, Thomas, 'A Syrian City Amid the Rubble of Rebellion', 29 May 1982.

19. For full SHRC statement published on 14 February 2006, see www.shrc.org/data/aspx/ d5/2535.aspx

20. Capaccio, Tony, 'Military aid to Yemen doubles as U.S. aims to boost fight against Al Qaeda', published by Bloomberg, 25 August 2010.

21. Zaks, Dmitry, 'Russia kills "Saudi al Qaeda leader" in Chechnya', AFP, 22 April 2011.

22. The details of Libya's hunt for bin Laden and his links to the Libyan Islamic Fighting Group have been widely reported, e.g. 'The untold story of Gaddafi's hunt for bin Laden', *Die Welt*, 2 May 2011, www.worldcrunch.com/untold-story-gaddafis-hunt-osama-bin-laden/2963

23. Published in 2006, the findings of the Commission of Inquiry into the Actions of Canadian Officials in Relation to Maher Arar clearly explain what befell Arar: www. sirc-csars.gc.ca/pdfs/cm_arar_rec-eng.pdf Another example is that of Abu Omar, a cleric kidnapped in Milan in 2003 and sent back to his native Egypt, where he was inter-rogated. For more details, see BBC story 'Egypt rendition cleric freed', published on 12 February 2007, http://news.bbc.co.uk/1/hi/world/africa/6352717.stm

24. This was widely reported. See Nordland, Rob, 'In Libya, former enemy is recast in role of ally', *New York Times*, 1 September 2011, http://www.nytimes.com/2011/09/02/ world/africa/02islamist.html?pagewanted=1&_r=1

25. See Wright, Robin and Baker, Peter, 'Iraq, Jordan see threat to election from Iran', *Washington Post*, 8 December 2004, www.washingtonpost.com/wp-dyn/articles/ A43980–2004Dec7.html
26. Bush gave his second inaugural speech on 20 January 2005.
27. 2010 Arab Opinion Poll, conducted by University of Maryland in conjunction with Zogby International in June and July 2010, published 5 August 2010.
28. Kassir, Samir, foreword to *Being Arab*, London: Verso, 2006.

Chapter 2: Bread, Oil and Jobs

1. De Tocqueville, Alexis, *The Old Regime and the Revolution*, 1856.
2. Report by Samba, a Saudi bank, released in December 2008. Figures refer to period from June 2003 to June 2008.
3. UNCTAD World Investment Report 2011, www.unctad.org
4. Dubai's oil production is estimated at 70,000b/d, less than 5 per cent of the UAE's total output.
5. UNCTAD World Investment Report 2011, www.unctad.org
6. Ibid.
7. Ennakhl, Le Moteur and Alpha are the three companies in question.
8. As described in WikiLeaks cables.
9. The corruption probe was widely covered in the local and international press and investigated various state-owned entities, including Nakheel and Sama Dubai. See, for example: Kerr, Simeon, 'Three held in Dubai corruption probe', *Financial Times*, 10 February 2009.
10. Cable entitled 'Troubled Tunisia: what should we do?' dated 17 July 2009, http://wikileaks.org/cable/2009/07/09TUNIS492.html#
11. US embassy cable leaked by WikiLeaks and quoted in www.crethiplethi.com/wikileaks-moroccan-royals-accused-of-corruption/usa/2011/
12. The idea of soft states is discussed at various points in Myrdal, *Asian Drama: An Inquiry into the Poverty of Nations*, 1968.
13. Galal Amin, *Egypt in the Era of Hosni Mubarak*, Cairo University Press, 2011.
14. World Bank data.
15. National Bank of Kuwait (NBK) report, cited at www.emirates247.com/business/economy-finance/gcc-remittances-to-egypt-exceed–4bn–2010–07–26–1.270952 (accessed 15 September 2011).
16. World Bank data.
17. Poll conducted by Abu Dhabi Gallup Center, available at www.abudhabigallupcenter.com/148229/tunisia-analyzing-dawn-arab-spring.aspx
18. Authors' interviews with employees of the institute, August 2011.
19. From 84 points to 151 points. CAPMAS statistics, www.capmas.gov.eg
20. Syrian Central Bureau of Statistics, www.cbssyr.org
21. Haut Commissariat au Plan (Moroccan statistics authority), www.hcp.ma/Indice-de-cout-de-vie_r104.html. The subsidies bill rose by 78 per cent and the grain price index rose from 148 points to 180 points.
22. Tunisian National Statistics Institute data. Food and drinks rose from 105 points in 2006 to 128 points in 2010, while transport rose from 106 to 131 points over the same period. The overall index rose from 104 to 122.
23. US embassy cable released by WikiLeaks in December 2010.
24. Central Bank of Tunisia data, www.bct.gov.tn/bct/siteprod/english/indicateurs/credits.jsp#beneficiaire
25. IMF April 2011 World Economic Database. Figures are in real terms.
26. US Wheat Associates report January 2011. North Africa is defined in the report as Morocco, Algeria, Tunisia, Libya and Egypt.
27. Ibid.

28. UN Food and Agricultural Organisation (FAO) overall food price index, accessed at www.fao.org
29. BP Statistical Review of World Energy 2011.
30. Saudi Central Department of Statistics.
31. Abu Dhabi Gallup poll, as cited above.
32. World Bank report cited in Dubai School of Government paper 'Missed by the Boom, Hurt by the Bust', available at www.dsg.ae/PUBLICATIONS/PublicationDetail. aspx?udt_826_param_detail=676
33. As quoted in BBC News report at www.bbc.co.uk/news/business–14006885
34. Pierre Puchot, *Tunisie, Une Revolution Arabe*, Galaade, France, 2011.
35. As reported in *The National* newspaper, www.thenational.ae/news/uae-news/unemploy-ment-rate-for-emiratis-stands-at–13
36. *Al Watan* newspaper, as quoted in August 2011 in www.iloveqatar.net/forum/read. php?28,29516
37. http://news.gulfjobsmarket.com/native-workers-in-the-uae-still-avoid-working-in-the-private-sector–7861475-news
38. Saudi Arabian Monetary Agency (SAMA), www.sama.gov.sa
39. 24.6 million estimated by CAPMAS in July 2010 census, compared to 22.8 million in the 2006 census.
40. CAPMAS statistics. 35 per cent of the unemployed population had degrees.
41. www.eces.org.eg/Uploaded_Files/events/ per cent7B9717DAA4-FA14–49B7–91DB–6E24FF8B6E62 per cent7D_Sahay_MacArthur_ECES_Final-Janu_23_2011.pdf
42. Report by Al Arabiya website, http://www.alarabiya.net/save_pdf.php?cont_id=58209
43. Al Sayegh, Hadeel, 'Syria grows into new Bourse', *The National*, 14 February 2011.
44. Bourse de Tunis, 'Rapport Annuel 2010'. Saudi statistics are taken from www.tadawul. gov.sa
45. Central Bank of Egypt statistics.
46. UNCTAD World Investment Report 2011, www.unctad.org
47. Tunisian official statistics showed arrivals were 6.9m in 2009 and 2010 compared to 7.05m in 2008.
48. Syrian Ministry of Tourism figures quoted by The Syria Report (www.syria-report.com).
49. Abu Dhabi Gallup poll, as cited above.
50. IMF figures from April 2011 World Economic Outlook database at www.imf.org

Chapter 3: The Media Revolution

1. Wael Ghonim interviewed by CNN's Ivan Watson, 9 February 2011.
2. Noueihed, Lin, 'Syrian Court Postpones Trial of Leading Dissident', Reuters, 19 May 2002.
3. The journalist in question was co-author Lin Noueihed.
4. See the Open Network Initiative report on Syria published 7 August 2009 for a fuller picture of Syria's internet censorship, http://opennet.net/research/profiles/syria (accessed 16 September 2011). Both internet censorship and the role of ONI will be discussed in more detail later in the book.
5. 3G services cost the equivalent of $50 a month, according to the Open Network Initiative report on Syria, 7 August 2009, http://opennet.net/research/profiles/syria (accessed 16 September 2011).
6. http://shaam.org/ (accessed 16 September 2011).
7. James, Laura M., 'Whose Voice? Nasser, the Arabs and Sawt al-Arab Radio', TBS 16, 2006, www.tbsjournal.com/James.html (accessed 16 September 2011).
8. Miladi, Noureddine, 'Satellite News and the Arab Diaspora in Britain: Comparing Al-Jazeera, the BBC and CNN', *Journal of Ethnic and Migration Studies* 32(6), August 2006, pp. 947–60.
9. Ibid.

10. Ibid.

11. For an excellent study of the role of Al-Jazeera and its coverage of the 2003 Iraq war in transforming the Arab public sphere, see Lynch, Marc, *Voices of the New Arab Public: Iraq, Al-Jazeera, and Middle East Politics Today*, New York: Columbia University Press, 2006.

12. Miles, Hugh, *Al-Jazeera: How Arab TV News Challenged the World*, London: Abacus, 2005, pp. 38–48.

13. Transcription by the authors from the original video.

14. Miles, Hugh, *Al-Jazeera: How Arab TV News Challenged the World*, London: Abacus, 2005.

15. Ibid.

16. 2010 Arab Public Opinion Poll, conducted by the University of Maryland in conjunction with Zogby International, published 5 August 2010, www.brookings.edu/~/media/Files/rc/reports/2010/08_arab_opinion_poll_telhami/08_arab_opinion_poll_telhami.pdf (accessed 16 September 2011).

17. Prodger, Matt, 'Superstar Muslim preacher Amr Khaled Battle Al Qaeda', BBC, 7 December 2010, http://news.bbc.co.uk/1/hi/programmes/newsnight/9264357.stm (accessed 16 September 2011).

18. Demonstrations continued over two years, until concerns over the build-up to the invasion of Iraq took precedence on the Arab streets.

19. Sachs, Susan, 'Unleashed, Anger Can Bite its Master', *New York Times*, 22 October 2000.

20. Arab Human Development Report 2002, UNDP and Arab Fund for Economic and Social Development, pp. 74–5 (accessed 19 September 2011).

21. International Telecommunications Union statistics, from www.itu.int (accessed 23 December 2011). User numbers rose from 25 million in 2005 to 105 million in 2011.

22. Wheeler, Deborah, 'The Internet and Youth Subculture in Kuwait', *Journal of Computer-Mediated Communication* 8(2), 2003.

23. All statistics from International Telecommunications Union, www.itu.int (accessed 23 December 2011).

24. Mourtada, Racha and Salem, Fadi, 'Facebook Usage: Factors and Analysis', Arab Social Media Report, Dubai School of Government, vol. 1, no. 1. January 2011, pp. 4–5 (accessed 17 September 2011).

25. Ibid.

26. All statistics from International Telecommunications Union, www.itu.int (accessed 23 December 2011).

27. Scholars have theorized this phenomenon from a rational choice perspective. See Lohmann, Susanne, 'The Dynamics of Informational Cascades: The Monday Demonstrations in Leipzig, East Germany, 1989–91', *World Politics* 47(1), 1994, pp. 42–101, and Kuran, Timur, 'Now Out of Never: The Element of Surprise in the East European Revolution of 1989', *World Politics* 44(1), 1991, pp. 7–48.

28. Gladwell, Malcolm, 'Small Change: Why the Revolution will not be Tweeted', 4 October 2010.

29. Morozov, Evgeny, 'Facebook and Twitter are Just Places Revolutionaries Go', *Guardian*, 7 March 2011.

30. Dickinson, Elizabeth, 'The First Wikileaks Revolution?', 13 January 2011, http://wikileaks.foreignpolicy.com/posts/2011/01/13/wikileaks_and_the_tunisia_protests (accessed 18 September 2011); 'First Wikileaks Revolution: Tunisia Descends into Anarchy as President Flees after Cables Reveal Country's Corruption', *Daily Mail*, 15 January 2011.

31. Courbage, Youssef and Todd, Emmanuel, *A Convergence of Civilizations: The Transformation of Muslim Societies Around the World*, New York: Columbia University Press, 2011.

Chapter 4: Tunisia's Jasmine Revolution

1. Translation from the Arabic by Elliot Colla, associate professor of Arabic and Islamic Studies at Georgetown University, http://arablit.wordpress.com/2011/01/16/two-translations-of-abu-al-qasim-al-shabis-if-the-people-wanted-life-one-day/ (accessed 29 September 2011).

2. Others accompanied them to the airport but these are the family members who are believed to have boarded the plane for Saudi Arabia. For a blow-by-blow account of the day of Ben Ali's departure, see 'Al Arabiya enquiry reveals how Tunisia's Ben Ali escaped to Saudi Arabia', Al Arabiya, 13 January 2012, http://english.alarabiya.net/articles/2012/01/13/188093.html (accessed 16 January 2012).

3. 'France says Tunisia Ex-leader not Welcome', Reuters, 14 January 2011.

4. See 'France Intercepted Riot Gear Shipment to Ben Ali', Reuters, 19 January 2011. See also 'France Replaces Tunisia Envoy with Sarkozy Ally', Reuters, 26 January 2011.

5. For a full account of Alliote-Marie's activities in Tunisia on the eve of revolution, see Pape, Eric, 'Le Scandal', *Foreign Policy* magazine, 25 February 2011: www.foreignpolicy.com/articles/2011/02/25/le_scandal?page=full

6. Love, Brian, 'French minister under attack over Tunisian trip', Reuters, 2 February 2011, www.reuters.com/article/2011/02/02/uk-tunisia-france-idUKTRE71147320110202 (accessed 17 January 2012).

7. As note 2, see 'Al Arabiya enquiry reveals how Tunisia's Ben Ali escaped to Saudi Arabia', Al Arabiya, 13 January 2012, http://english.alarabiya.net/articles/2012/01/13/188093.html (accessed 16 January 2012).

8. 'Tunisia: 2010 Article IV Consultation', IMF, conducted August 2010, released September 2010, www.imf.org/external/pubs/ft/scr/2010/cr10282.pdf (accessed 3 October 2011).

9. 'The Global Competitiveness Report 2010–11', World Economic Forum, 2010: www3.weforum.org/docs/WEF_GlobalCompetitivenessReport_2010–11.pdf (accessed 3 October 2011).

10. 'Tunisia: Analyzing the Dawn of the Arab Spring', Abu Dhabi Gallup Poll, June 2011, www.abudhabigallupcenter.com/148229/tunisia-analyzing-dawn-arab-spring.aspx (accessed 3 October 2011).

11. Authors' interviews with Tunisian protesters in January, February, July and August 2011.

12. Figures taken from Zartman, William, 'Report on the First Tunisian Multiparty Legislative Elections', International Foundation for Electoral Systems (IFES), April 1989, www.ifes.org/Content/Publications/Reports/1989/~/media/Files/Publications/VRC/Reports/1989/R01910/R01910.pdf

13. 'Opposition Contests Election Results', Reuters, 8 April 1989.

14. In its press release from 4 March 1992 entitled 'Tunisia: Thousands Held Illegally, Torture Routine in Crackdown on Islamic Opposition,' Amnesty International states that at least 8,000 people had been arrested over the previous 18 months: www.amnesty.org/en/library/asset/MDE30/005/1992/en/7d2ed1fa-f93b–11dd–92e7-c59f81373cf2/mde300051992en.pdf

15. 'Repression of Former Political Prisoners in Tunisia: A larger prison', 24 March 2010, Human Rights Watch.

16. Noueihed, Lin, 'Tunisian Muslims Worship Freely after Revolution', Reuters, 21 January 2011.

17. Hibou, Beatrice, *The Force of Obedience: The Political Economy of Repression in Tunisia*, Cambridge: Polity, 2011, pp. 97–8; Heydemann, Steven, 'Upgrading Authoritarianism in the Arab World', Analysis Paper No. 13, October 2007, Saban Center for Middle East Policy, Brookings Institution, p. 9, www.brookings.edu/~/media/Files/rc/papers/2007/10arabworld/10arabworld.pdf (accessed 21 September 2011).

18. Hibou, Beatrice, *The Force of Obedience: The Political Economy of Repression in Tunisia*, Cambridge: Polity, 2011, pp. 97–8.
19. World Report 2009, Human Rights Watch: http://www.hrw.org/world-report–2009/tunisia (accessed 13 October 2011).
20. According to UGTT website: http://www.ugtt.org.tn/en/presentation3.php (accessed 13 October 2011).
21. Figure provided by Adel Jelil Bedoui, former union official, in an interview with the authors, August 2011.
22. Hibou, Beatrice, *The Force of Obedience: The Political Economy of Repression in Tunisia*, Cambridge: Polity, 2011, pp. 123–6.
23. According to Tunisian political activist Sofiane Chourabi in an interview with the author, August 2011.
24. According to interviews by the authors with PDP members and communists in Sidi Bouzid in January 2011.
25. 'Popular Protests in the Middle East and North Africa: Tunisia's Way', International Crisis Group Middle East/North Africa Report No. 106, 28 April 2011.
26. Interview with the authors, August 2011.
27. Ibid.
28. Ibid.
29. 'Popular Protests in the Middle East and North Africa: Tunisia's Way', International Crisis Group Middle East/North Africa Report No. 106, 28 April 2011, p. 11.
30. Ibid.
31. Bouazizi's family says he was slapped. The policewoman denies this and was later found innocent.
32. Noueihed, Lin, 'Peddler's Martyrdom Launched Tunisia's Revolution', Reuters, 20 January 2011.
33. Awad, Marwa and Chikhi, Lamine, 'Burnings Spread to Egypt, Algeria in Tunisia Echo', Reuters, 17 January 2011.
34. Noueihed, Lin, 'Peddler's Martyrdom Launched Tunisia's Revolution', Reuters, 20 January 2011.
35. Ibid.
36. Interview with the authors, August 2011.
37. 'Tunisia Frees Rapper Critical of Government', Reuters, 9 January 2011.
38. 'Popular Protests in the Middle East and North Africa: Tunisia's Way', International Crisis Group Middle East/North Africa Report No. 106, 28 April 2011, p. 11.
39. 'Violence Breaks out in Tunisia Capital', Reuters, 11 January 2011.
40. 'Five More Killed in Tunisia Clashes – Witnesses', Reuters, 12 January 2011.
41. Tarhouni gave a press conference to this effect on 8 August 2011.
42. 'UN Says 147 Killed in Tunisian Uprising', Reuters, 1 February 2011.
43. Noueihed, Lin, 'Thousands Await Return of Tunisian Islamist Leader', Reuters, 30 January 2011.
44. Moore, Clement Henry, *Tunisia Since Independence: The Dynamics of One-Party Government*, California University Press, 1965, pp. 50–52; see also Tamimi, pp. 9–10.
45. Ibid. See also Tamimi, pp. 9–10.
46. King, Stephen Juan, *The New Authoritarianism in the Middle East and North Africa*, Indiana University Press, 2009.
47. As cited in Moore, p. 55.
48. Noueihed, Lin, 'Islamists Emerge as Powerful Force in New Tunisia', Reuters, 2 February 2011.
49. Noueihed, Lin and Perry, Tom, 'Tunisian Islamists Show Strength at Chief's Return', Reuters, 30 January 2011.
50. Henegan, Tom, 'Tunisian Women Rally to Defend Rights Against Islamists', Reuters, 3 November 2011.
51. Interview with the author.

52. Interview with author, 3 February 2011. Part of this quote was published in Noueihed, Lin, 'Tunisia Islamists say Excluded, Call for Unity Government', Reuters, 3 February 2011.
53. Amara, Tarek and Lowe, Christian, 'Tunisia Islamists Send Business-friendly Message', Reuters, 26 October 2011.
54. 'Tunisia Warns of Tough Action Against Troublemakers', Reuters, 30 October 1990.
55. Tamimi, Azzam S., *Rachid Ghannouchi: A Democrat within Islamism*, Religion and Global Politics Series, Oxford University Press, 2001, pp. 4–7.
56. Ibid., pp. 17–23.
57. Ibid., pp. 28–33.
58. Ibid., pp. 46–52.
59. Ibid., pp. 56–7.
60. Ibid., p. 72.
61. Ibid., p. 47.
62. Ibid., pp. 61–2.
63. Wright, Jonathan, 'Tunisia Launches Anti-Islamist Campaign', Reuters, 23 April 1990.
64. Ibid.
65. Ben Ghazi, Myriam, 'Hopelessness, desperation and marginalization: five attempted suicides in Kasserine', Tunisia Live, 17 September 2011.
66. www.investintunisia.tn (accessed 15 December 2011).
67. 'New Regional Development Strategy Centred Around Three Axes', TAP, 29 September 2011, www.tap.info.tn/en/en/economy/5948-new-regional-development-strategy-centred-around–3-axes.html (accessed 17 October 2011).
68. Interview with the authors, August 2011.
69. Amara, Tarek, 'Tunisia President Asks for 6-month Political Truce', Reuters, 14 December 2011.
70. Interview with the authors, August 2011.
71. '4 Billion to Tunisia for 2011–2013: EU Offers Financial Support, Trade Openings and Improved Mobility', ENPI, 30 September 2011, .www.enpi-info.eu/medportal/news/latest/26539/%E2%82%AC4-billion-to-Tunisia-for–2011–2013:-EU-offers-financial-support,-trade-openings-and-improved-mobility (accessed 17 October 2011).
72. Interview with the authors, July 2011.

Chapter 5: Egypt: The Pharaoh Falls

1. *Taxi* was first published in Arabic in 2005. This foreword was penned in April 2011 for the new English edition published the same year by Bloomsbury Qatar Foundation Publishing, and translated from Arabic by Jonathan Wright.
2. See 'Unrest in Egypt: Strange Ongoings', 10 February 2011, www.economist.com/blogs/newsbook/2011/02/unrest_egypt (accessed 16 September 2011).
3. 'Egypt's Military Discusses Measures in Crisis – TV', Reuters, 10 February 2011.
4. 'Mubarak Likely to Step Down this Evening – CIA chief', Reuters, 10 February 2011.
5. 'Egypt Ruling Party Head Says Mubarak Must Go', Reuters, 10 February 2011.
6. 'Mubarak Definitely not Going to Step Down', Reuters, 10 February 2011.
7. Perry, Tom, 'Mubarak Speech Pulls Plug on Tahrir Square Party', Reuters, 11 February 2011.
8. 'Mubarak Says Heading to Peaceful Power Transfer', Reuters, 10 February 2011.
9. 'Opposition Party Pulls out of Egypt Dialogue', Reuters, 10 February 2011.
10. Blair, Edmund and Nakhoul, Samia, 'Rage in Egypt as Mubarak Hangs on', Reuters, 10 February 2011.
11. 'Egypt's Private Sector Country Profile 2009', African Development Bank, p. 3, www.afdb.org/fileadmin/uploads/afdb/Documents/Project-and-Operations/Brochure%20Egypt%20Anglais.pdf (accessed 2 November 2011).

12. See IMF's 'Arab Republic of Egypt: 2010 Article IV Consultation', April 2010.

13. Ministry of Finance: www.mof.gov.eg/English/Pages/Selected-Economic-Indicators. aspx (accessed 2 November 2011). Also see IMF World Economic Outlook database, September 2011.

14. Egypt's official Central Agency for Mobilization and Statistics: www.capmas.gov.eg/ pages_ar.aspx?pageid=851 (accessed 2 January 2012).

15. See 'Egypt's Progress Towards Achieving the Millennium Development Goals 2010', UNDP and Egyptian Ministry of Economic Development: www.mop.gov.eg/ PDF/2010%20MDGR_English_R51.pdf (accessed 8 November 2011).

16. Egypt's official Central Agency for Mobilization and Statistics: www.capmas.gov.eg/ default.aspx?lang=2 (accessed 8 November 2011).

17. Ibid.

18. Ibid.

19. CAPMAS statistics.

20. According to the IMF World Economic Outlook database, September 2011.

21. Egypt's official Central Agency for Mobilization and Statistics: www.capmas.gov.eg/ default.aspx?lang=2 (accessed 8 November 2011).

22. 'Payout over Egypt Ferry Disaster', BBC, 7 June 2006, http://news.bbc.co.uk/1/hi/ world/middle_east/5054358.stm (accessed 30 October 2011).

23. 'Egypt Ferry Owner Sentenced to 7 Years', Die Welt online, 11 March 2009, www.welt. de/english-news/article3358219/Egypt-ferry-owner-sentenced-to-seven-years.html (accessed 30 October 2011).

24. See Egypt: The Arithmetic of Revolution, Abu Dhabi Gallup poll, published in March 2011, www.abudhabigallupcenter.com/146888/BRIEF-Egypt-Arithmetic-Revolution.aspx (accessed 15 September 2011) and Tunisia: Analyzing the Dawn of the Arab Spring, Abu Dhabi Gallup poll published June 2011: www.abudhabigallup-center.com/148229/tunisia-analyzing-dawn-arab-spring.aspx (accessed 15 September 2011).

25. Williams, Dan, 'Egypt Frees an Aspiring Candidate', Washington Post, www.washington-post.com/wp-dyn/articles/A29477–2005Mar12.html (accessed 21 September 2011).

26. 'Egypt's Nour Released from Jail', BBC, 18 February 2009, http://news.bbc.co.uk/1/hi/ world/middle_east/7897703.stm (accessed 21 September 2011).

27. US cable by Ambassador Francis Ricciardone entitled 'Presidential Succession in Egypt', http://wikileaks-egypt.blogspot.com/2010/12/ricciardone-we-believe-gamal-did-not.html (accessed 9 November 2011).

28. This is certainly the conclusion US diplomats in Cairo had come to and is corroborated by conversations with various Egyptian activists and analysts. US cable by Ambassador Margaret Scobey dated September 2008 and entitled 'Academics See the Military in Decline but Retaining Strong Influence', http://wikileaks.ch/ cable/2008/09/08CAIRO2091.html (accessed 2 November 2011).

29. Amin, Galal, Egypt in the Era of Hosni Mubarak 1981–2011, Cairo: Cairo University Press, 2011. Despite its title, this book contains a thorough criticism of Sadat's economic policies.

30. According to a 2007 cable entitled 'Egypt in Transition: Mubarak and Sadat', released by WikiLeaks in December 2010: http://wikileaks.ch/cable/2007/09/07CAIRO2871. html (accessed 2 November 2011).

31. Amin, Galal, Whatever Happened to the Egyptians? Cairo: American University of Cairo Press, 2000.

32. Al Aswany, Alaa, The Yacoubian Building, New York: Harper Perennial, 2006.

33. Interview by the authors with Kamal Abu Aita, head of the Egyptian Federation of Independent Trade Unions established during the uprising, 8 October 2011.

34. Ibid.

35. Ibid.

36. See UNDP Program on Governance in the Arab Region for more on associations legislation in Egypt: www.pogar.org/countries/theme.aspx?t=2&cid=5 (accessed 21 January 2012).

37. Chick, Kristen, 'Egyptians unhappy with lenient sentence for Khaled Said's killers', *Christian Science Monitor*, 26 October 2011, www.csmonitor.com/World/Middle-East/2011/1026/Egyptians-unhappy-with-lenient-sentence-for-Khaled-Said-s-killers (accessed 21 January 2012).

38. Carnegie Endowment paper 'Egypt's Controversial Constitutional Amendments', by Nathan J. Brown, Michele Dunne and Amr Hamzawy, published 23 March 2007, www.carnegieendowment.org/files/egypt_constitution_webcommentary01.pdf (accessed 15 September 2011).

39. Lyon, Alistair, 'Egyptians Chafe under Mubarak's Protracted Tenure', Reuters, 10 January 2011.

40. Interview with the authors in Cairo, October 2011.

41. A full account of these tactics is in Levison, Charles and Coker, Margaret, 'The Secret Rally that Sparked an Uprising', *Wall Street Journal*, 11 February 2011, http://online.wsj.com/article/SB10001424052748704132204576135882356532702.html (accessed 30 October 2011).

42. Some twenty-five former NDP officials were sent to court accused of organizing the camel attack. They deny the charges. For details see 'Egypt begins trial over February protest camel charge', Reuters, 11 September 2011, www.reuters.com/article/2011/09/11/us-egypt-trial-charge-idUSTRE78A2J720110911 (accessed 21 January 2012).

43. For part of Ghonim's interview on Dream TV where he breaks down and leaves the studio, see www.youtube.com/watch?v=V690GO7YzgA (accessed 21 January 2012).

44. Perry, Tom and Wright, Jonathan, 'New Protesters Flood Cairo Square to Oppose Mubarak', Reuters, 8 February 2011.

45. According to labour union activists interviewed by the authors in Cairo in October 2011.

46. A breakdown of the civilian and military products manufactured by the AOI is available at www.aoi.com.eg/aoieng/ (accessed 1 November 2011).

47. The NSPO is notoriously opaque but a brief outline of its activities is at www.nspo.com.eg/Untitled-1.htm (accessed 1 November 2011).

48. Topol, Sarah A., 'Egypt's Command Economy', 15 December 2010, www.slate.com/articles/news_and_politics/dispatches/2010/12/egypts_command_economy.html (accessed 1 November, 2011).

49. 'Egypt's Private Sector Country Profile 2009', African Development Bank, pp. 13–14, www.afdb.org/fileadmin/uploads/afdb/Documents/Project-and-Operations/Brochure%20Egypt%20Anglais.pdf (accessed 2 November 2011).

50. For an assessment of Egypt's military, see Cordesman, Anthony H. and Nerguizian, Aram, 'The Egypt Military and the Arab-Israeli Military Balance: Conventional Realities and Asymmetric Challenges', February 2011. Also see the Stockholm International Peace Research Institute's tally from 1988 to 2010.

51. 'Egypt: Retry or Free 12,000 after Unfair Military Trials', Human Rights Watch, 10 September 2011; 'Work on him Until he Confesses: Impunity for Torture in Egypt', Human Rights Watch, January 2011.

52. Kamel, Ahmed, 'Egypt NGOs May Fade if Denied Foreign Funding', *Egyptian Gazette*, 28 September 2011.

53. Beach, Alastair, 'HSBC Accused of Helping Egypt Generals Stifle Dissent', *Independent*, 31 October 2011, www.independent.co.uk/news/world/africa/hsbc-accused-of-helping-egypt-generals-stifle-dissent–6255002.html (accessed 12 November 2011).

54. Zayed, Dina and Hammond, Andrew, 'Egypt State Media Changes Tune After Mubarak's Fall', 15 February 2011.

55. For a good explanation of how the elections were organized see Hassan, Mazen, 'The Effects of Egypt's Election Law', *Foreign Policy*, 1 November 2011, http://mideast. foreignpolicy.com/posts/2011/11/01/egypts_electoral_cunundrum#.TrB8ahHnKGE. Twitter (accessed 3 November 2011).

56. Osman, Tarek, *Egypt on the Brink: From Nasser to Mubarak*. London/New Haven: Yale University Press, 2010, p. 105.

57. 'Egypt Elections: Low Turnout for First-round Runoffs', BBC News, 5 December 2011.

58. 'Supra-constitutional Debate Heats up Again', Al Masry Al Youm, 3 November 2011, www.almasryalyoum.com/en/node/511527 (accessed 3 November 2011).

59. 'Fear Skyrockets as Reported Crime Holds Steady in Egypt', Abu Dhabi Gallup Center, www.abudhabigallupcenter.com/149738/fear-skyrockets-reported-crime-holds-steady-egypt.aspx (accessed 3 November 2011).

60. Mogahed, Dalia, 'Winning Back the Revolution', *Foreign Policy*, 28 November 2011.

61. See US cable by Ambassador Margaret Scobey dated September 2008 and entitled 'Academics See the Military in Decline but Retaining Strong Influence', http://wikileaks.ch/cable/2008/09/08CAIRO2091.html (accessed 2 November 2011).

62. El Gundy, Zeinab, 'Egypt's 29 July Protests Finally Named: The Friday of Unity and Popular Will', Aramonline, 27 July 2011: http://english.ahram.org.eg/News/17496.aspx (accessed 11 November 2011).

63. Shadid, Anthony, 'Islamists Flood Square in Cairo in Show of Strength', *New York Times*, 29 July 2011, www.nytimes.com/2011/07/30/world/middleeast/30egypt. html?pagewanted=1&_r=1&hp (accessed 11 November 2011).

64. Voll, John O., 'Fundamentalism in the Sunni Arab World: Egypt and the Sudan', in Marty, Martin E. and Appleby, R. Scott, *Fundamentalisms Observed*. Chicago and London: The University of Chicago Press, 1994, pp. 345–90.

65. Ibid.

66. Wright, Lawrence, 'The Man Behind Bin Laden', *New Yorker*, 16 September 2002. In his article, Wright describes the relationship between Bin Laden and Zawahri.

67. Programme of the Freedom and Justice Party 2011 (Arabic): http://hurryh.com/ Uploadedimage/files/mainsystem.pdf (accessed 11 November 2011).

68. Fadel, Leila, 'Egypt's Muslim Brotherhood Could be Unravelling', *Washington Post*, 7 July 2011, www.washingtonpost.com/world/egypts-muslim-brotherhood-could-be-unraveling/2011/07/06/gIQAdMZp1H_story_1.html (accessed 6 November 2011).

69. 'Egypt's Army Appeals for Unity after Christian Clash', Reuters, 12 October 2011.

70. Interviews with the author, and author's eyewitness account of events.

71. Interviews with the author in Cairo, October 2011.

72. 'Former Regime Remnants Instigated Maspero Violence', Ikhwanmisr, http://ikhwan-misr.org/iweb/index.php?option=com_content&view=article&id=32578:mb-chairman-to-german-press-agency-former-regime-remnants-instigated-maspero-violence&catid=10387:newsflash&Itemid=858 (accessed 5 November 2011).

73. 'Egypt Bomb Kills 21 at Alexandria Coptic Church', BBC, 1 January 2011, www.bbc. co.uk/news/world-middle-east-12101748 (accessed 6 November 2011).

74. 'Attacks on Christians in Egypt', Reuters, 10 October 2011, http://uk.reuters. com/article/2011/10/10/us-egypt-clashes-coptic-idUKTRE7992W420111010 (accessed 6 November 2011).

75. Zayan, Jailan, 'Egypt Warns of "Iron Hand" to Halt Religious Unrest', AFP, 7 May 2011.

76. Osman, Tarek, *Egypt on the Brink: From Nasser to Mubarak*. London/New Haven: Yale University Press, 2010, pp. 155–8.

77. The Salafist Noor Party denied covering up the statue but a banner clearly bears its logo and the party was holding a rally nearby. A photograph appeared in the independent newspaper *Al-Masry Al-Youm*, www.almasryalyoum.com/en/node/511759 (accessed 6 November 2011).

78. Interview with the author in Cairo, October 2011.

79. According to interviews with women's rights activists in Cairo, October 2011.

80. For a full interview with Ibrahim and an account of the case, see Deasy, Kristin, 'Egypt: Samira v. the military', *Global Post*, 23 October 2011, www.globalpost.com/dispatch/news/regions/middle-east/egypt/111023/egypt-samira-vs-the-military (accessed 7 November 2011).

81. Interview with the author, January 2012.

82. According to figures published by Egypt's Central Agency for Public Mobilization and Statistics, www.capmas.gov.eg/pages_ar.aspx?pageid=1317 (accessed 7 November 2011); 'Egypt's Tourism Revenue to Suffer 25 pct Drop in 2011, Minister Says', Reuters, 10 April 2011.

83. According to figures published by Egypt's Central Agency for Public Mobilization and Statistics, www.capmas.gov.eg/pages_ar.aspx?pageid=1317 (accessed 7 November 2011).

84. Egyptian Ministry of Finance, the Financial Monthly, October 2011, www.mof.gov.eg/MOFGallerySource/English/Reports/monthly/2011/Oct2011/a-b.pdf (accessed 7 November 2011).

85. CAPMAS figures.

86. According to figures from the Central Bank of Egypt (accessed 12 November 2011).

87. According to interview by the author with Adel Zakaria, spokesman for CTWUS union movement, October 2011.

88. Interview with the authors, Cairo, January 2012.

Chapter 6: Bahrain: An Island Divided

1. Cited in Heard-Bey, Frauke, *From Trucial States to United Arab Emirates*, p. 338.

2. Friday sermon by Issa Qasim attended by the author on 25 March 2011.

3. According to the accounts of those living in the neighbouring building, who showed the author the room where Abdulaziz was found.

4. According to former parliament members from Wefaq who gave the author a list of missing people in March. Many more were later arrested.

5. Figures given by Interior Minister Sheikh Rashid bin Abdallah Al Khalifa in speech to parliament. See Sambidge, Andy. 'Bahrain Minister Says 24 people Dead in Uprising', *Arabian Business*, 29 March 2011, www.arabianbusiness.com/bahrain-minister-says-24-people-dead-in-uprisings-390813.html (accessed 21 November 2011).

6. Neighbours interviewed by the author on 25 March 2011 described the concerns about taking the wounded to hospital. The author also interviewed several doctors from Salmaniya hospital who described the conditions they had worked under. See Noueihed, Lin, 'Bahrain Doctors, Casualties Caught up in Crackdown', Reuters, 21 March 2011.

7. See 'Bahrain: Investigate Shooting, Arrest of Man Caught up in Police Sweep', Human Rights Watch, 23 March 2011.

8. See 'A House Divided: The Scars from Bahrain's Protests are Still Felt on the Pitch', *Economist*, 13 August 2011, www.economist.com/node/21525932 (accessed 21 November 2011).

9. According to Mansour Jamri, editor-in-chief of *Al-Wasat*, March 2011.

10. Ibid. Also see 'Bahrain newspaper editors fined over unrest,' Reuters, 11 October 2011.

11. Interview with the author, March 2011.

12. Author's eyewitness account, March 2011.

13. Interview with the author, March 2011.

14. Cole, Juan R., *Sacred Space and Holy War: the Politics, Culture and History of Shi'ite Islam*, London: I.B. Tauris, 2002, pp.1–10.

15. Ibid.

16. Louer, Laurence, *Transnational Shia Politics: Religious and Political Networks in the Gulf*, New York: Columbia University Press, 2008, pp. 11–28.

17. Ibid., pp. 1–28.

18. Khuri, Fuad I., *Tribe and State in Bahrain: The Transformation of Social and Political Authority in an Arab State*, Chicago and London: University of Chicago Press, 1980, pp. 2–4.

19. Al-Baharna, Husain M., 'Iran's Claim to Sovereignty over Bahrain and the Resolution of the Anglo-Iranian Dispute over Bahrain', Shaikh Ebrahim bin Mohammed Al Khalifa Center for Culture and Research, 2008.

20. For more on Al Khalifa's system of rule and the challenges it faced see Khalaf, Abdulhadi, 'Contentious Politics in Bahrain: From Ethnic to National and Vice Versa', paper given at the fourth Nordic Conference on Middle Eastern Studies: The Middle East in a Globalizing World, Oslo, 13–16 August 1998, www.hf.uib.no/smi/pao/khalaf. html (accessed 22 November 2011).

21. Al-Baharna, Husain M., 'Iran's Claim to Sovereignty over Bahrain and the Resolution of the Anglo-Iranian Dispute over Bahrain', Shaikh Ebrahim bin Mohammed Al Khalifa Center for Culture and Research, 2008.

22. For more on the role of Shia in political activism in Bahrain see al-Mdaires, Falah, 'Shi'ism and Political Protest in Bahrain', *Domes* 11(1), Spring 2002, p. 20.

23. Razavi, Ahmed, Continental Shelf Delimitation and Related Maritime Issues in the Persian Gulf, *Publications on Ocean Development*, The Hague/Boston/London: Martinus Nijhoff Publishers, 1997, pp. 122–8.

24. See DeAngelis, Jackie, 'Bahrain's Saudi Links Vital to Economy: Minister', CNBC, 27 July 2011.

25. See official website of King Fahd Causeway Authority, www.kfca.com.sa/en/pages. aspx?pageid=288 (accessed 17 November 2011).

26. For instance, Najaf-based but Iranian born cleric Ali al-Sistani was instrumental in encouraging Iraqi Shi'ites to cast their ballots in that country's first elections after the ouster of Saddam Hussein even though he does not possess the Iraqi nationality that would allow him to vote in that country himself.

27. This question of loyalty to a *marjaa taqlid* is openly discussed by Sunnis in Bahrain and elsewhere.

28. For the activists' perspective on the plot, see this interview with Saudi Shi'ite activist Fouad Ibrahim: Abedin, Mahan, 'Saudi Shi'ites: New light on an old divide', *Asia Times*, 26 October 2006, www.atimes.com/atimes/Middle_East/HJ26Ak02.html (accessed 29 November). For an outline of the key political groups operating in Bahrain before and after the 2011 revolt, see 'Popular Protests in the Middle East and North Africa III: The Bahrain Revolt', Crisis Group Middle East/North Africa Report No. 105, 6 April 2011.

29. See 'Gulf states see threat from Iran', Reuters, 25 February 1982. For a detailed analysis of attacks and the move towards collective GCC security, also see Ramazani, Rouhollah, K. and Kechichian, Joseph A., *The Gulf Cooperation Council: Record and Analysis*, University of Virginia Press, 1988, pp. 33–8.

30. Qubain, Fahim I., 'Social Classes and Tensions in Bahrain', *Middle East Journal* 9(3), Summer 1955, pp. 269–71.

31. Interview with the author in Bahrain, March 2011.

32. Khuri, Fuad I., *Tribe and State in Bahrain: The Transformation of Social and Political Authority in an Arab State*, Chicago and London: University of Chicago Press, 1980.

33. Accounts of how the 1990s uprising began differ, with some authors citing the stoning of runners participating in a race that went past some conservative Shi'ite areas where demonstrators objected to the runners' attire. Other accounts cite the unemployment picket but the push for the restoration of the constitution had started before either of these incidents.

34. For more on the role of Shia in political activism in Bahrain, see al-Mdaires, Falah. 'Shi'ism and Political Protest in Bahrain', *Domes* 11(1), Spring 2002, p. 20. Also see Fakhro, Munira A., 'The Uprising in Bahrain: An Assessment', in *The Persian Gulf at the Millennium: Essays in Politics, Economy, Security, and Religion*, eds. Gary G. Sick and Lawrence G. Potter, New York: St. Martin's Press, 1997, pp. 167–88.

35. Notice, for instance, the excitement in blogger Mahmood Al Youssef's 2003 blog, which would be far more critical of the royal family by the end of the decade, at http://mahmood.tv/2003/12/28/Sitra-starts-to-breathe/

36. Parolin, Gianluca Paolo. 'Generations of Gulf Constitutions: Paths and Perspectives', pp. 65–70, in Khalaf, Abdulhadi and Luciani, Giacomo (eds), *Constitutional Reform and Political Participation in the Gulf*, Dubai: Gulf Research Center, 2006.

37. See National Action Charter 2001, www.pogar.org/publications/other/constitutions/bahrain-charter–01e.pdf (accessed 21 November 2011).

38. Kapiszewski, Andrzej, 'Elections and Parliamentary Activity in the GCC States: Broadening Political Participation in the Gulf Monarchies', pp. 108–10, in Khalaf, Abdulhadi and Luciani, Giacomo (eds), *Constitutional Reform and Political Participation in the Gulf*, Dubai: Gulf Research Center, 2006.

39. Parolin, Gianluca Paolo, 'Generations of Gulf Constitutions: Paths and Perspectives', pp. 65–70 in Khalaf, Abdulhadi and Luciani, Giacomo (eds), *Constitutional Reform and Political Participation in the Gulf*, Dubai: Gulf Research Center, 2006.

40. See 2002 constitution of Bahrain on ConstitutionNet, www.constitutionnet.org/files/Bahrain%20Constitution.pdf (accessed 21 November 2011).

41. Kapiszewski, Andrzej, 'Elections and Parliamentary Activity in the GCC States: Broadening Political Participation in the Gulf Monarchies', pp. 108–10 in Khalaf, Abdulhadi and Luciani, Giacomo (eds), *Constitutional Reform and Political Participation in the Gulf*, Dubai: Gulf Research Center, 2006.

42. Al-Derazi, Abdellah, 'Old Players and New in the Bahraini Elections', *Sada: Analysis on Arab Reform*, Carnegie Endowment for International Peace, 2 June 2011.

43. Opposition activists openly accuse the prime minister of corruption, which will be discussed in more detail later in the chapter. The prime minister's opposition to reform during the 2000s is well documented. It spilled into the open in 2008, when the king, urged by his son, the crown prince, was forced to step in and ask the government to cooperate with a body leading economic reforms.

44. According to a member of the royal family who spoke off the record.

45. Sager, Abdulaziz, 'End the Saudi-Bahrain FTA Row', Gulf Research Center, 1 January 2005, www.grc.ae/?frm_module=contents&frm_action=detail_book&sec=Contents&override=Articles%20%3E%20End%20the%20Saudi-Bahrain%20FTA%20Row&book_id=18463&op_lang=en (accessed 9 January 2012).

46. Fattah, Hassan, 'Report Cites Bid by Sunnis in Bahrain to Rig Elections', *International Herald Tribune*, 2 October 2006, www.nytimes.com/2006/10/02/world/africa/02iht-web.1002bahrain.2997505.html (accessed 29 November 2011).

47. Hamada, Suad, 'Bahrain Grants Citizenship to 7,012 People', *Khaleej Times*, 3 December 2008, www.khaleejtimes.com/DisplayArticleNew.asp?section—iddleeast&xfile=data/middleeast/2008/december/middleeast_december31.xml (accessed 29 November 2011).

48. 'Bahrain's Sectarian Challenge', Crisis Group Middle East Report, No. 40, 6 May 2005, pp. 8–9.

49. One leaked US embassy cable quotes a Shia cleric claiming 100,000 people had been naturalized for political reasons. It casts doubt on this figure, quoting an Al Wefaq official giving a number closer to 38,000. See Monroe, William, 'Prominent Shia

Paint Gloomy Picture of Shia Outlook in Bahrain', US embassy cable, WikiLeaks, 2007, http://wikileaks.org/cable/2007/04/07MANAMA328.html#par4 (accessed 29 November 2011).

50. Ereli, Adam, 'Opposition Protest Highlights Political Naturalization', US embassy Manama, WikiLeaks, 2009, http://wikileaks.org/cable/2009/11/09MANAMA639.html (accessed 29 November 2009).

51. Nakhle, Emile, *Bahrain: Political Development in a Modernizing Society*, Lanham/Boulder: Lexington Books, 2011, pp. 153–5.

52. 'Bahrain's Sectarian Challenge', Crisis Group Middle East Report, No. 40, 6 May 2005, pp. 8–9.

53. Monroe, William, 'Prominent Shias Paint Gloomy Picture of Shia', US Embassy Manama, WikiLeaks, 2007, http://wikileaks.org/cable/2007/04/07MANAMA328.html#par4 (accessed 30 November 2011).

54. 'Bahrain's Sectarian Challenge', Crisis Group Middle East Report, No. 40, 6 May 2005, pp. 8–9. Also a common complaint of protesters, one of whom said the royals behaved as if Rifaa was 'a slice of heaven' by not allowing Shi'ites to buy land there.

55. Central Informatics Organization, www.cio.gov.bh/StatPublication/11RecurrentRequest/AdjPop2001–2007.pdf and www.cio.gov.bh/cio_ara/English/Publications/Statistical%20Abstract/ABS2009/Ch2/2.37J.pdf (accessed 29 November 2011); Ereli, Adam, 'It Doesn't Add up: Shia MP Challenges GOB Population Figures', US Embassy Manama, 8 February 2008, www.telegraph.co.uk/news/wikileaks-files/bahrain-wikileaks-cables/8334481/IT-DOESNT-ADD-UP-SHIA-MP-CHALLENGES-GOB-POPULATION-FIGURES.html (accessed 30 November 2011).

56. Crabtree, Steve, 'Housing Shortage Stands out Among Bahrain's Woes', Gallup, 31 March 2011, www.gallup.com/poll/146912/housing-shortage-stands-among-bahrain-woes.aspx (accessed 28 November 2011).

57. 'Bahrain Announces $5.32 Billion Home Plan', AFP in *Khaleej Times*, 9 March 2011, www.khaleejtimes.com/DisplayArticleNew.asp?xfile=/data/middleeast/2011/March/middleeast_March160.xml&section—iddleeast (accessed 30 November 2011).

58. Interviews with the author, March 2011.

59. Ibid.

60. 'Bahrain National Guard to Recruit Former Soldiers from Pak', *Deccan Herald*, 11 March 2011, www.deccanherald.com/content/144961/bahrain-national-guard-recruit-former.html (accessed 29 November 2011).

61. The Saudis were open about their concerns. See for instance, 'Saudi king expresses support for Mubarak', Reuters, 29 January 2011, and 'Saudi minister denounces foreign meddling in Egypt,' Reuters, 10 February 2011. Some analysts have also said the Saudis feared losing Egypt as another ally against Iranian influence.

62. According to a source in regular contact with the crown prince during this period.

63. Author's eyewitness account.

64. For instance, blogger Mahmoud al-Yousef warned of civil war in his blog Mahmoud's Den.

65. Central Department of Statistics and Information, 2007. Also see Sfakianakis, John, 'Saudi Youth Struggle to Find Work Raises Urgency for Reform', *Arab News*, 17 February 2011.

66. Robinson, Simon, 'Special Report: US Cables Details Saudi Royal Welfare Programme', Reuters, 28 February 2011.

67. See 'Bahrain opposition says met Crown Prince on dialogue', Reuters, 14 March 2011.

68. According to a source in regular contact with the crown prince during this period.

69. See Noueihed, Lin, 'Bahrain Bans Lebanon Travel, Sectarian Tension Rises', Reuters, 22 March 2011.

70. See 'Bahrain says Iran Complaints Harm Gulf Security', Reuters, 17 March 2011. Also see 'Bahrain: Suspects say had Contact with Iran', Reuters, 13 November 2011 and 'Iran says Bahrain Plot Claim "baseless"', Reuters, 14 November 2011.

71. See, for instance, this interview on Ahlulbayt on 29 March 2011: www.youtube.com/watch?v—il7GuA1VkY (accessed 21 November 2011).
72. Interviews with the author in Bahrain in March 2011.
73. Hammond, Andrew, 'Bahrain King Approves Reforms, Opposition Rejects', Reuters, 28 July 2011.
74. Based on interviews with Bahrainis familiar with the candidates' backgrounds.
75. See 'Report of the Bahrain Independent Commission of Inquiry,' released 23 November 2011. The full BIC report is available at www.bici.org.bh (accessed 22 January 2012).
76. 'Bahrain hires British ex-top cop for reforms-report', Reuters, 3 December 2011.
77. 'US lawmakers seek to block US arms sales to Bahrain', Reuters, 8 October 2011.
78. Louer, Laurence, *Transnational Shia Politics: Religious and Political Networks in the Gulf*, New York: Columbia University Press, 2008, pp. 1–28.
79. Laessing, Ulf, 'Shi'ite Mosque Demolitions Raise Tension in Bahrain', Reuters, 22 April 2011.

Chapter 7: Libya's Revolution from Above

1. Schwartzman's visit was mentioned in 'Private Equity Firms Beat Path to Tripoli', *Financial Times*, 18 March 2009. Bashir visited Libya numerous times in the 2000s, as reported by state news agencies.
2. 'BP Agrees Major Exploration and Production Deal with Libya', BP Press Release, 29 May 2007, www.bp.com/genericarticle.do?categoryId=2012968&contentId=7033600
3. Original motives for Libyan involvement include France's support for Chad during the Libyan-Chad war of the time. In July 2011 former foreign minister Abderrahman Shalgam said they had blown it up because they (incorrectly) believed that Mohammed al-Megrief, then leader of the National Front for the Salvation of Libya (NFSL) was on board flight UTA 772.
4. 'French Air Force Rafales Attack Libya', *Aviation News*, 19 March 2011.
5. 'Tripoli Real Estate 2008' report by Frontier MEA, 2008.
6. Ibid.
7. UNCTAD World Investment Report 2010.
8. Libyan Ministry of Tourism and Handicrafts, obtained by Frontier MEA. Arrivals rose from 23,029 in 2003 to 125,480 in 2006. Figures refer to non-Libyans arriving specifically on tourist visas (rather than business visas).
9. www.telegraph.co.uk/news/worldnews/1561031/Gaddafis-son-calls-for-new-Libyan-constitution.html
10. This was reported in some international media, for instance http://af.reuters.com/article/libyaNews/idAFLDE70H1PK20110118
11. Interview with the author, 2010.
12. Report is listed by Human Rights Watch at www.hrw.org/en/news/2010/02/11/postcard-fromtripoli
13. As reported in the media, e.g. by AFP at www.canada.com/montrealgazette/story.html?id=e9214aea-d552–4f1b-ba51–1e5e943fac37
14. As quoted in www.guardian.co.uk/world/2010/feb/25/muammar-gaddafi-libya
15. 'Verenex Shareholders Approve Libya Takeover Deal', Reuters, 11 December 2009.
16. As related by the tourism official to the author in late 2010.
17. First-hand research by the author in 2010.
18. As recalled by a passenger who was on the flight and reported at www.businesstraveller.com/news/airlines-cancel-tripoli-flights
19. 'Libya's Gaddafi says Tunisia's ouster was too hasty', Reuters, 16 January 2011.
20. Transcription of Saif's speech on 20 February 2011 is at http://mylogicoftruth.wordpress.com/2011/02/20/full-text-of-saif-gaddafis-speech/
21. Belhadj launched a lawsuit against the British government in late 2011. His claims appeared widely in the press. See, for instance, 'Libyan commander Abdelhakim

Belhadj withdraws cooperation from British torture enquiry', *Daily Telegraph*, 12 January 2012.

22. Author's experience.

23. Author's visit to Benghazi, late 2010.

24. As cited at http://news.bbc.co.uk/1/hi/world/africa/4726204.stm (accessed 15 September 2011).

25. See, for instance, 'Sarkozy's Libyan surprise', *Economist*, 14 March 2011.

26. Henri-Levy made the comment in a 14 March interview with Al-Jazeera English, accessible online at www.youtube.com/watch?v—-tAmkKRVME.

27. As reported on 5 March in *Le Parisien*, www.leparisien.fr/election-presidentielle–2012/sondage-presidentielle-marine-le-pen-en-tete-au-premier-tour–05–03–2011–1344656.php

28. The rally took place in Nabatieh, southern Lebanon, in August 2008. It was reported in Lebanon's *Daily Star* at www.dailystar.com.lb/News/Politics/Sep/01/Berri-flays-Gadhafi-over-Sadrs-disappearance.ashx#axzz1ZdEKyNvS.

29. A transcript of Gates' speech can be found at http://blogs.wsj.com/washwire/2011/06/10/transcript-of-defense-secretary-gatess-speech-on-natos-future/

30. Press Statement issued on 19 March 2011, quoted in numerous sources, e.g. www.almasryalyoum.com/en/node/366790

31. Author's experience.

32. 'Libye: Seif al-Islam Kaddafi commence a parler', *Jeune Afrique*, 29 December 2011 (accessed 30 December 2011).

33. 'Nato Must Target Gaddafi Regime, Says Armed Forces Chief Gen Sir David Richards', *Daily Telegraph*, 14 May 2011.

34. Author's experience, April–May 2011.

35. Ibid.

36. There are conflicting death tolls, some higher, some lower. This one was issued by the interim health minister on 8 September 2011, reported at www.tripolipost.com/articledetail.asp?c=1&i=6862

37. See, for instance, 'Al-Jazeera footage captures "Western troops on the ground" in Libya', *Guardian*, 30 May 2011.

38. 'Qatar Fielded Hundreds of Soldiers in Libya', *Al-Ahram*, 26 October 2011, http://english.ahram.org.eg/NewsContent/2/8/25193/World/Region/Qatar-fielded-hundreds-of-soldiers-in-Libya.aspx (accessed 15 November 2011).

39. According to author's interview with Amazigh rebels in western mountains, and see, for instance, Black, Ian, 'Qatar admits sending hundreds of troops to support Libyan rebels', *Guardian*, 26 October 2011.

40. 'Holding Libya Together – Security Challenges after Qaddafi', International Crisis Group, December 2011.

41. Several such videos and photos were uploaded onto various internet sites. One graphic frame-by-frame analysis is at www.globalpost.com/dispatch/news/regions/middle-east/111024/gaddafi-sodomized-video-gaddafi-sodomy

Chapter 8: Disintegrating Yemen

1. Small Arms Survey 2007. Yemen is ranked second worldwide.

2. Author's visit in 2007.

3. Brian Whitaker, *The Birth of Modern Yemen*, Chapter 1. Published as an eBook in 2009: www.al-bab.com

4. US embassy cable released by WikiLeaks, www.guardian.co.uk/world/2011/apr/08/saudi-arabia-yemen-ali-mohsen

5. BP Statistical World Handbook 2011.

6. Yemen Armed Violence Assessment, Small Arms Survey, Issue Brief 2, October 2010.

7. 'Yemen: Towards Qat Demand Reduction', World Bank report, June 2007.

8. UNDP International Human Development Indicators, http://hdrstats.undp.org/en/countries/profiles/YEM.html (accessed 15 September 2011).
9. Congressional testimony by Petraeus on 13 September 2011 to Joint House-Senate Intelligence Committee, www.telegraph.co.uk/news/worldnews/al-qaeda/8760342/Al-Qaeda-in-Arabian-Peninsula-most-dangerous.html
10. Human Rights Watch.
11. Interview with the authors, October 2011.
12. Quoted in the *New York Times*, www.nytimes.com/2011/07/24/magazine/yemen-on-the-brink-of-hell.html?pagewanted=all (accessed 17 September 2011).
13. As reported at www.reuters.com/article/2011/03/18/us-yemen-idUSTRE72H2Z720110318
14. 'Saleh Orders Rival Tribal Chief's Arrest', Al-Jazeera International, 26 May 2011, http://english.aljazeera.net/news/middleeast/2011/05/201152691014710948.html
15. Interview with the authors, 29 September 2011.
16. Ibid.
17. Details at www.asharq-e.com/news.asp?section=3&id=23755
18. The Arabic translation of the interview was published by the International Centre for the Study of Radicalisation and Political Violence, accessed at www.icsr.info
19. As reported in Human Rights Watch report,www.hrw.org/news/2011/07/09/yemen-dozens-civilians-killed-southern-fighting
20. 'UNHCR Worried About Refugees and Displaced People in Strife-torn Yemen', 3 June 2011, www.unhcr.org/4de8ec1d6.html (accessed 19 September 2011).
21. Some details on 2010 pro-secession protests at www.upi.com/Top_News/Special/2010/04/28/Yemen-Secession-drive-becomes-violent/UPI–12361272477397/
22. Referenced in 'Breaking Point – Yemen's Southern Question', International Crisis Group, 20 October 2011.
23. Interview with the authors, 3 November 2011.
24. 'Yemen: Fragile Lives in Hungry Times', Oxfam briefing paper, September 2011.
25. Ibid.

Chapter 9: The Struggle for Syria

1. This translation was published by the official Syrian state news agency, SANA, at www.sana.sy/eng/337/2011/06/21/353686.htm (accessed 17 November 2011).
2. 'War is Only Option to Topple Syrian Leader: Colonel', Reuters, 7 October 2011.
3. Cited in Seale, Patrick, *Asad, the Struggle for the Middle East*, University of California Press, 1989, p. 40.
4. The pupil was Mohammed ibn Nusayr. The Alawites were and still are sometimes called Nusayris.
5. Salah Jadid remained in prison from 1970 until his death in 1993. Muhammed Umran was shot dead in 1972. Abdel Karim al-Jundi killed himself in 1962. Ahmad al-Mir had been sent to Madrid as ambassador in 1968.
6. The co-founders of the party were Salaheddin Bitar and Michel Aflaq. Both had previously been schoolteachers in Damascus.
7. The cleric was Imam Moussa al-Sadr, the spiritual founder of Lebanon's Shi'ite Muslim *Amal* movement, who disappeared in Libya in 1978.
8. The 1973 constitution did, however, state that Islam was the source of jurisprudence. An English translation of the document is available at www.servat.unibe.ch/icl/sy00000_.html
9. Cited in Seale, Patrick, *Asad, the Struggle for the Middle East*, University of California Press, 1989, p. 171.
10. Reporters Without Borders website: http://en.rsf.org/press-freedom-index–2010,1034.html (accessed 23 November 2011).

11. Average production fell from about 575,000 barrels per day (b/d) in the late 1990s to around 375,000 b/d in the late 2000s, according to the BP Statistical Review of World Energy, 2011.

12. Interview in Damascus with the author in 2008.

13. In 2001 Ghassan al-Rifai, a former World Bank executive, was appointed as Minister of Economy and Foreign Trade. Ali Kanaa, an economist, was put in charge of the state-owned Industrial Bank, while the French-educated Sadallah Agha al-Qalaa became Minister of Tourism.

14. The first ATMs were opened in 2001 by the Real Estate Bank: www.albawaba.com/business/first-atm-machine-opens-syria

15. Damascus Securities Exchange website: www.dse.sy

16. 'Syria Among Fastest-growing Tourist Destinations in Mideast', SANA news agency, 5 April 2011, www.sana.sy/eng/33/2011/04/05/339958.htm (accessed 18 November 2011).

17. Interview with the author, 2010.

18. Cited in Blanford, Nicholas, *Killing Mr Lebanon*. I.B. Tauris, 2006, pp. 89–90.

19. Syrian Central Bureau of Statistics figures, accessed through: www.cbssyr.org

20. Central Bureau of Statistics, 2010 Statistical Abstract.

21. Ibid., www.cbssyr.org/yearbook/2010/Data-Chapter15/TAB-5-15-2010.htm

22. Interview with the author, 2006.

23. The full text of the resolution can be found on the UN website at www.un.org/News/Press/docs/2004/sc8181.doc.htm.

24. 'Interview with Syrian president Bashar al-Assad', *Wall Street Journal*, 31 January 2011.

25. A video of the protest can be seen at www.youtube.com/watch?v=i41MjEGqprI (accessed 20 November 2011).

26. 'Inside Deraa', Al-Jazeera, 19 April 2011, www.aljazeera.com/indepth/features/2011/04/201141918352728300.html

27. 'Syrian City of Deraa Hit by Protests', BBC News, 24 April 2011, www.bbc.co.uk/news/world-13016843

28. 'Rami Makhlouf Sells Syrian Duty-free Businesses', *Duty Free News International*, 20 June 2011.

29. 'Makhlouf to Focus on Charity', *Syria Today*, July 2011, www.syria-today.com/index.php/july-2011/838-business-news/16152-makhlouf-to-focus-on-charity

30. 'Syria Opens up to Social Networks', BBC News, 11 February 2011.

31. 'Instigating Channels Lacking Coverage of Raising Largest Syrian Flag Betrays their Involvement in Conspiracy', www.sana.sy/eng/337/2011/06/15/352885.htm (accessed 23 November 2011).

32. Interview with the author, November 2011.

33. 'Syria Faces More International Pressure after Assad Speaks', Bloomberg, 21 June 2011.

34. 'Background Note: Syria', US State Department, 18 March 2011: http://www.state.gov/r/pa/ei/bgn/3580.htm (accessed 20 September 2011).

35. Bhalla, Reva. 'Making Sense of the Syrian Crisis', Stratfor Global Intelligence, 5 May 2011: www.stratfor.com/weekly/20110504-making-sense-syrian-crisis?utm_source=GWeekly&utm_medium=email&utm_campaign=110505&utm_content=readmore&elq=2ef73758a9434404bd465acd3490d5fe#ixzz1LTPFUuuw (accessed 20 September 2011).

36. 'Syria's Military: What does Assad Have?', Reuters, 6 April 2011 (accessed 20 September 2011).

37. Bhalla, Reva. 'Making Sense of the Syrian Crisis', Stratfor Global Intelligence, 5 May 2011, www.stratfor.com/weekly/20110504-making-sense-syrian-crisis?utm_source=GWeekly&utm_medium=email&utm_campaign=110505&utm_content=readmore&elq=2ef73758a9434404bd465acd3490d5fe#ixzz1LTPFUuuw (accessed 20 September 2011).

38. While there are no official figures on the size of the various minorities, the two provinces of Lattakia and Tartous had a combined population of 2.1 million in 2010, about 9 per cent of the total, according to official statistics. When taking into account the Sunni and Christian population in those provinces, plus the Alawites in other parts of the country, it seemed unlikely that Alawites made up no more than about 10 per cent of Syria's population.

39. Noueihed, Lin, 'Exclusive: Second Arab monitor may quit Syria over violence', Reuters, 11 January 2012.

40. Syrian Central Bureau of Statistics.

41. Hourani, Albert, *A History of the Arab Peoples*. London: Faber and Faber, paperback edition 2002, p. 454.

42. 'Christian Support for the Ba'athists', Al-Arabiya, 27 November 2011, www.alarabiya. net/views/2011/11/27/179364.html

43. 'Kurds Step into Syria's Protest Mix', *Wall Street Journal*, 10 October 2011, http://online. wsj.com/article/SB10001424052970203499704576620443224171146.html

44. 'Syrians Would Support Turkish Intervention – Brotherhood Leader', Reuters, 17 November 2011.

45. Interview with Hala Jaber in the *Sunday Times*, 20 November 2011.

46. 'Syrian Elite to Fight Protests to "The End"', *New York Times*, 10 May 2011, www. nytimes.com/2011/05/11/world/middleeast/11makhlouf.html?pagewanted=all (accessed 24 November 2011).

47. 'US Criticizes Syria for "Cynical" Golan Heights Incident', *VOA News*, 17 May 2011, www.voanews.com/english/news/middle-east/in-transition/US-Criticizes-Syria-for-Cynical-Golan-Heights-Incident–121985054.html (accessed 24 November 2011).

48. 'Israel Sees Syrian Hand in Golan Clashes, 23 dead', Reuters, 6 June 2011.

49. 'Muslim Brotherhood Breaks with Khaddam and NSF', Syria Comment, 6 April 2009, www.joshualandis.com/blog/?p=2627 (accessed 1 December 2011).

50. 'Assad under Pressure from Qatar Embassy Closure, EU', Reuters, 18 July 2011.

51. 'Shell, Total Cut Syrian Oil Output amid Sanctions', Reuters, 11 November 2011.

Chapter 10: The Kings' Dilemma

1. Population figures according to the UAE National Bureau of Statistics 2005 census. The population has risen significantly since then.

2. Some 6,700 UAE nationals were given the vote in 2006. For the elections of 2011, coming after the Arab uprisings and amid growing domestic calls for wider suffrage, 129,000 nationals were given the vote.

3. 'Dubai sets a 7% rent cap for 2007 to curb inflation', Reuters, 1 January 2007.

4. Dubai Statistics Center, Household Income and Expenditure Survey, 2009.

5. From author's interview with UAE then-Minister of State for the Federal National Council, Anwar Gergash, published by Reuters, 22 November 2006.

6. Qatar Statistics Authority, www.qsa.gov.qa/QatarCensus/HistoryOfCensus.aspx on 7 October 2011.

7. Kuwait census agency, www.kuwaitcensus.com

8. UAE Statistics Bureau (the number of Emiratis at end of June 2011 was 948,000 out of a total population of 7.3 million); Central Statistical Bureau of Kuwait, at www.kuwait-census.com (accessed 15 October 2011).

9. Oil and gas revenue figure taken from Qatar Central Bank, 2010 Annual Report. Qataris are estimated to account for 14 per cent of the total population of 1,069,756 recorded in the 2010 census.

10. Kuwait Census statistics, IMF World Economic Database. Author's own calculations based on 2008 figure of Kuwaiti nationals.

11. As reported in http://gulfnews.com/news/gulf/qatar/public-sector-in-qatar-to-get–60-per-cent-pay-rise–1.862595 (accessed 12 September 2011).

12. 'UAE: Government Detains Human Rights Defender', Human Rights Watch press release, 9 April 2011, www.hrw.org/en/news/2011/04/09/uae-government-detains-human-rights-defender (accessed on 14 October 2011).

13. Taken from page 5 of the UAE constitution, available online at www.unhcr.org/refworld/category,LEGAL,,,ARE,48eca8132,0.html (accessed 14 October 2011).

14. The original petition in Arabic is available at www.ipetitions.com/petition/uaepetition71/; Ibtissam Ketbi, as quoted in the *Wall Street Journal* article 'UAE Citizens Petition Rulers for Elected Parliament', 9 March 2011, at http://online.wsj.com/article/SB10001424052748704132204576190012553500944.html (accessed 14 October 2011).

15. 'UAE: Activists Arrested for Opposing Government', Human Rights Watch, 25 April 2011, www.hrw.org/news/2011/04/25/uae-activists-arrested-opposing-government

16. 'UAE: Trial Observer Says Case Against "UAE5" has been Grossly Unfair', Amnesty International, 3 November 2011.

17. BP Statistical Review of World Energy 2011. Production was 865,000 b/d in 2010 compared to 813,000 in 2009 and 754,000 in 2008.

18. Oman Central Bank, Annual Report 2010. Debt was about 5 per cent of GDP in 2010.

19. 'Oman to Spend $2.6bn to Satisfy Protest Demands', Reuters, 17 April 2011.

20. Oman Census 2010 preliminary results.

21. 'Deaths in Oman Protests', Al-Jazeera English, 27 February 2011, http://english.aljazeera.net/news/middleeast/2011/02/2011227112850852905.html (accessed 12 October 2011).

22. 'Oman Protesters Call for Political Reform, Pay Rise', Reuters, 19 February 2011, www.reuters.com/article/2011/02/19/us-oman-protests-idUSTRE71I0V920110219

23. 'Oman Police Kill 2 Protesters, Sultan Offers Jobs', Reuters, 27 February 2011.

24. Jordan received soft loans and grants worth more than $1 billion in 2010. Central Bank of Jordan, Annual Report 2010, www.cbj.gov.jo (accessed 30 September 2011).

25. Central Bank of Jordan, Annual Report 2010.

26. Ibid.

27. According to official Jordanian government figures, in the final quarter of 2010, the male unemployment rate was 10 per cent compared to 20.1 per cent among females. Overall unemployment was 11.9 per cent in the final quarter of 2010, www.dos.gov.jo/dos_home_e/archive/emp_12_2010.pdf

28. Combined current and capital expenditure rose from SR285.2 billion in 2004 to SR596.4 billion in 2009, according to the Saudi Arabian Monetary Agency, Annual Report 2010, Statistical Appendix; cited in 'Saudi Arabia's coming oil and fiscal challenge' Jadwa Investment, July 2011.

29. Carey, Glen. 'Saudi Arabia's economy will expand 5.3% on oil prices, NCB says', Bloomberg, 15 May 2011.

30. April 2010 government census listed 27.1 million people. Assuming continued growth, it is likely to have reached close to 28 million by 2012.

31. 'Saudi Arabia's Coming Oil and Fiscal Challenge', a report published by the Riyadh-based Jadwa investment bank, July 2011.

32. 'Airport Highway to Become Kingdom's First Toll Road', *Jordan Times*, 6 October 2011 (accessed 13 October 2011). The other toll roads in the region are in Dubai and Tunisia.

33. 'GCC Agrees Five-year Aid Plan for Morocco and Jordan', the *National*, 13 September 2011, http://www.thenational.ae/news/worldwide/middle-east/gcc-agrees-five-year-aid-plan-for-morocco-and-jordan

34. 'Tiny Kingdom's Huge Role in Libya Draws Concern', *Wall Street Journal*, 17 October 2011, http://online.wsj.com/article/SB10001424052970204002304576627000922764650.html

35. Comments were translated from the Arabic and reported at http://blog.foreignpolicy.com/posts/2011/11/04/libyan_diplomat_unloads_on_qatar

36. 'King Abdullah Interview Transcript', *Washington Post*, 16 June 2011, www.washington-post.com/national/national-security/king-abdullah-interview-transcript/2011/06/15/AGHQpjWH_story.html (accessed 25 September 2011).

Chapter 11: The Islamist Resurgence

1. From Ghannouchi's *Al-Hurriyat al-'Amma fid-Dawla al-Islamiyya* as quoted in Tamimi, Azsam S., *Rachid Ghannouchi: A Democrat within Islamism*, Oxford University Press, Oxford, 2001.

2. For a thorough examination of Algeria's revolution and the army takeover, see Evans, Martin and Phillips, John, *Algeria: Anger of the Dispossessed*, New Haven and London: Yale University Press, 2007.

3. Ibid., p. 150.

4. Kirkpatrick, David, 'Military flexes its muscles as Islamists gain in Egypt', *New York Times*, 7 December 2011, www.nytimes.com/2011/12/08/world/middleeast/egyptian-general-mukhtar-al-mulla-asserts-continuing-control-despite-elections.html?_r=1&pagewanted=all (accessed 25 January 2012).

5. Many articles appeared, mostly from the second half of 2011, that made this point. Many were published in traditionally right-of centre publications. See, for instance, 'EDITORIAL: From Arab Spring to Islamist Winter', *Washington Times*, 25 October 2011, www.washingtontimes.com/news/2011/oct/25/from-arab-spring-to-islamist-winter/ (accessed 25 January 2012) and Bradley, John, 'Arab Spring? This is turning into the winter of Islamic jihad', *Daily Mail*, 22 November 2011, www.dailymail.co.uk/debate/article-2064503/Arab-Spring-This-turning-winter-Islamic-jihad.html (accessed 25 January 2012).

6. Voll, John O, 'Fundamentalism in the Sunni Arab World; Egypt and the Sudan', in Marty, Martin E. and Appleby, R. Scott, *Fundamentalisms Observed*, Chicago and London: The University of Chicago Press, 1994, pp. 345–90.

7. See Wright, Lawrence, 'The Man Behind Bin Laden', *New Yorker,* 16 September 2002, in which Wright describes the relationship between Bin Laden and Zawahri.

8. See 'Al Zawahri: Egyptian Militant Group Joins Al-Qaeda', CNN, 5 August 2006, http://articles.cnn.com/2006-08-05/world/zawahiri.tape_1_zawahiri-al-jazeera-al-qaeda-terrorist-network?_s=PM:WORLD

9. 'The 2001 Arab Public Opinion poll', Brookings Institution, October 2011, www.brookings.edu/reports/2011/1121_arab_public_opinion_telhami.aspx

Chapter 12: Embracing the Void

1. 'Mideast Power Brokers Call for "Marshall Plan" After Unrest', Reuters, 22 October 2011.

2. Harrigan and al-Said, 'The Economic Impact of World Bank and IMF Programs in the Middle East and North Africa: A Case Study of Jordan, Egypt, Morocco and Tunisia', *Review of Middle East Economics and Finance* 6(2), 2010, http://www.relooney.info/0_NS4053_1226.pdf

3. Cited in Dresch, Paul, *A History of Modern Yemen*, Cambridge University Press, 2000, p. 198. Data is also in 'Yemen: Transactions with the Fund' at IMF online database, www.imf.org/external/np/fin/tad/extrans1.aspx?memberKey1=1069&endDate=2011-10-31&finposition_flag=YES (accessed 4 November 2011).

4. An assessment of the programmes is discussed in the IMF's Article IV consultation on Syria, published March 2010.

5. US Census Bureau Annual Report 2010. Poverty is classed as an annual income of below $22,314 for a family of four, and $11,139 for a single person. Overall poverty was 15.1 per cent, 26.6 per cent among Hispanics and 27.4 per cent among the black community.

6. Data on income inequalities are incomplete, but the Gini coefficient rankings published by the CIA lists the US as the 40th most unequal in the world. In comparison, Tunisia is ranked 63, Egypt 92 and Turkey 64. The rankings are published at www.cia.gov/library/publications/the-world-factbook/rankorder/2172rank.html

7. 'Remarks at Opening Press Conference', 14 April 2011, http://web.worldbank.org/WBSITE/EXTERNAL/COUNTRIES/MENAEXT/LIBYAEXTN/0,,print:Y~isCURL:Y~contentMDK:22888974~menuPK:410789~pagePK:2865066~piPK:2865079~theSitePK:410780,00.html (accessed 2 November 2011).

8. Institut National de Statistique, Repertoire Nationale des Entreprises.

9. US Census Bureau figures, www.census.gov/econ/smallbus.html (accessed 2 November 2011).

10. 'Jordan Ex-CBank Head Says Ousted by Force', Reuters, 21 September 2011.

11. Cited in 'The Syrian People's Slow-Motion Revolution', ICG, July 2011, p. 6.

12. The footage appeared on Tunisia state TV in November 2008 and can be viewed online at www.youtube.com/watch?v=xEA9X6j7b_U (accessed 3 November 2011).

13. 'Egypt T-bill Yields Surge, May Need Foreign Cash', Reuters, 20 September 2011.

14. 'Declaration of the G8 on the Arab Spring', press release, 26–27 May 2011, www.g20-g8.com/g8-g20/g8/english/live/news/declaration-of-the-g8-on-the-arab-springs.1316.html (accessed 3 November 2011).

15. 'Tunisia: EIB Signs Its First Post-Deauville Loan', EIB Press Release, 24 June 2011, www.eib.org/projects/press/2011/2011-091-la-bei-signe-son-premier-financement-de-lapres-deauville-en-tunisie-163-meur.htm (accessed 3 November 2011); 'African Development Bank Gives Tunis $500m Loan', Reuters, 10 June 2011; 'Obama Faces Obstacles in Aid to Arab Nations', *Washington Post*, 25 September 2011. http://seattletimes.nwsource.com/html/nationworld/2016319063_arabspring26.html

16. US Treasury Department figures. The historical debt outstanding is listed at www.treasurydirect.gov/govt/reports/pd/histdebt/histdebt_histo5.htm.

17. 'Arab Attitudes 2011', published by Arab American Institute Foundation and conducted by Zogby International.

18. 'Obama Presses Egypt's Military on Democracy', *New York Times*, 11 February 2011.

19. SAMA Annual Report 2010, Statistical Appendix. Export values to China rose from SR5, 630m in 2000 to SR112,210m in 2010. 2010 figures are listed as provisional. Imports from China rose from 4.4 billion riyals in 2000 to 46.85 billion riyals in 2010.

20. Saudi Aramco Annual Report. Exports to China in 2009 were estimated at approximately one million barrels per day.

21. US Energy Information Administration (EIA) figures.

Afterword

1. www.tunisia-live.net/2012/12/17/festivities-mask-disillusionment-in-birthplace-of-arab-spring/

Bibliography and Sources

Newspapers, magazines, television stations, agencies and other outlets

AFP (*Agence France-Presse*, French news agency)
Agence Tunis Afrique Presse (Tunisian state news agency)
Ahlulbayt (Iraqi-owned Shi'ite TV channel and news service)
Al-Ahram (Egyptian daily)
Alalam (Iranian state-owned TV station broadcasting in Arabic)
AP (Associated Press, news agency)
Arabian Business (Dubai-based Gulf business magazine)
Arabist.net
Al-Arabiya (Saudi-owned pan-Arab TV channel)
Ash-Sharq al-Awsat (pan-Arab newspaper published in London)
Bahrain TV (state-owned TV channel)
BBC News
Bloomberg
Business Today Egypt
Christian Science Monitor
Daily Star (Lebanese English-language daily)
Daily Telegraph
Deccan Herald
Dream TV (Egyptian TV channel)
Economist
Economist Intelligence Unit
Egyptian Gazette
Euromoney (London-based financial magazine)
Financial Times
Foreign Policy
Foreign Affairs
Guardian
Gulf Daily News (Bahrain-based daily)
Gulf News (UAE-based daily)
Hannibal TV (Tunisian TV channel)
Al-Hayat (pan-Arab newspaper based in London)
Independent
International Herald Tribune
IRIN (UN-run news source focussed on humanitarian news)

Al-Jamahiriya (Libyan state-run newspaper, now believed defunct)
Jamahiriya News Agency (Libyan state news agency, now believed defunct)
Al-Jazeera
Jeune Afrique (French-language current affairs magazine based in Paris)
Jordan Times
JO (Jordan-based English language magazine)
Khaleej Times (UAE-based newspaper)
Kuwait Times
Al-Libia (state-owned Libyan TV channel)
Libya Al-Youm (newspaper founded in 2011)
Al Manar (Hezbollah-run satellite TV station)
Al-Masry al-Youm (Egyptian newspaper)
Le Matin (Moroccan daily newspaper)
MEED (pan-Arab economic and business news source)
Le Monde
Moody's (ratings agency)
National (Abu Dhabi state-owned daily)
Nawaat.org (Tunisian political and economic news and analysis website)
New Yorker
New York Times
Al Nil (Egyptian TV channel)
Oman Observer
Petroleum Economist
Reuters
Russia Today (state-owned TV station and website)
Saudi Economic Survey
Saudi Press Agency (state news agency)
Slate
Al Shorouk (Egyptian newspaper)
Sunday Times
Syrian Arab News Agency (state news agency)
Syria Report (economic and business news website)
Syria Today (English-language magazine based in Damascus)
Le Temps (Tunisian daily)
Time
The Times
Tishrin (Syrian state-owned newspaper)
Tripoli Post
Wall Street Journal
Al-Wasat (Bahrain's first independent daily newspaper)
Washington Post
WikiLeaks
Xinhua (Chinese state news agency)
Yemen Times
Yemen Observer

Other local information sources

Abu Dhabi Gallup Center
Abu Dhabi Statistics Centre
African Development Bank
Bank Audi (Lebanese bank)
Bourse de Tunis (Tunisian stock exchange)
Capital Markets Authority (Saudi stock market regulator)

Central Agency for Public Mobilization and Statistics (CAPMAS, Egyptian statistics agency)
Central Bank of Bahrain
Central Bank of Egypt
Central Bank of Kuwait
Central Bank of Libya
Central Bank of Morocco
Central Bank of Oman
Central Bank of Qatar
Central Bank of Syria
Central Bank of Tunisia
Central Bank of Yemen
Central Bank of the United Arab Emirates
Central Bureau of Statistics (Syria)
Central Informatics Organization (Bahrain)
Central Statistical Office (Kuwait)
Central Statistical Organization (Yemen)
Damascus Securities Exchange
Department of Statistics (Jordan)
Dubai Financial Market
Dubai Statistics Centre
Dubai School of Government
Haut Commissariat au Plan (Moroccan statistics agency)
Institut National de Statistique (Tunisian statistics authority)
Jadwa Investment (Riyadh-based investment bank)
Libyan Information Authority
Ministry of Finance (Egypt)
National Oil Corporation (Libyan state energy company)
Qatar Statistics Authority
Samba (Saudi bank)
Saudi Arabian Monetary Authority (Saudi Central Bank)
Saudi Aramco (state energy company)

International organization, think-tanks and NGOs

Amnesty International
Brookings Institution
BP (Statistical Review of World Energy)
Carnegie Endowment for International Peace
Centre for Strategic and International Studies
Chatham House
Congressional Research Service
Council on Foreign Relations
German Institute for International and Security Affairs
Gulf Research Center
Human Rights Watch
The International Centre for the Study of Radicalization and Political Violence
International Crisis Group
International Energy Agency
International Foundation for Electoral Systems
International Monetary Fund
International Telecommunications Union
Organization for Economic Cooperation and Development
Organization of Petroleum Exporting Countries

Oxfam
Project on Middle East Democracy
Reporters Without Borders
Royal United Services Institute
Small Arms Survey
Transparency International
United Nations Conference on Trade and Investment
United Nations Development Programme
United Nations Food and Agriculture Organization
World Bank

Selected books and articles

Ahmed, Leila, *A Quiet Revolution*, Yale University Press, London and New Haven, 2011

Al Aswany, Alaa, *The Yacoubian Building*, Harper Perennial, New York, 2006 (originally published in Arabic in 2002)

Al Khamissi, Khaled, *Taxi*, Bloomsbury Qatar Foundation Publishing, Doha, 2011 (originally published in Arabic by Dar al Chorouk, Cairo, 2006)

Amin, Galal, *Egypt in the Era of Hosni Mubarak*, American University of Cairo Press, Cairo, 2011

Amin, Galal, *Whatever Happened to the Egyptians?* American University of Cairo Press, Cairo, 2000

Ansari, Ali M., *Modern Iran Since 1921*. Pearson, Harlow, 2003

Ayubi, Nazih N., *Overstating the Arab State*, I.B. Tauris, London, 1996

Al-Baharna, Husain M., *Iran's Claim to Sovereignty over Bahrain and the Resolution of the Anglo-Iranian Dispute over Bahrain*, Shaikh Ebrahim bin Mohammed Al Khalifa Center for Culture and Research, Manama, 2008

Barber, Benjamin R., *Jihad vs McWorld*, Random House, New York, 1995

Bayat, Asef, *Life as Politics*, Stanford University Press, 2009

Beau, Nicolas and Graciet, Catherine, *La Régente de Carthage*, Editions La Découverte, Paris, 2009

Beau, Nicolas and Tuqoui, Jean-Pierre, *Notre ami Ben Ali*, 2011 edn, Editions La Découverte, Paris, 1999

Blanford, Nicholas, *Killing Mr Lebanon*, I.B. Tauris, London, 2006

Blundy, David and Lycett, Andrew, *Qaddafi and the Libyan Revolution*, Corgi Books, London, 1988

Bouebdelli, Mohamed el Boussari, *Le jour ou j'ai réalisé que la Tunisie n'est plus un pays de liberté*, Tunis, 2009

Bradley, John, *Inside Egypt*, Palgrave Macmillan, New York, 2008

Cole, Juan R., *Sacred Space and Holy War: the politics, culture and history of Shi'ite Islam*, I.B. Tauris, London 2002

Cordesman, Anthony H. and Nerguizian, Aram, 'The Egypt military and the Arab-Israeli military balance: Conventional realities and asymmetric challenges', *Center for Strategic and International Studies*, February 2011

Courbage, Youssef and Todd, Emmanuel, *A Convergence of Civilizations: The Transformation of Muslim Societies Around the World*, Columbia University Press, New York, 2011

Davidson, Christopher, *Dubai: The Vulnerability of Success*, Hurst, London, 2008

Dresch, Paul, *A History of Modern Yemen*, Cambridge University Press, Cambridge, 2000

Evans, Martin and Phillips, John, *Algeria: Anger of the Dispossessed*, Yale University Press, New Haven and London, 2007

Filiu, Jean-Pierre, *The Arab Revolutions: Ten Lessons from the Democratic Uprisings*, Hurst, London, 2011

Fromkin, David, *A Peace to End all Peace*, André Deutsch, London, 1989

Fukuyama, Francis, *The End of History and the Last Man*, Penguin, London, 1992

Gardner, David, *Last Chance: The Middle East in the Balance*, I.B. Tauris, London, 2009

Gurr, Ted, *Why Men Rebel*, Princeton University Press, Princeton, NJ, 1971

Hammond, Andrew, *Popular Culture in the Arab World*, American University of Cairo Press, 2007

Hamzeh, Ahmad Nizar, *In the Path of Hizbullah*, Syracuse University Press, New York, 2004

Hassan, Hamdy A., 'Civil society in Egypt under the Mubarak regime', *Afro-Asian Journal of Social Sciences* 2(2), Quarter II, 2011

Heard-Bey, Frauke, *From Trucial States to United Arab Emirates*, Motivate Publishing, Dubai, 2004

Heydemann, Steven (ed.), *Networks of Privilege in the Middle East*. Palgrave Macmillan, 2004

Heydemann, Steven, Upgrading authoritarianism in the Arab world', Analysis Paper No. 13 Brookings Institution, Saban Center for Middle East Policy, October 2007

Hibou, Beatrice, *The Force of Obedience*, Polity Press, Cambridge, 2011 (first published in French as *La Force de L'Obéissance*, Editions La Découverte, Paris, 2006)

Hiro, Dilip, *After Empire: The Birth of a Multi-polar World*, Nation Books, New York, 2010

Hobsbawm, Eric, *The Age of Extremes*, Michael Joseph, London, 1994

—, *The Age of Revolution*, Abacus, 2002 (originally published by Weidenfeld and Nicolson, London, 1962)

Hourani, Albert, *A History of the Arab Peoples*, Faber and Faber, London, 2002 edition

Huntington, Samuel P., 'Democracy's third wave', *The Journal of Democracy* 2(2), 1991

Ibn Khaldun, *The Muqaddimah*, Princeton University Press, Princeton, NJ, abridged 1989 edition

Ismail, Salwa, *Rethinking Islamist Politics*, I.B. Tauris, London, 2006

Kapiszewski, Andrzej, 'Elections and parliamentary activity in the GCC states: Broadening political participation in the Gulf monarchies', in Abdulhadi Khalaf and Giacomo Luciani (eds), *Constitutional Reform and Political Participation in the Gulf*, Gulf Research Center, Dubai, 2006, pp. 108–10

Kassir, Samir, *Being Arab*, Verso, London, 2006

Kerr, Malcolm H., *The Arab Cold War: Gamal 'Abd al-Nasir and His Rivals 1958–1970*, Oxford University Press, 3rd edition, 1971

Khuri, Fuad I., *Tribe and State in Bahrain: The Transformation of Social and Political Authority in an Arab State*, University of Chicago Press, Chicago and London, 1980

King, Stephen Juan, *The New Authoritarianism in the Middle East and North Africa*, Indiana University Press, Bloomington, 2009

Kuran, Timur, 'The economic impact of Islamic fundamentalism', in Martin E. Marty and R. Scott Appleby (eds), *Fundamentalisms and the State*, Chicago University Press, Chicago, 1993

—, 'Now out of never: The element of surprise in the East European revolution of 1989', *World Politics*, 44(1), 1991, pp. 7–48

Lacey, Robert, *Inside the Kingdom*, Arrow Books, London, 2010

—, *The Kingdom*, Hutchinson, London, 1981

Lankester, Tim, '"Asian drama": The pursuit of modernization in India and Indonesia', in *Asian Affairs*, XXXV (III), November 2004

Leverett, Flynt, *Inheriting Syria*, Brookings Institution Press, Washington, 2005

Lewis, Bernard, '*What Went Wrong?*' Weidenfeld and Nicolson, London, 2002

Lohmann, Susanne, 'The dynamics of informational cascades: The Monday demonstrations in Leipzig, East Germany, 1989–91', *World Politics*, 47(1), 1994, pp. 42–101

Louer, Laurence, *Transnational Shia politics: Religious and Political Networks in the Gulf*, Columbia University Press, New York, 2008

Lynch, Marc, *Voices of the New Arab Public*, Columbia University Press, New York, 2006

Lynch, Marc, Glasser, Susan and Hounshell, Blake (eds), *Revolution in the Arab World: Tunisia, Egypt and the Unmaking of an Era*, Foreign Policy, 2011

Mackintosh-Smith, Tim, *Yemen*, John Murray, London, 1997

Madelung, Wilferd, *The Succession to Mohamed*, Cambridge University Press, Cambridge, 1997

Matar, Hisham, *In the Country of Men*, Penguin, London, 2007

Al-Mdaires, Falah, 'Shi'ism and political protest in Bahrain', *Digest on Middle East Studies* 11(1), Spring 2002

Miladi, Noureddine, 'Satellite news and the Arab diaspora in Britain: Comparing Al Jazeera, the BBC and CNN', *Journal of Ethnic and Migration Studies* 32(6), August 2006

Miles, Hugh, *Al-Jazeera: How Arab TV News Challenged the World*, Abacus, London, 2005

Moore, Clement Henry, *Tunisia Since Independence: The Dynamics of One-Party Government*, California University Press, Berkeley, CA, 1965

Morozov, Evgeny, *The Net Delusion*, Penguin, London, 2011

Mottahedeh, Roy, *The Mantle of the Prophet*, Oneworld Publications, Oxford, 2000

Mourtada, Racha and Salem, Fadi, 'Facebook usage: Factors and analysis', *Arab Social Media Report* 1(1), Dubai School of Government, January 2011

Myrdal, Gunnar, *Asian Drama: An Inquiry into the Poverty of Nations*, Allen Lane, 1968

Nakhle, Emile, *Bahrain: Political Development in a Modernizing Society*, Lexington Books, Lanham/Boulder, 2011

Onley, James, *The Arabian Frontier of the British Raj*, Oxford University Press, Oxford, 2007

Osman, Tarek, *Egypt on the Brink*, Yale University Press, New Haven and London, 2010

Palmer Harik, Judith, *Hezbollah, the Changing Face of Terrorism*, I.B. Tauris, London, 2004

Parolin, Gianluca Paolo, 'Generations of Gulf constitutions: Paths and perspectives', in Abdulhadi Khalaf and Giacomo Luciani (eds), *Constitutional Reform and Political Participation in the Gulf*, Gulf Research Center, Dubai, 2006, pp. 65–70

Pennell, C.R., *Morocco from Empire to Independence*, Oneworld Publications, Oxford, 2003

Perthes, Volker, *Syria under Bashar al-Asad*, Routledge, 2005

Peterson, J.E., 'The United States and Yemen: A history of unfulfilled expectations', in Robert E. Looney (ed.), *Handbook of US–Middle East Relations*, Routledge, London, 2009

Puchot, Pierre, *Tunisie, une révolution Arabe*, Galaade Editions, Paris, 2011

Al Qaddafi, Muammar, *The Green Book*, Tripoli, Libya, 1983 edition

Alqadhafi, Saif al-Islam, 'The role of civil society in the democratization of global governance institutions', PhD thesis at the London School of Economics, submitted 2007

Qubain, Fahim I., 'Social classes and tensions in Bahrain', *Middle East Journal* 9(3), Summer 1955, pp. 269–71

Ramadan, Abdel Azim, 'Fundamentalist influence in Egypt: The strategies of the Muslim Brotherhood and the Takfir groups', in Martin E. Marty and R. Scott Appleby (eds), *Fundamentalisms and the State*, Chicago University Press, Chicago, 1993

Ramazani, Rouhollah, K. and Kechichian, Joseph A., *The Gulf Cooperation Council: Record and Analysis*, University of Virginia Press, 1988

Razavi, Ahmed, *Continental Shelf Delimitation and Related Maritime Issues in the Persian Gulf*, Publications on Ocean Development, Martinus Nijhoff Publishers, The Hague/Boston/London, 1997

Rodenbeck, Max, *Cairo*, Random House, New York, 1998

Ronzitti, Natalino, 'The treaty on friendship, partnership and cooperation between Italy and Libya: New prospects for cooperation in the Mediterranean?', *Bulletin of Italian Politics* 1(1), 2009

Saad-Ghorayeb, Amal, *Hizbullah, Politics and Religion*, Pluto Press, London, 2002

Said, Edward W., *Culture and Imperialism*, Chatto and Windus, London, 1993

—, *Orientalism*, Penguin, London, 2003 edition

Salibi, Kamal, *A House of Many Mansions*, I.B. Tauris, London, 1988

Seale, Patrick, *Asad: The Struggle for the Middle East*, University of California Press, Berkeley and Los Angeles, 1989

Sharp, Gene, *From Dictatorship to Democracy: A Conceptual Framework for Liberation*, 4th edn, The Albert Einstein Institution, Boston, May 2010

Shlaim, Avi, *The Iron Wall: Israel and the Arab World*, Penguin, London, 2000

—, *Lion of Jordan: The Life of King Hussein in War and Peace*, Penguin, 2008

St John, Ronald Bruce, *Libya, from Colony to Independence*, Oneworld Publications, Oxford, 2008

—, *Qaddafi's World Design*, Saqi, London, 1987

Taleb, Nassim Nicholas, *The Black Swan*, Random House, 2007

Tamimi, Azzam S., *Rachid Ghannouchi: A Democrat within Islamism*, Oxford University Press, Oxford, 2001

Traboulsi, Fawwaz, *A History of Modern Lebanon*, Pluto Press, London, 2007

Tueni, Ghassan and Khoury, Eli, *The Beirut Spring*, Dar an-Nahar, Beirut, 2005

Van Dam, Nikolaos, *The Struggle for Power in Syria*, I.B. Tauris, London, 2011 edition

Vandewalle, Dirk, *A History of Modern Libya*, Cambridge: Cambridge University Press, 2006

Voll, John O., 'Fundamentalism in the Arab world: Egypt and the Sudan', in Martin E. Marty and R. Scott Appleby (eds), *Fundamentalisms Observed*, Chicago University Press, Chicago, 1991

Whitaker, Brian, *The Birth of Modern Yemen*, 2009, published as an e-book on www.al-bab.com

—, *What's Really Wrong with the Middle East*, Saqi, London, 2009

Wilson, Mary C., *King Abdullah, Britain and the Making of Jordan*, Cambridge University Press, Cambridge, 1987

Winograd, Morley and Hais, Michael D., *Headwaters of the Arab Spring*, ebook, June 2011.

Wright, John, *A History of Libya*, Hurst, London, 2010

Yergin, Daniel, *The Prize*, Free Press, New York, 2008

Index

Yemen (*cont.*)
  Islamist resurgence 19, 263, 276, 279
  media revolution 46, 53, 54
  militant Islam 199–200
  political structure 199
  Al-Qaeda 19, 195, 197, 205, 206, 210, 279
  Qatar 294
  southern independence movement 206–8,
    211, 212
  unemployment 38
  US support 16

Yemen Arab Republic (YAR) 197, 199
youth bulge 35, 38
youth unemployment 2, 36, 42, 100, 153–4

al-Zaitouna 80
Zakaria, Adel 105
al-Zawahri, Ayman 122, 267
Zaydi community 197
Zayed Al Nahyan, Sheikh 139
Zeidan, Ali 188
Zoellick, Robert 286